D1613135

Crossroads at Clarksdale

THE JOHN HOPE FRANKLIN SERIES IN
AFRICAN AMERICAN HISTORY AND CULTURE

Waldo E. Martin Jr. and Patricia Sullivan, editors

Crossroads
at Clarksdale

*The Black Freedom Struggle in the
Mississippi Delta after World War II*

Françoise N. Hamlin

THE UNIVERSITY OF NORTH CAROLINA   Chapel Hill

UNIVERSITY OF WINCHESTER
LIBRARY

Library of Congress Cataloging-in-Publication Data
Hamlin, Françoise N.
Crossroads at Clarksdale : the black freedom struggle in
the Mississippi Delta after World War II / Françoise N.
Hamlin.
p. cm. — (The John Hope Franklin series in African
American history and culture)
Includes bibliographical references and index.
ISBN 978-0-8078-3549-4 (cloth : alk. paper)
1. African Americans—Civil rights—Mississippi—
Clarksdale—History—20th century. 2. African
Americans—Segregation—Mississippi—Clarksdale—
History—20th century. 3. Civil rights movements—
Mississippi—Clarksdale—History—20th century.
4. Segregation—Mississippi—Clarksdale—History—
20th century. 5. National Association for the Advancement
of Colored People. Coahoma County Branch—History.
6. Henry, Aaron, 1922–1997. 7. Pigee, Vera Mae, 1924–
2007. 8. Clarksdale (Miss.)—Race relations—History—
20th century. I. Title.
F349.C6H36 2012
323.1196'073076244—dc23

2011045259

The author wishes to thank the National Association for
the Advancement of Colored People for authorizing the
use of Table 2 and Figures 3.4 and 4.2.

Poems in chapter 5: Elnora Fondren, "Changing the
American Stage," and Allan Goodner, "Segregation Will
Not Be Here Long," from *Letters from Mississippi*,
edited by Elizabeth Sutherland Martínez. Original edition
© 1965 and renewed by Elizabeth Sutherland Martínez.
New edition © 2002 by Elizabeth Sutherland Martínez.
Reprinted with the permission of The Permissions
Company, Inc., on behalf of Zephyr Press, www.zephyr
press.org.

16 15 14 13 12   5 4 3 2 1

MIX
Paper from
responsible sources
FSC
www.fsc.org   FSC® C013483

FOR ELIJAH

In memory of
Corine Bradley (1929–2005)
Aaron E. Henry (1922–1997)
Vera Mae Pigee (1924–2007)

Mississippi has always been a bewitched and tragic ground,
yet it's also a land of heroism and nobility; a land which has
honored those of us of all our races who possess the courage and
the imagination of the resources given us on this haunted terrain.
I love Mississippi, and I hope the best of it will endure.

—Willie Morris (1986)

Contents

Figures, Maps, and Tables

Figures

Preface

*It is by knowing where you stand that you grow able to judge where you
are. Place absorbs our earliest notice and attention, it bestows upon us our
original awareness; and our critical powers spring up from the study of it and
the growth experiences inside it. . . . One place comprehended can make us
understand other places better. Sense of place gives us equilibrium;
extended, it is sense of direction too. — Eudora Welty*

Drive the approximately seventy miles south to Clarksdale, Mississippi, from
Memphis, Tennessee, on U.S. Highway 61 through Tunica County. Fields
dominate the landscape, broken only by lines of trees between properties or
crops. Depending on the time of year, crop dusters might zigzag low across the
asphalt and telegraph poles as they drop their loads of fertilizers and pesticides
on the once-rich soils of the Mississippi Delta. In the fall, the fields dress in
white as cotton bursts from straining bolls.

Coming in from the east along Route 6 from Batesville, the view is more
dramatic. Fields still dominate this landscape too, but the road winds grace-
fully around smaller plots, where the trees seem taller and the buildings hug
the road. At night there is no light, no distinction between the land and the
heavens. The lights from Clarksdale, Coahoma County's seat, illuminate the
sky, like a stadium rock concert, miles before the city comes into view. Turning
the last bend, hidden by a bank of tall mature trees, the city crouches low on
the horizon.

My favorite Delta entrance, though, is from the south. Route 49 East cuts
through the Delta diagonally from Yazoo City to Clarksdale. Yazoo City sits
amid rolling hills and marks the southern tip of the Delta. The traffic falls away

Mississippi

as the car points north out of the city and the landscape suddenly straightens, like a person stretching from top to toe in the first waking moments after a good night's sleep. The topography marks the location. Swamps sometimes come perilously close to the blacktopped two-lane road. Driving in the early hours of the morning, mists hover over the murky waters and kudzu drapes the trees, reminiscent of the bayous of Louisiana or Florida. Behind those small untamed swaths of nature, the fields take over for miles and miles, interrupted only by small towns of rundown buildings and wandering, emaciated dogs.

On the way to Clarksdale on this road, Parchman, the state penitentiary, appears on the left, just before the Coahoma County line. Fenced in by barbed wire, razors, and steel, the prison is huge, spread over several hundred acres in satellite compounds, surrounded by a treeless, barren expanse, a no-man's-land. It scars the landscape. Leaving the prison behind, Clarksdale is only thirty miles down the road and comes as a welcomed sight. Those one hundred miles are emotionally draining. It is very easy to fall in love with the beauty of the Delta, its uniqueness and its landscape. The reality of its poverty and exploitation, visible from the road, strikes a blow that leaves many visitors breathless. It is one thing to travel through, pausing to let the senses experience the Delta's history, and quite another to eke out a living, or struggle with the demons of the past and present, as a resident.

Descriptions of Clarksdale written by the Federal Writers' Project of the Works Progress Administration in 1938 illustrate how little has changed to the landscape: "Viewed from a distance, the bare and treeless business district of stores, gins, warehouses, and loading platforms appears squat and dwarfed; yet silver-leaf maples and water oaks line the residential streets giving the homes a secluded air." The writers omit that these homes belong to white citizens. They continue: "Fringed by dark cypresses and bright willows, the narrow Sunflower River winds through the city eastward and westward. Along its banks are many of the oldest homes of Clarksdale—large, comfortable frame houses, with wide front galleries."[1]

The land defines the region. It defined the people who settled here, adventurers seeking wealth in the richest topsoil in the country. It defined those brought here in chains to level the abundant forests, to build levees against the mighty river, or to drain the swamps for planting. It defined the thousands who died from malaria, snakebites, or sheer exhaustion, their bodies reuniting with the land. Even now, as those conditions have disappeared, the land bears the scars of its inhabitants. Banished from the land and pushed west onto reservations, the native peoples left names for counties and towns. Coahoma is the Choctaw name for the once-plentiful red panther. Clarksdale is named after John Clark, son of an English architect, who landed in Coahoma County in 1839 and incorporated the town in 1882. The Europeans made the county the Golden Buckle on the Cotton Belt, retaining the wealth they drained from the soil and the slaves, now invested in machines and chemicals rather than in black muscle and sweat. The slaves' descendants still struggle to survive. As historian John Dittmer noted, "The Delta is both a clearly defined geographical area and a state of mind."[2]

The geography of the city of Clarksdale in the postwar years followed natural and manmade boundaries, the Sunflower River and the train tracks. Downtown Clarksdale, north of the tracks, east of the river, boasted the best the town had to showcase. Wide, tree-lined streets offered ample parking for the latest models of vehicles and space for traveling vehicles to pass without clipping wing mirrors or scratching polished paintwork. Many storeowners maintained flower boxes or potted plants on their premises, enticing customers with their brightly lit wares and cheerful greetings. Laid out in a typical grid, most of the important business of Clarksdale took place within the approximately fourteen small blocks. The major banks with the Civic Auditorium clustered around Second Street on Delta Avenue; the Carnegie Library and the seed and supply store shared the block with city administrative offices; and a block further stood the historic Alcazar Hotel. The Greyhound Bus Terminal's landmark sign was illuminated above the entrance on the corner of Issaquena and Third Street. A few national department store chains, like Woolworths, had franchises, and customers came from counties across the Delta to shop on these protected streets.

A block south of this lovely picture of southern charm and hospitality, the Illinois Central Railroad Station marked the line in the dirt, as it were. Historically black Clarksdale across the tracks has significantly narrower streets where storefronts pressed together tightly as if holding each other up by sheer will. Streets and blocks were laid out with a little less care and precision here. Potholes and mud made travel treacherous for motorists and pedestrians alike. Most of the black businesses in town collected on Issaquena Avenue and Fourth Street (renamed Martin Luther King several decades later). Curtis Wilkie, a reporter for the *Clarksdale Press Register* during the 1960s, noted that the vibrant black businesses "operated like outposts of African civilization."[3] Two blocks further on Fourth Street, passing Aaron Henry's Fourth Street Drugstore, the majority of the city's larger black churches stood. Their close

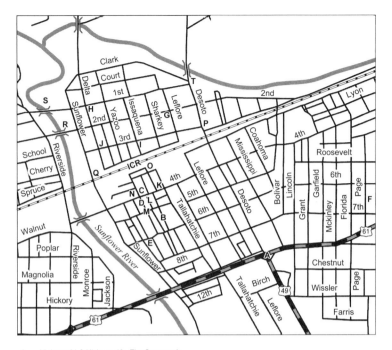

A   Highway 61 & Highway 49 - The Crossroads

B   407 Ashton Avenue - Pigee's Beauty Salon

C   213 4th Street - Fourth Street Drug Store

D   459 Yazoo Avenue between 4th and 5th Streets - Freedom House

E   611 Baird Street - Vera Pigee's home

F   636 Page Avenue - Aaron Henry's home

G   Leflore Avenue & East 2nd Street - Civic Auditorium

H   Delta Avenue & 1st Street - Carnegie Public Library

I   Issaquena Avenue & 4th Street - Greyhound Bus Terminal

J   Delta Avenue & 3rd Street - Alcazar Hotel

K   Issaquena Avenue & 4th Street - nexus of black commercial district

L   404 Yazoo Avenue between 4th Street & Ashton Avenue - Haven Methodist Church

M   200 5th Street (5th Street & Yazoo Avenue) - Centennial Baptist Church

N   4th Street & Harrison Avenue - First Baptist Church

O   Issaquena Avenue & South Edwards Avenue - Reverend Trammell Crossroad (chapter 3)

P   Desoto Avenue & 3rd Street - Aaron Henry Crossroad (chapter 3)

Q   Sunflower Avenue & The Illinois Central Railroad - R. L. Drew Crossroad (chapter 3)

R   Second Street Bridge - John Melchor Crossroad (chapter 3)

S   First Street Bridge - Reverend J. D. Rayford Crossroad (chapter 3)

T   Cutrer Hill - Vera Pigee Crossroad (chapter 3)

ICR   Illinois Central Railroad Station

The Crossroads and Downtown Clarksdale

proximity encouraged spaces for social and spiritual interaction on Sundays, and as the mass movement grew, they hosted most of the mass meetings.

Residential neighborhoods fanned out from these cores. Zoya Zeman, a college student from Nebraska volunteering in Clarksdale during Freedom Summer in 1964, captured the essence of segregation in Clarksdale succinctly on the pages of her diary:

> The sections of town are divided very distinctly. Even in areas where the neighborhoods are "mixed" there are Negroes on one side of the street and whites on the other. Very graphic picture—blond children playing on their driveways, and thirty-five yards away their counterparts are also playing, but the two not exchanging or sharing or possibly noticing. There are five Negro neighborhoods, all located on one side of the viaduct where the railroads run. The one small white community on this side . . . is set between Riverton . . . and the Brickyard area.[4]

North and west of downtown the houses are larger and stately, with carports and better-kept lawns and flower beds. Back then if black people were seen there, they carried rakes, brooms, dusting cloths, hedge trimmers, buckets, or white children. In black neighborhoods, houses were close enough together so that mothers and grandmothers could watch their children play and have conversations with each other across the dirt patches that separated them. With only a handful of black people owning air conditioners, windows were flung open to catch a wisp of a breeze, advertising to the world outside all the angst and drama going on inside.

Clarksdale and the Delta redefined me. That place created its own drama in my life. I was the first black exchange student from England to arrive in the town, and I did my senior year at Coahoma County High School after finishing my Advanced Levels (A Levels) at home. Coming from London in 1991, I was assigned to a black woman in Coahoma County, Mississippi, because a faceless and nameless someone thought that "I'd feel at home there." Sixty-three-year-old Corine Bradley lived in the Delta all her life and rarely slept out of arm's reach of her rifle. Poorly educated, she labored as a domestic and occasionally as a school bus driver, while raising two sons on her own. She left her husband at thirty, after fourteen years of marriage, neglect, and abuse, and gave birth to their son some months later. Worried about raising him as an only child, she adopted another baby. Her devout faith and love of people convinced her to open her home to me. By the time of my arrival, her birth son lived in California after a navy career took him from Mississippi years before. Her adopted son was only thirty miles away, in Parchman.

Together, we spent many nights, over bowls of popcorn, as I listened to her stories of life in Mississippi. What she lacked in education she made up for in wisdom and common sense. Fiercely independent and always poor, she had worked hard all her life and still struggled to work despite her worsening health. She taught me tolerance, forgiveness, and the power of faith. With her, I changed. I wanted to know more about her life—and those of her friends and family. At Coahoma County High School, I (re)defined my identity as I struggled to make sense of my environment. I was hooked, turning down a guaranteed university slot to study law for an application to read United States Studies. All of these roads, the ones covered in asphalt, the ones soaked in memories, and the ones bathed in music, protest, blood, or tears, meet at the Crossroads. This book is a rest stop on my quest to understand the Delta I experienced then and to pay homage to the people who enabled me to see more clearly. It honors Corine Bradley, who now finally rests and never has to work in someone else's house again. It also honors Vera Mae Pigee, one of the pioneers of the mass movement in Coahoma County, who also now rests from her earthly fight for freedom and fairness.

Crossroads at Clarksdale

The Black Freedom Struggle at the Crossroads

Ours is a hell of a story, but freedom is worth every adversity.
—*Aaron Henry (1963)*

Every significant change that came about in the civil rights movement is linked
to Mississippi. You should be proud to say you're a black Mississippian.
—*Nelson Rivers III (2003)*

The claim to fame for Clarksdale, Mississippi, is as the home of the blues. In
the first half of the twentieth century, many men, and a few women, gathered
there to develop the blues as a musical form and consume it with pleasure.
W. C. Handy, Gus Cannon, Charley Patton, Son House, John Lee Hooker,
Jack Johnson, Frank Frost, Bessie Smith, Ike Turner, Howlin' Wolf, Muddy
Waters, and Robert Johnson, among others, carved their mark on the local
and national music scene in Clarksdale.[1] Today, the most famous landmark,
the Crossroads—where Robert Johnson supposedly sold his soul to the devil
in exchange for mastery over his music—is proudly demarcated by a decora-
tive pointer of four guitars, with each neck pointing toward the geographical
compass points: north and south along Highway 61 (now 161); east and west on
Route 49. Yet Clarksdale's African American history resonates much deeper
than the musical melodies emanating from juke joints and the fields. The fact
that the blues, a musical form documenting hard life and harder knocks, found
a fertile home here speaks to the stories of struggle and survival on the ground
where it matured.

A fuller history of African Americans in Clarksdale illustrates how a community organizing during the mass civil rights movement found, chose, or ap-

propriated opportunities in order to survive. These (real, rather than legend-ary) crossroads existed on various planes—across time and place and within personal (and sometimes communal) lives. This metaphor, which Johnson's lonely meeting conjures, helps us remember the uncertainty in the choices, opportunities, and decisions that black people made as they worked for better futures, highlighting agency and strategic organization over declension and de-feat.

Crossroads at Clarksdale chronicles the black freedom struggle in Clarks-dale, Mississippi, from 1951 to the mid-1970s. The narrative, however, spills backward into the 1940s and forward to the turn of the twenty-first century. At the national level, while mass movement strategies forced the enactment of desegregation laws and case decisions and took down major barriers to equal economic opportunities, the reality of life for most African Americans did not change dramatically. Risky choices led to relatively slow change at the local level, with steady battles for gains, at times in tiny incremental steps.

The larger national portrait of the mass civil rights movement leaves out this local story and the personal narratives and drama that permitted the everyday push for a more just society. This partially explains the indifference to the past in today's Clarksdale. During my stay there as an exchange student at Coa-homa County High School in the early 1990s, in a school that was easily 90 percent African American, hardly any black history was taught, nothing be-yond specific leaders and inventors. Once in graduate school and specializing in African American history, the one book I found on Clarksdale's history, written in 1982 and published by the city's Carnegie Library, did not reflect history as African Americans remembered it. Rather it showed an unrealistic and sanitized version of social harmony and the blues.[2] The youth of Clarks-dale, starting with my peers, knew nothing of the history, the struggle, and the sacrifices made by their neighbors and relatives. This book recovers for the first time those forgotten or discarded memories.

Looking at one place provides a window for analyzing the complexity of movements even *within* the locales. It complicates our understanding of a mass movement, or, more accurately, a mass of movements throughout the nation, each peculiar to its locale and population. This portrait uses Clarks-dale as its canvas.[3] By keeping this study local, the project conducts a cross-organizational comparison through time, showcasing Clarksdale's residents and the triumphs and tragedies that occurred there as they arrived at various crossroads. These accumulative stories about the sustained push for substan-tive change during the mass civil rights movements are a continuation of the black freedom struggle, one that is unique to the history of African Americans carrying the legacy of slavery. Themes around organizing, victories, persistent problems, and the nature of coalition building, past and present, are distilled in this one town's story.[4]

As a Delta town, Clarksdale typified many movement sites, yet for many reasons it is unique. Clarksdale's movement was more homespun than in other Delta towns—the National Association for the Advancement of Colored People (NAACP) had its strongest branch there, founded in the early 1950s by local people. For that reason, other organizations like the Student Nonviolent Coordinating Committee (SNCC) did not have as big a presence as they did in the adjoining Sunflower County directly south, or less than sixty miles away in Greenwood. In Clarksdale itself, there were relatively more possibilities for African Americans because as a larger urban area it offered more employment possibilities. For example, Coahoma County Junior College and Agricultural High School, locally known as Aggie, became one of the first institutions of its kind in the state in 1949 when grades thirteen and fourteen were added to the curriculum to create a black public junior college serving adjacent Delta counties. With a more diverse and better-educated population, Clarksdale generally had an aura of relative progressivism in the Delta—a handful of African Americans could register to vote and a few black businesses and professionals constituted a middle class. Yet violence existed and was used as a deterrent by those upholding Jim Crow.

People were raped or killed there just as they were in Greenwood, Sunflower County, Hattiesburg, or Jackson, making Clarksdale representative as well. Community leader, World War II veteran, pharmacist, and state NAACP president Aaron Henry confirmed that "the fear of the unknown kept the Negro community in place."[5] The black community suffered the indignities of segregation just like its neighbors and remained mindful of the repercussions that most civil rights activity faced. During the postwar years, as more local people began to protest, white leaders reacted negatively and, at times, without mercy. Yet agitators persevered, risking life and livelihood for the sake of their own families and communities, with little national attention. The nation's iconic civil rights figure, the Reverend Martin Luther King Jr., came to Clarksdale (and Mississippi) only a few times for rallies, and he was whisked away immediately, oftentimes with the national press right behind him.

A story has to have a beginning, and this one starts at the end of World War II, when many black veterans returned home and took advantage of the GI Bill to escape from the plantation economy. They had already faced crossroads, where they could have started afresh elsewhere or returned home. As these men, foremost among them Aaron Henry, chose to return to their communities, many steeled themselves to challenge Jim Crow. A close look at the fifties in the Delta, and particularly in Clarksdale, reveals a hotbed of African American activity, mostly under the radar. NAACP branches formed or revitalized with the work of local women and men, and children became empowered through the NAACP youth councils, guided by advisors like Vera Pigee of Clarksdale.

This is not a story with neat vignettes and big solutions packaged in chapters with pithy lessons for the wise. Movements do not operate according to schedules or blueprints. They are untidy, layered, contentious, and oftentimes disappointingly unfulfilled. A strategy might work once and fail the next time, or what looks like success might wind up causing strife in other arenas or for later generations. This is a narrative in which the characters (be they organizations, policies, or leaders) fade in and out; they are not constantly on stage for the whole performance. A variety of acts unfold in the chapters, and they are layered rather than linear, linked by some characters and goals but with some narrative threads breaking at points as collisions and collusions reshape the landscape. The stories meet and overlap in places, but the routes to them are from all directions, like the roads to Clarksdale itself.

Some narrative threads remain constant throughout, and they include inter- and intra-organizational relationships and local leadership dynamics. What becomes clear in the wide view of Clarksdale over time is the intense and at times painstakingly slow pace of activities at the local level—and the constant pressures people endured. The most common media images of the mass movements of the sixties, those of activists holding hands and singing modified and politicized spirituals, masked the internal conflicts that occurred daily. Instead of civility, listening to the voices reveals deep adversarial rifts from the beginning.

Clarksdale's story belies assumptions about the distinctiveness of the "Big 4" organizations: the NAACP, SNCC, the Congress of Racial Equality (CORE), and the Southern Christian Leadership Conference (SCLC). While there were differences between and competition among the leaders and group strategies nationally, in Clarksdale, and probably in other towns and communities across the South, some people served in several organizations simultaneously, illuminating the malleability of activism and the subsequent complexity and unpredictability of local movements. The Coahoma County NAACP remained the dominant and constant presence in Clarksdale, and this local study provides the best vantage point to see its intricate intra-organizational cogs and the interaction between national, state, and local entities, especially when other civil rights groups enter the state.

Two local leaders stand out in this book: Aaron Henry and Vera Pigee. Civil rights leaders were self-defined in Mississippi—they were those who put their names to paper as organizers and speakers. Not many were able to stand up to this task, but these two did. Aaron Henry was a World War II veteran and the most noted black Clarksdalian leader. He held the presidency in the local and state NAACP and adeptly manipulated the competition between civil rights organizations to garner resources for Clarksdale and Mississippi. Historian John Dittmer referred to Henry as the "most ecumenical" of Mississippi's activists.[6] To the chagrin of the national NAACP office, which was ever mindful of its dominance in the state, Henry was pivotal in introducing the SCLC and increasing SNCC's numbers in Mississippi. He was a broker among civil rights groups through his flexible associations, which he used to harness resources from several competing groups at the same time, rising above the fray to adapt to and fulfill constituent needs while navigating among the larger organizations.[7]

Vera Pigee represented another type of leadership. Highly visible in the early years from 1955 to the late sixties, her life encompassed the range and depth of black women's local leadership during the civil rights movements in Mississippi. She did not have opportunities like Henry to pay for an education that could allow her to ascend to formal leadership positions by virtue of her class status. It is only when experiences like hers are analyzed in conjunction with the male leadership, not in competition, that women's roles as mothers, wives, and daughters become part of their leadership styles. In 1976, when historian Jacquelyn Hall asked activist Septima Clark (a teacher who had traveled throughout the South recruiting for citizenship schools) about outstanding vocal black women at the local level, Clark listed Pigee alongside Daisy Bates and Fannie Lou Hamer, two of the too few black women to be recognized for their leadership.[8] Despite the fact that her story is not well known, Vera Pigee always knew her own worth. As one of the founding members of the local NAACP branch, its secretary, and a beautician, Pigee played a prominent role in Clarksdale. Many of the civil rights initiatives there can be traced to her initiation. She defined herself as a churchgoer, a professional woman, a mother, and an activist. Her self-definition empowered her through what she called her "struggle of struggles," the title she chose for her self-published autobiography.[9]

Pigee worked with children, orchestrating the strongest and most active NAACP youth council in the state. She utilized her mothering role to be an organizing and mobilizing tool that enabled her to implement radical social change. Vera Pigee's story sheds light on alternative ways of thinking about the broader debate on the gendered and racialized leadership of civil rights movements, and social movements in general, through the context of mothering and women's empowerment and resistance.

The story in Clarksdale does not rise and fall on Pigee, however (or even on Henry), but rather on all the community efforts in the long period of mass activism, especially those that outlast the sixties and Pigee's tenure in Clarksdale. The backgrounds of Henry and Pigee are revealed as the narrative moves forward and events expose elements best understood through personal details. Pigee's presence and departure before the book's conclusion encourages a critical discussion about opportunities and the gendered dimensions of leadership. Neither leader conducted his or her activities without fault—both had egos, which were necessary to motivate them when the stakes were high and dangerous in the fifties but which caused them to stumble later when collaboration may have worked best. So while both leaders get their due accolades, their personal limitations also complicate their professional narratives and fracture narrative threads in places.

Collecting and organizing these layered narratives required varied and extensive research. My high school year in Clarksdale greatly enriched my sense of place. The archive collections—from the Sovereignty Commission Papers in Jackson, to the minutes of the mayor and the Board of City Commissioners and the school board, to the *Clarksdale Press Register* in Clarksdale—all laid a foundation, but oral history brought the story to life. Interviews gave texture and insight into the motivations, attitudes, and fears that elude the formal written record.[10] Used extensively to record the memories of an aging population of activists, oral history (along with autobiography and biography) became invaluable for uncovering, for example, how school desegregation really happened, for black and white teachers and students.[11] Vera Pigee was the oldest surviving activist interviewed, and her advanced age clouded details in her memory of the fifties. Indeed, most of my interviewees remembered the ruckus days of the sixties best, particularly from the mid-1960s onward, so more first-person voices appear in the chapters on later years, underscoring the immediate importance of collecting local oral histories from these decades.

Crossroads at Clarksdale complicates civil rights history. Historian Jacquelyn Hall insisted that history should be "harder to celebrate as a natural progression of American values. Harder to cast as a satisfying morality tale. Most of all, harder to simplify, appropriate, and contain."[12] Clarksdale's story demands a rethinking of the dominant King-driven narrative, of the SNCC-driven Mississippi movement narrative, and of the traditional temporal boundaries often placed on this era. The struggle continues, so the book purposefully leaves frayed ends, just as it picks up strands from a long history of African American resistance that set the foundation for the mass movements.

This book tells many interweaving stories. It lays out how members of civil rights organizations worked on the ground with their disagreements between constituencies and between groups. The narrative also gives details about how mainstream and national student protests worked with local people, particularly during the well-publicized Freedom Summer in 1964. A fuller picture of the scale of protest emerges through the simultaneous local struggle for school desegregation and the acquisition and impact of federal antipoverty programs. By tracing the leadership styles of just two individuals, the gendered complexity of organizing and managing a movement deepens.

Finally, *Crossroads at Clarksdale* shows how the local defense of Jim Crow worked, engaging with the local white leadership and law enforcement as activists continuously tried to secure meetings, compromises, and cooperation with them. These (mostly) men are also characters who influenced the trajectory of local mass movement activities by their racism and belligerence and their own organizing. Indeed, as the stories unfold and the book ends, the power of these men, supported by the state and national politics, remains.

Ultimately, this is a story of people and change in a community in one place over a long period of time. It is a story of people in organizations, in government, in schools, and on the streets. It is the story of Clarksdale beyond the history of the blues or the glorious days of the white pioneers—public histories that dilute or ignore other narratives. This is another Clarksdale, one with faces pressed into dirty floors at the police station after a beating, or seated in Vera Pigee's beauty salon, or gathered in Aaron Henry's drugstore sipping cold sodas on a hot day, or congregated in church basements, or meeting at the Freedom House. These stories are also national stories. They illustrate how people utilized organizations, not how organizations directed their members. They also portray the power of individual actions. They are continuing stories of hope and despair, of triumph and tragedy. They are the stories that made the blues.

CHAPTER ONE

Washington Was Far Away

DEFINING A DIFFERENT POSTWAR DELTA

*As protest began to stir among local Negroes in the early fifties, it became
more acceptable to express dissatisfaction with the status quo. This change was
significant, because so many Negroes had been willing to accept conditions
rather than question them and gamble with reprisals.*
—*Aaron Henry,* Fire Ever Burning

*The only thing I knew about the NAACP was that it is something that
is supposed to make these Mississippi white folks act like human beings and I
want to be a part of that monster.* — *Vera Pigee,* Struggle of Struggles

In Mississippi, the violence of white supremacy stained the land as in few
other places in America. The brutal murder of fourteen-year-old Emmett Till
in Money, Mississippi, in August 1955 embodied, then transcended, that violence. The crime stunned even those who had grown accustomed to everyday
white terror, but it also galvanized a generation in Mississippi and beyond.

One of those responding to the violence was Aaron Henry, president of the
Clarksdale/Coahoma County branch of the National Association for the Advancement of Colored People (NAACP). "The Coahoma County Branch found
itself at the Rail Head of activities relating to the murder of Emmett Till in
1955," Henry recalled.[1] Members of the NAACP leadership, most of whom were
not normally found in the fields, donned overalls to comb the area looking for
witnesses who either saw the murderers with Till or witnessed the theft of the
cotton gin that pinned him down in his watery resting place. Henry remembered, "We all knew we moved under a cloud, and we moved cautiously."[2] He

told an interviewer in 1969 that "in trying to find out who the witnesses were, who saw what [happened], day after day, [we went] into the cotton fields and chopping cotton with the hands, and picking cotton with the hands, wandering through the crowds just to find out what we could about Emmett."[3] The organization also provided safe passage north for these witnesses after the trial.

As northern journalists descended on the Delta, reporting to a rapt national audience on the alien, backward conditions in postwar Mississippi, one of that state's native daughters came back home. Vera Mae Pigee had recently returned to Clarksdale from Chicago, where she had studied cosmetology. As an active member of the Coahoma County NAACP, she journeyed to Sumner, the site of the trial and about thirty miles from Clarksdale, to observe and offer support to fearful locals: "I was in touch with the people when the trial was over, they wouldn't stay in a little town like Sumner, they would come to Clarksdale and go other places to stay, and some wouldn't tell anyone where they were. They were just that afraid," Pigee remembered. "They were black people and maybe it wasn't like they were so afraid of one white person, but of a crowd, coming with their white sheets on to kill somebody, like these people had killed Emmett Till."[4]

Henry and Pigee are emblematic of postwar grassroots black freedom movements. Virtually unknown on the national stage, they are two of many who devoted the greater part of their adult lives to the struggle for racial justice in Mississippi. Yet Henry and Pigee, by organizing and sustaining the local movement in Clarksdale, were not simply local representatives of a national mass movement. They were, in complex ways, architects of the movement's foundation, the kind of people without whom a mass uprising against Jim Crow would have been impossible.

Aaron Henry, the most celebrated civil rights leader in Clarksdale, was born in the Coahoma County town of Dublin in 1922. His father took shoe carpentry courses at the Tuskegee Institute in Alabama, enabling him to work his trade in the county. His mother, Mattie, was a member of the Women's Society of Christian Service, one of the few biracial organizations in Mississippi.[5] The family had the means to pay tuition for a decent high school education, and with no black public schools available, boarding at Coahoma County Agricultural High School was the only option. While there, Henry became involved in the NAACP. He credited one civics teacher in particular, Miss Thelma K. Shelby, newly graduated from Dillard University (where she had joined the NAACP), as a major influence on his maturing political sensibilities. She spent extra time with her seniors, assigning Richard Wright's *Black Boy* and *Native*

Son, along with *Uncle Tom's Cabin*, speaking French to them, and sharing her indignation over the state of racial affairs. Henry recalled that Shelby talked the "total incoming senior class into taking out a junior membership in the NAACP."[6]

Serving in the U.S. Army during World War II, he sought out the NAACP as he struggled between the discrimination in the military and the patriotism black soldiers felt and exhibited through their service and sacrifice. Henry grew impatient with the segregated facilities and the blatant racism. On his ship, the army had segregated movie showings: the whites had one night and African Americans had the next. As a result, black servicemen boycotted the movies. Henry recalled a particularly ornery chaplain in Honolulu, Hawaii. While preaching, he described the weather as "raining pitch forks and nigger babies." The black congregants walked out and never returned, preferring to attend services in town. A year later, Henry tried to talk to his fellow servicemen about Marcus Garvey (the Jamaican-born black nationalist and Pan-Africanist who founded the Universal Negro Improvement Association in 1914), but "hardly anyone else in the whole company knew who I was talking about." They seemed only versed in the contributions of Booker T. Washington and George Washington Carver, he noted. "They hadn't heard of Benjamin Bannicar [Benjamin Banneker, 1731–1806, African American mathematician and astronomer] . . . and Harriet Tubman and Nat Turner and many of these great Americans who were black and who helped to shape the destiny of this country."[7] They obviously had never had exposure to someone like Thelma Shelby in the classroom. He returned to Mississippi open-eyed and politically prepared to tackle Jim Crow.

Henry used his veteran's benefit provided through the GI Bill, one of the few postwar pieces of legislation or federal funding that trickled down into the hands of African Americans. Designed to reward veterans for their service, the GI Bill provided tuition and subsistence pay, and it educated a new generation of southern black men, elevating them out of the narrow occupational niche available to blacks in the region.[8] Henry enrolled at the Xavier University pharmacy school in New Orleans, determined to be his own boss. He served as student body president for two years, and at a 1948 meeting of the U.S. National Student Association (founded by veterans in 1947), he met and established a relationship with Allard Lowenstein, who would erupt on the political scene and in Mississippi with force in the sixties.[9] Henry graduated and became an independently employed pharmacist in Clarksdale, a man whose middle-class status had been forged with government assistance and who, in the coming years, would challenge Mississippi to make the kind of opportunity he enjoyed open to all. He was, as writer and activist Constance Curry put it, a "conservative militant," able to work his way up the social and political ladder while fighting it all the way in order to improve and expand its range.[10]

Vera Mae Pigee was born Vera Berry, the daughter of sharecroppers from Tutwiler, in Tallahatchie County. Wilder Berry, the father of Vera and brother W. C., succumbed to alcoholism and a wanderlust that led him to abandon his family. Their mother, Lucy Wright Berry, spent her time working the farm, raising livestock, growing vegetables, and exercising her impressive voice in the church choir, while instilling in her two children a fear of God and a solid work ethic. Young Vera absorbed both her mother's religious faith and her strength, especially in the way she stood up for herself in a hostile segregated South.[11] At a time when black people tended to "take things off of white folks," her mother had once delivered "a backhand whooping" to a white boy who continuously and contemptuously bumped her with his bike. The blow "knocked him plumb off his bike!"[12] Those opportunities to assert one's humanity (and not have it painfully stripped away) were rare. Lucy Berry, like many black Mississippians unable outwardly to resist Jim Crow most of the time, found alternative ways, particularly through spirituality, to voice discontent and ease everyday pressure.[13] By example, this mother's resourcefulness and endurance influenced her daughter, who grew up fast as she helped to run the household. Unable to go further than the ninth grade at the Rolenwald School in Tallahatchie County, she married Paul Pigee when she was fifteen and he was eighteen. "I'd set my cap for Paul Pigee the very first day I laid eyes on him," and their love survived the families' objections. Their daughter, Mary Jane, arrived a year later, but their second daughter died less than three weeks after birth the following year.[14] Pigee recalled traveling to Memphis from Clarksdale on the bus with baby Mary Jane in the mid-1940s: "I had to stand on a bus, where I had paid up fare. . . . It's approximately 100 miles and there were seats available on the bus, and because I was a black woman, I had to stand there and hold my baby."[15] Wearied by the journey and insulted by the injustice, she never forgot that day.

The Pigees wanted to improve their life chances and not be dependent on the land (and on landowners), as their parents had been. They moved briefly to Chicago so that Vera could study cosmetology and have a sustaining trade. Preferring to live closer to family, they returned to Clarksdale. Honing her skills at a beauty salon, her meticulousness and leadership acumen impressed the shop owner, Lillie Pharr, who, upon moving to California because of declining health, promptly promoted her to manage the business. Pigee rose to the occasion and learned how to run a business, then located at 407 Ashton Avenue. Pigee remembered how Pharr "took me aside and said that if anything happened to her, she wanted me to have the shop." When she passed, Pharr's husband honored his wife's wish and sold the business to Pigee, and in this way she became an independent business owner.[16]

Each in his or her own way, Henry and Pigee helped birth the modern black freedom movement in Coahoma County. As time moved on, it becomes clear how they were contrasting figures whose life trajectories bespeak the mass movement's dependence on distinct, yet malleable, modes of organizing. Both leadership styles, and the distinct gendered spheres in which they operated, were crucial to the movements' lifeblood — in Coahoma County and through-out the South. This chapter focuses more on Henry, since Pigee was away in Chicago for much of the county's early organizing, returning in 1955 and join-ing him on center stage.

In the meantime, four years before the Till murder, in 1951, another act of racial violence had spurred the founding of the Clarksdale/Coahoma County branch of the NAACP. The rape of Leola Tates and Erline Mills, two young African American women from Clarksdale, like the later lynching of Till, had galvanized the local community and had transformed ad hoc, disparate resis-tance to Jim Crow into the early stirrings of a movement. The perpetrator of the assaults walked away free, a gift to a white man that was all too common in southern justice. That crime changed the fate of Coahoma County forever and amplified a rich history of local organizing and activism that already existed. Despite living under the calloused thumb of Jim Crow, African Americans in the immediate postwar years found ways to voice their concerns (from voting to education) and minister to one another's needs and complaints.

Early Postwar Organizing

The national NAACP had always had an embattled relationship with the state of Mississippi. So much so that in May 1948, Gloster Current, national director of branches for the NAACP, wrote to Executive Secretary Walter White caution-ing that "the state is devoid of a spokesman, white or Negro, who can speak out against [Governor Fielding L.] Wright."[17] Wright, who that year would be the vice presidential candidate of the Dixiecrat revolt, had appeared on state-wide radio "advising" black people in his state to go elsewhere if they con-templated eventual social equality.[18] The following year, in March 1949, John

Bell Williams, congressman from the Magnolia State and devout Dixiecrat, published an article in *Speakers Magazine* about the threat of "Civil Rights," expounding on the internal Communist attack driven by "selfishly organized minority groups." He tapped into a growing national hysteria generated by the escalating Cold War—a hysteria that would be used against civil rights organizations.[19] "Through the conscienceless racketeers who head these parasitic groups," Williams wrote, "they are asserting their political strength as never before—attempting to bring about a forced amalgamation of the white and black races."[20]

The virulent racism of Wright and Williams, and the ever-present threat of white violence it inspired, intimidated many black people into a public silence. Yet Current misjudged the extent of local African American agitation. Lamenting the absence of one clear spokesman in Mississippi, he had overlooked the leaders then working long hours within black communities, discreetly and safely out of general view. Local black civil rights groups worked to improve their members' life choices in the everyday, given the opportunities (which were lacking) available. Thus organizations rose and fell in visibility and activity, and memberships shifted, depending on the ebb and flow of success, activism, and leadership. Flexible loyalties and alliances to organizations helped local people adapt to their current crises and pool resources quickly and as needed. It helped them to survive. Within four years of Current's comment, local leaders would become more vocal and visible in public, and many would gain national recognition.[21]

During the war years, the most dominant black activist organization of the era, the NAACP, had remained predominantly middle class in membership and legalistic in strategy. Conventional political lobbying in Washington, D.C., in the end, produced few gains; and the courts eventually provided the NAACP with its most durable successes.[22] It chose its cases carefully, selecting plaintiffs who could withstand the pressure of a prolonged, public battle and the inevitable recrimination. Likewise, with thinly spread resources and staff, the national office of the NAACP concentrated its attention on certain cases and places that had a fighting chance. It seemed safer and more expedient to make the courts of law the battleground than to see the bloodshed of the world war replicate itself in the streets and fields of America. The organization would remain somewhat stuck in this model, subsequently drawing criticism from newer civil rights groups with younger constituencies eager for direct and immediate action. Concentrating resources and personnel outside of the Deep South and building up urban branches where the institution maintained a strong base worked, as the NAACP sustained surging membership figures during the war.[23]

With a comparatively small African American middle class in the Deep South, the NAACP membership there grew less robustly. Although World War II accelerated urbanization and industrialization across the country—the South, especially, benefited enormously from the huge injection of resources and jobs—the economy still ran on the low-waged labor of an undereducated black working class. In addition, the ever-present and real fear of losing standing in a volatile society dominated by the codes of Jim Crow made the African American middle classes cautious. Most opted to work at improving conditions within the system rather than overhauling it. The first option was radical; the second was potentially fatal.

As the black South awaited an opening at the national level, the effects of cracks in white supremacy had become more visible. The NAACP's legal strategy, albeit restricted to a few signature cases, rang Jim Crow's first audible death knell. *Smith v. Allwright* (1944); *Morgan v. Virginia* (1946); *Sweatt v. Painter* (1950); *McLaurin v. Oklahoma* (1950); and *Henderson v. United States* (1950) extracted the legal linchpins from segregation as the Supreme Court increasingly confirmed that segregated institutions were not equal.[24] Joining forces with President Truman's 1947 President's Committee on Civil Rights report, "To Secure These Rights," and publications like Gunner Myrdal's 1944 *American Dilemma*, the life expectancy of white supremacy, at least at the national level, had seemed to shorten.[25]

National improvements during the war had passed over the Delta, and many World War II black veterans returning home reacted with dismay. They found out that German prisoners of war had been shipped to the United States and that ten camps had formed in the Delta in 1944. Camp Como, in northern Mississippi, had a satellite camp in Clarksdale, where prisoners were sent out to work in the cotton fields, replacing the black men sent overseas to fight them. German prisoners enjoyed better treatment than the darker-skinned Americans who had toiled there in intolerable conditions. A son of Josef Menden, a prisoner held in Clarksdale for one year in 1944, visited in 1980 after his father had gushed about the region. Menden remembered the Delta as "a land where cotton grew abundantly and the people were as warm as summer evenings," and he said "wonderful things" about Mark Ham, the owner of the plantation on which he labored.[26] No African American could gush about their experiences on these plantations, and black GIs bristled at the insult to their patriotic service.

Most returning African Americans had witnessed the transforming possibilities of a different, and in many cases better, way of life during the war. Haywood Stephney, a native of Clarksdale, recalled: "When you're not exposed to much you don't get much. But after seeing what some of the other world was doing then I realized how far behind I was. As we began to move and stir around and learn other ways then we had a choice—a comparison."[27] Yet returning brought practical considerations. Veterans needed jobs to feed families and to survive in an environment hostile to their presence. The South had changed little socially and politically in their absence, and many servicemen suffered low morale and despondency in a situation outside of their control.[28] Nevertheless, through their experiences abroad, many minds had grown attuned to a more defined racial consciousness that would no longer stay silent about inequality. This consciousness seeped into those with whom the soldiers came into contact and sped up the possibility that change would come.

Three pugnacious soldiers who came home searing from the brand of military segregation were Aaron Henry, Medgar Evers, and Amzie Moore.[29] Medgar Evers would come to focus his attentions statewide on behalf of the NAACP. He returned from the war, registered to vote with his brother Charles, and attended Alcorn A&M as a business major—like Henry, thanks to the GI Bill. Amzie Moore worked hard in Cleveland, Mississippi, as president of the local NAACP branch and is credited with welcoming Robert Moses and thus introducing the Student Nonviolent Coordinating Committee (SNCC) into the state. In Clarksdale, Henry would become a leader. All three directly credited the war for their ardor to fight at home for what they had fought for abroad. Henry recalled, "Ex-soldiers told their friends and families things that they had seen in their travels and the word had spread that conditions in Coahoma County had not been ordained by God." Furthermore, he added, "the situation was ripe for leadership and someone was needed whose livelihood was not dependent on the white community."[30]

Shortly after returning from the war in 1946, taking full advantage of Mississippi legislation that exempted veterans from the poll tax requirement, Henry tried to register to vote in the city of Clarksdale's mayoral election. When he approached, the circuit clerk began to stall. "The first time I went to the circuit clerk's office to register, he told me he knew nothing about the poll tax exemption for veterans. He was very nice but insisted that I was confused," Henry remembered. He found some white veterans, who had been given poll tax exemption certificates by the same court clerk when they had gone to register. They lent Henry a copy and he tried again: "I got the same innocent ignorance of any knowledge about poll tax exemption until I pulled out the certificate."[31] On 23 December 1949, nine months after Congressman Williams's article, Aaron Henry, now twenty-seven years old, registered as a voter of Coahoma County in the south Clarksdale precinct. Standing first in a neat, orderly line of white veterans and older men who had paid their required poll taxes, he registered without hindrance.[32] Presumably the numbers were small enough not to warrant undue anxiety.

His actions served as an example as he worked to get other black people out to register in his hometown, with the help of the Mississippi Progressive Voters' League. The league had formed in 1946 to implement the *Smith v. Allwright* Supreme Court decision, which had outlawed the whites-only primary. As the organizational base for postwar voter registration drives, its headquarters were in Jackson, with major branches in Clarksdale and Hattiesburg. Focusing solely on voter registration and relying on preexisting networks, the organization urged the payment of poll taxes and "the pursuit of civic studies" but avoided the kind of door-to-door campaigning that raised white suspicion. The league enjoyed a small measure of impunity because it focused on the disproportionately small black middle class, hardly a threat to Jim Crow at the polls. Officially stressing a no-party preference, the organization emphasized the importance of registering black people and then voting, but for the most part, few wanted to "upset the applecart." A prosperous local dentist, Dr. Purvis William Hill Sr., established in the area for twenty years, had founded the Coahoma County branch while Aaron Henry attended college in Louisiana. By June 1947, it boasted 168 members and a paid secretary. It aided black attempts to pass the literacy tests and encouraged local teachers, ministers, and educators to assist, helping to qualify 600 African Americans for the 1946 primary.[33] In 1950, Henry began to work earnestly with the league as it "mounted a non partisan effort to educate and motivate potential black voters."[34] By then he had graduated and moved back to Clarksdale permanently with his new wife, Noelle. It would not take long before his sights were set on finding resources to overturn the applecart completely.

Mississippi's Postwar NAACP

The NAACP, founded in 1909 in New York City, had long struggled to create some semblance of its national presence in the South. Battered by a downturn in membership during the Great Depression, the NAACP had come back aggressively in the 1940s. Most of the branches in the region organized around membership drives and tours by the director of branches.[35] Unlike most of the country, where the NAACP operated more confidently, in the South the national office had to wear down considerable shoe leather in order to spread the word and convince local blacks to join. Nevertheless, the NAACP had not gained a strong foothold in Mississippi (apart from a branch in Jackson) during the war years as it had in other states, including many in the South.[36] The organization planted sustaining roots in Mississippi only after the war.

In March 1951, the Southeast Regional Office opened its first temporary office to coordinate membership campaigns in Birmingham, Alabama.[37] Establishing offices throughout the country kept the New York City office in touch with far-flung branches. Regional outposts also provided legal and organizational expertise and support, while creating and strengthening new branches.[38] Ruby Hurley, on a three-month assignment, had the task of keeping in touch with the local branches and working to develop programs for a growing membership.[39] Like the blueprints for the headquarters, the goals were short term: to augment membership during the spring campaign and to improve the bonds between local and national offices. But by the beginning of 1952, the Southeast Regional Office had become permanent. Leaving their options open, and reluctant to commit resources in a region not expected to yield significant results, the national officers recognized that progress in the South would not happen overnight. Indeed, it was not guaranteed to happen at all.[40]

The only definite commitment made by the national office was to Hurley, whose job was extended indefinitely. Born Ruby Hawkins in 1909 in Washington, D.C., she had been active in the NAACP since the late 1930s—she was a charter member of the branch in Washington, D.C. One of her first campaigning experiences was with the Marion Anderson's Citizens Committee, which had found an alternate site, the Lincoln Memorial, for an integrated concert after the black soprano was denied the use of the Daughters of the American Revolution Constitutional Hall.[41] Unsure of a professional path, she graduated from Miners Teachers College in Washington, D.C., and attended Terrell Law School at night, while working full time at the Industrial Bank after a stint at the federal government. She married Lieutenant William L. Hurley of the U.S. Army Engineer Corps. The war took him away for long stretches of time, and she spent that time in her local community.[42] Hurley worked her way up the NAACP organizational ranks—from branch member, to member of the executive committee, and finally to organizer and sponsor of the youth council.[43] Her contacts among influential African Americans in the nation's capital secured her the post of national youth secretary.[44] Relocating to New York City in 1943, she began her new job developing NAACP youth councils and college chapters, which she did successfully for the next eight years.

She was an intensely private person who was cognizant of her status as a woman in the South, and her life remains shadowed behind her work.[45] Yet she was sent to battle a leviathan: maintaining the southern NAACP infrastructure in the face of massive opposition. In a region where African American women were treated in the same ungracious way as men, not protected from physical and emotional violence due to their sex, the NAACP entrusted her with its southern offensive. Acknowledging her double vulnerability as an African American and as a woman in a violent climate of repression that dissuaded many black people from emerging as political activists, Hurley nonetheless gripped the baton with both hands.

The NAACP was often a haven of unreconstructed patriarchal masculinity, and women rarely broke through the male ranks to executive, decision-making positions in the organization. Lucille Black and Ella Jo Baker were the most prominent NAACP women during this time, serving in the national office in New York City, but they were in charge of the membership and branches, as opposed to organizational policy or the financial purse strings. Likewise, Hurley's first temporary assignment was to boost membership numbers in the South. Her position became full time and permanent when she became entangled with the social and political issues that dissuaded black southerners from signing their names to the membership rolls. While her sex would have done little to dilute the hatred of segregationists, it may have aided in her appeals to ordinary black folk in southern counties and towns, where she effectively leaned on her femininity to motivate women and convince men to take on the struggle. Thus, even as the NAACP maintained its own glass ceiling for women, it came to depend heavily not only on female staffers like Hurley, Baker, and Black but also on women in local southern communities (as mothers, church members, and nurturers) as well. Indeed, Vera Pigee's experiences would exemplify these women.

Yet, as the NAACP took its first real steps in the Deep South in 1951, in the Delta, the Regional Council of Negro Leadership (RCNL), one of the first indigenous black organizations in Mississippi, also began its work. The leadership here was profoundly male and traditional too. The RCNL founder, Dr. Theodore Roosevelt Mason (T. R. M.) Howard, born in 1908 in Murray, Kentucky, came to Mississippi as the chief surgeon of the Knights and Daughters of Tabor Hospital. He completed his undergraduate work at Union College in Lincoln, Nebraska, and earned his degree in medicine at the College of

Medical Evangelists in Loma Linda, California. Hired by the Taborian hospital in 1942, in the all-black town of Mound Bayou, in Bolivar County, Howard climbed quickly up the social ladder, accumulating substantial wealth through numerous business enterprises.[46] Mound Bayou, founded in 1887 by an ex-slave, had remained a safe bastion in Mississippi for African Americans to vote and hold local office. With such a concentration of aspiring black leaders and egos, competition caused conflict, and Howard was dismissed from the hospital. A rival fraternal organization, the United Order of Friendship of America, opened a hospital across the street from the Taborian hospital and installed Howard as the chief surgeon.

Under Howard's leadership, the Mississippi RCNL took its first breath. The collective sought to bring local black leaders in the Delta counties together under one organization with the stated goals of guiding "our people in their civic responsibilities regarding education, registration and voting, law enforcement, tax-paying, the preservation of property, the value of saving and to guide us in all things which will make us stable, qualified, conscientious citizens, which will lead to first class citizenship for Negroes in the Mississippi Delta and the State of Mississippi."[47] Befitting an organization composed largely of middle-class strivers with a Booker T. Washingtonian orientation, the RCNL emphasized working within the system rather than fighting it. "This is the most opportuned time for the formation of an organization of this type," leaders explained optimistically, "for the common good of all citizens in the Delta area, and the State, regardless of race or creed."[48]

They organized in order to seek cooperation with the white Delta Council for a mutually satisfying solution to regional issues: "The chosen leaders of the masses in Mississippi and the Delta [must] get together in a great organization through whose committees, working with the white Delta Council and other proper agencies in our State and Nation, may arrive at a solution to most of our problems which will lead us into the more abundant life." The Delta Council, formed in 1935 as the region struggled to recover from the Great Depression, in fact set out to be a regional chamber of commerce. Concerned primarily with white agricultural issues, the group provided strong voting blocs in elections, and some of the most powerful planters in the state were members. Serving eighteen Delta and part-Delta counties, it boasted a large membership, and the Delta Council noted that because of its service to the counties, they received financial contributions from governmental bodies and that honorary memberships were regularly bestowed on officials who acted in their interest.[49] Focusing on self-improvement and conservative practicalities like saving money, property preservation, and tax paying, the RCNL sought to ally with the Delta Council rather than be a civil rights group.[50]

Indeed, in a 1952 memo to Walter White in New York City, Ruby Hurley labeled the RCNL doctrine as "separate but equal."[51] It was true that the RCNL's early analysis of problems in Mississippi downplayed the two most basic barriers to black advancement: mass political disfranchisement and economic inequality. Agricultural mechanization, for example, had rendered increasing numbers of blacks unemployed and unemployable in the new industrial and urban markets. Racism kept the black working class uneducated, shut out of apprenticeship training, and confined to impoverished agricultural cycles. The RCNL's written aims failed to articulate how any attempts to transform black opportunity in Mississippi would have to address the way that race and class were intertwined within the state's pernicious white rule. In order to survive in the viper pit, it could not stick out its neck.

Nonetheless, the RCNL's policy of open arms made the NAACP take note, as it would again when SNCC formed eight years later. As another method of survival, RCNL membership was conceived broadly to include as many local African American groups as possible. The standard advertisement for the organization welcomed any black person not affiliated with a Communist organization who supported the development of leadership and the welfare of black citizens.[52] Ruby Hurley observed the threat of the RCNL to the NAACP, citing the RCNL's wide membership (500 people in twenty-nine counties) and the assertive local leadership. She wrote, "One of our presidents has talked with Dr. Howard in an effort to bring him around to our way of thinking, but to no avail."[53] Educated men like Aaron Henry, either landowners or businessmen, led the RCNL and worked to build a society on the foundations of self-help. The RCNL stressed a local loyalty based on local politics and community needs. Although many of these same men also organized under the auspices of the NAACP in city and county branches, Hurley rightly assessed that they might undermine the NAACP by favoring the local group over the larger national organization.

Hurley distrusted what she considered appeasement by the RCNL. "Our people are so thoroughly conditioned to accept the segregated pattern that they are easy prey for what appears to me to be an organization set up for self-aggrandizement reasons," she wrote.[54] In some ways, she was right. The risks of joining the NAACP before World War II always outweighed the possibilities that protest would succeed.[55] Recalling the early fifties in the Delta, Henry observed that "communication continued in the traditional master-servant relationship. On our part, the Negro would lie to his white boss when the boss asked if he was happy with the status quo—he knew he needed to say what the white man wanted to hear."[56] What appeared to be acquiescent behavior may have masked strategies of resistance—lying kept you in good favor, which kept you alive—but black Deltans were always aware of the lie, and they kept their organizational loyalties and affiliations close to their chests.

In the thirties, anthropologist, author, and folklorist Zora Neale Hurston called this behavior "featherbed resistance," in which African Americans would give partial information in order to satisfy those outside the community, while keeping their real feelings and thoughts hidden.[57] "Featherbed resistance" gave African Americans up and down the socioeconomic ladder in the Delta the leverage to negotiate, albeit minimally, in their daily lives. The RCNL provided the space for more vocal resistance, in part because it was perceived as less of a threat than the NAACP, with which the white Mississippi establishment fought tooth and nail. Howard recognized the native xenophobia of white Mississippians and decided that they would be more likely to talk to their "own Negroes" than with strangers from New York City.[58] Given the reputation of the NAACP in the South among whites—as pro-Communist and aggressively anti–Jim Crow—black Mississippians were reluctant to put their eggs into such a fragile basket.

White resistance to the NAACP across Mississippi dissuaded public organizing as well. Dr. B. E. Murph, a dentist and president of the Laurel, Mississippi, branch, wrote: "The NAACP is about as welcome as a rattlesnake in these circles." He continued with pride, "We have very little support from our white citizens, and I would say that about 90 per cent of the Negroes in our state are skeptical. . . . Many of our people are afraid to be seen at a NAACP meeting. . . . Yet we are willing to fight and fight uncompromisingly."[59] The dire membership figures reflected the woes of the NAACP in the Magnolia State. In 1951, there were a total of 1,486 members in twenty organized branches, due in part to Hurley's hard work, but by the middle of 1952 the number had fallen to 593. Ruby Hurley's lack of resources exacerbated the problem: she could not sustain the momentum, which also slowed because of white resistance.

In much of the internal correspondence between the regional and the national offices, Hurley complained about the lack of money and the slow flow of supplies from New York City. With the structure centralized, urgently needed funds had to be requested formally in order to receive authorization before delivery to the finance department.[60] The hierarchical structure created bottlenecks that handicapped the work of the NAACP in the Deep South. For example, during the early years of grassroots activities in Mississippi, both Ruby Hurley and Medgar Evers (who had served as the state's field secretary since late 1954) received administrative slaps on the wrist, meted out by Gloster Current, for embarking on projects without seeking proper counsel from NAACP headquarters.[61] Burdened with the necessity of "procedure" that comes with running a national organization, the NAACP could not meet the needs of the people, who required direct, urgent help in their particular situations. It is not surprising then that local people, eager for relief, sought other avenues, such as the RCNL, through which to channel their activities.

The NAACP grounded its reputation on victory in the courtroom.[62] While no one involved disputed the value of this approach, litigation in Mississippi against Jim Crow at this point was suicide. Yet Current's actions, like his comments in 1948 about the state's black leadership, are important because they illustrate the national office's general disconnect with the state conference and local branches, a friction that would continually create sparks within the organization and further isolate grassroots activism. Current features prominently at these contested moments, given his position as the main point of contact in the New York City office for the branches. When narrating the story of movement-building, which required quick decision making at the local level, Current appears obstructive, a northern middle-class professional who probably never experienced profound terror of the sort that black southerners had, and he issued commands from afar in New York City, dictating how things should be. Born in Indianapolis, Indiana, educated at West Virginia State University and at Wayne State University (master's degree in public administration), he served as executive director of the Detroit NAACP branch from 1941 to 1946 before joining the national office. His trajectory could not have differed more from that of most black Mississippians, and the fact that he grew up away from the tentacles of the South, just as Roy Wilkins had grown up in St. Louis, clarifies (but does not excuse) his experiential disconnect. Certainly the national office had to juggle the needs and demands of branches in all regions, but Current's inability to recognize, appreciate, and trust the differences among locales, branches, and organizers frustrated members at the grass roots and led to constant tensions between field staff like Evers and the New York City office.[63]

Meanwhile, immediate relief for the visible and visceral suffering in Mississippi could not be delayed. Despite her views of the RCNL, Ruby Hurley, whose own opinions shifted after she relocated south, acknowledged that the NAACP had not addressed the needs of the masses.[64] She persisted and even broke through in many places as she traveled extensively during May 1953 recruiting for the NAACP. Her trip to Mississippi, accompanying the state president, the Reverend Amos O. Holmes, was not her first. A year before, she had toured the state to assess the extent of membership campaigns and reported to the national membership secretary a healthy interest in establishing branches.[65] This trip took her to towns where branches did not exist—Fulton, Tupelo, Starkville, Holly Springs, Clarksdale, and Canton—as well as to established branches to observe campaigns to support local membership efforts.[66] Scheduled midway through her itinerary, Hurley made a stop in Clarksdale, "a Delta town with a large Negro population," where she participated in a "very well-attended meeting."[67] Still, in her monthly report to Gloster Current, she noted, "The feeling had been that the citizens of the community could take care of things themselves which is the philosophy of the [RCNL]."[68]

The NAACP in Clarksdale/Coahoma County

Hurley's first perceptions of Coahoma County had developed during her associations with RCNL members. With Mound Bayou located in the next county on Highway 61, activists did not have to travel far to find allies, but they could also function locally. Two years before formal admission into the NAACP, the Progressive Voters' League in Clarksdale sponsored a public program at the courthouse so that the small number of registered black voters could hear the invited candidates. Such public performances of organization and initiative existed early in a relative climate of tolerance, where even the local newspaper, the *Clarksdale Press Register*, advertised the meeting.[69]

Indeed, white Clarksdale prided itself on the extent of its interracial cooperation in comparison to its neighboring counties. The city's population in 1950 was just over 16,500, with roughly equal distribution between the two races. In the rural parts of the county, blacks outnumbered whites two to one.[70] Henry provided a useful illustration of the mechanics of race relations in Clarksdale with his description of the local Civic Music Association. This group, responsible for hosting artists and organizing concerts, had a membership of about five hundred white and fifty black citizens and was chaired by Rosemarie Clark, a wealthy white woman who had married into one of Clarksdale's founding families. The central interracial committee, which included four or five local blacks, met regularly at members' homes to plan musical events. Some of these conferences occurred at the palatial home of Mrs. Clark, which had been built from the sweat of slave labor. Here, all members sat at the same table and ate together. The irony was not lost on Henry: "People like the Clarks were immune to the law inside their own homes, but out in public where we had the concerts, we found ourselves in the poorer segregated seating enforced by law." Henry grimly recorded, "White people completely controlled politics, finances, and employment. They held a tight grip, and we knew that our fight for equality was going to be long and difficult."[71] Those at the top of society's class structure could be tolerant and open-minded—their status was untouchable. Their tolerance extended to affairs that valued black cultural contributions to the civic art-appreciating community—but only behind closed doors and only with a select few. Sharing political or economic power with blacks never entered the picture.

In his personal life, Henry's association with the white community remained minimal. After finishing college, he had needed a financial partner to open his pharmacy, but his public push for equality turned potential investors away. K. William Walker, whom Henry described thirty years later as "a young white boy in business on Issaquena [the black business district]," offered to go into partnership. From 1950 to 1954, the men maintained good relations and mutual respect for each other. Eventually, the pressure from the white community got to be too much for Walker, and he let Henry buy him out, dissolving the partnership and then purchasing a Walgreens store. Henry had few white friends beyond Walker. Most whites just saw him as a rabble-rouser. "The reason for this was that so few whites took seriously our claims about achieving equality," Henry reasoned. "Washington was far away."[72] But white Clarksdale's selective tolerance and the black community's sense of isolation were about to change. Henry began to see signs shortly after the rape trials in 1952.

In August 1951, thirty-five-year-old Leola Tates and twenty-two-year-old Erline Mills, two black Clarksdalians, separately accused the same white man of assault and rape. Police apprehended Greenville resident E. L. Roach, a truck driver, through the work and persistence of black citizens in Clarksdale. However, three justices of the peace swiftly dismissed the rape charge based on alleged discrepancies and conflicts in the victims' testimonies. Roach's witnesses included the Coahoma County deputy sheriff, Noble F. Black, who swore that the incident could not have taken place, despite Roach's admission to having had intercourse with the women. They disregarded a third woman, Freddie Lee Smith, who also testified that Roach had attempted to assault her.[73]

Recalling the case, Henry reasoned that "the outcome was normal for similar cases throughout the state and generally accepted as part of the system."[74] The Progressive Voters' League, the existing local black organization best equipped to respond, met soon after Roach's release to discuss forcing the case to a grand jury. Henry's presence in the league radicalized it somewhat. He pushed members hard at a critical crossroads to take the path of challenge rather than the well-trodden path of resignation and retreat. "We felt the need to express our outrage, or it would amount to just another case of white men raping Negro women and getting away with it." Henry, however, was realistic: "We also felt that nothing would come out of our efforts." The victims wanted to drop the case, fearful of retaliation and the publicity, which would destroy their privacy and wreak havoc on their families.[75] But Henry and others continued to apply pressure. With no black lawyers in town, they hired George F. Maynard, a liberal white attorney whose status as one of the grandsons of Clarksdale's founding families shielded him from threat and reproach. He charged $10,000 to take the case, an astronomical figure, but the community scraped together enough to take the case to court.[76] On 14 January 1952, Roach was indicted on two counts of kidnapping and two counts of pointing and aiming a pistol. On 28 January, after just fourteen minutes of deliberation, however, the all-white jury found him not guilty of kidnapping Leola Tate. Following the dismissal of the most serious charge, and after twelve hours of testimony and arguments, Maynard advised his clients to consent to drop the three remaining charges. Roach walked free two days later.[77]

The outcome of the case, despite its inevitability given the racial and sexual politics of the South, ignited a local fire.[78] As that fire burned, it revealed another subtle crack in the Delta's seemingly impenetrable Jim Crow façade. African Americans in Clarksdale had felt empowered enough to raise funds to hire special counsel, pursue the arrest, and convince two fearful and reluctant women to put their lives on the line for a larger cause. To challenge a centuries-old precedent that condoned the abuse of black women and sanctioned rape across the color line required a strong public stance of resistance. The judge in the case had ordered the trial closed to the public, aware that too much exposure made "southern justice" potentially vulnerable. The nervous behavior of the local white leadership, evident in the court proceedings, betrayed an increasing sense that white privileges, usually taken for granted, had to be guarded and monitored—a small opening, indeed, created by larger general trends in race politics and local black action. But black Clarksdalians had seized the opportunity.

The rape case marked a first set of crossroads for the segment of Clarksdale's black community now no longer willing to be silenced by the abuses and threats of Jim Crow. Aaron Henry wrote: "The straw that broke the camel's back was the complete insensitivity of the city of Clarksdale and Coahoma County to the Brutal Beatings and Rape."[79] Moreover, local media felt it newsworthy to report that the white attorney's services were paid by "interested Negroes of Clarksdale," emphasizing that "there is no evidence that the National Association for the Advancement of Colored People has taken any part in the case."[80] The local white community dreaded the NAACP using its litigation skills in Mississippi. It was this public display of fear that unwittingly prompted local black leaders to contact the NAACP's national offices to secure more protection. White nervousness in regard to the NAACP actually gave the organization an entryway into Clarksdale and also put leading whites on high alert.

Within months of the verdict, Denzill Turner, an epileptic, had a seizure on the street. Concerned whites called the police to report a perceived drunken black man on the loose. In the presence of the young man's father, who was frantically explaining the circumstances of his son's behavior, Turner died from multiple police gunshot wounds to the back. When the three arresting officers were exonerated, Henry led a group of concerned black citizens to protest the killing to the mayor. They encountered belligerence and a lack of interest. As Henry recalled, one of the white people present in the meeting mentioned that Henry "spoke as though [he] had been trained to refute arguments," referring to possible NAACP influence.[81] Shortly after the mayoral meeting, police and city officials approached Henry's business partner, K. William Walker, to "persuade" him to curb Henry's tongue—a request Walker promptly refused. Three days later, the FBI sent a representative to question Henry about his whereabouts for the past ten years. "The agent told me the bureau was trying to track down ten communists who had jumped bail and that they had reports that one of them was in Clarksdale."[82] The case, again not necessarily unique in its details, demonstrated not only the new, sustained level of activism in the black community but also the creeping coldness seeping from the mayor's office.

Many African Americans in Clarksdale, frustrated by the results in the rape trial and Turner murder, recognized the need for broader legal protection. At the next Progressive Voters' League meeting, the decision was made to organize a local NAACP branch, "with an eye to their history of legal protection."[83] Aaron Henry noted that the much-loved principal of the black high school in Clarksdale, Wallace A. Higgins (for whom the school was named), had in fact raised the issue at the Progressive Voters' League meeting but deferred the organizing and leadership to Henry, a common stance for many city employees.[84]

Instead, Higgins led pragmatically, making and maintaining spaces in schools for people like Thelma Shelby, but now he recognized that the time had come to bring in additional support. "My concept of our role," Henry wrote, "was at long last to get legal assistance when we needed it and perhaps remedy the frequent abuses our people suffered at the hands of whites."[85]

Henry and a few other black leaders contacted Ruby Hurley, and in May 1953 she came to Clarksdale with Rev. Amos Holmes (from Amory). The meeting drew an estimated 200 charter members, the result of persistent door-to-door campaigning in the community. "The existence of the branch opened our eyes to other civil rights issues," Henry recalled. "Speakers came to our meetings and made statements that seemed unbelievable to us. Thurgood Marshall came shortly after we had organized and promised that Ole Miss would be open to Negro students in the foreseeable future."[86] By the end of 1953, the branch had added 104 paid-up senior members, including Medgar Evers, and two youth members.[87] The swelling membership and the wholehearted participation of constituents in activities and fund-raising led Henry to report that "Clarksdale Negroes became recognized throughout the state and nation as citizens Determined [*sic*] to be free."[88]

While the fledgling NAACP branch busied itself with building membership, meeting regularly in private homes, the more established Mississippi Progressive Voters' League ran a voter registration drive in Coahoma County. Launched in September 1953 during a meeting of the Coahoma County chapter at Haven Methodist Church, the campaign hoped to secure 1,200 black voters by February 1954, signaling Clarksdale's emergence as a central site for black activity in the state.[89] League members stepped out a little further publicly, emboldened by the new NAACP branch, with whom most also held memberships. In March 1954, the local paper announced plans for the league to hold its state convention in Clarksdale in April at the Metropolitan Baptist Church, the first such meeting in the city.[90]

As Clarksdale became a beacon for growing black activism in the area, the light attracted the *Clarksdale Press Register*, which for the first time mentioned the Coahoma County NAACP. On the evening of Monday, 29 March 1954, a work night for most, the paper reported that New Orleans attorney Daniel Byrd, a regional officer of the NAACP, spoke before 300 people at Haven Methodist Church. He was a member of the counsel for the plaintiffs in the current Supreme Court case, *Brown v. Board of Education of Topeka*, consuming the interest of the South. Aaron Henry introduced Byrd, in town to promote voting registration as the way to raise standards of education and living conditions for African Americans. Also present was Medgar Evers—the new applicant to the University of Mississippi's law school—who spoke about his reasons for pursuing admission.[91] Byrd's participation in Clarksdale's program reflected surging NAACP activity, which would become even more pronounced after the *Brown* decision came down in May.

That surge also came from Ruby Hurley, who was applying pressure, sending regular newsletters through the summer with month-by-month action plans for branches, ending with the slogan, "LET'S DO MORE IN '54 BECAUSE WE WANT TO BE FREE BY '63."[92] The Mississippi State Conference of Branches held a meeting on 25 July with "state leaders, representing every major fraternal, civic, social, labor, religious, educational, business and professional organization in Mississippi" to develop a plan of action to deal with the state's racial issues.[93] The Mississippi NAACP had developed the habit of accommodating other organizations, much like the RCNL. This strategy, strongly discouraged by the national and regional office, became the method through which the maximum number of activists with malleable associations could coordinate efforts effectively and draw strength in numbers against a strong, united, pro-segregation force in Mississippi.

In this increasingly, though cautiously, aggressive context, the RCNL had begun to shift its aims. Ten days before the *Brown* decision, the RCNL held its third annual meeting in Mound Bayou, where it revealed a newfound partnership with and commitment to the NAACP, honoring the keynote speaker, Thurgood Marshall.[94] Many speakers were known NAACP men, including Jackson attorney Jack Young, who served on the RCNL committee on state and national legislation.[95] Pressed by the newly arrived NAACP, the RCNL had evolved from being concerned with black standing within the Jim Crow framework to being increasingly for dismantling it.[96] By the end of the decade, as members increased their roles in the NAACP, its membership and activities would be totally absorbed by the larger national group.

Mississippi's Education Battle before *Brown*

While the local NAACP members built the branch and organized voting drives, the *Brown v. Board of Education* case was pending in the U.S. Supreme Court. These two activities, one at the local level in the Delta, the other on the national stage, were not mutually exclusive or a coincidence in timing. The success of each depended on the other and both aimed to kill Jim Crow. Desegregating schools, major sites of socialization and cultural learning, threatened white supremacy at the root. The possibility that young children would naturally form friendships with each other in the classroom, across racial lines, from kindergarten to adulthood, deeply troubled segregationists. How could parents maintain prejudicial views in the home, insisting that black people were inferior, when school opened up the possibility of black classmates studying with their children, side by side on equal terms? The specter of sex, social equality, and "race mixing" could become a reality in the classroom. It could never happen. The future of white supremacy was at stake. The defiance of governors, legislators, and lawyers blazoned across the pages of the local press for days after the *Brown* ruling and buttressed white citizens' resolve to fight.[97]

Impetus created by the cases leading up to the 1954 *Brown* decision became evident in Mississippi, stimulated in part by the increased militancy of local African American groups in the postwar years. The lawsuit brought by Jackson teacher Gladys Bates in 1948 to equalize teachers' salaries, although defeated, brought attention to the extent of the educational inequalities in the state, ringing warning bells throughout Dixie. Then the RCNL had evolved from the desire to carve improved spaces for themselves within the existing system (like Bates had tried to do) to overhauling the system altogether. Jim Crow's legal protectors also changed tactics and began to take this task more seriously in the early 1950s. The extroverted bravado of the segregationists, who projected their confidence in maintaining Jim Crow, masked genuine concern that their way of life might change. Rather than leave it up to the Supreme Court, legislators got to work to try to forestall the inevitable.

In Coahoma County and in Clarksdale (the county had had two separate school districts since 1890), local efforts to both maintain segregation and make conditions equal (to finally uphold the 1896 *Plessy v. Ferguson* "separate but equal" clause) moved in tandem to the state's, including the idea of consolidating white schools to pool and upgrade resources and facilities.[98] The local paper noted, "The South is willing to pay dearly for the privilege of clinging to a custom that has been cherished—and fought over."[99] Studies and budgets conducted statewide projected just how much custom would cost and acknowledged just how unequal the schools were. In 1951, initial estimates made by Mississippi's Department of Education calculated an outlay of $144,410,809 to equalize school facilities immediately.[100]

Several groups formed by the Mississippi Education Association and the Department of Education toured the state to address teachers and school boards and galvanize support for the program, stopping in Clarksdale in October 1951. The superintendent of Clarksdale's public schools, H. B. Heidelberg, sent word to hundreds of white parents encouraging their attendance. The message included the following incentive: "The menace of a U.S. Supreme Court decision compelling equality of schooling for the two races, or else — the abolishment of separate schools for white and Negroes hangs like a black cloud over the people of Mississippi."[101] An estimated 500 people attended the meeting. The discussions around the state and in Jackson continued for years, with several plans drafted to lay out how the program would materialize.[102]

The program's ultimate failure can be boiled down to five factors. First, there was never money to close the gap. White taxpayers balked at the huge financial burden that equalization would impose. Second, the proposals were designed for minimal adjustment in state spending to deflect desegregation challenges — the rhetoric of equalization was just that. Third, the immense educational gap that had existed since the turn of the century between black and white school systems could never be equalized in any real way without years of real commitment and financial investment. Fourth, changes to the system had to come at the local level, where implementation remained poor and halfhearted at best. Finally, white leaders wanted to see their black counterparts explicitly pledge support for equalization before they funneled large sums of money into black education. The rising levels of black activity clearly showed that black support was not forthcoming, despite many black educators pushing for state spending in their institutions at the expense of desegregation and a few black citizens promoting voluntary segregation. Despite all this, however, white segregationists in Mississippi still felt in total control of "their" black people.[103]

In July 1954, an overconfident Governor Hugh White invited black leaders to Jackson to discuss black interests in the schools. The NAACP elected T. R. M. Howard to speak.[104] Believing he could still manage African Americans with plantation-based condescension, the hubristic governor imagined that black Mississippians would support his plan to continue segregation, despite the Supreme Court's decision that spring. Indeed he had actively supported the 1953 equalization plan passed through the state legislature, the first serious effort to end inequalities in the dual system. On the spectrum of those legislators (most, if not all) who supported segregated education, White was one of those who believed in actually equalizing education — as a boon to the state and as an act to comply with *Plessy*.[105]

The governor was in for a surprise that hot July day, because, as historian Numan Bartley observed, "the day of Booker T. Washington had passed."[106] Howard got to the podium, eager at last to address the governor. Taking a deep breath, he spoke: "Fundamentally, there is no such thing as separate but equal in a matter as vital as the education of our children. We believe that it is morally and legally wrong for those who have sworn to uphold the laws of our land to talk about abolishing the public school system, in order to evade the laws of our land."[107] He added, "We seriously recommend that competent Negroes be appointed to all policy-making Boards affecting both races on a State and local level. The day is past and forever gone when one race can work out all the problems affecting another group and bring it to him as a 'take it or leave it' proposition. We are demanding a chance to help shape our own destiny."[108] To calm a potentially violent negative reaction to his demands, he made a point of adding: "There is not a thinking Negro in Mississippi today that bothers about social equality, but we are mighty concerned about equality of educational opportunity. We recommend that instead of the term voluntary segregation that we use and follow the path of voluntary integration, until the Supreme Court says 'when and how.'"[109] Not only did this public statement embarrass the governor, but it also demonstrated confidence not heretofore exhibited in the past by African Americans in Mississippi.

"Real Violent in Words and Deeds"

In equal parts, *Brown* validated the courage of black Mississippians and enraged whites. A few border states had quietly begun integrating as the NAACP won lower court decisions, but on 27 May 1954, a few short weeks after the *Brown* decision, James O. Eastland from Mississippi stood on the Senate floor and declared: "Let me make this very clear. The South will retain segregation!"[110] Vicious reprisals from state and local white groups provided fuel for an already blazing fire. Aaron Henry noted, "During the era of 1954 and 1955— came the founding of the White Citizens' Council and several of our members were targeted for extinction."[111] Citizens' Councils emerged in Indianola, in Sunflower County (about sixty miles from Clarksdale), in the summer of 1954, a direct result of *Brown*. Native white Clarksdalian Robert Patterson, after hearing Mississippi Supreme Court judge Thomas P. Brady's "Black Monday" tirade against the U.S. Supreme Court decision, "went to work to save the South," organizing the first council explicitly to prevent integration. Ironically, Henry and Patterson had known each other on more amicable terms in earlier years.[112] Standard Citizens' Council recruiting rhetoric adhered to the popular white myth of the black male rapist: "When the NAACP petitioned to Court for integration, it was to open the bedroom doors of white women to Negro men."[113] Tactically, the Citizens' Councils organized economic reprisals while publicly renouncing violence. Council leaders hoped in particular to destroy the NAACP. A declaration of war had been issued.

On one side of that brewing war were the Citizens' Councils, the state's white elected officials, the state Democratic Party, the white business community, and the more violent vigilante types. On the other side were the NAACP, with its small but growing local networks in places like Clarksdale, and a handful of organizations like the RCNL. It hardly seemed a fair fight.

The Citizens' Councils never set out to be a secret society. Lawmakers in the counties and at state levels openly discussed the Citizens' Councils and their "persuasive tactics." Patterson maintained, "We felt that our position could be defended without hurting anyone, on purely legal and constitutional grounds."[114] Councils with the largest memberships in the Delta had leaderships composed of the most prominent, well-educated, and conservative businessmen in the community, all of whom pledged to maintain segregation and to forswear violence.[115] Designed to be a gentleman's club of respected citizenry, the organization publicly sought to legitimize its existence around civic duty and ideals, separate from groups like the Ku Klux Klan. One unidentified Yazoo County planter summed it up: "We won't gin their cotton; we won't allow them credit; and we'll move them out of their rented houses if necessary to keep them in line."[116]

Voter registration records reflected the effects of heightened anxiety. County registrars, the continuing barrier to black voter registration, stepped up efforts to enforce legislation that tightened voting requirements. By late August 1954, only 22,104 black people were registered to vote in the state's Democratic primary. Attorney General J. P. Coleman ordered a poll of county registrars to assess the threat against segregation. The figures reassured him, and he wasted no time releasing the report to the press. This number of registered black voters represented only 4 percent of the state's potential voters of both races; thirteen counties had no black voters; several more had fewer than ten. "Heavy" black voter registration existed in Coahoma (1,268), Washington (1,783), and Warren (1,480) counties, where numbers equaled one-third of these counties' total. However, on the agenda for the upcoming November general election was a proposed state constitutional amendment to further strengthen voting requirements.[117]

The NAACP had the unenviable task of blocking and parrying these blows, keeping its defenses up despite not knowing the direction of the next punch. The organization felt the strain as it became the principal target of the hatred and frustrations of thousands. Without the national NAACP, there would have been no lawsuits, and especially no *Brown*. By maintaining an active public role in promoting and filing lawsuits for desegregation, the NAACP inadvertently painted a target on every branch door and officer in the state.[118] In an effort to stem the bleeding locally, black people met and strategized. The Coahoma County branch of the NAACP advertised a legal symposium run by NAACP attorneys titled "How Can We Make Democracy Work" at Haven Methodist Church in late September.[119] The Sunday before, the RCNL had held a special meeting with 2,000 in attendance to criticize the Citizens' Councils and to present a united front in the face of pressure to deny the right to vote or to attend desegregated schools.[120]

African Americans engaged in, or even suspected of engaging in, NAACP activities faced reprisals, which included the calling in or refusal of loans, eviction, closure of credit, exorbitant utility rates, and even the disconnecting of utilities. Some of the local Citizens' Council leaders were bank presidents, and their actions caused many black people to leave the state.[121] But many more stayed and prepared to fight. Ruby Hurley issued a press release and reported "numerous complaints about threatening telephone calls and visits by white persons to our branch officers in several sections of Mississippi, but although the Negroes are terribly annoyed they are not frightened as they might have been a few years ago."[122] Her defiant stance accomplished two goals. It positioned the NAACP squarely on the battlefield, apparently ready to fight in the local arena, armed with the threat of federal protection through the organization's contacts in Washington. But it also gave courage to those who were suffering and provided a circle of support and encouragement.

Many African Americans in Mississippi did suffer for their defiance. Two of the Delta's prominent leaders, Dr. Howard, RCNL president, and Amzie Moore, found themselves targeted. Howard was threatened with the military draft to reduce his influence by physically removing him.[123] Moore, in an affidavit signed on 29 December 1954, chronicled how his newly opened service station, café, and beauty shop, located on Highway 61 in Cleveland, had been targeted for economic ruin because of his refusal to post "All Colored" or "Colored Only" signs as segregation laws demanded.[124]

Ordinary people, not in or near the spotlight, also felt the wrath of segregationists. Clarksdalian Lurleaner Johnson, for instance, was fired in January 1955. Employed by the Coahoma County hospital since November 1952 as a maid and nurse's aide, she was in the process of training to become a nurse in the hospital's segregated wing. According to her affidavit, filed with the Coahoma County NAACP branch, the hospital administrator, Reed Hogan, did not find anything about her work unsatisfactory: "He told me that because of my husband's activity with the NAACP, and because he signed a petition stating that the recent supreme court decision outlawing segregation in the public schools be complied with, that he must let me go."[125] The administrator further informed her that he had received pressure from the hospital board and the Citizens' Council. She testified defiantly, "If I am to be a victim of 'economic pressure' because my husband has displayed a spark of manhood and asked that Negro children be admitted to attend the best schools in the community, which all parents should desire for their children, then I accept it painfully but unashamed."[126]

In response to this all-out war, which played out in the local papers, in offices and boardrooms, and on the streets, the national NAACP turned its full attention to Mississippi for the first time.[127] In order to meet the challenge toe to toe, serious institutional adjustments had to take place. By the second half of 1954, the Southeast Regional Office served 290 branches but had insufficient numbers of field workers. Personnel in the Southeast Region, including Hurley, totaled only four. "The NAACP is entering into a new phase in its activities," Gloster Current wrote in a memo to his staff; "it has become increasingly evident that the emphasis must be shifted from the national to the regional and local levels."[128]

Help arrived in the person of Medgar Evers. After his World War II service, Evers graduated from Alcorn A&M College and then began work immediately as an insurance salesman for Dr. Howard's Magnolia Mutual Life Insurance Company. There he cut his teeth on the harsh realities of Mississippi life while traveling the back roads visiting sharecroppers and tenant farmers. His training began in Mound Bayou, where he and his bride, Myrlie, relocated. Here Evers met other like-minded veterans such as Moore and Henry and joined the Coahoma County NAACP branch, in 1953. The turning point came after he heard Thurgood Marshall's speech in 1953 espousing the necessity of litigation as a method for attaining freedom.[129] On the spot, Evers volunteered to desegregate the University of Mississippi, the bastion of white education in the state. His university application was rejected on a technicality by J. P. Coleman, state attorney general and soon-to-be governor.[130] His audacity and courage, however, impressed Henry and Dr. Emmett Stringer of Columbus, a long-time member of the NAACP in Mississippi, who immediately recommended Evers to the national office. "The applicant is not only qualified, but courageous and impressive," wrote Current to Executive Secretary Roy Wilkins, asking for procedural approval of the hiring. "With his experience and interest in our work, I am convinced that he will be the type of worker that we need in Mississippi."[131]

Employed as NAACP assistant field secretary assigned to Mississippi, Evers assumed formal duties in December 1954. The post, designed to increase the NAACP presence, demanded someone who could withstand the pressure. By publicizing his presence, Evers not only became a leading black spokesman in the state but also a leading and open target for hostility. Less than six months after his appointment, his name headed the death list circulating among the state's extremist groups.[132]

In Clarksdale, the Coahoma County branch solidified as a local organizational bedrock, and the members felt strong enough to publicly defy the Citizens' Councils. Sending a press release to the *Clarksdale Press Register*, the branch announced its annual Emancipation Proclamation Program, to be held Monday, 10 January 1955, at Haven Methodist Church. Not shying away from the risks, Aaron Henry declared the return of speaker Daniel Byrd, legal defense counsel for the NAACP.[133] Driven and strengthened by the winds of change and the NAACP's newfound focus on Mississippi, coupled with strong local leadership, the branch's confidence increased.

The growth and sustenance of NAACP branches in the state, despite white opposition and threats, illustrates the tenacity of communities and the realization that the time to organize had arrived. A renewed faith in the national organization emerged, given the NAACP's highly public legal successes and its prominence and attention on the state. By March 1955, the regional office newsletter proudly announced that Mississippi topped the region in growth and had won the organization's first Harry T. Moore Award: "In spite of threats, intimidation and pressure, Mississippi showed more than 87 percent increase in memberships during 1954 over the previous year."[134] The impressive figures of growth attest to the organization's consolidated commitment and attention in the state. In 1950, only 849 members signed membership cards in Mississippi. The state with the next highest number of members in 1950 was Florida, with 3,077 members. The state with the most members was South Carolina, with 6,186. While all the states showed increases over the next few years, by 1954 Mississippi recorded a relatively large jump to 3,101 members (1,657 in 1953). The total of active branches in the state more than doubled in four years, from fourteen in 1950 to thirty in 1954.[135]

To encourage membership drives, NAACP leaders got creative in their strategic organizing. For example, they enacted a series of certificates of merit for all workers reporting twenty-five or more added memberships during campaigns. Likewise, frequent letters of thanks and praise sent to branch committees buoyed spirits and gave encouragement.[136] The rewards, though small, and the constant correspondence put goals in place and connected branches and regions through friendly competition, fostering a sense of personal pride and achievement for individual workers struggling everyday against oppressive forces. Crossing organizational boundaries to get the job done, the Coahoma County branch members operated at times under the auspices of the Coahoma County Citizens' Association citing its long establishment in the county since 1934 and its membership of 2,563.[137] The Mississippi NAACP communities drew closer and pooled their strengths.

Black students in Clarksdale did not sit back and wait for salvation from the national NAACP legal teams or the adult branch members. Even at this early stage after the passage of *Brown*, they sought to be heard as they watched their elders bear the brunt of white retaliation. The NAACP youth, the children of the World War II generation, presented a plan for gradual integration at a meeting held in the Chapel M. B. Church at the end of March 1955.[138] The proposed nine-year plan would begin with the first three grades, and expand annually by one grade. Bennie Stone Gooden, president of the group (and someone who would step forward in the mid-sixties as an influential figure in the local antipoverty program), gave recommendations on how to zone the city to achieve desegregation. He was joined by NAACP youth council members Diane McNutt, Mary Ratliff, Peggie Watts, Joseph N. Richardson, Yvonne Cannon, and James Carter.[139] Showcasing the growing crisis in black education, the panel presented the glaring inequalities in the dual school systems: the lack of kindergarten education for black youngsters and the decaying facilities and play areas. The meeting illuminated the level of activism and consciousness of politicized young black people in early 1955, defying mainstream white stereotypes of apolitical and apathetic black youth unwilling or unable to try to change their own destinies. They were way ahead of their time, as the school board did not even consider such plans until forced to do so in the mid-sixties. Vera Pigee would harness that energy as she formally organized the NAACP youth council later that year.

NAACP growth was a promising sign, but, by the time the Supreme Court issued its *Brown II* decision in 1955, one year after the initial ruling, Mississippi had desegregated virtually nothing. Indeed, the state's white power structure had one year to build its legislative and figurative blockades to ensure that "all deliberate speed" meant indefinitely. "The white community used the time to fan the fires of a reaction that would stave off compliance for years," Henry wrote regretfully.[140]

The onslaught from the Citizens' Councils forced many groups like the RCNL and the Progressive Voters' League underground and nearly out of business. Henry observed that at this time white people generally regarded the RCNL as a homegrown NAACP. He noted: "Whites were also slowly becoming aware that the NAACP was making progress through the courts, and they began to view [the RCNL] with suspicious eyes."[141] Therefore the smaller, local groups, buckling under the pressure, pooled their resources like never before. Recognizing the NAACP's growing influence in the state, T. R. M. Howard reported that the RCNL voted unanimously to defer all matters of school integration to the NAACP. Now there was a common goal and method: attain first-class citizenship in the state and improve children's education. Pooling efforts and resources under the umbrella of the NAACP proved more effective than parallel campaigns.[142]

The next stage for the litigation team included securing petitions from as many local communities as possible to push for the desegregation of schools. At this point, the organization aimed to seek school integration by September 1955.[143] The national office circulated a list of key cities to regional directors, indicating where officers felt that the leadership could complete the task and where favorable factors conducive to immediate action existed. In Mississippi, the thirteen branches listed included the Coahoma County branch.

Clarksdale, along with Vicksburg, Natchez, Jackson, and Yazoo City, filed petitions in Mississippi that summer. More than 400 black Clarksdalians added their families' names to the sheets posted in churches and local black businesses for a month. The eventual document, sent by registered mail, totaled 316 signatures, according to School Superintendent Robert Mayo—342 according to Aaron Henry.[144] On 11 August, the Clarksdale school board accepted the petition and placed it on file.

The 12 August edition of the *Clarksdale Press Register* printed all of the names as they appeared on the petition.[145] In hindsight, Henry realized the mistake of exposing so many unprepared people to intimidation. Quantity and consensus had been the goal, but the results created publicized open targets. He said, "Some of the signers were forced to flee the state, others could not buy even basic staples, and carpenters and plumbers in the building trades were no longer hired by whites. . . . Whites looked at the petition list, and if your name was on it, you just caught hell."[146] "It got to be real violent in words and deeds," he remembered with much regret. It pained him that he could not help the people who had jeopardized themselves doing what he had advocated: "That was a bad time."[147] Most signers removed their names, and ultimately the local branch suffered. The NAACP, particularly the national office, had misjudged its enemy and found itself at another crossroads.

In August 1955, in the context of this struggle, this all-but-declared war, photographs of Emmett Till's mutilated young body hit the newsstands all over America and across the world. A belligerent and defensive state would now have to face the glare of international attention.[148] The image of this beaten and waterlogged child's body, pulled out of the Tallahatchie River near Money, became a rallying cry to take up the fight.

Many activists in subsequent years cited this episode, among the countless other lynchings that black Mississippians had endured, as a turning point in their activism, their own personal fork in the road. Till's death galvanized a generation. Due in part to the publication of the postmortem photographs, most African Americans felt the death profoundly.[149] The news of the murder quickly reached the furthest backwoods of Mississippi. Anne Moody, from Wilkinson County, Mississippi, learned of the murder while coming home from school and overhearing a group of boys similar in age to Till, saying: "Everybody [is] talking about that fourteen-year-old boy who was killed." Later that day, as Moody worked as a domestic at a white woman's house, her employer asked her directly if she had heard the news. After being subjected to the full tirade of Mrs. Burke's anger toward Till, Moody recounted, "Now, there was a new fear known to me—the fear of being killed just because I was black."[150] Black children lost their youthful innocence, but so did many adults, during those dark days, which were infused with increased psychological terror. J. W. Milam and Roy Bryant murdered Till because they could, and in that hideous act they defiantly stated that despite mounting gains in Washington's courts, Mississippi would not bend.

The NAACP worked hard to keep Till's death from being in vain, while promoting the organization as the vehicle through which protest should take place. On 27 September 1955, Roy Wilkins sent memos to the staff regarding the plan of action for Mississippi and the South.[151] Coupled with the continued campaign to counteract the economic squeeze and promote school desegregation, a new fund-raising program emerged using the Till murder to focus attention. Indeed, in the months following the death and trial, the NAACP received a significantly increased number of contributions.[152]

And so the NAACP took root in Mississippi—although this was not the organization that New York City had imagined. Tactics at the local level changed as people sought to survive in an environment far removed from the Northeast. Local branches, like Clarksdale's, grew away from the parent organization as memberships in and loyalties to other groups proliferated out of necessity. This would become a common pattern over the following years. By the time of Till's murder, the organization had to fight battles on several fronts: to iron out national-local tensions within the association, to fight white violence, and to deal with black people's fears. As an example, Ruby Hurley herself adapted, suspended between the national office and the local branches. By the fall of 1955, after months of feeling out of her element, she had modified her Northeast-inflected speech to speak more like the locals. The NAACP at all levels had to confront the fear and suspicion of ordinary black people and convince them that the organization would deliver them from their strife, while fighting to itself survive in a South increasingly hostile to the group, as the protest trajectory became increasingly clear.[153]

In Clarksdale, members of the new local NAACP branch, created in order to funnel national resources to the Delta town for local issues, juggled their attentions between groups, depending on the particular needs of the moment. Within the ranks of the NAACP, Aaron Henry was seen as a force to be reckoned with by 1955 and had established a reputation as a fierce enemy of Jim Crow among white supremacists in the Delta. Vera Pigee, returning to Clarksdale to work in her cosmetology trade, was just beginning to find her niche as a youth council advisor and an active NAACP member. She would in time come to be as important to Clarksdale's struggle as Henry.

In its early years, the local movement in Clarksdale depended on three crucial things. First were World War II veterans, who proliferated throughout the membership rolls of these organizations after the rude awakening of their homecoming. Veterans like Amzie Moore, Medgar Evers, and Aaron Henry met in Mound Bayou and befriended each other, forming bonds based on their defiance of Jim Crow. Hundreds of veterans like them exuded a brand of hope that helped change a generation. Organizationally, they provided a leadership class unknown in the South until then. Second were the flexible associations of local activists, who moved between organizations as circumstances demanded. Whether organizing under other organizational banners to disguise NAACP activities or maintaining memberships in different organizations, activists found ways to safely strategize and reach the largest possible audience. Finally, the movement depended on the capacity of local people to use the resources of the national movement in ways that conformed to and served local conditions.

"A majority of both races accepted segregation as a way of life that was going to be with us forever," Henry recalled of the immediate postwar years. "Until people outside the system—or independent of it—helped fashion new ideas and a fresh spirit of hope, there was little effective agitation for change. But once there was hope, then came the bright vision and the swelling tides for change."[154] Those tides had brought in men like Aaron Henry and women like Vera Pigee, who would work in their own communities, strengthening and organizing activities that shifted the racial shoreline forever.

CHAPTER TWO

M Is for Mississippi and Murder . . . and Mother

In order to organize a town you must win over two people: the
beautician & the midwife. — Sheila Shiki y Michaels (2001)

Stand firm then, with the belt of truth buckled around your waist,
with the breastplate of righteousness in place, and with your feet fitted with
the readiness that comes from the gospel of peace. — Ephesians 6:14-15

The "Mississippi Situation," as the national NAACP referred to the crisis at the
end of 1955, focused national attention on conditions in the state. In addition to
Emmett Till, three other black males were murdered that year in widely publicized attacks. Emotions ran high, and the whole world, it seemed, was increasingly watching. The NAACP's 1955 pamphlet, "M Is for Mississippi and Murder," disseminated to publicize its work and solicit support for beleaguered
members, captured the sentiment.[1] Years later, Amzie Moore recollected, "It
was a real rough year for Mississippi."[2] However, for all those black Mississippians reluctant to join the NAACP for fear of retaliation, many others found
themselves drawn into the action—the murders had dissuaded some and empowered others. In 1954, official NAACP statistics put membership in Mississippi at 3,101, up from 1,657 in 1953; by 1955, the numbers had risen to 4,639.[3]
Till's death, in particular, struck the state's African American population like a
lightning bolt. For some, it sparked a flame that drew them to the organization.

Vera Pigee was drawn in. She had just begun working with the youth councils and had been elected Coahoma County NAACP branch secretary when the
Till trial in September motivated her to direct action. Clarksdale served as a
hub for reporters covering the trial in nearby Sumner. Pigee felt compelled to

assist in finding justice for Till's grieving mother, and she helped the NAACP comb the Delta for witnesses, approaching frightened strangers and gently asking questions. Once the trial began, Pigee accompanied U.S. congressman Charles Diggs (D-Mich.) to the courtroom each day, sitting with him and absorbing the energy around her.[4] Later in the year, as she attended her first Mississippi State NAACP Conference in Jackson, she raised her hand to assist some more and was elected a state youth council advisor. The NAACP field secretary, Medgar Evers, had been trying to organize the youth more effectively, and he directed Pigee to start a chapter in Clarksdale. She then spent the better part of the next four years building the local youth council and the broader youth movement statewide, which under her direction asserted itself in the early 1960s as one of the leading edges of the civil rights struggles in Mississippi.[5]

From 1955 to 1960, the rising temperature of protest lent new urgency to what was a local emergency and an increasingly national crisis. White Clarksdale had established its own Citizens' Council in 1955, reacting to local black activism. Angered by the *Brown v. Board of Education of Topeka* decision, which was perceived as increased federal interference, state authorities had ironically begun to intrude more vigorously on the individual rights of citizens. As the reality of the *Brown* decision grew more obvious, opposition to desegregation also strengthened. The state reached new levels of surveillance in the civil war against its own citizens, as it watched the federal government "violate" southern prerogatives in the *Brown II* decision in 1955, in Little Rock in 1957, and in its defense (however tepid) of the Freedom Riders later in 1961. In these five years, as "massive resistance" built, a new relationship between the federal government and African Americans, who had grown more critical of the old order and more militant in hastening its demise, tested the South.

In this context, four black students in Greensboro, North Carolina, further changed the game rules when their own brave protest initiated waves of sit-ins across the South. They helped to make 1960 the dawn of a constellation of mass direct-action movements involving large numbers of young people around the country. Yet the beginnings of an earlier youth movement in Mississippi had already surfaced in the NAACP youth councils under the guidance of Pigee. If men like Aaron Henry and Medgar Evers expressed leadership through male channels and institutions, black women exercised a similarly gendered form of activism. The concept of "activist mothering," like Vera Pigee's work in the youth councils, comes closest to capturing this style of political engagement. Women like Pigee expanded their niches within the hierarchical and male-dominated NAACP and developed strategies particular to their communities by continuing (or expanding) work they were already engaged in, especially the nurturing of youth. A successful beautician running a business independent of whites, Pigee occupied more than a niche, however. She made one, and made herself indispensible, working at the center of an immense web of local contacts and information streams, a space from which she could maximize the return on her gendered social position.

In the five years between Till's murder and the Greensboro sit-ins, Pigee's efforts to organize youthful energies in Mississippi stand out. White retaliation against growing opposition to Jim Crow made the local NAACP even more crucial, as activists sought refuge and resources to battle the forces of segregation. However, when the local branch scrambled to respond to immediate situations, knowing that failure to do so would undermine its support, tensions with the national office were exposed. Over the course of these five years, black Mississippians grew increasingly frustrated with the inability, or unwillingness, of the NAACP to engage fully with the problems of Mississippi. This ultimately pushed members to extend their alliances, loyalties, and memberships to other places, either by creating new groups or by inviting other organizations to enter the state. In this way, the Southern Christian Leadership Conference (SCLC) found an entrance into Mississippi early in its organizational existence in 1957, as local people nurtured the activist environment and a growing momentum that made the 1960s so ripe for the mass movement. All of these stories—Pigee and gendered patterns of leadership, the NAACP and its recalcitrant bureaucracy, the early stirrings of a mass protest movement—wove together in these formative years.

Stepping Up the Ante

The combination of the Till murder, growing militancy in the black population, and northern media coverage was a potent and dangerous mix. As much as the Till case inspired black activism, it also fired white resistance. Both black activists and white defenders of segregation found themselves on the defensive, albeit for very different reasons and from different positions of power. For Aaron Henry, 1955 was "the bloody and death-pocked year," when the sale of guns in Mississippi rose rapidly and there was "a whole solid mass of violence."[6] On the eve of Emmett Till's death, over 300 of Clarksdale's black parents had already begun to feel the heat from their signing of the school petition requesting desegregation. W. J. Simmons, Jackson's Citizens' Council leader, recalled that in Clarksdale "the good folks there had said, 'We don't need a Citizens' Council, our niggers are good niggers, they don't want to integrate, if we organize a Citizens' Council it'll agitate 'em.'" He continued, "But one bright morning they woke up with a school petition and three hundred three signers, including most of their good ones. So they organized a Council. . . . The petition collapsed. They all started taking their names off." Indeed, the formation of the Clarksdale Citizens' Council, the second-to-last city in the Mississippi Delta to organize one (Greenville was the last), had prompted more than a dozen people to withdraw their names from the petition.[7]

Over 1,000 white Delta residents descended on Clarksdale's civic auditorium on the night of 16 August, eager to fight desegregation and encouraged by the release of the names of the petitioners. Judge Tom Brady, author of "Black Monday," a pamphlet distributed by the Citizens' Councils denouncing the *Brown* Supreme Court decision, spoke at this first public gathering, whipping the crowd into a frenzy with the perceived threat of interracialism. A sea of raised hands endorsed the formation of a single Citizens' Council for Clarksdale and Coahoma County. Of those present, 261 completed applications on the spot and paid their five dollars in annual dues. Brady made clear the effectiveness of economic pressure to discourage black participation in elections and NAACP activities. The Citizens' Council's board acquired forty-one members in less than four months, and by June 1956 the group boasted a membership of 1,130. While there is no surviving list of those who completed the applications, given the mandate of the council—to employ economic tactics to stamp out progressive activism—those with the means and position to effectively carry out this task probably joined. It is no surprise that among the leaders of this group, bank presidents dominated the top positions. The most powerful man in Clarksdale, Eddie Peacock Jr., the president of the largest bank in town (the Bank of Clarksdale), became the council chairman.[8] African Americans in Clarksdale now had a great deal more to fear.

The Citizens' Councils defended segregation, but they also cared about the state's economy. The NAACP's national spotlight on the "racial tyranny in Mississippi" resonated in business conference rooms throughout the state. Cheap black labor, coupled with black spending in white-owned businesses, made the black population central to the overall health of Mississippi's economy. The Citizens' Councils, whose membership came from the ranks of the state's business community, had to tread carefully, lest boycotts, both local and national, threaten the state's already weak economy.[9]

Reinforcing efforts to maintain the state's status quo, in March 1956, Governor James Coleman and the state legislature created the Mississippi Sovereignty Commission, designed to preserve white supremacy and prevent the encroachment of the federal government.[10] Equipped to be a public propaganda program, the agency sought to reach national audiences. With unlimited powers of investigation, officers plotted and communicated with private groups such as the Citizens' Councils to help maintain states' rights. In doing so, they sought to conceal evidence of hatred and blatant white supremacy to improve the state's image. Indeed, its defined role was to "pacify racial hysteria in the state, thus removing Mississippi's racial incidents from national attention."[11] Investigators came to Clarksdale frequently to meet with city officials and bankers, most of whom were on the board of the Citizens' Council. As a result of their careful documentation and reporting, much of the day-to-day civil rights activities not reported in the daily newspaper appear on the record, though oftentimes embellished, but these documents nevertheless provide a useful glimpse into the thoughts and motives of city leaders behind closed doors.

In addition to the creation of the Sovereignty Commission, the state also passed anti-NAACP laws disguised as protection against subversive Communism. In truth, these laws reflected the policy of discouraging NAACP membership. The 1956 session of the state legislature approved a bill requiring all state teachers to "file affidavits listing the organizations to which they belonged for the past five years." No longer could teachers like T. K. Shelby, who had influenced Aaron Henry in high school, openly discuss the NAACP, let alone recruit members, without the fear of being reported. By marking the NAACP as seditious and Communist, the state hoped to cloak its opposition to desegregation in nationalist, patriotic terms (and subsequently portray the NAACP and its allies as unpatriotic), as was the language in the era of more pronounced red-baiting.[12]

NAACP branches in Mississippi suffered as a result. Constant white repression, particularly threats against families' economic security, sent membership numbers, rising since 1950, into a nosedive in 1956, despite the national office's publicity campaign and an extensive tour by Ruby Hurley.[13] Still in his first year as state field secretary, Medgar Evers traveled around the state organizing new branches and reporting local incidents. He was "thrust into the middle of intensive activities by White Citizens' Councils and a series of incidents including shootings and murder of NAACP officials, denial of voting privileges, [and] economic pressure upon signers of petitions," the national office acknowledged.[14] His success hinged on local black cooperation and willingness to talk. But, as Evers's biographer Adam Nossiter stated, "fear shut mouths," and "it atomized the community, making any kind of association a frightening undertaking."[15] As a marked man for his visible position in the NAACP, Evers found that many black people shunned him, hoping to avoid potential stray bullets. "People were afraid," Vera Pigee remembered; "it was more than people feeling sad. People knew what had been done in Clarksdale . . . and in the state of Mississippi, and they might have not just said it, but they were so afraid."[16]

Despite these obstacles, black Clarksdale continued efforts in 1956 to apply pressure on the foundations of segregation. The news of the Montgomery bus boycott had spread fast in Mississippi. If change could happen in Alabama, why not in Mississippi? The theme of the three-hour NAACP branch gathering on 2 January as part of the annual Emancipation Proclamation Program at Haven Methodist Church defiantly cut to the point: "The Status Quo Must Go."[17]

An imposing, ruddy-complexioned white man took to the podium that evening, shortly after two solos by sixteen-year-old Mary Jane Pigee, daughter of Vera, before a sea of expectant black faces.[18] Riding the crest of the emotions whipped up by spiritual word and song, John Bolt Culberston from Greenville, South Carolina, addressed a captivated audience of about 300 from Coahoma and two neighboring counties. An attorney from a family with state prominence who had once served in the South Carolina legislature, Culberston had rededicated his life to fight for justice for the oppressed. Now spurned by his peers, he faced physical threats for his actions. He spoke passionately for over an hour that night, encouraging audience members to continue to seek their rights, starting with registering to vote.[19] The message, be active or be quiet, was clear: "Pay your poll tax. Register and vote, or stop Squaking [squawking]."[20] Thunderous applause ended the evening.

In Clarksdale, mass meetings continued, and African Americans attended in increasing numbers. But the meetings were often accompanied by violence or tragedy. An assault on thirteen-year-old Ray Stack, for instance, a student at Higgins High School, provoked angry community reactions. Stack, working after school, was struck on the head by the butcher, Byron M. "Doc" Sanderson, with a jar of mayonnaise, for not immediately carrying out an order. Stack had been busy performing a task for the storeowner. His injuries required multiple stitches at the emergency room. Stack's guardian, Mrs. Eva Porter, told the audience that she had been advised to settle out of court for the sum of $500 before it was revealed that her lawyer also represented the storeowner. According to Henry, over 2,000 people came out for the meeting called by the Coahoma

County Negro Citizens Association, a probable pseudonym for the local NAACP branch, at Bell Grove Baptist Church in May 1956. The crowds spilled out of the church into the parking lot and the churchyard, forcing latecomers to park blocks away. After Stack's testimony at the meeting, the crowd voted to boycott the grocery store and set up a committee to investigate Abe Sherman, Porter's attorney. Boycotting one store, a small act of defiance less than a year after the murder of Emmett Till, signified growing confidence in community action.[21]

Local activists also worked behind the scenes to reach sympathetic whites. The NAACP branch regularly invited white citizens to meetings, in part to publicize activities and minimize accusations of subversiveness. By the end of June 1956, the branch had sent seventy-five letters to white organizations and individuals requesting improved communication at the local level. Utilizing a different form of persuasion, calm common sense, the letter confirmed that "Negroes of our community are not interested in mingling socially with white people nor with other Negroes, for that matter, who do not desire our presence or company. . . . The Supreme Court decision did not demand integration. . . . It forbade discrimination."[22] The letter cautiously made a plea for practicality and ended by extending a warm invitation to a meeting of the local NAACP branch, on 3 July at Haven Methodist Church: "We are not interested in so-called outside interference . . . but we are very much concerned about inside neglect." They desired, at least on paper, to have the opportunity for local people to respond and sort out local situations and issues for the communal well-being of all in the county. In effect, the local branch had issued a subtle ultimatum to city fathers: either deal with them directly or face outsiders more likely to expose the dirty laundry. The *Clarksdale Press Register* did not publish any response to this request but continued to publicize the activities of the Citizens' Councils.[23] No evidence suggests that any invitee ever darkened the doorways of any of these meetings.

As the crisis in Mississippi deepened, the state and national offices of the NAACP wrestled with the limits of organizational resources and the challenges of managing a mass movement—a sea of local movements—over vast distances against determined opponents. In so doing, they also revealed the gendered and class assumptions that shaped the NAACP's vision of leadership. A hierarchical and centralized organization, the NAACP trusted its national leadership to design policies for, and explain them to, the field staff and local branches. This almost always meant that information and directives flowed in one direction, from the top down, and that traditional local male leaders—ministers, businessmen, and attorneys—remained the valued local contacts.

In 1956, the direction of the state NAACP in Mississippi had shifted to accommodate the quickening crisis. This is an example of how the organization functioned. The sole Mississippi NAACP field-worker, Medgar Evers, traveled across the state to gather growing numbers of complaints, especially of economic pressures applied on farmers in the Delta. At the end of January, Evers, along with project coworker and at-large field staff member Mildred Bond, submitted a report to Gloster Current outlining the economic needs of local farmers.[24]

Two complaints came from Clarksdale, signed by Robert L. Drew and Walter Jones. Drew's summary indicated that he owned a funeral home and farmed ten acres while also employed by the United Order of Friendship.[25] The president of the Coahoma County Bank (with which he had done business for twenty years) refused to loan him $800 to plant his crops that year because he had signed the school board petition. Ralph Baltzer, executive vice president of the bank, served on the local Citizens' Council executive board.[26] Similarly, Walter Jones worked eighty acres of land and owned a house and two lots in Clarksdale and a house and a lot in Greenwood. He had a loan with the black-owned Tri-State Bank in Memphis but needed $3,670 for his mortgage and tractor, which local banks would not loan him.[27]

By singling out landowners for assistance above far more destitute sharecroppers and tenant farmers, however, the NAACP confirmed the limits of its reach and resources. Targeted for political activity, Drew and Jones were clearly victims. But both men were also substantial property owners. Gloster Current had written to Roy Wilkins that "the consensus . . . is that a program should be inaugurated to aid Mississippi landowners on an emergency basis who might be victimized by the squeeze or suffering from reprisals because of association with the NAACP."[28] Maintaining the leadership and protecting those who worked for the NAACP or attended member churches took precedence over assisting the more numerous, and poorer, laborers in the fields.[29] A meeting among executive NAACP officers, Thurgood Marshall, and the Tri-State Bank in Memphis in February 1956 did secure NAACP funds under the Committee on Emergency Aid to Farmers in Mississippi for both landowning farmers and longtime tenants, but only a handful ultimately benefited.[30]

Reconstruction II and the SCLC

Historians have argued that the "national office of the NAACP considered Mississippi a lost cause," and it "responded to this defeat by dropping Mississippi like a hot potato."[31] Economic reprisals and threats paralyzed the momentum generated by the Till case. The school petition drive proved to be a costly error, for which many paid dearly. The mistake also cost the organization financially, and it had to invest thousands of dollars in the Memphis Tri-State Bank to aid those who faced reprisals. However, the national office's lack of attention also proved to be a blessing and allowed (or forced) local NAACP leaders to develop homegrown, adaptable strategies and alliances — in order to be flexible. Amzie Moore, for instance, contacted Bayard Rustin and Ella Baker in the New York–based organization, In Friendship, to plead for clothing for the Delta. In response, the American Friends Service Committee agreed to send a shipment of children's clothes.[32] That correspondence initiated an exchange between Moore and Robert Moses in 1960. Ella Baker had given Moses the task of recruiting young people from the Deep South to attend the second Student Nonviolent Coordinating Committee (SNCC) conference and had put him in touch with Moore, who subsequently attended the conference and made the case for SNCC's presence in Mississippi for voter registration.[33] Local activists, out of touch most of the time with the national office, forged ties with other organizations willing to help with material relief.

The forces against change loudly defied civil rights legislation and court orders. A civil rights bill had begun to make its way through the U.S. Congress in the early months of 1957. Mississippi governor J. P. Coleman, speaking in front of a House Judiciary subcommittee in the first week of February 1957, vigorously criticized the federal government's interference as "wholly unnecessary." Patterson defended the Citizens' Councils against the encroachment of the NAACP: "When one group organizes to tear down and destroy . . . another group has the right to organize to defend." The resulting landmark Civil Rights Act of 1957, although weak, prohibited action to prevent voting in federal elections and authorized the attorney general to bring suit. The act created the Civil Rights Commission and also set up the Civil Rights Division in the Department of Justice.[34] It failed, however, to provide federal power to punish lawbreakers. Nevertheless, Citizens' Councils denounced this "force bill, coercive and vicious." The group's statement read like a declaration of war: "Reconstruction II has now been officially declared upon the former Confederate states by the adoption of the first force bill since Reconstruction I of the 1870s."[35] Another front in the battle had officially opened, as now the federal government had a legal responsibility to become involved in state elections — all this happening at the same time that nine black children walked up the steps of Central High School in Little Rock, Arkansas, under the protection of federal troops.[36]

Activists in Clarksdale scrambled to organize a statewide program to test the new provisions, taking advantage of the psychological euphoria produced by the legislation and the events in Little Rock. Under the auspices of the RCNL, a daylong meeting on Sunday, 8 December 1957, at Metropolitan Baptist Church established a letter-writing campaign in all counties to protest discrimination in voter registration and initiated an appeal to the governor and a plea to the federal Civil Rights Division. The *Clarksdale Press Register* noted that the real test, however, would be at the clerk offices and in the clerk's discretion in the examination and enrolling of voters. The *Register* also published the names of everyone on the RCNL's program, and the Coahoma County Citizens' Council reproduced the handbill in a paid newspaper advertisement to alert white residents of the aims of the meeting.[37] Once again, the newspaper exposed black citizens. Any vigilante with a tendency for violence now had precise targets.

Still, Medgar Evers reported the conference as a rousing success to the national NAACP office. The lines between the RCNL and the state's NAACP leadership had blurred sufficiently for Evers to write confidently that "many of our influential NAACP members in the Delta are key members of the Council [the RCNL]." Nonetheless, he urged the national office to file a suit to keep black support strong and to send a tangible message to the governor. He claimed that "most people now are interested in some type of positive action, even here in Mississippi, especially with regard to these segregation laws and this new voter amendment." To help the process, he listed three counties (Jefferson Davis, Forrest, and Clarke) that were struggling with voter registration as "excellent starting points," but chided, "We *must* get off center if we are to maintain our influence here in the state and get more financial support."[38] He recognized that local people's loyalty to the NAACP could waiver if the national office did not pick up the pace in the state. The national office did not heed his advice, and it would be well into the next decade before the lawyers initiated any suit in Mississippi.

As a result, disillusionment with the national NAACP came quickly after the 1957 Civil Rights Act high. Frustrated, Ruby Hurley reported a loss of a thousand members in Mississippi and declared, "We are almost back to where we were in 1950 before the Region was established."[39] Apart from gains in Laurel, Gulfport, and Amite County, most other branches reported significant losses, including the Clarksdale/Coahoma County branch (see table 1). The figures mirrored those in the rest of the South. With regionwide "massive resistance" in place, the NAACP had lost its branches entirely in Alabama, and injunctions

TABLE 1. NAACP Membership in County and City Branches
in Mississippi, 1956 and 1957

Some Mississippi County and City Branches	1956	1957
Amory	33	15
Claiborne County	27	18
Clark County	94	41
Cleveland	439	67
Coahoma County	31	16
Columbus	6	51
Florence	69	39
Hattiesburg	25	20
Jackson	481	259
Kemper County	14	13
Lawrence County	29	4
Louisville	24	20
McComb	211	115
Meridian	114	31
Mound Bayou	6	14
Panola County	15	10
Pascagoula–Moss Point	19	9
Pass Christian	20	None
Prentiss	None	14
Vicksburg	138	86
Walthall County	42	23
Washington County	59	27
Yazoo City	44	3

Source: Ruby Hurley to Medgar Evers, memorandum, 14 January 1958, NAACPP II C172,
   Southeastern Regional office correspondence.

TABLE 2. Declining NAACP Membership in Southeastern
Region, 1955–1957

1955	1956	1957
349 branches	342 branches	221 branches
52,365 members	36,726 members	26,775 members

Source: Gloster Current, Report and recommendations on membership
and staff, 1958, NAACPP II C279, Membership campaign losses
1957. (Used by permission of The National Association for the
Advancement of Colored People)

crippled activity in Louisiana and Texas.[40] Table 2 shows the steady membership decline in the NAACP Southeast Region since 1955.

With the NAACP in decline, the SCLC emerged in 1957 as a new force in the
region, testing the flexibility and malleability of organizational loyalties anew.
Aaron Henry and Medgar Evers, eager to engage with the ministers from Alabama who had successfully boycotted there, were elected to the SCLC board.
Evers, the new assistant secretary, however, received curt instructions from
Roy Wilkins to resign from the SCLC. Holding a salaried NAACP position, he
had little choice, but he told Wilkins that he was "sincere in trying to do what
I possibly could to bring first-class citizenship to our section of the country as
hurriedly as possible."[41] Like his fellow Mississippian activists, he felt the end
justified the means.

Aaron Henry, on the other hand, openly accepted the SCLC offer. As a non-
salaried NAACP officer, Henry served as an SCLC representative for Mississippi,
along with Evers's replacement, R. L. Drew. In 1968, Henry was still on the
SCLC board and quipped that he was the only man in America to serve on the
national boards of both the NAACP and the SCLC: "I have responsibilities of
keeping each group honest to the other. . . . It's a great tribute in terms of the
respect and the trust that I enjoy from both organizations and I work tremen-
dously hard to try to put over the programs of both." Henry remembered,
"The SCLC program and philosophy advocated nonviolence and appealing to
the moral conscience of the community to do right for the sake of doing right.
They wanted to 'love the hell out of Mississippi.'" Writing to Martin Luther
King Jr. directly in August 1957, Henry asked for the organization to hold a
meeting in Mississippi, "the state where it is perhaps needed most."[42] These
links, forged early, allowed the SCLC some room to operate in Mississippi, despite the active opposition of the NAACP's national officers.

Organized by Ella Baker, the SCLC's opening southern campaign, the "Crusade for Citizenship," began on 12 February 1958, with simultaneous meetings in twenty cities throughout the South. By January, Clarksdale had its spot on the itinerary, the only Mississippi city on the roster. With a program of education and action, the crusade sought to double the number of qualified black voters in the South.[43] Four days after King opened the campaign, Evers reported that efforts had been made to establish a movement in Jackson, which he had managed to thwart. Evers bristled from what he saw as an attempt to pit the Crusade for Citizenship against the NAACP-sponsored "Jackie Robinson Day Program" on 12 February, and he wrote, "It will be our design through the NAACP and the Progressive Voters League, of which our leaders are in key positions, to control the present state of affairs."[44] Even though he saw the value of SCLC and had welcomed the ministers, he did not want to see NAACP work overshadowed by the newcomers. As a result of his labors, the Crusade for Citizenship had only a minor presence in Mississippi, and the SCLC was unable to establish a major foothold in the state.

As it fought for survival in Mississippi, the NAACP had more immediate concerns than the SCLC. In late February 1958, Mississippi state senator George Yarborough, with twenty-five other senators, helped pass a bill to make public the membership roll of the NAACP, copying a law passed in Louisiana the previous year.[45] As a result, many NAACP members made use of their other membership affiliations to organize. For example, in March, Aaron Henry, acting as executive secretary of RCNL, told a reporter that a smaller organization had sponsored a series of citizenship classes held in Clarksdale, although in reality the classes, instructing students on the state constitution, were part of the RCNL's drive to register voters.[46] Henry warned that as more and more students enrolled, registrars should take notice because the RCNL would make a formal appeal to the federal Civil Rights Commission if attempts to register were repeatedly thwarted. The RCNL waited until April and then voted to seek an audience with the new Civil Rights Commission in Washington to challenge the restrictions on black voting.

In addition to the Civil Rights Commission, Mississippians who exercised flexible alliances encouraged other groups to enter the Delta. Responding to calls, Martin Luther King Jr. journeyed to Clarksdale on 29 May 1958 for the first major meeting of the SCLC. The conference attracted delegates from ten states, 130 from Mississippi. Afterward he exclaimed, "This was the finest meeting that the Southern Christian Leadership Conference has ever had. . . . The whole trip, with its rich fellowship, has sent me back to Montgomery with renewed strength and enthusiasm to tackle afresh the stupendous job that we all know must be done." The Mississippi links with the SCLC through Coahoma County thus began strong and remained firm with Aaron Henry as the head of SCLC's Clarksdale committee.[47]

"Mississippi Must Change"

Sensing the shift in national attention and the ebb of activities in Mississippi, the Clarksdale NAACP branch held an October program called "Mississippi Must Change" to promote as many organizations in the city as possible, to the chagrin, once again, of the national NAACP office. Much had happened in the months leading up to the program, from the state's direct attacks on the NAACP, to teachers fired from schools, to police murdering citizens. Local people needed support and reassurance. Held at Haven Methodist Church, the mixture of scripture readings, song, and speakers endeavored to reclaim the organization's slipping momentum. Fifteen citizens and leaders, representatives from five local churches, and the top-ranking NAACP officials in the region congregated in one place to encourage the rank and file. The program read like a Who's Who of prominent black Clarksdalians in the NAACP, united, at least on the list, against state-sanctioned harassment. It opened with "Lift Ev'ry Voice and Sing," the black national anthem, and prayer from the church's pastor, Rev. Theodore Trammell. Then Mary Jane Pigee stood alone and sang "Bless This House." Following scripture readings by Rev. S. H. Jones, the pastor of Metropolitan Baptist Church, two choirs offered selections to prepare the audience for the message. Vera Pigee, as branch secretary, outlined the purpose of the program and presented the local youth council.[48]

Such meetings brought needed sustenance to the local movement, but they hardly forced the opposition to relent. With the help of city officials and the local Citizens' Council, the tentacles of the Sovereignty Commission had snaked their way into the lives of black Clarksdalians, seeking to neutralize movement leaders where they could. Attorney Joe Hopkins, based in Clarksdale and a member of the Sovereignty Commission, kept a close watch on the NAACP branch. Reporting to investigator Zack J. Van Landingham (a former FBI agent), Hopkins named Henry and activist John C. Melchor as "principal agitators," not forgetting to mention Melchor's economic independence as president of the Delta Burial Corporation. Van Landingham also reported that both men's wives worked in the public school system. The confidential document pulled no punches. He wrote, "Subsequently the Citizens' Council of

Clarksdale obtained the information regarding these two Negroes and threw pressure on, and both were either fired or the school declined to renew their contract."[49]

The Citizens' Councils were not the only groups that opposed the rising black movement. The local police force in Clarksdale did too. Many police departments across the state, and particularly in Clarksdale, did the dirty work for the Citizens' Councils and the Sovereignty Commission and perhaps are the reasons why Mississippi's Ku Klux Klan remained relatively quiet.[50] Elnora Causey related the events of a particularly brutal police incident to the local NAACP branch, which urged the FBI to investigate.[51] During the week previous to Sunday, 10 May 1959, for reasons unknown, two white men, Orville Bailey and Bunion W. Knight, had driven a blue Ford pickup by the shack where she and her husband, Jonah Causey, lived, located south of the city on the Montgomery Farms Place, threatening physical harm. Called to the scene after the incident, the police (as usual) found no evidence of a disturbance. Returning the following Saturday, now incensed that the couple had had the audacity to report them, the two cursing white men reportedly discharged weapons randomly for most of the night. Leaving briefly on Sunday morning around 9 A.M., they returned soon, firing directly at the house, grazing Elnora Causey's thigh. Her husband, shocked by the sight of her blood and determined to protect her, ran out of the shack with his shotgun aimed directly at Bailey and Knight. Bailey fell at the scene. Knight, struck by birdshot, fled.

The call to the police came from a neighbor, a mile away from the Causey home. This neighbor had answered the persistent knocking on her front door and stood facing a bloody, intoxicated Knight. When Sheriff Leighton Miller arrived around 11:25 A.M., the Causeys had barricaded themselves inside their home. Miller called for backup, including shotguns, rifles, a tear gas gun, and ammunition.[52] The siege continued past midnight, when the desk sergeant at the precinct received a call for more shotgun shells and tear gas in preparation for a forced entry. Driven out by tear gas bombs thrown through the windows, Elnora staggered out, leaving her husband inside. Knowing the fate that awaited him for killing a white man, Causey refused to leave his home. Showing no interest in taking him alive, fifteen police officers shattered the house with bullets until he lay dead. Acting on behalf of the widow, the NAACP blamed the shooting and death of Causey on the initial threats and shots of the white men harassing his home. The police countered that Elnora Causey's wound was not only superficial but that the doctor who treated her could not verify that it came from a gunshot. Furthermore, they placed doubt on Causey's sanity because of a brief stay at the state mental hospital.[53] No one was ever charged for harassing the Causeys.[54]

Though he had yet to face bullets himself, Henry suffered at the hands of Mississippi's white backlash. The Citizens' Council plotted to destroy his business. Henry's pharmacy faced difficulty, as local distributors refused to sell him supplies and some white doctors stopped sending prescriptions to him. Forced to buy from Memphis at a higher cost, he gradually lost trade. Van Landingham was clear in his intentions: "It is believed that if Henry leaves this area, the NAACP will die, as he is the main one and keeps it alive." This had been done before to Dr. T. R. M. Howard. Reacting to threats against his life, by the end of 1955 Howard had sold his home and farmland in Bolivar County.[55] Henry, however, managed to stay in business with the community's support.

Van Landingham feared the potential of the local youth council as well. Unidentified informants assumed that the black school system promoted membership and activities, as Henry's teacher had in the 1940s. Many of the teachers in the segregated school system attracted the attention of the Sovereignty Commission and the local Citizens' Council. Crawford McGivaren, vice president of the Bank of Clarksdale and treasurer of the local Citizens' Council, served on the Clarksdale school board, which had fired Noelle Henry and John Melchor's wife in late 1958, and now McGivaren targeted Lillian Rogers Johnson, an administrator in the black schools in Clarksdale and an active NAACP member.[56] The superintendent of education, L. L. Bryson, moved too slowly for the Citizens' Council's liking, and so the next step was to campaign vigorously to remove Bryson himself from his position in the upcoming election.[57] Focusing on black schools as a site of struggle permitted the Citizens' Councils to attack activists employed by the city or state. This emphasis on controlling the teachers and their influences in the community kept many from openly supporting or joining the NAACP or similar civil rights organizations.

The school attack had two fronts. Not only did city leaders seek to gag black teachers, but they feverishly worked to find ways to circumvent *Brown* and retain the separate and unequal, dual education systems. The history of segregated education in Clarksdale and Coahoma County mirrors the dreadful history across Mississippi.[58] Black educational development always lagged behind in terms of physical spaces, resources, and staffing. Indeed, this is an understatement. The system would only change with federal intervention, because education remained a state-funded mandate. When the *Brown* decision came down, however, it did not take long for African Americans to realize that the struggle had just begun. State and local governments across the

South fought to ensure that "all deliberate speed," the provision granted by the Supreme Court in 1955, successfully translated into strategies of avoidance. As Aaron Henry ruefully wrote, "The relatively quiet years of the early fifties were only the calm before the storm. The Supreme Court had given us a beautifully wrapped gift, but when we removed the shiny wrappings, the box was empty."[59]

The struggle of the Little Rock Nine across the Mississippi River sent searing messages to the NAACP about the strength of opposition to school integration.[60] In spite of the students' eventual entry into Central High School, following President Eisenhower's reluctant intervention, the event never became a clear-cut victory for the NAACP. Indeed, Arkansas governor Orval Faubus's landslide reelection that year highlighted the fervor of the opposition. Historian Adam Fairclough affirmed that Little Rock "foreshadowed years of dogged white resistance that not only delayed large-scale integration for more than a decade, but also ensured that schools were eventually integrated under the worst possible circumstances."[61] In other states, despite the ranting of governors and the local threats, federal troops did not appear. Even in the later crisis produced by James Meredith's enrollment at the University of Mississippi in 1962, troops were called in to stop riots, not to enforce integration.[62] Federal intervention to force school integration was not in the offing—the push would continue to originate from NAACP court challenges.

Van Landingham's fears about black schools as recruiting centers for the NAACP youth councils were not completely baseless. Youth council members attended the local schools, putting them in direct unrestricted contact with their classmates. Cora Lee Hicks, a youth council member in the late 1950s, remembered: "In my classroom at school and my classmates, many of them were not members of the Youth Council or even active in the movement . . . so it made us stick out at school because we were very few in numbers."[63] Understanding the world of teenagers and peer pressure, it is not a stretch to assume that youth council members, by their mere presence and notoriety, presented avenues through which information circulated in spite of parental and school board control.

The impetus to recruit came not only from within the schools but also from the national office. At the end of 1958, with NAACP membership in the South wavering, Ruby Hurley again felt the pressure to increase memberships and dues.[64] Threatened with budget cuts and office closings, workers in the field faced 1959 with a degree of dread. Medgar Evers slept even less than before as he worked to "not remain at the bottom of the list in this fight."[65]

Mothering the Movement

Evers enthusiastically promoted a new "Mother of the Year Campaign" to raise funds in time for the national convention in July 1959. Appeals targeted women. Like the "Miss NAACP" contest, this one sought to engage older women, the mothers, to become more involved. As a strategy to further stimulate the activities of women at the grassroots level, such contests, awards ceremonies, banquets, freedom dinners, Christmas seal campaigns, and the like served as fund-raising initiatives and encouraged the participation of women of all ages, albeit in secondary, service roles. These campaigns mirrored the NAACP's continued ambivalence about female authority. Adam Clayton Powell Jr. characterized the organization as standing "in the full virility of manhood."[66] The organization mirrored the national emphasis in the postwar decades on the supposed naturalness of female domesticity and mothering. For instance, after Emmett Till's brutal murder, although the NAACP gave his grieving mother, Mamie Bradley, a national platform around the country to speak about her loss as a respectable mother, once she began to assert herself and attempt to manage her own image the NAACP promptly dropped her from its speakers' roster. Similarly, the "Mother of the Year" campaign sought to elevate women's roles as mothers but in tightly controlled definitions of respectability. Only a rare few, like Ruby Hurley, Lucille Black, and Ella Baker, broke through the male ranks to the executive positions.

It was in this context that Vera Pigee began to play a prominent role in the movement in Clarksdale, in the state, and beyond. Using Bolivar County public school letterhead, Sovereignty Commission informant and neighboring Cleveland's black high school principal B. L. Bell reported on the RCNL annual meeting on 27 April 1959. Outlining the time and place of the gathering, he noted the small number present—between seventy and one hundred persons. He named Vera Pigee as "a top official in the NAACP in the state and who is also Director of the Young People's Dept of the State of Mississippi NAACP Chapter."[67] He targeted her as an enemy of the state, and in doing so he recognized and validated her authority and leadership.

Pigee now worked as the advisor at the state and regional levels, organizing youth councils throughout the state and speaking across the nation. Mary Jane Pigee, then around sixteen years old, stayed with her mother on the frontlines for most of her teenage years. Many activists, fearing for their families, kept their children in the background, protecting them from harm and sometimes sending them out of state. Pigee, on the other hand, saw this movement as the

ultimate education for her daughter, developing life-saving skills that also promoted self-image and self-worth. It was a lesson in tough love taught to Pigee
as a child by her mother. In fact, Pigee treated all in the council as her children
and as siblings of her only child. Members held meetings at her beauty salon
and her house, and Pigee would give the youth keys to her home to find food if
they had walked some distance into town to attend events. She trusted them as
she would her own child with her possessions, protecting them as her own by
giving them access to shelter and food.

Still, parents in Clarksdale instinctively balked at the idea of their children becoming open targets of race hatred. The 1958 Coahoma County Youth
Council consisted of only five members, rising to thirty-four, enough for a
charter, in 1959. It took Pigee four years to receive the official charter, and
many parents requested that their children remain anonymous.[68] The local
youth council in 1959 ranked fifth out of the state's fourteen.[69] The first official president was Steve Abraham; Mary Jane Pigee served as vice president.
Members ranged from twelve to twenty-one years of age. Clarksdale's NAACP
was one of only a few branches that actually improved membership figures that
year, rising from 54 members in 1958 to 180 by the close of 1959.[70] This level of
youth activity confirmed the Citizens' Council's fear of black schools as institutions where organizing took place. However, outside of the schools, strong
leadership and parental participation proved crucial in making youth councils
work and flourish.[71]

The youth council labored diligently with the senior NAACP branch members to mobilize the community. Performing tasks that working adults could
not or would not execute, the youth served as ushers in mass meetings; distributed flyers; held raffles, dances, street rallies, workshops, and public programs;
sponsored events for fund-raising; participated in boycotts and sit-ins; and
helped with mailings.[72] The work the youth councils undertook in the early
years galvanized local people. Seeing their own young put themselves on the
line in the shadow of Emmett Till's murder, and in the face of massive resistance from the Citizens' Councils, lifted parents out of their own fears. These
increasingly visible activities of the local youth influenced many adults to try
to register to vote, or to support the movement in some way.

Pigee's role in the local movement shows that black women utilized their
everyday social roles (in her case as a mother) to promote activism and radical change by example and in conjunction with her other role as branch secretary. She was a bridge leader, a bridge between community and lectern, rather
than a formal figurehead leader, to use the idea of sociologist Belinda Robnett,

working on the ground with the community while holding positions in formal structures, using knowledge and contacts to be most effective. By integrating this model with the politics of mothering, activist mothers become visible. No spotlight or camera illuminated Vera Pigee for all to see, but her presence helped to drive the local movement, and her guidance of the youth movement, specifically the youth council, enabled her to reach larger numbers of local people.

The concept of activist mothering is complicated and can operate in many directions, some in complete opposition to women like Pigee. For example, consider the Mothers' League of Little Rock Central High, formed in 1957 in support of white supremacy and against desegregation. This group represented a conservative, right-wing form of activist mothering, yet it was highly influential and successful in organizing the local white community. Members galvanized and influenced their children, students at the high school, and made their presence felt every day outside the school as they picketed and protested.

It is important to state, however, that a woman who is an activist and a mother does not necessarily equate to an activist mother. Many mothers were campaigners for many causes, some even motivated by situations affecting their children, but would not fit into the category of activist mother. Similarly, a woman who is a leader is not necessarily maternally driven. Neither Ella Baker nor Ruby Hurley could be read as activist mothers as easily as Pigee can. Their activities did not engage with gendered familial and communal norms. In fact, they defied them. They did not adhere to the gendered roles of their time, assuming high profile positions in their organizations and eschewing domestic "stability." But Baker (and probably Hurley and Lucille Black) recognized the relative institutional openness to women at the local level to craft and shape their specific leadership acumen and sought to exploit that for the organization and for themselves.[73]

Mothering is a process of nurturing, of rearing, of bringing up. By making nurturing gendered, it is easy to fall into the quagmire of decades-long feminist debates about the construction of motherhood and the tension between mothering as liberating and empowering the community and mothering as oppressive, caught in biological determinism and directing rigid gender roles. It is best to avoid assigning labels and categories that those so designated may not recognize or accept; rather, it is more productive to look at African American women's lives as they existed. They were mothers, daughters, and wives in a society that imposed heightened value on domesticity and women's traditional roles. It becomes clear that many African Americans repositioned and

transformed seemingly static stations into weapons of resistance, empowerment, and maneuver, rather than dwelling solely within the four walls of narrow Eurocentric constructions of domestic space.[74]

While avoiding the ongoing feminist debates, however, it is necessary to
acknowledge the fundamental difference between the historical hegemonic
perceptions of black mothering and white mothering. Both black women and
white women manage the public and private divide—but not in the same way
or in the same spaces. Motherhood is generally understood to be the moral
incubator for the family (and, by extension, society), but that is framed as
"white." Black mothers have always been cast as deficient, "breeders" of a
race marked as inferior and unworthy. As such, black women's access to the
privileges of motherhood has always been limited. Enslaved, they had had no
ability to protect their children, all legally deemed the property of another.
White women's work, on the other hand, has always been seen as political—
they are affirmed by their ability to protect their offspring and identify as such.
The Mothers' League of Little Rock Central High is a dramatic case in point.
However, because black mothers are not affirmed by the status quo, they could
make changes and transform mothering to incorporate alternative elements.
They are equipped with tools, almost by default, to resist social hegemonic
norms.

Pigee's activist life embodied activist mothering, where "the blurring of
community work and family-based labor by those women frequently meant
opening their homes to those in need," something she did regularly and without question.[75] Roy Bell Wright, one of the first Coahoma County Youth Council presidents, remembered, "She was a mother to hundreds of us over a twenty
year period," as she sustained the group with her brand of personal care.[76]
Such alternative kin networks and "other mothering," common in African
American communities, provided young people in Clarksdale with not only
a safe space but also a nurturing adult to aid in their socialization.[77] Pigee became the community's mother, able to dispense criticism and advice and to
direct others with good results. A product of a strong mother, who raised two
children and provided enough food and materials to disguise their poverty
from her youngsters, Pigee already knew the skills of survival, hard work, and
female independence. The importance of the foremother to African American
women's activism as a source and model of pride, motivation, and inspiration
had clearly shaped Pigee's younger life.

Not only did Pigee run her own household, but by adding more children to
her family through the youth councils she engaged in a much broader model

of mothering that encompassed the community and local politics. Activist mothering includes more than biological kinship. In a climate of threat and actual violence, political mothering becomes all the more important. Nancy Naples wrote that "*good mothering* [comprises] all actions, including social activism, that addressed the needs of their children and the community."[78] For Pigee, mothering became an organizing tool, harnessing youthful energies and shepherding them (hopefully safely) down constructive paths. Her activist mothering, in turn, reared activist offspring.

The younger Mississippians in the youth councils were impatient for change, angered at seeing their elders constantly humiliated by the bonds of Jim Crow. Indifferent to the risks and the very real danger that lay in wait for them, the youth felt it was now their turn. They avidly watched the tactics of the college students elsewhere. With increasing access to television sets, Mississippians who had not traveled out of the state could take a peek into a new world not so far, geographically, from their own, even if their own local terrain proved more perilous. In Clarksdale, without SNCC, the sturdy NAACP youth council took the initiative in instigating direct action.

Clarksdale saw its first public demonstration in the spring of 1960, not long after the Greensboro sit-ins in North Carolina in the first week of February.[79] Pigee had contacted the national NAACP youth director, Laplois Ashford, who generally discouraged sit-ins, in accordance with NAACP policy.[80] In Mississippi, no resources were available to pay for bonds or attorney support. Nevertheless, in a compromise, a group of youths, including Mary Jane, went on a shopping trip to buy a Bible and a frame for the youth council's charter. Although the local Woolworth's sold goods to black customers in the store, it maintained segregated lunch counters.[81] The "observation tour" occurred without incident. The young people showed the charter in need of a frame to the stunned saleswoman, who quickly carried out the transaction and encouraged them to leave the premises promptly. Other customers "had frozen in their tracks, others had a look of surprise, and still others had hate stares on their faces."[82] The action tested the system—by entering the store in a group and presenting the charter these young people demonstrated their existence and their fearlessness, but the trip also tested the black community's support for direct action. Vera Pigee remembered, "We termed this experience a semi-protest, or trial run, and we also watched the action and reaction of the parents and the public."[83] Under Pigee's direction, the youth council went on to participate in direct action with gusto and enthusiasm. She utilized her negotiating leverage with the national office, reasoning that the youth should at least have proper guidance rather than have them seek leadership from another organization. By supporting them, they would remain in the youth council and continue their NAACP work.

Vera Pigee's occupation and social position helps to explain her motivation to act so decisively and with such determination. Longtime activist Sheila Michaels described a gathering at the SNCC head office in Atlanta sometime in late 1963. "It was the late Cordell Hull Reagan, who told me that in order to organize a town you must win over two people: the beautician & the midwife. And I thought, of course, they're in touch with everyone, they're necessary & they hold all the secrets. There is no minister who can touch that."[84] This acknowledgment of the location of black community power had come long before. The Highlander Folk School, a training site for liberal southern activists nestled in the hills of Tennessee, recognized the leadership possibilities of beauticians in the early sixties and sought to train them in the art of propagating information and strategic organizing.[85] Myles Horton, organizer and director of Highlander, seeking leaders among African Americans in the fifties, noted that leaders typically came from sectors of the workforce not reliant on white patronage or jobs. Self-employed service providers, serving the segregated black population, had less to lose and could rise to positions of visibility in their communities. Horton discovered, quite by accident, the importance of black beauticians: "A black beautician, unlike a white beautician, was at that time a person of some status in the community. They were entrepreneurs, they were small businesswomen . . . respected, they were usually better educated than other people, and most of all they were independent. They were independent of white control." He confessed, "Just by sheer accident I noticed that some of the people that came to Highlander were beauticians, and I followed up that lead and used to run beautician's workshops at Highlander, just for beauticians."[86]

Septima Clark, who ran citizenship schools and training workshops across the South, held a three-day workshop for beauticians in January 1961, for the purpose of finding "the things which need to be done in a community that cannot be done by city and state employees or churchmen. . . . The Beauticians can speak out openly and can publicly promote the cause for justice and equality in the South."[87] Clark reached out particularly to beauticians because of their independence in a space that also served as a community center.[88] Although Pigee never attended Highlander during the meetings specifically for beauticians, Clark had already identified her leadership possibilities (Pigee had attended other workshops in 1960) and encouraged her to attend further training sessions for citizenship classes in 1961 in Dorchester, Georgia, under the auspices of the SCLC.[89] In fact, Clark was so impressed by Pigee's efforts in the local NAACP branch that she took out a life membership through its chapter "because they were really getting something done."[90] By the end of 1961, four citizenship schools ran in Clarksdale under Pigee's tutelage and direction, teaching the Mississippi state Constitution, along with general literacy skills.[91] By the middle of 1965, Pigee had supervised twenty schools in the previous four years, stating that in 1965 alone 100 had registered to vote under her direct influence. Clark was right in her high level of confidence in the hardworking beautician.[92]

Pigee's beauty shop in the heart of a black neighborhood in downtown Clarksdale sheltered strategy meetings and activists from the fifties through the seventies. Located at 407 Ashton, right in the heart of the black business district, it became an organizing site and a safe house for civil rights meetings. It was a space to discuss, cajole, and persuade, and it was "the birthing room for civil rights in Clarksdale."[93] The beauty shop culture aided in the dissemination of news. At times, Pigee could literally hold clients hostage to a continuous barrage of information and persuasion while working on their hair. The salon served as a center of female economy that catered to a diverse class of clientele. The beauty shop became the public household, where the mothering of the domestic sphere was renegotiated in a public, yet special place outside of white surveillance.[94] For working-class women in particular, the beauty shop remained a space for economic, political, and social empowerment outside of both the man's world and the white world. In short, the beauty shop culture demonstrated mothering to mothers, while also nurturing techniques and work that fostered activism.

As women entered, sat, and waited for their turn in the chair—a process that took at least two hours, if not half a day—they talked to each other, caught up on current events, laughed over stories about their children and men, and lamented deaths and departures. Charles Moore's photograph of Pigee's salon gives a sense of the atmosphere the women created and occupied (see figure 2.1). Crates of Coca-Cola stacked on the floor indicate that clients stayed awhile, needing sustenance to tide them over until the next meal. There they talked and gossiped about work and family and also shared news about the mass meeting the night before and the rumors of police incidents following protests and made plans for that day's activities. On the lap of Pigee's client, voting registration papers initiated a lesson in citizenship and strategy, a conversation shared with other clients or kept private between beautician and

FIG. 2.1. Vera Pigee at work in her beauty salon, 1963. (Charles Moore/Black Star)

client. On the wall, a poster advertising the Freedom Vote in November 1963 makes clear the work to be done.

The photograph perfectly illustrates the significance of the beauty shop in the circulation of information. Moore presents the image of an image. The photographer is not visible through the mirrored image and the women are not looking at/for him either. The audience's gaze, like Moore's, remains indirect. The mirror, overtly ornate for a beauty shop, was probably recycled from a bedroom set, the domestic space of a home rather than from a supply store. Its nonutilitarianism adds to the incongruity of the scene. On the surface, viewers witness the serenity of a female space, two women participating in the creation of beauty. But another transformation was occurring. A political transformation is realized through the conversation that viewers cannot hear or see. Two kinds of work were occurring: the work of creating beauty and the work of creating a movement, both of them marked here as distinctly female and effectively masked. The only clue is the stack of papers on the lap of the client. There were two kinds of preparation taking place, the preparation of the body and the preparation of the fighting mind. It was an act of a process, not of a product. The poster interrupts the creation of beauty with the reality of ugliness and violence. Clients could not help but see the epitome of ugliness, demonstrating the tensions within the photograph and the overlapping realities in people's lives.

Black women's activism has been rendered invisible in too many instances because strategies of nurturing are oftentimes confused with notions of "naturalness" or the ordinary activities of women in their communities. In fact, it is this misunderstanding that permits many women to engage in subversive activities—they are not suspected, their activities are not prone to arrest for inciting lawlessness or civil disobedience because of the protected space they inhabit, safe from violence. Maternal strategies of nurturing and organizing in a patriarchal movement are taken for granted as "natural," not radical. Indeed, much more is known about the potentially radical spaces of barbershops for male politicization. The space of the female-centered beauty shop, ignored *because* of its seemingly benign, gossip-filled façade, proved to be the space for debate and discussion on current events and a major organizing site. A woman who utilized and expanded the role society and culture assigned her sex in order to organize groups of youths and adults is rarely recognized in the official record. In fact, black women's activism denaturalizes gender roles. Like men, they are leaders, yet they willingly maintain their other gendered identities as mothers and wives. Just as Myles Horton stumbled on the reality of black beauticians as community leaders because of their initiative in attending Highlander in large numbers, historians too have come to appreciate that community nurturing can have a political, even radical, dimension.

Class, as well as gender, shaped the possibilities of black women's activism. Most working women, struggling to make ends meet for their families, organized and became active in areas relevant to their lives only when it became urgently necessary.[95] If their livelihood depended on whites, they could little afford to be too active in public. Vera Pigee thus benefited enormously from her status as a property owner and businesswoman. Her position as self-employed, owning the property on which her business operated, allowed her to take risks others could not. If her husband (who stayed uninvolved publicly) had lost his job at the North Delta Compress due to her activities, the family contingency plan included setting up a catering business in the back room of their property where they could profit from his culinary skills (which also fed the family when his wife worked late into the night). Fortunately he never had to.[96] But, by serving others, his wife also worked to improve her own class position. The duties she performed sought her own uplift as much as it did that of others.

Once the beauty shop closed for business for the night, people entered not looking for new hairstyles but seeking knowledge. Figure 2.2 shows a voter registration class in progress in the shop's alcove. A bare lightbulb illuminates the table, as four students, two men and two women, and Pigee intently read from manuals. She sits erect, wearing an NAACP youth council T-shirt. This is her domain. And it is a safe learning space. To her left, tucked behind the mirror, her diploma and business licenses decorate the walls with two hair-styling advertisement posters. Moore's earlier photograph of her working in her salon shows the same mirror, indicating the same salon with the display of her professional qualifications. Behind Pigee is a window, the blinds pulled tightly closed, and a tiny clock on the wall next to the window indicates that it is 7:45. Given the opposition to African Americans registering to vote, such classes could have been potentially dangerous. Employers could (and did) fire employees if they found out about their involvement and participation, so a covered window also provided safety and a degree of anonymity. To discover the activities in the salon, intruders would have had to enter through the front door.

Beside the window, a corner table indicates that this alcove was where Pigee and her assistants perhaps took their breaks during the workday. This was after-hours work. The people look wearied, the stress of learning after a day's work plain on their faces. What could be Pigee's handbag sits on a chair behind

FIG. 2.2. Vera Pigee leading an adult voter registration class after hours in her beauty salon, 1963. (Charles Moore/Black Star)

her as though readied for departure. The woman seated closest to the camera wears a wedding band, indicating that she has left a family to be present. But they were there to learn, and Pigee extended her own day to work with the adults to increase the numbers on the registration rolls. Her T-shirt also illustrates the extent and reach of her work—she worked with children and adults for freedom.

Located in a prime position in the black community, among other black businesses, churches, and homes, Pigee's property was somewhat protected from harm. The community surrounded her, literally. Her position, recognized by the community, enabled her to shape strategies and activities, endowing her with community-based power from which her authority derived. Pigee's position as a leader, therefore, prompted many in the black community to form a cocoon around her business, a site of resistance and strategy-building too precious to risk losing. When asked if she was concerned about unwelcome visitors when she kept her doors unlocked so that anyone could enter for shelter, she laughed, "They knew better than to come down there!" By providing services for the black community, the beauty salon did well enough for her to be able to employ up to six assistants at one point, allowing her the opportunity to work with the movement full time.[97] Indeed, she attended many conferences, traveling throughout the state and the nation (even abroad) under the auspices of the NAACP, with the youth or as branch secretary.[98] Having the time to invest in the movement, in turn, consolidated her local power, earning her the respect she needed in order to fulfill her "other mother" duties.

Competing for Youth Loyalties

Young people held the key to the movement's future, and this was all the more apparent in the wake of the successful organization of SNCC in April 1960 and the initial relative success of the NAACP youth councils in Mississippi. To an older national NAACP leadership, these changes in the political and social landscape did not bode well for the organization, and they reached another crossroads. Nonviolent direct action overtook litigation as the primary form of resistance—spurring instant reactions and media images by relying on emotion and rhetoric to reach wide audiences. Change would come from the political arena rather than sluggishly through the courts.[99]

With three significant organizations, the SCLC, the Congress of Racial Equality (CORE), and SNCC, vying for the spotlight through their direct-action strategies, the NAACP's premier position, especially in Mississippi, appeared to be in peril. NAACP leaders in New York debated the effects of the new organizations. Gloster Current and youth director Herbert Wright discussed the relevance and appeal of the NAACP to contemporary youth, recognizing that the organization's size hindered adequate communication. NAACP youth councils and college chapters saw the grinding bureaucracy as a fatal flaw in the organization. As Wright traveled to state youth conferences, he noted the presence of numerous other organizations and how the youth division spent much time discussing the sit-ins and activities happening elsewhere. Even in the much-lauded Clarksdale/Coahoma County Youth Council, in a state where SNCC had yet to penetrate, the youth created a furor when they were "observed surveying downtown stores to ascertain the number of Negro patrons in that community." Wright reported, "The sit-ins have aroused unusually high interest among our youth and college units in sending representatives to the National Convention at St. Paul this year. Accordingly, we are expecting between 400–500 youths to be in attendance at the national meeting." Not surprisingly, membership figures at the close of 1960 echoed the flurry of activities in the senior branches. In 1960, national membership increased to 388,347, an increase of 13 percent over the previous year, due in part to direct-action activities in the South.[100]

Working under the careful tutelage of ex-NAACP officer Ella Baker, SNCC attracted many members from NAACP chapters throughout the region. The NAACP in turn vied to retain youth, stressing their homegrown successes, including Montgomery's bus boycott (which they claimed as their victory following the successful court decision), and writing to field secretaries and state presidents to send groups to the retreats, like the one at Boggs Academy on 17 August, in Georgia. In a joint letter from Hurley and Wright to the youth councils and adult branches encouraging participation on the retreat, they advertised, "You will also hear firsthand about the exciting sit-ins which our councils and chapters are participating in this summer. The wonderful successes which we have scored at Winston-Salem, Durham, Greensboro and Charlotte, in recent weeks will be reported on in detail."[101] Trying to capitalize on the college student movement started that spring, the organization sought desperately to stem the resulting membership hemorrhage.

Young people were not the only ones critical of the NAACP. Amzie Moore battled continued economic pressure to oust him from Bolivar County and became embittered toward the NAACP, the organization he had loyally promoted for so many years. His subsequent correspondence with Bob Moses in 1960 brought about the arrival of SNCC in Mississippi. Moore had grown critical of the NAACP bureaucracy's inability to react quickly in times of crisis. In an effort to save his businesses, he had petitioned several banks and organizations, including the NAACP, for loans—mostly to no avail. Resentful of what he considered a lack of response to his loyalty and sacrifices for the cause, meeting Moses was a turning point. Speaking to journalist Howell Raines, he said, "Nobody dared move a peg without some lawyer advisin' him," and because the base of operation resided stubbornly in Jackson with Medgar Evers, the organization in Mississippi remained fettered, not functioning at its full potential.[102] To Moore, SNCC represented the opposite of the legalistic NAACP: "SNCC was for business, live or die, sink or swim, survive or perish. They were moving, and nobody seemed to worry about whether he was gonna live or die."[103]

And so the sixties began, with the blossoming of direct public protests among black youth in the South, who were tired of waiting for change five years after the *Brown* decisions. Mississippi had yet to witness the tenacity of the college youth movement, which would descend on the state in the next few years. Nevertheless, the movement's landscape had been redrawn yet again. With new organizations, particularly CORE, SNCC, and the SCLC, competing for resources and national attention, the NAACP tripped on its own red tape and missed opportunities to act and form coalitions. The inflexibility in the national office, far away from the realities of fierce repression from Citizens' Councils and state legislatures, handicapped its effectiveness when events occurred quickly, with no time for consultation or elaborate planning. Little substantive progress toward equality had been made. The internal tussle over strategies between those in the national office (Wilkins and Current) and those at the grass roots (Evers and Henry) hindered the organization's future as the cutting-edge leaders in the crusade for civil rights.

The NAACP's inability—or unwillingness—to promote mass protest opened a void quickly occupied by the generation born during and immediately after World War II and now in high school and college. Mississippi youth, watching these events from afar, grew restless, encouraging state and local NAACP leaders, unfettered by many of the bureaucratic restrictions placed on paid staff, to find spaces for them to vent their desires for direct action. At the helm of the state youth councils, Vera Pigee oversaw this process. She drew on her strengths as a mother, a community leader, and an independent beautician to maintain a watchful eye on her wards and find protection for them, despite the hostility of their immediate landscape and the aloofness of the national organization. In the coming years, her strength would be tested and tried as she herself tussled with groups entering the state vying for the attentions of her youth councils and as she herself became a target through her activities.

CHAPTER THREE

I Think Freedom and Talk Freedom

DEMANDING DESEGREGATION, 1960–1963

It appears that the Negroes in Mississippi have been given a do-it-yourself
kit to carve out for ourselves those freedoms that America and Mississippi
guaranteed to all other citizens. — Aaron Henry and Medgar Evers (1961)

I am Mrs. Vera Pigee, a wife, a mother, political prisoner, business
and professional woman. Wherever I go, even if I am brought in handcuffs,
my name is still Mrs. Vera Pigee. — Vera Pigee (1961)

"What can a mother, a professional woman, and a Christian contribute to the struggle for human dignity?" asked Vera Pigee. Answering her own question, Pigee mused: "It was my first commitment as a mother to see her [daughter Mary Jane] more fully equipped to cope with the problems of today. Youth is our greatest resource. Daily, I try to impress this simple truth on parents in my community, and the National Association for the Advancement of Colored People has provided a vehicle whereby I have been able to do this with considerable success. A professional woman in Mississippi is something of a rarity. My work is hard but it is never dull, and for this reason: it has a goal, it is not an end in itself. . . . I think freedom and talk freedom with my customers."[1]

Pigee had also demonstrated freedom. She and Idessa Johnson, a member of the NAACP branch, had put their bodies on the line in support of the youth. Dressed immaculately in their churchgoing attire, they walked with their carefully coiffed heads held high into the Clarksdale Greyhound bus terminal's white-only section in the fall of 1961. Pigee was the only woman on the Coahoma County NAACP executive board, and none of the men, whom she characterized as "black proud brothers," wanted to participate. Desegregating the bus terminal was a personal goal. Pigee knew that her daughter, Mary Jane, a student studying voice and music at Central State College in Wilberforce, Ohio, and former local youth council president, would not use the designated black side of the station traveling home for her Christmas vacation. So Pigee decided to protest "because no one in Clarksdale was willing to do what they should have done long before she was born."[2]

Pigee consulted her husband and then fasted and prayed all night. The following morning, she asked Idessa Johnson to accompany her. Rev. J. D. Rayford stood watching on the platform between the two segregated entrances. Taking deep breaths, the women walked to the window and asked for a round-trip ticket from Cincinnati, Ohio, to Clarksdale and for an express bus schedule. The transaction took place quietly. Turning on their heels, they walked slowly, pausing to marvel at the spacious, air-conditioned, white section. Lingering further, they bent to drink at the water fountain before visiting the ladies' room.[3] Satisfied, they pushed open the doors and walked out.

When Mary Jane came home for Christmas, she entered the white side, complaining only about the loss of one piece of luggage and the illegibly written ticket that delayed her journey. When it was time for her to return to school, however, four policemen entered the white waiting room where she sat with her mother and a family friend, Hattie Mae Gilmore. Harassing them with a barrage of questions, the officers threatened arrest. Mary Jane, following her mother's instructions, wrote down their names and badge numbers, while black men on the Jim Crow side began to leave, fearing the confrontation. Later, the women filed complaints with the NAACP, the Justice Department, the local FBI, the police, and the Interstate Commerce Commission. "We kept repeating the cycle until we won," Pigee remarked.[4] On 27 December 1961, the *Clarksdale Press Register* reported that all the segregation signs had disappeared from the Greyhound and train terminals. Federal sources confirmed that the police had voluntarily removed the signs after the Justice Department informed the city that it faced a lawsuit. After all, this was after the Supreme Court decision *Morgan v. Virginia* of 1947, the 1955–56 Montgomery bus boycott, and a year marked by the Freedom Rides sponsored by the Congress of Racial Equality (CORE).[5] Aaron Henry, with tongue in cheek, publicly acknowledged the wonderful Christmas present for black citizens.[6]

Pigee's desegregation of the bus terminal symbolized the beginning of a more aggressive style of protest in Clarksdale, one already practiced in other counties and southern states. Two women, both mothers and NAACP members, initiated adult participation in direct action. But Pigee and Johnson were not simply reacting to an obvious injustice. Their actions took shape against the backdrop of rising student-led protest across the South, a mass of movements that increasingly pushed well past the adult leadership of old-line civil rights organizations, like their beloved NAACP. Disillusioned with the snail's pace of school desegregation and frustrated at the deliberate thwarting of justice in "all deliberate speed," black students (from grade school to college) turned their attention to the desegregation of their towns, caught up in the sweeping tidal wave of youthful direct-action protests. Civil rights energies spun away from schools as activists recognized the futility of fighting segregationists standing guard over their white boys and girls, particularly with the federal government's energies focused elsewhere. Pigee's work as head of the Clarksdale Youth Council, as well as her relationship with Mary Jane, confirmed to her that the local NAACP branch had better march in tune with young people or risk losing credibility as the leading civil rights organization in the county. If something was afoot, Pigee and other local adult leaders realized they should take their place along the new battle lines.

Rather than work on membership drives, newsletters, and campaigns to remove racist language from textbooks and to integrate college faculties, southern youth wanted to be on the direct-action frontlines. With its younger, more energetic forces, the Student Nonviolent Coordinating Committee (SNCC) had begun to outpace the national NAACP, which had trouble retaining its young members and an even harder time controlling their activities in the rapidly shifting civil rights terrain. Pigee managed the situation locally in Clarksdale, but the national office teetered in the assailing winds. Herbert Wright, youth director in the national NAACP office, beseeched the national director of branches, Gloster Current, to establish "a definite, clear-cut policy on the question of young adult councils within the youth program."[7] NAACP youth councils had existed since the 1930s, predominantly at the college level, where the organization sought to benefit from an earlier generation's enthusiasm and energy.[8] But in 1960 a deepening inconsistency between the NAACP's objectives and the direction of that generation's youth had become fully apparent. The old guard, Current and Roy Wilkins, resisted the pull toward public protest and applied brakes to Wright's more ambitious plans for the NAACP councils.

If the sixties is a decade memorialized for its youth culture and the emerging national liberalism, in 1960 it was *black* youth who took the reins of leadership and set an ambitious agenda for the decade. Many older black leaders, particularly in the NAACP, failed to endorse direct action, wary of the physical dangers and the legal system's reluctance to protect black citizens against brutality. Yet the generation born after the Depression and in the midst of world conflict in the forties had begun to assert itself. This was the Emmett Till generation. Their parents, for the most part, responded by following their lead. As the story in Clarksdale unfolded, the Clarksdale Youth Council supported by Vera Pigee pushed the adults' safer boundaries and provoked them to act. Even Pigee had followed the youths' lead when she and Johnson desegregated the Greyhound bus terminal.

The local activism in Clarksdale attracted women and young people and made them the mainstay of the movement. At the local level, women drew upon available resources to propel their activism while remaining close to the youth in protection and solidarity. They extended familial activities in their churches and groups to include the civil rights agenda. Yet the mass civil rights movement was more difficult, bloodier, and more contested the closer one got to the grass roots. Local places were where boots met backs, fists smashed cheekbones, and police clubs cracked skulls. It was where women and men sacrificed jobs, limbs, and sometimes lives.

However, the story of Clarksdale would be incomplete without attention to the parallel struggles, albeit less violent and bloody, within and among civil rights groups, for resources, members, and prominence. The Clarksdale movement unequivocally benefited from Aaron Henry's contacts and national resources as he rose in the NAACP ranks. When he sought alliances with other groups, however, the national office continued to view such coalitions with skepticism and frustration. In Clarksdale, too often the national NAACP was its own worst enemy, even as it was the most respected organization and even as many locals, particularly Vera Pigee, faithfully propped it up.

In this context of an expanding mass movement, increasing danger, and intergroup tension and rivalry, this chapter follows Clarksdale's desegregation struggle from 1960 to the end of June 1963. At the end of that summer, many would march in Washington, D.C., and twenty-one parents signed a legal suit to end school segregation, signaling fresh confidence to restart the education equality campaign after the disastrous attempts immediately after the *Brown v. Board of Education of Topeka* decision. Focusing on a selection of events that serve as turning points and provide vivid portraits of the movement's landscape at a particular moment, this chapter illustrates how the fight for desegregation fell to a minority, including women and young people, and how, by mid-1963, little had been resolved.

The New Frontiers in the Delta

With the events in neighboring Little Rock in 1957 and 1958 still generating headlines, in 1959, white Mississippians elected the reactionary white suprema-cist Ross Barnett as governor. Barnett charged the state's Sovereignty Com-mission with a new and more explicit mission that went well beyond the image maintenance preferred by his predecessor, James Coleman. Now the state as-serted white supremacy in open alliance with the Citizens' Councils.[9] The Sovereignty Commission began to channel state funds directly to the Citizens' Councils, and together they sought to influence politics at the city and county levels.[10] Sovereignty Commission investigators would now work even closer with city officials than they had in the 1950s. They mingled openly with leaders who were Citizens' Council members and relayed strategies of opposition to specific communities.

One such investigator, Tom Scarbrough, traveled to Clarksdale to look into a rumored mass voter registration drive. Scarbrough had served as Chicka-saw County sheriff from 1944 to 1948 and as commissioner of public safety for the Mississippi State Highway Patrol from 1956 before his appointment to the Sovereignty Commission.[11] On 3 November 1960, he attended a Citi-zens' Council meeting in the directors' room of the Bank of Coahoma County. Robert B. Patterson, fellow Clarksdalian and founder of the Citizens' Coun-cils, was also present. Despite determining that rumors far exceeded the real numbers of those registering to vote, Scarbrough seemed perplexed that the leaders showed no alarm that any black citizens had registered to vote in the first place. "I am led to think Coahoma County leaders are responsible for their present Negro complications as there has been a long established cus-tom for white people to register Negroes to vote in order to defeat some indi-vidual whom they opposed or to defeat bond issues," he wrote in his report.[12] According to Scarbrough—there is no evidence to corroborate his claims about a long-established custom—Clarksdale's whites had played with fire by using the black vote for their own purposes. He criticized them further for not putting sufficient economic pressure on black "agitators," such as firing more schoolteachers who had relatives involved in the movement.

Race relations in Coahoma County had always maintained the semblance of gentility in comparison to other Delta counties. In fact, Aaron Henry noted that the city "considered itself quite progressive in the thirties," for example, when the white Association of Church Women sponsored a recreation pro-gram for black youth. Similarly, he had noted the existence of a working interracial board for Clarksdale's Civic Music Association in the 1950s. Despite the strong paternalistic attitudes that accompanied any "good deeds" that whites rationed out to blacks, these gestures were few and far between in the Delta.[13] As a relatively large county, Coahoma had a disproportionately higher number of African Americans who could be called middle class—those who owned their own viable businesses or who taught at the segregated Coahoma County Junior College. With a more diverse black population than other Delta counties, white city fathers had long manipulated class divisions by permitting a chosen few to prosper and even, on occasion, to vote.

When Jim Crow was breached, however, a tight network of local elites and police ensured that the threat was eliminated and not publicized. On a Saturday afternoon in July 1960, for instance, twenty-four-year-old, Clarksdale-born, Irene Lloyd and twenty-three-year-old Myra Jones, two black women visiting from Chicago, tried to desegregate the local Woolworth's lunch counter. Entering the store, they completed a small purchase before taking seats at the far end of the counter during a lull in the day's business. The waitress immediately notified the manager, who instructed her to ignore the women. When one of the protesters approached the waitress for service, the manager politely advised the women that they did not serve Negroes and asked them to leave the store. By his account, the women became boisterous and argued but left the store. Someone called the police, but the manager declined to file a complaint and chose not to accompany the officers to the headquarters where the two women were held in the custody of Clarksdale's police.[14]

Lloyd and Jones had come to Clarksdale for the funeral of their grandmother, scheduled for the following Monday morning. After an investigation, the police officers and Judge Leon Porter (once described as "a pinch-faced, middle-aged attorney whose sour disposition reflected his antipathy toward blacks") concluded that the protest was unplanned and that local agitators had played no role in its execution. After a search of their possessions turned up no money or identification, both women were charged with vagrancy, and bail was set at $100 (this indicated a spontaneous protest—had they been trained for this kind of action, both would have had money and identification in the probable event of their arrest, as well as contacts ready to assist them). When no one came to post their bond, they remained in police custody and went before the city court on Monday morning at nine. Judge Porter released them to attend their grandmother's eleven o'clock funeral but ordered them to report to city hall prior to their departure for Chicago. A patrolman tailed the 1958 dark gray Ford with Illinois license plates until it left Mississippi at the Tennessee state line near Memphis.[15] The editor of the *Clarksdale Press Register* was instructed not to print details of the incident. There is no evidence that local black activists knew of the events since the branch made no note of the arrest—it tended to publicize any protest that occurred in town in order to maintain momentum. The situation had been cleanly and quietly managed.

The year after the more extreme Ross Barnett became Mississippi's governor, John F. Kennedy was inaugurated as the nation's thirty-fifth president.[16] Kennedy's advisors wanted calm on the civil rights front also. Attorney Harris Wofford's memo from the Democratic National Committee to President-Elect Kennedy on 30 December 1960 warned him to initiate "little or no legislation this year aside from the extension of the Civil Rights Commission, and a large measure of executive action." With executive action, Wofford explained that the president could "overcome the disappointment of Negroes and civil rights groups, although they [would] holler for a while." Wofford then went on to explain the importance of keeping in touch with black leaders, given their support in the election—in short, appease black voters but do not involve Congress in controversial legislation.[17]

Kennedy could not have foreseen the spreading wildfire of direct-action protests across the nation that began days after the inauguration.[18] The growing clamor for civil rights forced the president's hand, despite his desire not to further agitate white southern Democrats. Harris Wofford, now the president's special assistant, recognized that barriers to black voting had to be broken in the Deep South, which would free at least 1 million blacks to register. He even suggested that the Democratic National Convention announce the voting drive rather than Martin Luther King Jr. or the NAACP, because "the Southern Negro temper is changing fast and these state Democratic parties will need to adjust or risk losing the Negro vote." Furthermore, footholds of token desegregation in schools could be established in each southern state, "so that the solid front of massive resistance is broken." All of this could be done quietly, he imagined, with only a minimum legislative program for 1961, limited to extending the Civil Rights Commission and other less controversial measures. Wofford was overly optimistic about breaking massive resistance quietly, and he, like Mississippi's segregationists, was certainly unprepared for mass action by African Americans.[19]

In January, Aaron Henry, the Mississippi NAACP state president, wrote to the newly inaugurated president to extend his congratulations and the "well wishes of a grateful people." He promised the president that if black citizens had the opportunity to vote, Governor Barnett and the other officials in Mississippi would have to temper their diatribes against Kennedy, and "you would see a new man."[20] The election of Kennedy had restored hope that the tribulations of black Mississippi would not fall off the federal radar. Henry's letter reminded the president that direct executive action in the state would facilitate his reelection. Henry's claim had solid foundations. The SNCC newsletter, *Student Voice*, looked closely at the 1960 census. If black Mississippians voted en masse, they could control 36 percent of the seats in the Mississippi House of Representatives under present apportionment. Twenty-seven counties had a majority black population, equaling 49 seats of the House's total of 149.[21]

Local residents did not wait for the president to act. Even as Kennedy took the oath of office, activists pushed against the strictures of Jim Crow. In one of the most unique activities sponsored by the Clarksdale/Coahoma County Youth Council, Mary Jane Pigee, then a college sophomore, sang in Clarksdale's first interracial concert with renowned white folksinger Guy Carawan, accompanied by his wife, Candi.[22] Vera Pigee had met the Carawans at the Highlander Folk School, where she had attended a workshop with Mary Jane the year before. Candi Carawan fondly remembered her hosts and shuddered recalling the climate in the state: "It was very frightening in those days to go into Mississippi and other parts of the Deep South as well, but what really was so moving was how so supportive and welcoming the black community was once we got there . . . that feeling once you got into a black community how safe you really did feel. . . . It was wonderful." Staying with the Pigees, a week after the new year began, the Carawans experienced police intimidation firsthand when they were arrested on a trumped-up traffic violation, for running a stop sign and a red light.[23] Candi Carawan vividly recalled that night:

> For whatever reason, we were not going to stay the night. . . . Several men in the community were quite concerned about us getting out of town after dark, so they organized three cars to drive in front of us and three cars to drive behind us and kind of escorted us out of town. In spite of that, we had not gone very far at all when we were pulled over by the police and I was quite pregnant at the time with our first child, so it was really unpleasant to be taken to the police station! What I remember was the stark contrast between what it felt like to be in the black community and what it was like to be out of [it].[24]

Despite that treatment from the police, they returned for an encore in 1962.

Vera Pigee was also involved in a new voter registration drive. The Crusade for Voters resulted in 100 new voters in the spring of 1961, many garnered by

FIG. 3.1. Mary Jane Pigee and Guy Carawan sing in the first integrated concert in Clarksdale, January 1961. (Personal collection of Mary Jane Pigee Davis)

the youth council, whose members went door-to-door and announced the program in churches and schools. Black citizens attempting to register came to the courthouse dressed in their Sunday best. In order to pacify the black community, a handful of applicants were allowed to register, but many others were turned down in order "to keep a solid white majority," former *Clarksdale Press Register* reporter Curtis Wilkie wrote in his memoir. The circuit clerk since 1948, J. W. Smith, whom Wilkie described as "a cranky old man," shut down the program by refusing potential registrants, and the crusade itself petered out. Other activists then resolved to pay the three-dollar poll tax, attempting to appease the circuit clerk. So by the end of the year, Pigee had claimed some success in registering a few to vote in her annual reports to the national NAACP office.[25]

Nationally, buoyed by hopes in the new administration and growing grass-roots direct action, that spring the national NAACP launched Operation Mississippi. Aaron Henry, attorney Jack Young (a lawyer in Jackson), Medgar Evers, and Ruby Hurley, along with national officers Gloster Current, Robert Carter, John Morsell, and Roy Wilkins, gathered around a conference table in New York City that April. They discussed a program that focused on increasing registration and voting through citizenship training schools and legal challenges; desegregating public accommodations (for Tougaloo and Jackson State college students, for instance, to test facilities); challenging employment discrimination; and collecting and filing affidavits on police brutality with the Justice Department. The idea was to attack the structure of Mississippi white supremacy from multiple angles and to bring documentation of white resistance to the president's attention. The plan hinged on the two factors supplying hope at the grass roots: student activism and a new president.[26]

More than in the past, the NAACP recognized the need for immediate direct action. In order to maintain organizational supremacy over CORE and its highly visible and much-publicized Freedom Rides and hold off both the growing membership of SNCC and the momentum of the Southern Christian Leadership Conference (SCLC), the NAACP had to support the youth more convincingly, even in direct-protest action.[27] Indeed, Mississippi students had already forced the organization's hand in this regard. Undergraduates at all-black Tougaloo College had stepped up their direct-action protests in Jackson, and police had viciously attacked with imprisonment and the use of dogs.[28] The national NAACP hastily lent support and provided legal counsel after the fact. Young people were outstripping their elders, pushing at Jim Crow with their bodies, while the NAACP struggled to keep pace.

The Kennedys also scrambled to keep up with the youth who had refused to comply with the White House's minimalist agenda. The Justice Department's tepid support for the Freedom Riders had produced a flood of mail to Attorney General Robert Kennedy's office. As a result, Kennedy invited local black leaders, including Henry, to the White House to meet with the president on 12 July 1961.[29] As Henry recalled, "Our contention was that this intimidation and the fears associated with the exercise of basic rights were grounds enough for steps by the federal government." Their presence in Washington, D.C., had the desired effect. Robert Kennedy assigned John Doar to the position of special attorney in the Civil Rights Division. Doar, a registered Republican at the time, saw his work as nonpartisan but had the utmost respect for the attorney general's drive to uphold the law. Black leaders grew to trust him quickly, respecting his honesty and conviction. His job would involve gathering information in the Northern District of Mississippi about violations of civil rights laws.[30]

The Delta felt the Justice Department's new presence almost immediately. Rather than relying on FBI reports sitting on overworked attorneys' desks in Washington, D.C., awaiting review and action, Doar and others traveled south to meet people, collect their own affidavits, and assess the situation themselves. Within weeks, Robert Owens and a colleague from the Justice Department had entered Henry's drugstore and requested a meeting of local black activists. Recounting the day that they met with R. L. Drew, John Melchor, H. Y. Hackett, J. D. Rayford, and Vera Pigee in the back room of the drugstore, Henry recalled that the lawyers genuinely cared for the plight of African Americans, and he was convinced that the local situation would actually change.[31] He stated: "We complained to them about the years of these kinds of visits we'd had, and most of us considered that this was just one more. [They] promised us at that time that they were not coming just to talk, and that they would appreciate it if we would take them seriously and judge them by the results of what they were able to do, or what they got the Justice Department to do." The group talked at length about strategies. Henry remembered the discussion: "There is no panacea to the end of freedom road, and none of us know exactly how any of us are going to come out in any activities we take. But you have to be prepared to take the chances and prepared to take the punishment." With heightened federal presence, "civil rights activity began increasing back up to the 1955 level." But Henry was realistic as well. Filing affidavits and prosecuting violations county by county was slow. And it was sure to produce a backlash.[32]

Sure enough, the reprisals continued and intensified. However, retaliation was mostly discreet and individualized. For instance, Helen Anderson had picketed outside of the Mississippi State Capitol in Jackson on 19 July 1961. Two days later, in Clarksdale, Superior Laundry laid off a group of workers, including her mother. This was commonplace in the summer when business was slow, but usually employers reinstated staff soon thereafter. Mrs. Anderson was the only one who never got the call back. Black leaders believed that her daughter's activities caused her permanent redundancy. In response, the local NAACP branch launched a telephone-calling campaign directed at Gerald Commander, the owner. Vera Pigee made the first call, and after a series of other such encounters that day, Commander contacted Aaron Henry to cease the campaign, cognizant of the fact that half of his business came from the black community. He seemed willing to sort something out, even offering Mrs. Anderson a fill-in job for a sick employee (which she promptly refused). Pressure that he may have received from the Citizens' Council, however, caused Commander to hastily step back from the remediation. His business did not survive the subsequent branch-sponsored boycott.[33]

Motherhood, Respectability, and Civil Rights Activism

Anderson was not alone on the front line that summer. On 23 August, a Wednesday afternoon, after lunch, three black youths walked into the white waiting room of the Illinois Central railroad station in Clarksdale. They knew that they were not wanted or welcome—signs all around indicated that they had crossed the line—but they also knew that those signs were illegal. They pressed forward with determination, approaching Joe Collins, the ticket agent, and asking for tickets for the next Memphis-bound train. Collins turned to serve another customer while a bystander called the police and the local paper.

Mary Jane Pigee, age eighteen and a college student, Adrian Beard, age sixteen and attending Immaculate Conception Catholic School, and fourteen-year-old Wilma Jones, a student at Higgins High School, had planned their actions carefully. When Police Chief Ben C. Collins and his assistant chief, J. B. Mitchell, arrived, the solemn protesters refused to move to the "colored side" of the ticket counter and sat quietly in a (now) empty waiting room. The officers took them into custody under the charge of intent to disturb the peace.

The Clarksdale Youth Council had sponsored this demonstration, acting independent of the adult branch. It was its first formal direct-action arrest and was intended to test the breach of peace statute that so many young people had "violated" in the last twenty months since the beginning of the mass sit-ins across the nation. Indeed, Julia Wright, NAACP youth secretary for the region, had come to assist in the protesters' plans. It behooved them to keep this protest independent and not direct more animosity toward the NAACP, which might muddy the legal challenge. Aaron Henry insisted that he knew nothing of the plans or the event itself, but evidence suggests that he had an active role. As it happens, attorney Jess Brown had traveled from Jackson earlier that day to meet with Henry, so when the call came from Pigee informing him of the arrests, Brown was on hand to represent the youth. Prosecutors, police, and the national NAACP office questioned this coincidence.[34]

The young protesters sang freedom songs once arrested, filling the air with sound to soothe their nerves. After five hours at the police station, their parents escorted them out, with $500 bond each. At the Labor Day court case, Collins and *Clarksdale Press Register* editor Joe Ellis exaggerated the possibility for violence during the protest, despite no evidence to suggest a threat. The jury convicted the three on the charge that they had violated a Mississippi statute that segregated waiting rooms. Mary Jane received a ninety-day suspended sentence with a $200 fine and costs; the younger two got the same fine but only thirty days in jail (suspended). In the next few years, young people in Clarksdale and the state of Mississippi would become veterans in the ritual performance of the Mississippi legal system, but it always came at a cost and exposed them and their families to danger.[35]

Mary Jane Pigee had insisted that she be addressed as "Miss." Appearing before officers at the Clarksdale police station that August, she refused to be called by her first name. After all, at eighteen she was an adult. "Chief Collins kept tearing up Miss Pigee's sheets [for bond] all afternoon because she used the title, Miss," her mother remembered.[36] These kinds of conflicts and humiliations occurred daily in black people's lives during the Jim Crow era. Mary Jane got that tenacity from her mother, who repeated the scene the following December, when she was arrested for leading a boycott of downtown department stores. "I am *Mrs.* Vera Pigee, a wife, a mother, political prisoner, business and professional woman," Pigee wrote in her memoir. "Wherever I go, even if I am brought in handcuffs, my name is still *Mrs.* Vera Pigee."[37]

The incident at the Illinois Central train station pushed Mary Jane onto the Sovereignty Commission's radar. Since she was eighteen, the legal system could now pursue her. Investigator Tom Scarbrough noted that her longer jail sentence was because "she has been involved with other agitative activities." His report cast her as the main instigator of the sit-in, which he noted as consistent with her past NAACP activities. Listing some of the programs she had participated in since 1958, Scarbrough described her as "very insolent and arrogant when talking to white authorities." Sounding an ominous, even conspiratorial tone, Scarbrough reported that "more can be expected to be heard from Maryijane [*sic*] Pigee, as it is my thinking she is being trained for agitative purposes by the NAACP, and perhaps financed by them." Her mother had also gained increased notoriety in the Sovereignty Commission files. In the same report, Scarbrough pinpointed Pigee's beauty shop as the meeting place when several youths had gone to Woolworth's in the spring of 1960 to buy the frame and Bible. Ending his report, he stated, "Clarksdale is one of the 'hot spots' for racial agitators. The officials . . . recognize this and are joining together for an all-out fight to resist whatever efforts may be put forth by the NAACP and other agitators in the future."[38]

In a movement more famous for its "I am a Man" masculine heroics than for "I am Mrs." or "I am Miss," Mary Jane and Vera Pigee belie the conventional and inherited stories. As one-time Clarksdale Youth Council president Roy Bell Wright recalled, Vera Pigee thought like a mother, acted like a mother, and pleaded to mothers. He had written in 1964 to the national NAACP office praising her efforts and successes in Clarksdale to counterbalance the publicity generated by the Freedom Summer volunteers. Pigee's confidence convinced others that she did not ask of them what she was not willing to do herself. She could assure parents of their children's safety in her care and could gain their trust because of her own struggles. Wright, addressing the national youth secretary, Laplois Ashford, in July 1964, emphasized, "No one knows the scope of her work better than we do. Perhaps she does not turn the world on one end by doing magnificent feats, but to us it is the little things that one does everyday for the cause of Freedom that warrants merit." These smaller local and daily acts, which did not attract press attention, eroded the edifice of Jim Crow just as much as other more dramatic forms of direct action that made national and international news. Wright highlighted the sacrifices she had made: "Sacrifice in every shape, form and fashion mentionable."[39] Pigee encouraged her daughter's desire to agitate and sit in despite the obvious risks. To be a mother, to her daughter and to the movement, was for Pigee a duty and a great responsibility.

Vera Pigee fondly christened the NAACP "the grandmother of Civil Rights Organizations," confirming that "we called the NAACP mother. And mother would be there."[40] This confidence sustained her as she strode into the Greyhound bus terminal that December. Her own self-identification with mothering, exemplified as much in her work with the youth councils as with Mary Jane, must be understood within the larger framework of gender and race in the Deep South. Claiming motherhood and using it as an organizing tool enabled Pigee to reach more people and operate in concrete ways that they could understand and duplicate. Demanding the use of titles (Mrs. and Miss) became a simple way to insist on the recognition of human dignity and rights, particularly womanhood, when black femininity had long been denied and abused.

In regard to the beauty shop, in addition to "mother," Pigee claimed the title of "professional." In the class-circumscribed world of black Mississippi, Pigee had acquired a trade and owned her own business. This did not place her among the elite, a position reserved for male physicians and attorneys, but her claim to being a "professional" was a self-conscious assertion of status, a notice to whites and blacks of her dignity and command of resources. Serving an entirely black clientele in her beauty shop, Pigee's economic independence made her shop a node connecting different constituencies of Clarksdale's female networks—networks of professionals, domestics, field hands, mothers, and daughters. Reflecting on these different aspects of her life and position in the community, Pigee believed that "it was my first commitment as a mother to see [Mary Jane] more fully equipped to cope with the problems of today."[41] But she also acknowledged her more privileged position to work full time on the movement: "It would be unfair to ask all mothers, all professional women, and all Christians to eat, sleep, work and talk freedom, but more and more the opportunity not to do so is becoming less and less."[42] Mother and professional were woven through Pigee's identity and shaped her engagement with and nurturing of Coahoma County's movement activities.

Ironically, Pigee dedicated her life to championing the cause of the NAACP, an organization known for male chauvinism and sexism. However, over its long history, the organization had also championed women's suffrage and supported women's rights and recognized the role of women in communities, encouraging organizers and field-workers to exploit the resources women offered. These women did not wait to be asked. As historian Ruth Feldstein argues, "Civil rights activism that privileged masculinity [could not] keep black women from claiming their own rights as citizens and mothers."[43] "Mothering" was a complex process, one with limitations as profound as its potential.

As committed as Pigee was to the NAACP and as active as she was within its Coahoma County chapter, she was only one of the countless women active at the grass roots who carried out the branches' business. Many women were elected secretaries of NAACP branches. Not a woman to shy away from the spotlight or reject her due accolades, Vera Pigee's invisibility in history—despite her very real visibility in Clarksdale and the state—is typical of the women who worked in the NAACP, which poses interesting questions about community responsibilities, organizations, and leadership styles. Her exclusion from the official records of the mass civil rights movement stems largely from the omission of her name from most organizational reports about conferences and meetings. In NAACP field reports, she is noted as "an activist" and can be identified only through cross-referencing. In like fashion, reports promote the recognizable national names, not the local people also present (and delegated to perform the groundwork). While part of the NAACP clique—Pigee corresponded with and hosted most of the senior officers when they were in Mississippi and during national conventions—she did not share with them the national spotlight. The only Mississippians fully in the NAACP limelight were Medgar Evers and Aaron Henry, and later Charles Evers. The other famous movement activist from Mississippi was Fannie Lou Hamer, who worked for SNCC.

But did Pigee resent Aaron Henry's national prominence and did Henry resent Pigee? Compare the photograph of Pigee introducing Constance Baker Motley at a local meeting with the photograph of Aaron Henry at the 1964 Democratic National Convention (see figures 3.2 and 3.3). Clearly Pigee had a very robust sense of self and her value in Clarksdale. She had a strong command of the local youth and the local NAACP branch. She had a voice and a presence. Things rarely happened in terms of organizing without her input or direction. She had hosted the NAACP lawyer as she visited Clarksdale, taking care of every detail. Her invisibility enabled her to work locally and utilize female-centered spaces like her own beauty salon to organize, but that same invisibility denied her any credit when her colleague took center stage. Henry was not able to do what Pigee did—he was not plugged into the same networks in the community that facilitated organizing at the grassroots level. Similarly, she could not access his networks, which enabled him to receive the mantle of formal leadership in the national spotlight. She also knew that most of the resources and the impressive speaker roster that Clarksdale's branch accessed came in part because of Henry's national contacts. In the fifties, when Henry's circle was mostly confined to the Delta, relations were better—those early years and the intense dangers adjoined the officers, and they moved in lockstep, confined by their options and concerned for their own safety. Once Henry's circle widened, syncopated paces, interests, and influences caused more friction.

The relationship between Pigee and Henry was complicated—egos often clashed behind closed doors and off the record. There are few saints among

FIG. 3.2. Vera Pigee introduces the speaker, NAACP attorney
Constance Baker Motley, at a local branch meeting, 1960.
(Personal collection of Mary Jane Pigee Davis)

leaders. Larry Graham, one of her counselors in those years, remembered in
2003, as the branch prepared to celebrate fifty years, that Pigee "spoke out
when things weren't going right in the local NAACP branch." But Pigee bit
her tongue in public for the sake of the cause. Graham also wrote: "She and
Dr. Henry didn't see eye to eye at times, but they both worked to better the lives
of blacks, whites and other races of people."[44] Indeed, when Pigee's daughter
and two others protested in the train station, Henry insisted to the national
office that he had not known of the youth council's plans, especially as legal
counsel just so happened to be in town that day. Was this a cover to protect the
youth as they went to trial, so that the organization would not be vulnerable to
charges of conspiracy to break local laws? Or was it a moment to undermine
Pigee's work with the youth and reassert control? Finding proof of acrimony in
the archives is impossible, because the branch leadership properly maintained
a united front. Hints of conflict appear in these quiet moments when accounts
rest side-by-side and do not match. While both remained silent on paper about

FIG. 3.3. Aaron Henry testifying in 1964 before the Democratic Party Credentials Committee as to why Mississippi Freedom Democratic Party delegates should be seated. Henry was candidate for governor on the MFDP ticket. (© 1976 George Ballis/Take Stock/The Image Works)

the discrepancy in testimony and the obvious coincidence in events, the disjuncture underscores who had easiest access to the national officers and whom those officers chose to consult.[45] These moments of tension and discord would break through the public façade of unity a little more visibly during Freedom Summer.

Yet decades after the height of her involvement, Pigee remained unequivocal in her loyalty to the organization that had given her the resources and the space to make a place for herself and her activities. Organizing children, long deemed women's work, rose to the top of the list of new NAACP imperatives. Pigee could run the NAACP youth council in Clarksdale largely on her own terms and advise youth councils across the state. She probably could have carried out the same work without the NAACP's banner—it was, as all human institutions are, imperfect. But it was in this role that she received a little recognition internally between offices. Other NAACP national officers applauded, and often modeled, Pigee's performance. "Her commitment to the Association is total. . . . She requires very little guidance," wrote Calvin Banks (temporary program director of the Youth Branch Department) to Roy Wilkins. "She is articulate and effective at all times [and] projects a proper NAACP viewpoint." She knew the institutional ropes and did not press the already thinly stretched national staff and resources.[46]

On Thanksgiving Day in 1961, for instance, Mayor W. S. Kincade would not let the bands from black Higgins High School and Coahoma County Junior College march in the annual Christmas Parade, a tradition since the late 1940s. Merchants, who benefited from the extra business during the parade, had sent a delegation to the mayor and Board of Commissioners to try to reverse the decision, fearful of a boycott. The previous week, the junior college had canceled its homecoming parade when told that the procession could not move through the downtown area. However, on 2 December 1961, the Coahoma County Chamber of Commerce, responding to heightened civil rights activities and the alleged presence of "outsiders," endorsed the mayor's actions. If officials thought their actions would dampen civil rights activities, their plan spectacularly backfired. Working with the children in the youth councils, Pigee had immediate contact with the parents. Targeting the children during the holiday season provoked angry parents to act when they might not have before. To these parents, it was about more than a parade. Such processions and concerts, like churches and schools, are cultural realms, but they are also political sites of contestation. Not permitting the bands to play robbed the whole community of a degree of citizenship and a sense of local belonging. The mayor considered it a privilege, but the black community perceived it as a right to public space. Pigee noted, "This was the straw that broke the camel's back, as far as community involvement. . . . The white power structure gave the civil rights movement the momentum it needed." Aaron Henry remembered that "the announcement triggered our first major confrontation since 1955."[47]

The Clarksdale Youth Council debated its response, meeting at Pigee's beauty shop upon hearing the city council's announcement.[48] Standing along the walls, sitting on the floor, and leaning on the swivel chairs, the young people buzzed with excitement, talking all at once and angrily demanding militant protest. Understanding the increased tension in the air and the risk to their safety, Pigee calmed and encouraged the young activists to tell their parents to attend the mass meeting hurriedly called for the following night. "These are our children," she told the parents, a sentiment that sustained a two-year boycott of downtown businesses under the phrase, "No Parade, No Trade."[49]

More than one meeting convened that week. The initial reaction by the 2,000 students attending Higgins High School and Coahoma County Junior College was to picket and speak out against the mayor. In addition to protesting the parade, they asked that black women be employed as clerks in downtown stores and that store employees use courtesy titles of "Miss, Mrs., and Mr." rather than "uncle, aunt, boy, girl and nigger."[50] A flyer from the Coahoma

County Federated Council of Organizations (CCFCO) advertised a mass meeting for Wednesday, 29 November 1961, at 7:30 P.M., at the Metropolitan Baptist Church to continue the conversation and disseminate information.

The CCFCO was an organizing screen for those unable to work under the auspices of the NAACP. Aaron Henry confided in a letter to Gloster Current that "just between me and you [it] is a paper organization which the NAACP controls[;] but it offers an opportunity of expression for the Teachers[,] without them having the fear of participating in an NAACP only sponsored affair. Technically represented on the council is the president or chairman of all the organizations and Churches in the area which can aid cooperation in any project we desire." The chairmanship was rotated monthly to differ from the NAACP, but in reality most of the membership came from the branch.[51]

Pigee, Henry, and other local leaders mobilized parents to consider, and act upon, the future of their children. The call appealed to their sense of parental responsibility. Although sustaining the boycott and encouraging people not to shop in the holiday season proved difficult, Henry noted that "the best assist we have had is that the school children have won the support of their parents in not going down town."[52] As Pigee emerged as the key intermediary between parents and children, the Coahoma County Youth Council became the largest and most active in the state, with fifty-two members by 1962.[53]

Surprised by the boycott's fierce and rapid deployment, particularly at the height of the retail season, local white landowners and the city took drastic actions. A CCFCO flyer noted that many white farmers had brought their tenants in buses and trucks to spend their money downtown. But, the flyer asserted, "this forced spending will only last until the 'boss man's' settlement money last[s] and we all know how much that is. These people can not help themselves; but you and I can." City officials went further, publicly handcuffing and arresting many of the leaders of the local NAACP on 7 December.[54] Vera Pigee, John C. Melchor (president of the branch), Walter Wright (vice president), Robert L. Drew (chairman of the NAACP Executive Board), Rev. Theodore Trammell (NAACP chaplain), Laboyd Keys (truck driver), and Aaron Henry (state president) were charged with conspiring to withhold trade.[55] Pigee recalled how Chief of Police Ben Collins came into her house for the arrest and disrespected her by addressing her as Vera. It was at this moment that Pigee told him emphatically, "I am *Mrs.* Vera Pigee," mirroring the demands of the youth in the mass meeting two weeks prior.[56] A gathering held at Haven Methodist Church that evening informed the 500-strong audience of the day's actions.

> **Heed The Call, Negroes All**
> **Side By Equal Side —**
> **Brother, Trade In Dignity, Sister, Trade In Pride.**

We have all heard about how Negroes sticking together have gained rights and privileges *that for years have been denied.*

These Negroes suffered many hardships in cities like Montgomery and Tuskegee, Alabama — in Savannah, Georgia and just north of us in Memphis, Tennessee.

Now it is our turn — Can WE take it? — Do WE really want to be FREE? — And enjoy ALL of the blessings of LIBERTY?

Since the Downtown Merchants were not able to persuade the Mayor of Clarksdale to drop his racial bias and permit our two Negro School Bands to march in the Christmas Parade, although some of them tried very hard, let us not hold this forever against them.

If they will grant us now the PRIVILEGES OF EMPLOYMENT ABOVE THE MENIAL LEVEL, and COURTESY TITLES, we will be back down town to trade, *AND NOT UNTIL THEN.*

We are respectfully asking the Downtown Merchants now for two things, if they want Negro trade:

I. Hire Negroes in Clerk positions in stores desiring Negro trade.

We have enough maids and janitors already. There are many Negroes capable of handling a clerk's job. In all fairness, because of our patronage, we deserve some of the jobs in this category, something more than pushing a broom and a dust mop.

II. Treat Negroes courteously and with respect — just as you do any other customer.

This means to stop calling Negroes by their first or last names, or by such titles as "boy", "girl", "Auntie" or "Uncle."

Please refer to Negroes as Mr., Mrs. or Miss, just as you do in the case of your other customers — and when you send out statements, please place courtesy before the names. We are human, too.

A progress report will be given every Wednesday night at the mass meetings held every week at the Negro Churches, as to which stores desire and deserve our trade.

COAHOMA COUNTY FEDERATED COUNCIL OF ORGANIZATIONS

FIG. 3.4a. A Coahoma County Federated Council of Organizations flyer urging local people to support movement activities and goals, 1961. (Used by permission of the National Association for the Advancement of Colored People)

Pigee, Henry, and the others were charged but released on their own recognizance pending trial. On 18 December, African Americans descended onto the courthouse to the extent that Medgar Evers reported that "City and County Officials decided to move the trial from the Courthouse to a room in the jail house, where no spectators were permitted; only witnesses and defen-

To Every Negro Citizen Who Desires Fair Treatment:

The bands of HIGGINS HIGH SCHOOL and COAHOMA JUNIOR COL-LEGE have been denied the courtesy of marching down town in the Christmas Parade in Clarksdale this year.

This was done by the COAHOMA COUNTY CHAMBER OF COMMERCE under the direction of the MAYOR of the city, according to a letter sent to each institution.

If the DOWNTOWN MERCHANTS are not in accord with the action of the Mayor, we respectfully call upon them to influence the Mayor to alter his course and be the Mayor of ALL the people.

This big decision is:

If we can't PARADE down town—
'Should we TRADE down town?

If the DOWNTOWN MERCHANTS support the Mayor in this affront to the Negro citizens of our community (and he can't do this alone) — it appears a wise course to follow that we accommodate them and DO NOT GO DOWN TOWN TO TRADE.

Let's wear our old clothes this Christmas — Our Children can play with their old toys for another year —

And from now on, until Negroes are treated courteously and with respect in the DOWN TOWN AREA.

This area includes South Edwards to First Street and from Sunflower to Desoto Streets.

Coahoma County Federated Council Of Organizations

(This includes the various civic, fraternal, religious and social organizations of Negro i   Coahoma C

FIG. 3.4b. Another CCFCO flyer calling for action to gain courtesy and respect, 1961. (Used by permission of the National Association for the Advancement of Colored People)

dants." Despite the change, an overflow of 100 stood outside.[57] The initial case was postponed and rescheduled for 3 January 1962. Convicted mostly on Police Chief Collins's testimony, all but Pigee and Laboyd Keys received six-month jail sentences and $500 fines (although it is not specified why they were spared incarceration, Pigee was the only woman and Keys was not a branch leader). Investigator Scarbrough opined ominously, "The five Negroes convicted in this case are five of the most vicious agitators in Mississippi. . . . They are not going to remain quiet for long." He called them a "gang" and instructed white local officials to cut off as much of their income as possible.[58] Nevertheless, the boycott gathered fuel, generating nearly 90 percent effectiveness between December 1961 and March 1962. Weekly Wednesday movement and freedom meetings — regular mass assemblies to inform the people of breaking news and current activities — became a staple part of the Clarksdale movement through the first half of the sixties.[59]

Diabolical: Sex, Violence, and the Movement

At this point, Clarksdale's mass movement truly drew in more members of the black community, who became involved directly by boycotting and by attending rousing meetings. The arrest of the leaders, which fueled the boycott, and the way in which Pigee received a lesser sentence due to her gender aptly illustrate how her work was underestimated from outside the movement and also how she reasserted her femininity in the face of such uncouth and backward treatment. Indeed, leadership frameworks represent one way to view the gender dynamics of the mass of civil rights movements. Another way is to consider the ways in which sex and sexuality — and the gendered frameworks in which they operated — shaped the movements in the South. In 1951, the rape of two young women in Clarksdale served as a catalyst for the establishment of the local NAACP, which sought to end the sexual vulnerability of black women to white men. Women's bodies were the crucial site of contestation in the murder of Emmett Till in 1955 — the imagined desecration of a white woman by a child's whistle.

It did not take rape alone, however, to unleash the forces of sexual bigotry and oppression that guarded white supremacy. Sexual humiliations of a lesser, everyday order were practiced in ways designed to intimidate. Consider the case of Bessie Turner of Coahoma County. On Friday night, 19 January 1962, Turner had gone to Tutwiler with Luster P. Turner and Charlie Howard, where they patronized the Blue Moon Café, before returning to Turner's house around four in the morning. While she was laboring in the cotton fields on Saturday, her sister informed her that the police had called, so she telephoned the station after work. As she did not address the man on the other end of the line with "sir," he refused to give her any information. The next day around four in the afternoon, two officers, Paul Bratt and Ben Barrier, escorted her to a small room in city hall to question her about money Luster Turner allegedly reported as stolen.

Not satisfied with her denials of theft, the officers ordered her to lie on the concrete floor and to pull her dress up and her underwear down. One of them whipped her with a wide leather strap, demanding she tell him about the money. She reported, "He then told me to 'turn over and open up your legs and let me see how you look down there.'" As the other officer left the room, he hit her between the legs, threatening to beat her more seriously if she told anyone. After ordering her to straighten up and clean her tear-streaked face, he told her to pull down her dress to expose her breasts, under the pretense of searching for the cash. Delivering her home, the same officer searched her house without a warrant and issued a string of additional threats.[60]

The FBI investigated the charge in Clarksdale, interviewing another black woman, Mary Washington, who had been in the city jail at the time of the assault. No sooner had the federal agents left town than white city officers attacked Washington as they tried to force her into a squad car, attracting a large crowd. They also returned to Turner, renewing their threats and intimidation, no doubt peeved that they could not silence her. Both women, fearing for their immediate safety, voluntarily entered into the custody of the sheriff for protection against the city police. Rev. J. D. Rayford, acting as chair of the CCFCO, reported that racial tensions created by the Clarksdale police department were "very close to the breaking point."[61]

Vera Pigee accompanied Turner to Washington, D.C., to testify during a cluster of hearings before the Commission on Civil Rights.[62] This was part of a strategy by SNCC to generate publicity and to force the commission, the White House, or the attorney general to investigate racial incidents. Turner's case attracted a great deal of attention in the national civil rights community but failed to appear in the press, much to everyone's disappointment.[63] However, the violence inflicted on Bessie Turner, who later connected the incident to her attempts to register to vote, helped to sustain the local boycott. The CCFCO sent out a newsletter with the admonition that "any Negro that goes downtown to spend his money under these conditions has no self pride, no race pride, and is not deserving of the freedom Negroes all over the world are striving so hard to obtain. *You should be ashamed*!!"[64] The leaders applied more pressure on people to pay their poll tax by the 1 February deadline.

A second episode, this one concerning Aaron Henry, involved a different form of sexual violence but highlights important points about African Americans and sexuality in the South. On Sunday, 4 March 1962, Police Chief Ben Collins pounded on Henry's front door in the early hours of the morning. Wearing his nightclothes and instructing his frightened and confused wife to call NAACP lawyers, Henry was arrested and taken away. African Americans in the South knew that police raids at night spelled trouble. Under cover of darkness, people went missing and turned up in creeks, earthen dams, rivers, or ditches—if they were ever found. Henry knew that and feared for his safety. In an elaborate routine of imprisonment where police transferred him from place to place during the night and denied him his right to a call, it was impossible for his associates to locate him. The message reinforced who was in charge. The intricate maneuverings also reinforce Henry's claim that this was an organized "plot" to discredit him, a plot that involved the Sovereignty Commission— if not directly involved, it at least sanctioned local activity. The commission's constant surveillance of civil rights leaders had revealed Henry's vulnerability in the first place.

Hours later, well after the sun rose to its peak, Henry learned of the reason for his arrest. An eighteen-year-old white man, Sterling Lee Eilert, from Memphis, had apparently accused him of solicitation, first to find a white woman and later changing the story to Henry soliciting the boy himself in his car. Angered by the charges, Henry retorted: "There's not a soul involved in this except that goddam Ben Collins [police chief] and that chicken shit Babe Pearson [county attorney]." He continued: "I was convinced that they were trying to destroy my effectiveness in a movement in which most of the participants at the time were men. I felt that the arrest was an attempt to prevent people, particularly young men who were so very important to us, from participating in a movement where they might be accused of homosexuality."[65] Sodomy laws criminalized homosexuality. Scholar John Howard explains that automobiles were sites of movement and encounter for gay men in the South.[66] The alleged crime took place in a car, and, given Henry's mobility as a state leader, traveling often from Clarksdale to Jackson (and points between and beyond), there were opportunities for transgressions, which made him vulnerable to this accusation.

White supremacists in the South linked the increasingly liberal views about sexuality that the young white generation heralded in the early 1960s with the growing mass of black movement activity, a link strengthened when white youth loudly adopted civil rights battles. At the base of this connection, the prevailing attitudes about deviant and diseased black sexuality transferred to those who dared to ally with African Americans. It did not help that the proponents of white liberal culture were defined as "dirty beatniks" by older generations, and the "beloved community" of youth protest, particularly in SNCC, celebrated and advertised interracial meetings and negotiations. For white supremacists, therefore, the increased rhetoric and display of "deviant" sexuality and the long-standing fears of miscegenation went hand in hand—and creating scandal proved a useful way in which to silence and punish.[67]

Local police and the keepers of segregation had been looking for opportunities to take down this prominent leader. Henry's civil rights work went back to his years in the U.S. Army, but in the early 1960s, as his national visibility grew through his interaction with the Kennedy administration and his NAACP work, efforts to silence him stepped up. If the Sovereignty Commission and the white supremacist groups thought Henry to be a mild irritation in the fifties, he now became a real threat to the social order, and the rules changed. His enemies exploited his vulnerabilities as they tried to bring him down. His close friendship with William Higgs, a known homosexual and a traitor in the eyes of white supremacists, may have planted the idea for the ambush in their minds—indeed they successfully silenced Higgs in 1963 with accusations of sex with a minor, and he fled the state, never to return. E. Patrick Johnson asserts correctly that in the South "cultural and social transgression may render one silenced, physically harmed, or worse."[68] The morality charge was designed to make Henry an example, just as similar charges had been used to discredit Bayard Rustin at the national level—to dirty their names and disarm them, just as accusations of sexual deviance today continue to unseat leaders.[69]

Despite alibis placing him in the company of other leaders at the time of the alleged offense, Henry was charged, fined $250, and given a two-month jail sentence in a packed courtroom with Medgar Evers and others on the benches wearing NAACP pins. When Henry publicly accused the police chief of fabrication with his "chicken-shit" outburst, a lawsuit for $40,000 for defamation of character landed on his desk. In June 1963, the Mississippi Supreme Court ruled against the lower court, stating that he had been unlawfully arrested and his car unlawfully searched and that the affidavit was illegal and defective with no corroborating evidence to support any charges. A month later, the court reversed its decision, ruling that the defense had failed to enter an objection during the trial. Henry, reflecting on the case and the recent murder of his friend, Medgar Evers, stated, "The State of Mississippi is still trying to destroy us both—Medgar physically and Aaron Morally [*sic*]. However the death of Medgar has served as a great impulse to the freedom movement. I feel that to some extent my persecutions are having a similar effect." After successful appeals from prosecutors, the Supreme Court cleared him of the libel charges in 1965 (after the state Supreme Court had upheld the $15,000 judgment), but in 1968 after more appeals, the conviction in the morals case stood.[70]

Aaron Henry was a respected leader among black Mississippians. The besieged population looked to him for direction in the struggle for equality and appreciated his ability to communicate and get results. Bertha Blackburn, who grew up in Clarksdale, was a few years older than Henry, and became the branch president herself in 2001. She noted that "my father loved Aaron, he loved the ground he walked on. Anything Aaron said was the law of the land. . . . He was a civil rights man from his heart."[71] Henry was a teddy bear of sorts, tactile, courteous, and friendly, a powerful, commanding voice with a soft touch. To know him was to like him, even if opinions differed. Henry was a formalized leader, one who benefited from normative gendered relations (like the GI Bill, the male privilege that helped him procure an education in a profession that gave him middle-class status and economic independence) that gave him the authority to represent his people. Allegations linking Henry to homosexuality did not shock everyone, as his enemies had hoped. His proclivity for male company did not surprise many in the black community—in fact it was an open secret. Many in Clarksdale's black community knew of Henry's bisexuality, despite his domestic life with wife Noelle and daughter Rebecca, challenging preconceived notions about the nature (and nexus) of gender and sexuality and leadership, particularly in the South. Henry's personal life keeps the story messy and conflicting.

How was Aaron Henry able to negotiate (and be *allowed* to negotiate) his sexual double life, and how did this not affect his leadership abilities and effectiveness? Scholars of sexuality in the South assert that homosexuality coexisted with prevailing religious and conservative beliefs and practices. Henry had learned the lesson of tolerance and discretion behind closed doors at the white dining room table of Rosemary Clark in the 1950s, but he also knew it personally. Black homes were frequently violated, like his in the middle of the night, so they were not necessarily free and open spaces. But the omnipresence of the law and social rules remained outside.

Scholar Pete Daniel succinctly summed this up: "Southerners often accepted (or forgave) almost any eccentricity so long as it posed no threat to the established order."[72] In what amounts to an unspoken "don't ask, don't tell" societal rule, sexual liaisons, whether outside of marriage or same-sex (or, in Aaron Henry's case, both), could slide under the moral radar as long as perpetrators acted discreetly and followed through on their expected social performances. It was, in essence, a social compact.[73] For Aaron Henry, those performances included his roles as doting husband and father (and by all accounts he genuinely cared for his family) and as a loyal, self-sacrificing leader in the black freedom struggle. Indeed, it is not clear if Henry ever identified publicly as gay, nor did he explicitly support gay rights activism during his lifetime, even when it was clear that he lived with a man when he stayed in Jackson as a House representative in later years. Rather he espoused love and tolerance through his civil rights activism, easy foils for double meanings. His wife, Noelle, stayed married to him, and his personal papers reveal loving exchanges between husband and wife, alongside correspondence between him and various young men he had met on his travels. While he did not conform to sexual norms in that he had homosexual relationships, he made sure to conform to southern demands that he provide for his family, go to church, and live a public upstanding life. Leslie McLemore, who helped found and then led the Rust College chapter of the NAACP, meeting Henry during that process in 1962, claimed, "Doc. Henry is an upstanding dude. He's a good leader, he's a member of the church, leader in our community, in the church community, civil rights community, business community etcetera etcetera."[74]

A "complicity of silence" in the community kept Henry safe.[75] Black people closed ranks around him. Mary Jane Pigee Davis recounted that Henry's tendencies were no secret to those in his circle. Although she never heard her mother talk about his sexuality in front of her, among the youth, "everyone knew" that his "friend," whom he insisted stay and work in the NAACP office located next to his Fourth Street Drugstore, was a "flamboyant" type. McLemore corroborated Davis's assertions: "When you're in a movement you know it's a small circle of people. Everybody knows everybody indirectly or directly, right? So the word was that Aaron was actually gay. But it wasn't a topic that people discussed. It was something that a comment was made here and there and people accepted Aaron, because Aaron the man, Aaron the leader, Aaron the courageous crazy guy, outweighed any damn thing else, right?"[76] It was an open secret more than a closed closet, and southerners, in their genteel and polite way, figuratively averted their eyes and insisted on publicly practicing what John Howard has called a "pervasive, deflective pretense of ignorance."[77] The black community and a wider community of civil rights activists needed Henry's leadership and tenacity to continue to push for change, and that need and the respect he earned vastly outweighed any desire to oust (or out) him because of his transgressions.

Try as they might (and they did), white supremacists and other enemies could not discredit Henry as a leader or jail him for civil disobedience without fueling his popularity and leadership power, but in undermining him with morality charges—selectively asserting southern Christian integrity—they could tarnish him and make him a pariah. They took advantage of the oft-used image of the black man as a sexual predator, the specter of the black male aggressor, compounded by homosexual transgression. Or so they had hoped. Indeed, Henry was arrested for "homosexual sodomy or disorderly conduct" at least four times, yet he held elected office from 1960 (with his election to the state NAACP presidency) to 1993.[78] Also, rather than allowing incriminating and sensationalized press reports to pull him out of the closet, to strip him of his authority and voice, Henry made sure to write about his morality charges. The Clarksdale incident is called "The Diabolical Plot" in his autobiography. It is clear that in his version he included heterosexual relations in his defense, transgressions more palatable and "easier" for his image to shake off. By inserting his voice, he also made sure that readers of the local newspapers had a choice of what/who they wanted to believe.

In short, Aaron Henry was indispensable to black Mississippians at this crucial time in the freedom struggle. The public inquisition against him may have evoked deep sympathy from folks who frowned upon the acts themselves. Knowing that the motivation behind the arrest and subsequent court battles stemmed from his leadership, his supporters saw him as the sacrificial lamb, a mantle he took on himself for the greater good and one that consolidated rather than eroded his influence. He knew that most in the state would not take on his role as leader, and so it was in the interest of African Americans in Mississippi to support him rather than struggle without him. McLemore stated that "clearly it would have been even more harsh or harsher if Aaron had not been the person that Aaron was because nobody could question his credentials in the movement, nobody." As such, Howard astutely notes that overlooking the transgression "amounted to cultural self-protection, social self-preservation."[79]

Constance Curry, who worked with Henry on his autobiography and published it posthumously, made a special note at the end of the chapter dealing with the case. In her only footnote, she stated that Henry's bisexuality was known by friends and colleagues. Interviewing many people to complete the book, she summarized their comments: "We all knew it. It made no differ-ence to us, and it had no impact on his political life nor on his contributions to the freedom movement." With this short paragraph, she effectively acknowl-edged the presence of bisexuality but quickly rebuffed any criticism or dis-cussion by curtly informing the reader that his associates did not consider it a factor.[80] While it is fascinating to know that this man had, and got away with, a double life, engaging in transgressions that have taken down lesser leaders, particularly in the South, it has never been a topic of conversation or analysis in Clarksdale's (and Mississippi's) civil rights story among activists. The move-ment had to continue.

Coming to Coahoma: SNCC and CORE

The black boycott of downtown was holding steady—with participation rates as high as 90 percent, due to unifying events like attacks on the leadership—and white authorities increasingly looked for ways to disrupt the growing move-ment. Thus, the summer of 1962 looked to be a hot one in Clarksdale. The city had refused picketing permits for the downtown area and had adopted "beauti-fication'" ordinances (against leafleting), both designed to minimize the effects of the boycott by facilitating arrests. In response, protesters appealed to civic morality by drawing the "spiritual" lines at strategic crossroads leading to the district (see map 2). The leaders each had his or her own crossroad: one for the late Rev. Trammell at Issaquena and South Edwards; Aaron Henry's at Desoto and Third Street; R. L. Drew's at Sunflower and the Illinois Central Railroad; John Melchor's at the Second Street Bridge; Rev. J. D. Rayford's at the First Street Bridge; and Vera Pigee's "the symbol of womanhood" at Cutrer Hill.[81]

As tensions built in Clarksdale, new developments at the state level held out the promise of greater civil rights activity in the Delta as a whole. SNCC, which had done so much in just two years to spark and guide the student movement, and CORE, which had advocated nonviolent direct action since the forties, had both begun to step up their presence in Mississippi. Whether their new aggres-siveness would accelerate the state's burgeoning movement and unite disparate county-level activities remained to be seen. Open as well was the question of how the NAACP, in Clarksdale and statewide, would respond.

A year earlier, in 1961, state NAACP leaders had helped to create the state-wide Council of Federated Organizations (not to be confused with the local CCFCO, which served as the prototype for the statewide organization). COFO, as it came to be known, represented a strategic alias designed to facilitate a meeting with Governor Barnett, who refused to negotiate with the NAACP. As Henry observed, however, like in CCFCO, it was largely the same group of people: "Usually there was a casual overlapping of the membership of the organizations with the goal of equal rights as the common bond."[82] Although the meeting with Barnett proved fruitless, COFO, which included the majority of black leaders in the state, promised to unite the movement under a single umbrella, if in name only at that point. Henry noted, "We were convinced that COFO would increase our effectiveness in civil rights work all over the state, and at last the federal government had its eyes on Mississippi."[83] Then, in January 1962, Bob Moses, Henry, and Evers met to revitalize COFO for a broader and longer political assault.[84]

Bob Moses, who would emerge in 1963 as an inspiring force behind the 1964 Freedom Summer, came to Mississippi in 1961 to work on voter registration after contacting Amzie Moore through Ella Baker's introduction. Described by Evers as "a young man of Manhattan, New York City," Moses had set up offices in McComb, Mississippi. He was part of significant attempts to bring the energy of the mass movement from places like North Carolina, Alabama, Tennessee, and Arkansas to the state. Evers documented these efforts in a six-and-a-half-page report to the national NAACP in the fall of 1961, and he also took note of the visit of CORE's Tom Gaither to Jackson in May to rally the black community for donations to help the imprisoned Freedom Riders. Evers described the Jackson workshops conducted on nonviolence by the Nashville Christian Leadership Conference (Diane Nash, James Bevel, Marion Berry, Charles Sherrod, and Bernard Layafette working also under the auspices of SNCC) as having the sole purpose of involving the citizens in the Freedom Rides movement. CORE director James Farmer and Martin Luther King both came to Jackson to speak on the Freedom Rides in mass meetings sponsored by Woman Power Unlimited (a Jackson-based black women's group that supported civil rights activities) and SNCC.[85]

However, strong NAACP college chapters at Tougaloo and J. P. Campbell College thwarted attempts to organize stronger SNCC groups in Mississippi in 1961. Evers reported that SNCC maintained "a skeleton operation" in Jackson. Nevertheless, when arrested and harassed by the police, the leaders of SNCC came to the NAACP for legal assistance and bond support. The month before Evers's report, Roy Wilkins had written to Edward King, SNCC's executive secretary, to inform him that SNCC members working in McComb and in Walthall, Amite, and Pike counties had called the NAACP for bail money. He stressed, "We cannot commit ourselves to free-wheeling activity planned and launched by another organization. . . . If we are expected to pay the bills, we must be in on the planning and launching, otherwise bills will have to be paid by those who plan and launch."[86] King wrote back apologizing, prompting another response from Wilkins a week later to clarify his position: "I wish to emphasize that the NAACP is desirous at all times of working in all feasible ways with other groups who have the same objectives and which use, generally, the same methods." Eternally the politician and bureaucrat, he continued, "Our policy has been to work in this way on a project basis only and not to agree to any continuing formula for extended activity over a wide-ranging program."[87] NAACP Southeast Region director Ruby Hurley's own report in November 1961 highlighted the rise in violence in the counties where SNCC worked, a fact that worried local black residents. To decrease the violence in those areas, the NAACP urged locals not to attend SNCC meetings.[88]

All of this stood in the background in the summer of 1962, as COFO and the NAACP each tried to forge a path for Mississippi's movement. In Coahoma County, the Kennedy administration's Voter Education Program provided funding for a voter registration campaign, employing four part-time workers: Rev. J. D. Rayford, Idessa Johnson, Mary Jane Pigee, and Willie Griffin. Despite Henry's plea to the national office, the NAACP did not contribute financially to the project, even though all the workers came from the branch. Instead, the Taconic and Field Foundations gave grants to the Voter Education Program, which the Southern Regional Council distributed in Atlanta. The local leadership promoted the campaign as having "the backing of the President of the United States and the United States Department of Justice." The leaders' report from the summer of 1962 illustrated the frustrations African Americans faced trying to register—out of 1,234 people attempting to register, only 115 succeeded.[89]

The summer, however, brought the first outside workers directly into Clarksdale. SNCC's Charles McLaurin and fellow COFO worker James Jones led the way and attracted unwanted attention from the police department. Stopped while escorting a group home after a visit to the courthouse where they had tried to register, McLaurin was subjected to a curbside grilling. Officers wanted to know what he was doing and responded to his answer with a barrage of obscenities. Given an on-the-spot fine that they could not pay, McLaurin and Jones were hauled off to jail, where companions posted bond in the amount of $103. Rather than run the risk of a higher fine or mounting legal expenses pending an appeal, they forfeited the bond. But deliberate police harassment did not deter organizers. CORE also made further inroads into the county. David Dennis reported that his organization had branched into the area, through COFO, with six voter registration "clinics" opened in August in Bolivar, Sunflower, Leflore, Washington, Forest, and Coahoma counties.[90]

With SNCC in Coahoma County and other outside organizations funding the voter registration drive, Henry again approached Roy Wilkins, this time with resolve. He asked the NAACP for more legal assistance, stressing that without financial contributions from the national office, funds allotted for the program would only cover legal fees, fines, and bonds. To assuage Wilkins, Henry pledged to clear all projects with the NAACP. In 1962, the NAACP in Mississippi had a growing membership. The Coahoma County branch became the second largest in the state after Jackson, with 374 new members since 1 January (106 were Coahoma County Youth Council members). Henry dangled local loyalty in front of Wilkins, urging him to be flexible. Yet the NAACP national office continued to fret over the increased presence of other groups in Mississippi and worried about CORE as a competing group. Concerned about organizational turf, NAACP leaders also worried over the press received from Alabama's SCLC campaigns as the NAACP ban continued there.[91] Given the growing support of the organization by local African Americans and the other organizations stepping onto the stage, could the NAACP afford not to answer Henry's call?

Surging Violence

White Mississippi did not sit idly by. Threats, harassment, and intimidation all increased that summer and fall. Many who participated in voter registration or other civil rights activity were told that they no longer qualified for government commodity winter relief. In the Delta, still under the economic heel of sharecropping, many families relied on aid to stretch their meager crop payments through the winter. In 1962, the crops were picked early, and many black workers found themselves displaced by automation.[92]

To soften the winter hardship, particularly for sharecroppers, movement organizers successfully launched a nationwide campaign to bring in donated food and clothing. CORE started a donation drive in October 1962 and brought in over five tons of goods from fifteen states. In December, COFO adopted the program and organized the special welfare division, officially called the Emergency Welfare and Relief Committee. Dave Dennis from CORE and Vera Pigee from the NAACP co-chaired the organization, and distribution centers were set up in Coahoma, LeFlore, and Sunflower counties. The committee solicited information on needy families and speedily distributed goods and at times even

FIG. 3.5. Vera Pigee working with volunteers at a food and clothing drive in Clarksdale, circa 1961–63. (Personal collection of Mary Jane Pigee Davis)

rent or utility money. *Jet* magazine ran an article publicizing the project in the 21 February 1963 issue, printing a photograph of Vera Pigee (incorrectly called Pegues) and Aaron Henry with a fifteen dollar check from James Meredith.[93]

To counteract these efforts, the Clarksdale police worked to cut off the supply pipeline. On 27 December 1962, in the early hours of the morning, black twenty-one-year-olds Ivanhoe Donaldson from New York and Benjamin Taylor from New Jersey were apprehended as they rested in a truck full of donated commodities and medical supplies, which they had collected in Michigan and from a pharmacist en route in Louisville, Kentucky. Their truck was filled to overcapacity, and as the young men cruised south they had two flat tires along the way. Donaldson recalled, "We got in about two hours after when we were supposed to have been there. Doc [Aaron Henry] had closed up about an hour before."[94] They had no one to call and only had the drugstore address, so they parked outside at 213 Fourth Street and tried to get comfortable in the truck's small cab. The two students, juniors at Michigan State University, were rudely awakened an hour later by banging on the truck's doors and windows.

Donaldson, half asleep, rolled down his window and said, "What's up?" That was a bad move. The officer "looked at me, slapped me across the head, and said, 'Who do you think you're talking to,' that got me awake real fast. . . . I said, 'What's going on.' and he banged me again. 'So, when you talk to me nigger you say, "Sir."'"[95]

Promptly arrested, the police took the men to the police station a few blocks away. As they were denied their right to a phone call, no one knew to come to their aid. After three days at the city jail, they were transferred to the Coahoma County jail. Housed in a long, dorm-like room with multiple bunk beds lined up, of course the students were worried. They had not been charged with a crime, so the local paper had not recorded their arrest. Donaldson hatched a plan: "I discovered that some of the inmates there collected parking meter money on the street in front of Doc's store . . . so I said, 'Would you drop a note off for me?'" He worked hard persuading one prisoner to take the risk: "I wrote a note on a piece of toilet paper that simply said, 'Doc, I'm in the Coahoma County jail, get me out of here, Ivanhoe.'" His messenger returned from his duties and told Donaldson that he had simply run into the store, thrown the paper on the counter, and hightailed it out before anyone could see him. "You know but the next day I heard Doc's voice. . . . I could hear because he was speaking loud, and he says, 'I heard, I know he is here.'"[96] After an eleven-day sojourn, in the care of the Clarksdale and then the county police, and after a series of rib-breaking beatings, the men had their day in court and were released. They returned to their truck to find some of the contents destroyed, food spilled and ground into the dirt, and the clothes covered in oil. Anything that was salvageable made it to the distribution center.[97]

They were charged with possession of barbiturates, and bonds were set at $15,000 each, an astronomical sum. Donaldson insisted, "As it turned out, these things [the barbiturates] were bandages, band aids, aspirin, and things which anybody can buy over the counter."[98] Luckily, Henry secured NAACP lawyers to file a writ of habeas corpus, which reduced the bonds to nothing, allowing the students to leave. They were headline news all over the country. Invigorated rather than intimidated by the experience, the men did at least three more runs with the truck into Mississippi delivering goods. Now they knew better and managed to avoid further confrontations with the police.

The need for material aid to the poor in the Delta and the obstacles placed in the path of relief workers motivated African American comedian Dick Gregory to use his newfound position as a celebrity-with-means to help the movement. As a poor fatherless child in 1930s St. Louis, Gregory had been forced to use his wit as a cloak of protection. But when asked to go to Mississippi in 1963, his fear caught him: "I was afraid of the South, afraid of all the cities where I could fall down accidentally, break my head open, and be left to bleed to death in the gutter because the ambulance from the Negro funeral home had to come all the way across town." Still, his inner voice prevailed.[99]

In his first major contribution, Gregory organized a shipment of food from Chicago to help beleaguered Delta Mississippians. He used his influence to advertise the drive on the local radio station and collected 14,000 pounds of food. Chartering a plane on 11 February 1963, he flew with the food to Memphis, where it was loaded onto trucks. He then accompanied the shipment that went to Clarksdale and then onto Greenwood. He purposefully had picked that date to come to Mississippi because the next day was Lincoln's birthday, and President Kennedy had invited him and his wife to celebrate at the White House. No one would harm him, he figured, when they knew that the president of the United States expected him the next day. In his honor and in gratitude, Monday, 11 February 1963, became "Dick Gregory Day." Appearing at the First Baptist Church in Clarksdale at 7 P.M., Gregory entertained and encouraged the crowd.[100] By 7 March, so many provisions had collected at Haven Methodist Church that they were moved to a warehouse across the street, ultimately helping 8,000 families.[101]

Meanwhile, white resistance took new forms. The violence in Clarksdale had often stayed out of sight, in the jail cells or in the fields out of town. Now bombings and drive-by shootings became the norm. When a car in Greenwood was riddled with bullets, narrowly missing voter registration activists inside, and when in Clarksdale the front window display of Henry's Fourth Street Drugstore was smashed and the display of American flags desecrated, Henry wrote directly to the president requesting intervention. Members of Mississippi's advisory committee to the federal government's Civil Rights Commission did not meet in the state until 1963, and many members faced harassment. The vice chairman's home suffered a bombing, and another member and his wife were jailed on trumped-up charges.[102] In the open meetings that spring, the Civil Rights Commission's report noted that blacks were asserting their rights more vigorously but that the environment had intensified, with over 100 new complaints of brutality and voting violations. Two identifiable hotspots — the Upper Delta (Leflore, Sunflower, and Coahoma counties) and Jackson — prompted the commission to also appeal to the president for assistance, "employing the moral and legal powers of his office."[103]

The mask of civility once proudly flaunted by Clarksdale's leaders had been abruptly tossed aside. At the end of March 1963, police harassed four white undergraduates from the University of Iowa who had delivered supplies to Clarksdale. When orders to leave town went unheeded, a group of hired black "thugs" tried to fight with the volunteers. Some NAACP members uncovered the fact that the police had paid the black men to cause a disturbance in order to create an "arrestable" incident.[104]

One particular event, egregious because of its openness and the threat to so many lives, was a direct attack on a church. On 3 April, a gas bomb was thrown through the window of Centennial Baptist Church, which was filled with people attending a voter registration rally. Curtis Wilkie had just begun his assignment at the *Clarksdale Press Register* that month. He was the only white person in the church: "The sanctuary was filled that evening with several hundred blacks, an assembly of day laborers and domestic workers, ministers and morticians, bracing for their challenge to the status quo with songs of freedom and speeches to fortify morale."[105] Dick Gregory recalled the event in detail in his autobiography. After a protest march in Greenwood, Gregory had traveled up to Clarksdale with Jim Sanders to address the mass meeting. He remembered, "There were more than 800 people jammed into the Centennial Missionary Baptist Church there, and we had to push our way through the police to get inside. I was sitting on the stage, waiting to speak, when the bomb came flying through an open window. It hit a man on the head, bounced off a lady's hand, then rolled to the middle of the floor."

Thoughts of his wife and children flashed through his mind as he thought his life was about to end. He saw hundreds trying to flee through the door, and he jumped to the microphone: "Where are you going? The man who threw it is outside God's house. The Man who's supposed to save your lives [is] here." People stopped running, and someone picked up the bomb and threw it back out the window. When Gregory exited, he saw "cops lounging around outside, leaning on the hoods of their cars in the evening, talking softly and laughing." He found out that the bomb was a special U.S. Army gas grenade, more powerful than tear gas, capable of killing those nearby if it had detonated. Whoever threw it had not pulled the pin. "And people were surprised a few months later when they blew up that church in Birmingham," he mused.[106]

The situation balanced perilously on a knife-edge between order and chaos. Ten days later, on 12 April 1963, Good Friday, as Martin Luther King penned his famous letter from a jail cell in Birmingham, U.S. congressman Charles Diggs (D-Mich.) rested at Aaron Henry's home. The "adopted" congressman, who had witnessed the trial against Emmett Till's murderers in 1955, was a regular visitor to Clarksdale; he had come to see the situation in order to report directly to the president. After they had all retired for the night, Molotov cocktails came flying through the windows into the house and carport, shattering their sleep. The fire department took twenty-five minutes to arrive and loitered near the burning building. Luckily, no one was injured.[107] Two white men, Theodore A. Carr and Aubrey Cauthern, caught after an investigation, admitted guilt but insisted their prank was just for "fun" and that they did not know who lived in the targeted house.[108] Diggs, from Detroit, with access to a wide and varied audience in the North, could only damage the image of Mississippi. Indeed, he immediately appealed to the House Judiciary Committee to hold hearings in Clarksdale for firsthand testimony. A sign placed in the window of Henry's home, quoting scripture, read, "Father forgive them for they do not know what they do," feeding the drama to the press. Many white Mississippians fretted. Calling for swift and severe punishment of the culprits, an editorial in the *Vicksburg Evening Post* decried the act, stating that the "actions of these irresponsible and vicious persons do not reflect the attitudes of the overwhelming majority of Mississippians. Upon the picture which has been so cleverly and diabolically drawn of our people and of our state, this latest blot will be hard to erase." While condemning the individuals, the editorial worried more about reputation than the welfare of the victims. The bombing of a sleeping U.S. congressman was a terrible mistake on the part of white supremacists. Still, by 20 July, both bombers walked free.[109]

A month following the bombing of Henry's home, his drugstore was attacked again. With at least eight inside meeting and having supper, a huge explosion from above interrupted their repast. The roof suffered significant damage, which shattered glass behind the store, but the blast that Henry stated felt like "a concussion" was dismissed by Sheriff Ross as a lightning blast. Henry suspected nitroglycerin, but the police would claim otherwise. The *New York Times* reported on both of Henry's near misses, signaling his stature on the national stage.[110]

Violence continued beyond the national spotlight as well. In 1963, with the spirit of righteousness fueling her indignation, Vera Pigee grew increasingly bold. On Tuesday, 23 April, she drove with her husband, Paul, to the Lion Service Station on Highway 61 to service the vehicle with gas and oil. She asked to use the ladies' restroom. "He replied 'yes' and told me to go around to the rear of the station. I replied, 'I will be afraid to go around there in the dark, something might get me.'" Turning to leave, the young man called her back and said that even though he had only seen white ladies use the room, Pigee could get the restroom key. As she made her way there, another attendant, Percy Green, demanded she return the key and use the black restroom. She complied, but calmly told him to remove the gas and oil from her car. Enraged, Green told her to leave and never to return, to which she replied that she would also instruct black people not to patronize the station and would complain to his employers so that he would lose his job. When she asked for the change from the ten-dollar bill given for the service, which cost $5.70, he refused. Pigee continued to demand the change, and Green "advanced up on me and struck me in my left temple[.] I threw up my hand to keep him from hitting me in my eyes, and backed up. He followed me and hit me on the left side of my mouth." Seeing the violence, Paul Pigee ran into the service station and tried to get his wife to leave, but not before she received another blow to her right lower jaw. She refused to exit without her change, and Green grudgingly handed over the money while instructing the other attendant to phone the police.[111]

Returning to the home of Rev. Rayford, in whose car they had driven, Pigee followed procedure and called Police Chief Ben Collins to report the incident. She also called the FBI in Memphis. Fifty minutes after the call, Collins came to her home on Baird Street with a warrant for her arrest for disturbing the peace. She had to post bond in order to seek medical treatment. Evidently, white businesses would accept black currency, but those green dollars could not buy respect.

In the end, however, Pigee wreaked havoc on the business. She picked up the phone the next morning and demanded redress from the station owner, Mooneyhan. The owner told her in no uncertain terms that "he did not solicit nor care for niggers' business." She told him that he would not be getting any more of it, since she would instigate a boycott. By the beginning of May, the station had closed.[112] The local NAACP's newsletter made much of Pigee's service station incident and declared, "The rock throwing, shooting, bombing and beatings, by whites against Negroes in this community, without retaliation, are *over*," encouraging citizens once again to exercise their right to vote to rid the county of corruption.[113]

She earned respect by being fearless, although some would call her foolhardy. Brenda Luckett chuckled as she recalled Pigee's tenacity, but underscored Pigee's vital presence in the local movement:

They couldn't do anything with her. She wasn't afraid to stand up and say anything to any man or anybody and would get *loud*! . . . There were a lot of women that worked with her. I remember one lady who got fired from the bread house because she was working with Vera Pigee, and Vera got her hooked up with somebody in Jonestown who got her on some federal program and she got herself a better job, making more money! She would get other people involved. And she had safe houses, places where people in the county area who were trying to hide, she would have people who would keep them, house and feed them. . . . They couldn't scare her. . . . She lived in the heart of the black community, so they wouldn't have made it out alive. . . . She was the premier of women who would go anywhere and say anything and she was not intimidated.[114]

Despite her courageous audacity, Vera Pigee knew that the more involved she became in the freedom struggle, the more she subjected her family to attack. About 12:45 A.M. on 8 June 1963, she and her husband were asleep in bed when shots were fired into the home. Afterward, she found a bullet lodged under the piano, which had narrowly missed her bed on the other side of the wall. She remembered, "The piano is a constant reminder since it absorbed the bullet which would have spent itself in my bedroom otherwise." Evidence in the crime existed, but investigator Sheriff Ross never arrested a suspect.[115] Despite these attacks, her marriage held fast. Pigee's husband, confident in his wife's abilities and determination, supported her, although he stayed in the background. Maintaining his steady job at the North Delta Compress during her period of activism, his support and willingness to share his wife's notoriety made a difference. His boss withstood pressure from the Citizens' Council and never fired him. She recalled: "God bless his boss at that compress . . . [who] said 'His wife and daughter don't work for me. He does. And he's one of the best workers I've got—here every day, always on time.'" Parent of just one child, Paul Pigee watched numerous children and adults enter his home, eat his food, and sleep under his roof. He endured the physical dangers and constant harassing phone calls at all hours, and his wife credited him as her rock upon which the family stood, enabling her to go forth confidently.[116]

Late on 12 June, four days after the Pigee home was attacked, Byron de la Beckwith crouched down in the bushes, waiting for Medgar Evers to return to his home in Jackson. As Evers parked his car and walked wearily up the driveway, keys still in hand, Beckwith pulled the trigger on his high-powered rifle. Dragging himself to the door and into the arms of his screaming wife, Evers died before he reached the hospital. After the escalating lawlessness and near misses of the preceding few months, people like Pigee and Henry were devastated but not surprised that one of their number had been slain.

Evers's death closed a chapter for the NAACP in Mississippi. He had loyally fought long and hard to maintain the organization's prominence in the state. He followed orders and relinquished membership in other organizations to demonstrate complete dedication. Now the NAACP had lost its gatekeeper. In the end, Evers had been moving faster than his employer, the NAACP, but he had been doing it quietly, with the help of people like Henry and Pigee.

Despite his profound grief over the assassination of an old friend, the next day Henry testified at the subcommittee of the House Judiciary Committee in Washington, D.C. Evers had planned to meet him there to give his own testimony. Henry related the incidents of the past few years to the federal audience, from the antiboycott arrests, to his morality case, to the attacks on his home and business and other cases made known to him in his capacity as the Mississippi NAACP president. On the last page of his eight-page statement, Henry demanded help from the federal government. At the top of his list was civil rights legislation to give the Department of Justice authority to act when there was imminent danger, rather than having to wait for violence. He spoke in support of the Civil Rights Act, then before the Congress, and called for a voting rights bill.[117] Little did Henry know that it would take more brutality and deaths, many of them in Mississippi, for these legislative hopes to be realized in 1964 and 1965.

Meanwhile, the federal government sought to isolate lawlessness in Mississippi. One of the government's leverages against Governor Barnett was federal assistance. After the riots at the University of Mississippi following the enrollment of James Meredith, the state's businessmen recognized the negative impact this was all having on the economy. Mississippi had tried for twenty-five years to entice industry, and since the riots, four of the eight new plants scheduled to relocate to the state had withdrawn. Burke Marshall kept a file titled "Stick It to Mississippi" in his office research papers reviewing federal contracts. By the spring of 1963, the Commission on Civil Rights, thwarted repeatedly in its attempts to hold meetings in Mississippi, made a case to the president to withhold funds.[118]

Injustices continued at all levels. Four days after Evers's murder, on Sunday, 16 June, Fathers' Day, as part of the program to awaken the conscience of the city's church community, Hattie Mae Gilmore, a Pigee family friend and the chair of the branch's Voter Education Committee, led a group of five picketers to the largest white church in Clarksdale. Arrested and charged with parading without a permit, she told the police where she worked. This put Gilmore, a lifelong resident of Clarksdale, forty-one at the time and employed at Myrtle's Café, in the city officials' spotlight. Her employer, Myrtle Hamilton, did not object to Gilmore's activism, but the very next week two policemen entered the café to deliver a message from Chief of Police Collins. If Hamilton did not terminate Gilmore, the City Health Department would revoke the café's license. Unemployed, Gilmore became unemployable. Blacklisted as an activist and the chairman of the NAACP's Voter Education Committee, Gilmore could not secure work. Fortunately (as Brenda Luckett would later confirm), Pigee's work and influence in the community had given her a valuable list of contacts. When a person lost employment due to his or her activity in the movement, that person came to Pigee, who would burn up the phone lines to replace her or his job.[119] Through Pigee, Gilmore eventually found work as a domestic and later as a cook at Head Start.

Movement success at this point was relative. Activists roused and politicized a large population with displays of courage visible to the entire nation. Women, always active and vocal, took on local leadership roles when necessary, running citizenship classes and literally keeping workers fed and clothed. More and more local black people were demanding voting rights and desegregation. As children became more vocal and visible on the front lines, parents had a greater stake in the movements and more reason to overcome fear and self-protective habits of subservience. Inspiring local activists from afar and then joining them, organizations like SNCC, CORE, and the SCLC successfully organized in Mississippi. Their presence highlighted NAACP frustrations. Although not visible in front of photographers' flashes or reporters' microphones, while the organizations worked together under the auspices of COFO, inherent cracks, tensions, and terminal problems among them remained.

So many black people, spurred by the action of their youth, had fought so hard in Clarksdale for three years; yet, by some measures, they had accomplished little. For all the organizing and protesting, power relations remained frozen. By getting themselves arrested and provoking white supremacists' murderous responses, black Mississippians, nowhere more so than in Clarksdale, had drawn the federal government into the state for the first time since Reconstruction. And over these three years, federal representatives had come to realize the need for protection on the ground and legislation in Congress that would have a practical effect in Mississippi.

The mass movement stage was full of a host of characters moving in and out of the spotlight, improvising without a script or director. It was loud at times—the detonating pyrotechnics contained real dynamite. People talked and yelled all at the same time, to each other and across the stage, sometimes having conversations but mostly reacting to whatever barreled toward them. This "performance" would come to include even more characters in 1963 and 1964, adding to the chaos on and off stage.

CHAPTER FOUR

Fires of Frustration

SUMMERS OF 1963 TO 1965

Well, I want my freedom and I want it yesterday. — *Vera Pigee (1968)*

*He [Aaron Henry] believes that whosoever frees him and his
people should be used.* — *Gloster Current (1964)*

Vera Pigee was proud of Mississippi's youth councils, with good reason. She had toiled for years to build up the chapters and boost membership in local NAACP branches. By the middle of 1963, she had consolidated considerable strength among the state's youth, and the fruits of her labors were evident in Coahoma County's prominence in that year's national NAACP conference. However, she was continually swallowing her frustration as older youth from the Student Nonviolent Coordinating Committee (SNCC) and the Council of Federated Organizations (COFO) distracted her wards with their militancy, bravery, and organizing. Through Pigee's eyes, it became more and more apparent that SNCC sought wide-scale organization in the state—facilitated by COFO, the very organization she had helped to build two short years earlier— and she could not hold off its appeal forever. SNCC had new and bold methods of organizing and youthful charisma, and Pigee's Youth Council members knew it.

The climax would come in an extraordinary year in Mississippi, between June 1963 and the late summer of 1964. In the first weeks of that first summer, as the roiling streets of Birmingham compelled him to abandon political caution, President Kennedy told a national television audience that "the fires of frustration and discord are burning in every city, North and South, where legal remedies are not at hand." Warning the nation that it faced "a moral crisis as a country, as a people," Kennedy relayed from the Oval Office the message black demonstrators had been sending for years: "It is time to act in the Congress, in your state and local legislative body, and above all, in our daily lives." Late that night, an immediate rejoinder from white supremacists was forthcoming: Medgar Evers was gunned down in his front yard.[1]

Between Evers's murder and the Democratic National Convention in Atlantic City in August 1964, Mississippi's black citizens literally and dramatically entered the national struggle over civil rights. The stage expanded. And Clarksdale, where Pigee, Henry, and dozens of other activists had labored in the trenches, took much of the lead. In particular, Clarksdale's activists paved the road for COFO's statewide strength. Many of the campaigns waged at the state level before and during 1964's Freedom Summer originated in Clarksdale or Coahoma County. The county's federation of organizations (CCFCO), dating from the early sixties, and its Freedom Vote in August 1963 furnished prototypes for the larger state movement. Clarksdale's black residents thus fought a two-front war in these months. On one hand, they worked to desegregate Clarksdale itself, bringing into coordination and sharp focus the disparate local efforts of the previous decade. On the other, Clarksdalians eagerly joined statewide campaigns for voting rights, a massive organizing effort that carried Mississippi into the national conversation in the summer of 1964 in new ways.

The fires of frustration burned from every direction, not just from black communities tired by the slow process of desegregation. For Pigee and Henry, however, that two-front war barely concealed simmering organizational tensions within the movement itself. Although allies in the cause of freedom, conflicting organizational strategies and intramovement politics strained their relationship further, exacerbated by the increase in volunteers in Clarksdale. Compounding the local drama, the national NAACP office continued to tussle with state leaders, especially Henry and Charles Evers (who took over his slain brother's position). In an environment that more than ever favored flexible alliances and collaborations, national NAACP executives wanted the state officers to ensure that COFO would not undermine the NAACP in Mississippi. In this, they had an ally in Pigee, who labored long and hard to maintain NAACP prominence. It was often an uphill battle, however, as other COFO workers entered the county at Henry's behest. Henry's NAACP loyalties expanded to encompass his fervent desire to harness the enthusiasm and organizational energy of SNCC in the heady days leading up to Freedom Summer. Frustrated, national branch secretary Gloster Current commented in the fall of 1964 that COFO had "captured the imagination and most of the time of our state president [Henry], who offers little to his own organization except lip service. He believes that whosoever frees him and his people should be used."[2] Adding to the mix, community institutions, particularly the churches, did little to counter these tensions and divisions. Tangled amid their own internal politics and acrimonies, churches too often provided only organizational space and not solid leadership.

What emerges from these local stories is not a romantic image of a harmonious and cohesive movement bathed in sisterly and brotherly solidarity. Instead, the battles against segregation in Clarksdale and across the state in 1963 and 1964—a year immortalized in civil rights iconography—reveal a grittier reality. The campaigns of these years combined determined mass action and fractious organizational disagreements. The national NAACP took great exception to SNCC's and COFO's influence and organizing on the ground as they entered communities, which often brought the attentions of the national press to the state and their campaigns. Despite the unity against segregationists and the heart-wrenching losses, in lives and campaigns, and despite the ability to leave their collective marks on the national and international landscapes, discord in and between groups (at least at the top levels) came to a head during these years. It is an untidy story, with many characters and a cacophony of voices, but it reflects the urgency and passion (on both sides) that most movement veterans recall best.

Lighting the Fires: Summer of 1963

In June 1963, local leaders in Clarksdale organized a massive direct-action campaign for the summer. Hoping to force Clarksdale's mayor to meet with black community representatives, the local NAACP had begun preparing for a "jail-in," taking their cue from the Southern Christian Leadership Conference (SCLC) tactic of filling the jails in Birmingham that spring. Vera Pigee, willing to try new strategies, led in the preparations of the captains and organized outsiders who were invited to participate. A large sheet of paper fastened to the wall of the Freedom House served as a sign-up sheet for volunteers to be arrested. The fifty-nine names belonged to men, women, and youth: from old-timers like Rev. R. L. T. Smith, to indigenous COFO workers like Lafayette Surney, to Coahoma County Youth Council members like Roy Bell Wright, Cora Hicks, and Wilma Jones. Names on the list, not necessarily noted in earlier documents, would be etched in history on affidavits from that summer documenting the brutality that their nonviolent protests precipitated.[3]

Pigee had established (and rented) the Freedom House at 429 Yazoo the preceding December, after her election as state co-chair of the Emergency Relief Committee of COFO. It was now frequently monitored by local police, who parked outside or cruised by slowly. The one-story storefront building served as part warehouse, part community center, part meeting hall, and part library (well-stocked with donated books) and as a central movement space (also open to those not necessarily involved directly in the movement). The Freedom House was increasingly important to Pigee's vision of grassroots protest.

On the night of 8 July, with marches and rallies planned to begin the following day, an injunction halted events. Realizing, if not understanding, that tradition and fear no longer kept African Americans in line, like an invisible electric Jim Crow fence, white supremacists now required the reinforcement of legal bricks and mortar. The document issued by the chancery court of Coahoma County named as many activists and organizations as possible—fifty-nine in total. Along with locals like Pigee, Henry, Drew, and Melchor, it named Martin Luther King Jr., five visiting National Council of Churches (NCC) ministers and bishops, Charles Evers, Rev. James Bevel, the entire Coahoma County NAACP branch, the Congress of Racial Equality (CORE), the SCLC, COFO, and SNCC. Before the court, the city's attorney recounted the arrest of leaders in December 1961 for conspiring to boycott and claimed that similar activities had increased in recent months. Maintaining that it had only an innocent desire to maintain law and order, the city advocated stopping not just local leaders but also those "acting in concert." They must have known King was in town. The local NAACP branch had carefully planned a pep rally for the following day. Pigee had arranged for the visit—King attended a local luncheon, along with Ralph Abernathy, five black clergy, and thirty-five white clergy, before speaking to a crowd of 400. Pooling organizational strength from different sources, local leaders sponsored the ministerial assembly, building on the momentum generated from the Birmingham campaigns that spring and President Kennedy's civil rights speech in June. In his signature way, King took to the podium and encouraged the local movement but asked for patience in the face of the injunction and to allow leaders to work behind the scenes.[4]

Respecting the law, organizers obeyed the injunction for nearly three weeks, despite constant provocation and intimidation by the police and the white community.[5] The organizers changed their minds when the city denied the permit application to parade and demonstrate on 29 July. The first wave of protests, it was decided, would center on city government, beginning the next day, on Tuesday, 30 July; the second wave, on Clarksdale's churches, would

FIG. 4.1. Petition by Picket, 1963. (Courtesy of Robert Birdsong)

occur on Sunday, 4 August. Tired of waiting for city leaders to work with them around a table at a biracial committee meeting, black activists now wanted to capitalize on the publicity that direct action could generate. The only route for change, they believed, was to embarrass the city nationally. By creating an unstable environment of civil disobedience, mixed with anticipated police brutality, activists sought to mimic King's Birmingham strategy. Therefore, gratefully acknowledging that the NAACP had already spent $20,000 on bonds in the June demonstrations, Aaron Henry requested a further $50,000 to cover the activities of around 200 protesters.[6]

Working with CORE, particularly field secretary Thomas Gaither, local people also made the decision to step up the pace of their protest against segregated public eating establishments and other facilities and to continue pushing white leaders to form a citywide biracial committee. On Tuesday morning, as the meeting of the board of the mayor and commissioners convened, police arrested fifty-six demonstrators in downtown Clarksdale, including Henry. Most of those arrested were minors. Convicted on 1 August, each received a $200 fine and a thirty-day sentence, but they resolved to stay in jail rather than pay. This was carefully strategized—Gaither issued a press statement advertising the protest and the arrests and including a long list of objectives. Adults were immediately put to work on the chain gang, and all remained in jail for at least

Let's Clean Up CLARKSDALE
FROM THE
MISTREATIN' OF NEGROES

City prison chain gang

NAAEP - PRESIDENT

AARON HENRY And 80 – Others Arrested
Recently Started The JOB
YOU CAN HELP BY :
1. NOT SPENDING YOUR <u>MONEY</u> *in* DOWN-
   TOWN CLARKSDALE
2. REGISTERING & VOTING
3. COMING OUT TO A MASS MEETING
   SUNDAY AUG. 4th 1963 **8** P.M.
   at HAVEN METHODIST CHURCH
The Speaker Will Be Our OWN Dr AARON HENRY
FREEDOM **NOW** !

FIG. 4.2. Local NAACP flyer (August 1963) showing Aaron Henry on the city prison gang. (NAACP Papers III C75, Mississippi State, 64–65; used by permission of the National Association for the Advancement of Colored People)

FIG. 4.3. Police pose for a photograph as ministers from the National Council
of Churches march to a local church in Clarksdale, 1963.
(Danny Lyon/Magnum Photos)

one week, some longer. Henry made the most of his week's detail on a Clarksdale garbage truck, cheerfully chatting with observers as he swung the city's
trash. The bond tally in Clarksdale by September 1963 topped $100,000, dou-
bling Henry's estimates. The NAACP posted $70,000, the SCLC $10,000, CORE
$5,000, and local citizens the balance. More than simply an accounting detail,
the distribution of posted bonds demonstrates how civil rights groups coordinated more effectively under COFO.[7]

Affidavits document how Clarksdale's police department vented its frustration.[8] Local people, fueled by anger and indignation, expanded the volume of
complaints, and they built a clear case for federal intervention.[9] The affidavits
also document the local activity, introducing, albeit as snapshots, some otherwise unknown activists on the front line. As the local NAACP newsletter had
reasoned at the beginning of protests, "Apparently the Clarksdale Police Department has not learned that threatening and intimidating Negro citizens is a
great help to the Freedom Struggle."[10]

The "brighter side" advertised by activists does little to mask the horror
many experienced. One story stands out in particular, and COFO used it to spotlight the extent of the cruel and inhuman treatment inflicted on women, de-

spite the loud complaints issued to the local FBI and the Department of Justice. On 30 July, Police Chief Ben Collins arrested Mrs. Odessa Brooks with nine others as they wore antisegregation signs and walked in an orderly line toward City Hall. Pushed and prodded by the police, between twenty and twenty-five females were placed in a nine-by-nine cell built for a maximum of eight. They were not given any food or water for the rest of that sweltering day, and the next day's inedible breakfast consisted of a spoonful of unseasoned cold grits and one slice of cold bread. Conditions in the cell were intolerable, with overcrowding, no ventilation, and excessive heat. The minors were released that day, which left eight in that cell on the night of 31 July. The police, intent on breaking the resolve of the jailed women, turned on the heating system to heighten their discomfort. Brooks stated two weeks later, "My hair was as if it had been washed and sweat rolled down my face like rain." As the women tried to cool off, probably removing as much clothing as modestly possible, the male officers paraded in front of the cell, shouting curses and sexually charged epithets. Brooks recalled: "Police officers were always violating our privacy by peeping in the cell saying 'man if we could get in there—nigger women have some good ——.'"[11]

The next day, attorney R. Jess Brown appeared before a judge, who convicted the women of parading without a permit and sentenced each to thirty days plus a $101 fine. Brown entered a plea of nolo contendere (no contest), in keeping with the campaign's goals. The women's tormentors had every intention of shattering their spirit. Brooks, suffering profoundly from the heat and poor nutrition, asked for some aspirin, and after another uncomfortable night, Ben Collins ordered them outside in the Mississippi heat to cut grass with sling blades and hoes. Brooks said, "We were ordered to work under the threat that if we did not work we would be taken back to the cell and the heat would be turned on again." She became very ill, and a jail doctor saw her, dismissing her request for her own doctor's evaluation. She had suffered a heat stroke. When her husband attempted to visit her, Collins spat at him, saying, "Can't you keep that Bitch from up here marching?" Despite the severity of her symptoms, she remained in jail that night and most of the next day. At approximately 5:30 the following evening, after more than four days of torture, she was forced to post a $400 bond for her release and was immediately hospitalized for a week at the Sarah Brown Memorial Hospital at Mound Bayou.[12]

Police Chief Collins figured prominently in these complaints, as he had in previous years. African American activists in Clarksdale placed him on par with the infamous Eugene "Bull" Connor in Birmingham. Collins did not mind the comparison. He had become police chief the day before independence celebrations, 3 July 1961, after the resignation of Police Chief H. D. Sherck. Called "comically ignorant" by Aaron Henry, Collins did not have a good reputation, even among the white people of Clarksdale, although they averted their faces as he eagerly did their unpleasant business for them. *Clarksdale Press Reporter* Curtis Wilkie mused, "Long before hippies began to call cops 'pigs' later in the decade, Collins had the misfortune to look porcine." The board of the mayor and commissioners had voted to replace him, less than a year into the job, not for police brutality but for insubordination in relatively petty matters. The black population in Clarksdale had celebrated, revisiting a selection of Collins's "crimes" against the community—the arrest of the leaders, the arrest of Guy and Candi Carawan, and the incarceration of the youth a year earlier—and proclaimed that he would "forever be remembered and resented by freedom loving Negroes and whites of Clarksdale." Nevertheless, by the end of July he had been cleared of all charges, his services deemed too valuable to lose.[13]

Of all the blatant acts of brutality inflicted by the police that summer, and there were many, one in particular shocked activists. More than a dozen Clarksdale police savagely murdered a young black man named Ernest Jells on 20 September 1963.[14] Jells had argued with the shopkeeper of the Fair Deal Grocery over an alleged theft of some bananas. Earlier in the evening, he had been spotted slightly intoxicated at a local football game. Jells left the store between eleven and twelve that night, and the clerk followed him out and fired several shots in his wake. Police continued the chase and peppered him with bullets as he perched on top of a low building in Commerce Alley. Witnesses swore that Jells had no visible weapon, and one saw officers Petty and Mooreland driving and shooting while Jells ran for his life. Another source claimed that Jells suffered wounds before pleading with police to stop firing as he climbed the building. As the police shot indiscriminately, killing Jells, a resident of the Alley complained that bullets entered her home, barely missing her.

The local NAACP responded swiftly to the tragedy. Pigee and Charles Evers went to the funeral home to inspect the body. It affected Pigee profoundly. "I had gone to the funeral home and put my finger in the bullet holes in his back. I was trying to keep from hating anything white. After I left . . . I took the white sheets off my bed." Dismissing police claims, the NAACP stressed that "this murder cannot possibly be classified as self-defense."[15] Urging calm amid the boiling anger over the death of a popular young man, local leaders advocated nonviolence, directing the frustrated energy of the community toward supporting the ongoing boycott.

Leaders held up Jells's murder to the light. Knowing who had killed him, they pushed to explain *what* had killed him. Concluding that the system of segregation had the blood of Jells on its hands, the editorial in the branch's newsletter, probably written by secretary Pigee, provided a useful analogy of the bear and the snake to clarify the point and feed the fire:

> Negroes who are still foolish enough to believe that Mr. Charlie is their friend, is in for the same lesson that the bear learned when he picked up the rattlesnake on that cold day. When the snake got warm (doing pretty good on Negro patronage as the merchant of Fair Deal Grocery was) the snake then began to bite the bear (in this case the merchant shot the Negro). When the bear began to try to console the snake, with words of how kind the bear had been to the snake when the snake was cold and nearly dead, the answer that the snake gave was the answer Negroes can expect from the White Man, Mr. Bear, you knew I was a snake when you *picked me up*.[16]

Churches: A Mixed Blessing

As black Clarksdalians mourned the killing of Jells, many did so in the sanctuary of a church. If walls and pews could talk, those in church sanctuaries in black communities would wail with the memories of many a memorial or loss and rejoice with every communal victory. They could also tell us the names, dreams, and woes of every person who participated in the movement and attended the mass meetings. All of the city's civil rights leaders, including Pigee and Henry, faithfully occupied pews every Sunday. In Clarksdale, however, unlike in more urban parts of the South, black ministers did not stand at the forefront of the movement. Those in larger cities, sustained solely by their ministry, could afford to go against white leadership.[17] By 1963, at the height of the SCLC's national influence, prominent ministers like King, Ralph Abernathy, Fred Shuttlesworth, Jim Lawson, and Jim Bevel were the most visible civil rights activists in the country. But in rural and small-town Mississippi, most black ministers did not enjoy the financial independence that might have allowed them to preach any kind of liberation theology that denounced white supremacy as vigorously and defiantly as Shuttlesworth had in Birmingham. In other parts of the South, the murder of Jells might have propelled local ministers into action. That it did not in Clarksdale confirmed the tenuous position occupied by the black clergy in Mississippi.

Aaron Henry's tepid opinion of black religious organizations, and the lack of local political power they exerted in Clarksdale, dated to the 1950s. "Negro preachers in Mississippi during this era were a mixed blessing," he recalled. "They did most good for the spirit but not much for the problems on earth." He pointed out that the huge number of smaller churches, born out of internal strife and dissension, diluted the resources and strength of each. He criticized black ministers for not fighting for white concessions. "Still it seemed that preachers were always borrowing money or getting into situations where they were beholden to the white community. And most disgusting to me were the Negro preachers who frequently considered it their duty to assure whites that Negroes were happy living on the white man's terms," Henry remembered.[18] Vera Pigee criticized some black churches for never hosting meetings. After the bombing of Centennial Church, many institutions vacillated between activity and hesitation, as fear chipped away at faith. Disparaging that part of human nature that craves attention, Pigee dismissed those churches that took credit for projects like citizenship classes, turkey drives, and clothing and food drives, despite their lack of hands-on support.[19]

In a co-authored history of the movement activities of the local NAACP branch, Pigee, Henry, and H. Y. Hackett (branch treasurer) wrote that local ministers worked under a "veil of fear and apathy." They noted the lack of communication between the white clergy and the black clergy. In black churches, many clergymen did not reside in Clarksdale (probably they were traveling preachers with several churches) and therefore showed little interest in the local community. Ironically, many clergy who did reside in Clarksdale pastored outside of the city limits. All this, Pigee and the others concluded, resulted in "little real aggressive leadership" coming from the pulpit.[20]

Nevertheless, religion permeated African American political and secular life in Mississippi, across class lines. The name of God was frequently invoked as a source of strength. Pigee's written words, in particular, are liberally peppered with references to God and her faith. The often-celebrated religiosity of southern African Americans embodied a unique way of faith, where people, especially of older generations, lived, in author Melissa Greene's description, "on close, practical, and well-understood terms with God . . . where they expect justice in exchange for a lifetime of devotion."[21] In Clarksdale, some black ministers, affiliated with the larger congregations, lent their expertise, time, and energies to activism. R. L. Drew, Theodore Trammel, and J. D. Rayford were quiet movement leaders in the Clarksdale NAACP. They were exceptions to the rule in Coahoma County and other rural Bible Belt locales. Church sanctuaries and basements served as organizing sites for mass meetings, but laypeople, not the pastor, led the way.

Haven Methodist Church, the spiritual home of Henry and Pigee and less than a block from Centennial, hosted most of the mass meetings in Clarksdale. Established in 1880, the church had been debt free since 1946 and was therefore immune to the economic pressures that hamstrung many institutions seeking to be active in the movement. An imposing structure, with one of the largest sanctuaries in town, serving a large African American congregation over the years, the church was an important organizing site that boasted an impressive roster of speakers, ranging from outside ministers (King, Abernathy, and Shuttlesworth) to politicians (governors Cliff Finch and William Winter, attorney L. A. Ross, Congressman Mike Espy, and more recently Mayor Henry Espy) to movement figures (Roy Wilkins, Kivie Kaplan, Ruby Hurley, Aaron Henry, and Fannie Lou Hamer). The sanctuary frequently echoed with both religious and secular calls for freedom.[22]

The National Council of Churches gave strong support to the civil rights movement, establishing a Commission on Religion and Race in early June 1963, and President Kennedy's meeting with NCC leaders that June heightened its visibility. Trying to work on race relations in segregated churches remained an uphill struggle, and Mississippi became a focal point for the organization.[23] At Medgar Evers's funeral, Aaron Henry had approached the ministers to come to Clarksdale soon thereafter as it offered assistance in local struggles in its initial summer of operation. He categorized the NCC as "an organization with a seemingly unlimited supply of funds," and once again his flexibility opened a way for it to begin a ministry in Mississippi through Clarksdale, in his direct sphere of influence. In early July 1963, five white ministers from the NCC came to Clarksdale to "listen and do a little talking." A. Dale Fiers, Arthur W. Walmsely, Eugene L. Smith, Grover Bagby, and A. Dudley Ward received a warm welcome from black Clarksdalians but were completely rebuffed by white ministers and laypeople. At the end of July, yet more NCC representatives came seeking an audience with the mayor, who had nothing to say, later instructing them to stay out of local matters.[24] Approximately thirty ministers came to Clarksdale from ten other states on 6 August 1963 for a "service of Christian unity" at the First Baptist Church, with invitations extended to white and black ministers from across the state and from the city. Each minister received an injunction to obstruct any participation in demonstrations in the city (they were not spared the wrath of Ben Collins), and so all attempts at attracting publicity and promoting spiritual understanding failed.[25]

Given its failure to directly appeal to church members, the NCC offered legal aid in Clarksdale to support activists and sent a full-time lawyer, Jack Pratt, to Mississippi to forge stronger links with other civil rights organizations.[26] Thus the NCC served as minister-counselors to activists rather than continuing attempts to reason with local white church members. Wanting to provide a more permanent and long-lasting service to Mississippi, in the fall of 1963 discussions for a comprehensive community development program in the Delta led to the creation of the Delta Ministry, headquartered in Greenville, on 1 September 1964.[27] The tiny staff of up to fifteen full-time people served the Delta region extensively, from providing direct relief for displaced farmworkers to establishing the Freedom Information Service. With no coordinators in Clarksdale, however, its institutional presence in Coahoma County remained negligible. These people continued to lean on and draw from their faith and to use local churches as sites of relative safety, but rarely did their pastors use the pulpit to organize for civil rights.

"We Stand at the Crossroads": The 1963 Freedom Vote

Pigee, Henry, and Hackett's narrative document, dating from around the end of September 1963 and outlining the civil rights activities of the branch since its inception, clearly indicated the summer's frustrations. They wrote: "We stand at the crossroads of what must be done in the future."[28] Activities in the summer of 1963, from the jail-ins to the NCC presence, also included continued and robust efforts around voting rights. The chosen road to the future taken in the fall months of 1963 galvanized these efforts further.

Throughout this story, from the Progressive Voters' League in the postwar years to 1963, voter registration campaigns dominated the civil rights agenda in the South. The vote had been denied since the 1890s, mostly by local registrars, who rebuffed would-be black voters using both state law and creative chicanery. Most white supremacists believed that black people did not have the ability to participate in civil society—that they lacked the wherewithal or the education to exercise their civic duties responsibly. Moreover, many whites argued that African Americans did not want to vote. Black registration figures for Coahoma County were dismal. In 1899, 990 whites were over twenty-one, and 89 percent were registered voters, whereas of the 6,388 potential black voters, only 240 (3.8 percent) were registered. Black voter percentages hovered between 3.8 and 4.5 percent for the next sixty-five years (white percentages dropped to an average of just under 50 percent). By 1962, despite years of voter registration campaigns, the figure rose only to 7.6 percent (of 14,004 potential black voters, only 1,061 were registered). Interestingly, the white percentage rose dramatically, from 57 percent in 1960 to 73 percent in 1962.[29]

Aggravated by the constant obstacles and fired up by the surging activism across the South and in their back and front yards, activists in Mississippi decided to prove their critics wrong for the record. They aimed to demonstrate that, given a fair opportunity in a safe environment, African Americans would register and vote in large numbers. The result was the Freedom Vote, a campaign in which unofficial registration and mock voting would demonstrate black ability and desire as well as the potential power in numbers.

Many veterans have credited Allard Lowenstein with the origination of the Freedom Vote idea. After Evers's slaying, Aaron Henry called on the friend he had met in college, a political scientist and lawyer, to brainstorm how to resuscitate movements beaten down by legal and physical repression, like Clarksdale's injunctions stalling direct action and then the intense police cruelty there. With Bill Higgs, the only white lawyer in Mississippi who dared take civil rights cases, driven out by scandal, Henry went to his extensive Rolodex list of contacts and solicited the help of someone already proven in his activism and well prepared for the task. Called a "peripatetic Pied Piper," Lowenstein's charisma among students nationwide had created a network of followers through the National Student Association. He now called on them to raise funds and gather resources, traveling to Stanford and Yale to personally recruit students to work on this specific project in early October of the new academic year.[30] Lowenstein may have provided extra hands, schooled minds, and added visibility, but COFO activists already in the trenches did most of the legwork and took on all of the risk.

By the end of October 1963, preparations for the statewide Freedom Vote were well under way, and notices went to black communities to turn out the vote on three consecutive days in early November (2, 3, and 4 November). Clarksdale's Aaron Henry was on the ballot for governor; the lieutenant governor candidate was Rev. Edwin King, Tougaloo College's white chaplain. Henry's hometown hummed with increased movement activity. Indeed, that August, a prototype for the statewide Freedom Vote had already taken place in Clarksdale. The day before thirty-eight local activists, including Vera Pigee, boarded a chartered Greyhound bus bound for the historic March on Washington, thousands of Coahoma County's unregistered African Americans took part in a mock vote for governor concurrent with the actual primary.

After weeks of picketing and marching and then the severe and persistent police brutality, activists were fired up during what they had called Freedom Week (25 to 31 August). Organized quickly through church networks and mass meetings, Coahoma County's Freedom Ballot Campaign on 27 August had attracted 5,121 ballots in local churches, businesses, and block precincts. Of the votes cast, 5,047 went to candidate Aaron Henry, thirty-three went to Paul Johnson, and forty-one went to J. P. Coleman.[31] The local practice run proved that the campaign was more than a gimmick to allow black people to "act like" white people, as the press had mocked earlier. The local branch had done its homework. The next newsletter had quoted a policeman harassing citizens exercising their right to vote: "Niggers are up here voting and on welfare!" Mocking the officer for "feeling a basic insecurity," the writer, probably Pigee (as secretary), continued that "he was in violation of Federal Law when he interfered with the right of these citizens to peacefully cast their ballots. We feel that this ignorant soul did not realize the implications of his actions." Satisfied with the high turnout and the successful trip to Washington, the writer added, "When Negroes, in reality, begin to go to the polls in this manner, the day will come when Justice and fair play will be the by word of this community."[32] This experience also offered COFO a successful model to replicate across Mississippi.

The statewide Freedom Vote in November dramatized the eagerness of thousands of Mississippi blacks to take up their positions in the political arena and defend themselves against violence, wielding a ballot rather than a picket sign or a rifle. For those fortunate to be formally registered, organizers urged that they write in Aaron Henry's name on the ballot rather than vote for the official race-baiting candidates. Highly organized and involving all of the COFO constituent organizations, leaders wanted eligible black voters to have the full experience of and power that comes from voting, insisting on formal procedures. Clarksdale became a campaign headquarters, and approximately sixty Yale and fourteen Stanford University students drove south to help, running errands and dispatching information to newspapers and their contacts around the country.[33]

The Freedom Vote campaign was short and effective. Estimates of numbers of actual votes cast vary from between 82,000 and 85,000, but even at the lower figure these results are impressive, particularly with the harassment and hostility that workers experienced and the fact that only 20,000 African Americans were actually registered to vote. Police arrested and threatened activists and the students statewide, interactions that surprised the students, who had had little idea about what to expect and no idea that their privilege would not shield them. These police actions actually did two things that provided fuel to what had been an ebbing fire. First, the stunned students rallied their peers in their home institutions, who raised money and raised hell. Second, COFO activists closely watched the hysterical reaction from white Mississippi to the students' presence and the heightened surveillance (from the police on the students and from the national press on Mississippi) that the campaign generated, all of which planted the seeds for Freedom Summer in an election year.[34]

An oft-told story of police activity during the Freedom Vote occurred in Clarksdale. Lowenstein, Stephen Bingham, and John Speh were arrested there on 23 October. Two integrated cars had traveled around town that day, with Aaron Henry and Bob Moses campaigning with them. Bingham remembered that they had been careful to comply with traffic laws, knowing that the police were looking for any excuse to stop cars. After they paused at Vera Pigee's house to drop off some students staying overnight, the police's patience ran out. Pulled over first for running a nonexistent stop sign, they paid the eight-dollar fine on the spot before dropping off Henry and Moses at Henry's home. Then, as the last three searched for a hotel, the police arrested them for loitering and violating the city curfew as they crossed the street from their car to the segregated Alcazar Hotel. Inside of the Coahoma County jail, officers verbally threatened them. Thinking on his feet, Lowenstein loudly identified himself as a lawyer, demanding his right to a phone call. Placing a collect call to Franklin D. Roosevelt III in the middle of the night, making sure to spell out his full name slowly for emphasis, Lowenstein quickly improvised an animated conversation, casually invoking the name of President Kennedy for all to hear. Not knowing if he was bluffing (and accounts vary about whether or not Lowenstein had dialed a fake number) but not willing to take the risk, the police did not touch them for the rest of their jail stay, which ended when Aaron Henry posted bail.[35]

Organized by COFO and its constituent organizations, the statewide Freedom Vote was an enormous step for black Mississippi, harnessing the fires burning brightly around the state. In local beauty salons, barbershops, churches, living rooms, and businesses, local folks congregated to retell their stories of voting for the first time. They marveled at the sight of so many people waiting in line, chatting to each other, and anticipating their next opportunity to repeat the exercise. The campaign amassed thousands of addresses, names, and contacts for activists (around 70,000, in fact) and politicized whole communities in civic action.[36] It also initiated a suit against WLBT television station, whose owners refused to allow COFO to purchase on-air advertising time. Eventually, the station would lose its license because of its discriminatory policies.[37]

These roaring fires reduced to a flicker with the assassination of President Kennedy just before Thanksgiving. Convulsed with grief, African Americans looked earnestly yet warily to the hastily sworn-in southerner, Texan Lyndon Baines Johnson. During the 1960 election, staffer Harris Wofford had characterized Johnson as "an essential ingredient" to carry most of the civil rights load that Kennedy inherited.[38] Now a new president himself, what would he do?

While the stunned nation mourned and watched LBJ ascend to the highest office, the national NAACP's leadership felt threatened. The Freedom Vote campaign had solidified COFO as the dominant civil rights organization in Mississippi and fanned the anxieties over turf. Henry's written assurances to Wilkins that the state NAACP maintained institutional prominence barely masked the fact that, in reality, SNCC, with numerous grassroots workers in local communities, now had the most direct influence. The orientation toward direct action led by younger people had pulled more locals into movement activity. In 1964, most, if not all, direct activity siphoned through COFO from the different constituent groups. Indeed, within the state, most activists wore their COFO hats rather than differentiate themselves by their home organizational affiliations.[39] Only in Clarksdale, Jackson, and a few other towns with strong NAACP branch presence did the NAACP's influence prevail. The national officers considered themselves to be at a crossroads and scrambled to reassert the organization through Charles Evers, given that the national office was not part of COFO. Writing in February 1964, Gloster Current directed Evers that "with respect to COFO, please convey to Mississippi branches that this temporary organization is not to assume the functions of the NAACP branches except in the area of registration and voting and only in those areas where COFO has been assigned by Southern Regional Conference the job of coordinating the registration campaign." Clearly demarcating the line between COFO's role and the NAACP's, Current continued, "We shall expect NAACP branches to carry out the education, housing, transportation, employment, and other activities in the name of the organization which chartered them and no other group."[40]

Sensing the national office's panic over turf, some members of COFO maneuvered around the situation. For example, COFO co-chair of the Welfare and

Relief Program, Annell Ponder (who also worked with SCLC), wrote to Wilkins in early 1964 that although the program had existed under Vera Pigee and Dave Dennis in Clarksdale and Greenwood for the past few years, aid was desperately needed to reach low-income counties. She asked Wilkins to enlist local NAACP chapters by conducting clothing drives, cleverly manipulating the headquarters to contact and instruct the branches—in reality, as membership in the organizations remained fluid, such drives most likely already existed.[41]

Anxiety about Henry's leadership and involvement with other organizations increased nonetheless. Henry's national visibility, his popularity, and his penchant for the limelight made it almost impossible to stay ahead of him as events on the ground moved quickly and demanded immediate response. The national office fretted about the ramifications Freedom Summer would have on the organization, particularly when Henry and Charles Evers flagrantly practiced flexible associations and embraced COFO's constituent parts and strategies.[42] Henry, the unpaid state president, remembered: "I feel that my role as a volunteer gives me much more freedom or levity to do those things that Aaron wants to do. . . . You see, nobody can fire me 'cause there ain't nobody hired me. . . . I earn my living at the Fourth Street Drug Store, and that's the thing that pays the bills."[43] Representing the national office, a frustrated Gloster Current wrote to Evers, the highest-ranking paid NAACP officer in the state: "Every effort should be made to encourage Dr. Henry to wean himself away from that group. This has to be done carefully, because Aaron belongs to the school of thought that we can carry our own NAACP work by being involved in a lot of organizations. We know, this cannot be done. For it merely confuses things and distributes credit among other organizations."[44] COFO, or at least the NAACP's engagement with COFO, was not to survive this conflict.

Henry managed his roles in the NAACP and in COFO in a delicate balancing act. The friction between the NAACP and COFO was about more than turf, although that remained a primary concern for the NAACP. There were deep ideological differences also. The national office suspiciously eyed SNCC's funding sources, noting contributions from extreme leftist organizations. COFO workers in Mississippi, however, held Henry in high regard. His open attitude and lack of concern for organizational purity or loyalty won their trust. Ivanhoe Donaldson recalled: "Despite the general contempt in SNCC ranks for NAACP 'conservatives,' Aaron Henry enjoyed a personal respect like that accorded to Amzie Moore." As Donaldson articulated, many of the young people in SNCC saw the NAACP as conservative, slow-moving, and pompous. Amzie Moore shifted his attentions to the youthful organization, and Ella Baker's experiences with the

FIG. 4.4. Aaron Henry's Fourth Street Drugstore. (Aaron Henry Collection, T/013, Tougaloo Civil Rights Collection, Mississippi Department of Archives and History)

NAACP and the SCLC motivated her to nurture SNCC's organizational foundation to develop local leadership and participatory democracy wherever it could. For Henry, organizations functioned to serve the community, not the dictate of the leaders. His personal influence in managing the Mississippi movement through his state NAACP presidency and his leadership of COFO rendered his Fourth Street Drugstore in Clarksdale an "important SNCC way station in the Delta."[45]

The Fourth Street Drugstore was, as Curtis Wilkie described it, an "old-fashioned pharmacy," a one-story, red brick building bearing a neon sign, "4th St. Drugs," and a Borden's Ice Cream sign. A jukebox stood near the door next to a rack of civil rights literature. On the left, a fountain counter ran halfway to the back, and during the summer, civil rights workers escaped the heat by sipping Coke or ice water or licking ice cream cones. The rest of the left side and all of the right contained full display cases. Behind them, floor-to-ceiling shelves held goods, with the prescription section at the back. Henry wrapped the medicine he sold in the latest issue of the *Student Voice* (the SNCC publication), which he piled on one counter. Scenic Mississippi postcards were sold side by side with pictures and descriptions of Fred Shuttlesworth and Martin Luther King Jr.[46]

The drugstore was the organizing site where COFO's energy circulated in Clarksdale. Aside from the Freedom House, the drugstore, and Aaron Henry's backyard, the location of many outdoor cookouts and parties, volunteers who came to Clarksdale in the summer of 1964 had little interaction with the local NAACP branch. The angst of the national office had seeped into the chapter through Vera Pigee and her own real issues with what she saw as a breach of etiquette and authority. As such, Clarksdale became the microcosm of the clash of ideologies between and within groups, despite the common goal—the pursuit of freedom.

Clarksdale's Freedom Summer: Fire and Friction

The national office of the NAACP did not hold the monopoly on the internal frustrations swirling around and within the Mississippi movements. Some local NAACP workers expressed mixed feelings about the plans for predominantly white volunteers to work in the state in the summer of 1964. On the one hand, they knew the students would attract national attention to their locale, but they also feared that they, and their work, would get lost in the shuffle. Members and their local movements found themselves at another crossroads. In Clarksdale, Vera Pigee did not mince words as the arrival of summer volunteers in the Delta signaled the end of state youth councils' unchallenged dominance. She had worked alongside CORE's Dave Dennis with relief campaigns and with SNCC staff like Lafayette Surney the previous summer as Clarksdale's direct-action campaign swung into full gear and numbers of arrests rose into the triple digits. In 1964, however, Pigee wrote that what she called the "SNCC kid catch" had helped destroy virtually every youth council in the state except, due to her presence, Coahoma County's.[47]

Roy Wright, a devoted Clarksdale Youth Council member in the early 1960s, wrote to the national NAACP office, protesting the volunteers' presence: "As you know, other organizations are now working and seeking members in the South. We too would have changed over had it not been for the additional efforts of Mrs. Pigee to encourage us to hold on to the ideas, tactics, etc., we fought for before these organizations were conceived." He blamed SNCC "ego-trippers" for going into a town with no resources and creating "unrest toward the people in the community who had emerged as leaders of the civil rights movement, who made it possible for SNCC to move into the communities." Wright, who graduated from high school that June, had inadvertently caused his family to have to leave the land they had farmed for forty years—his civil rights activities had brought his father a series of excessive traffic fines for imaginary violations. Yet Wright continued his activism and made full use of Pigee's warm welcome to her home when he came into town, as did many in the Youth Council. His own personal sacrifices for the movement translated into complete loyalty to Pigee, and subsequently he chose his path at his own personal crossroads when the students arrived.[48]

The volunteers pulled into Clarksdale in two organized waves, completing training in Oxford, Ohio, and traveling south through consecutive Saturday nights, arriving on Sunday mornings. It was, as Henry later proclaimed, "the greatest sociological experience this country has ever had," and no one really knew what would happen.[49] The students specializing in voter registration were mostly trained in the first session, and they arrived first.

Matthew Zwerling, a twenty-year-old senior studying general science at the University of Rochester, who had set up a Friends of SNCC Chapter there when he had met John Lewis, came in the first wave. His family was close friends with the Goodmans—both families lived in the same apartment building—and he had driven to Ohio from New York with Andrew Goodman (one of the three workers murdered soon after). Both were excited and eager to get to work. Thinking back to that car ride, the last time he saw his friend, he said that they were "anticipating the goals of the summer program being met and happy to be a part of it." Instead of fear, "we just focused more on the positives."[50]

Zwerling was one of the few who drove a personal car down to the Magnolia State. He was careful to change his New York license plates promptly to decrease suspicion, but local officials knew his car immediately anyway. After his safe return, his parents showed him a list they had acquired from the police showing that the Ku Klux Klan had tagged his car straightaway, as it had most of the volunteers' vehicles. Meticulous plans did not always prevent information from reaching trigger-happy hands—the abduction and murder of Goodman with his compatriots during the project's first week proved that.

Bob and Lisa Mandel, a young married couple from California, and James Jones, a local African American working in Clarksdale who had gone to the training sessions, traveled in the car with Zwerling. Zwerling drove most of the way, across the Tennessee mountains through the night, reaching the Delta around daybreak, ahead of the bus. He recalled: "I was driving along looking at the cotton fields, I had never seen cotton fields and just taking it all in, I was driving about like maybe 30 miles an hour, for about five minutes or so. James Jones who was sitting next to me said, 'Listen are we going to speed up and drive here or what?'" Aware that dawdling attracted attention, particularly in an integrated car with New York tags, the local Mississippian pushed the visitor to speed up past the scenery that he took for granted. Driving straight to the Freedom House, exhausted, they awaited their assignments and lodging information. In one of his first letters home, Zwerling was not impressed with his summer hometown: "Clarksdale is not only a place you wouldn't want to live in—you'd never want to visit here."[51]

Charles Stewart also came to Clarksdale as part of the first batch of volunteers from Ohio. He recalled his arrival: "Our entry into Clarksdale was something less than spectacular. We arrived shortly after dawn, after an all night trip by chartered bus, which left us on the sidewalk in the midst of a crowd of Negroes who, apparently not knowing what to make of us, ignored us studiously." Aaron Henry was not present because of miscommunication about their arrival time. The police surrounded them immediately, ordering the now-alert travelers to move on and not block the sidewalk. They retreated to a black church, circled by police cars, until someone called the pastor to help them get to the Freedom House.[52]

Nebraskan Zoya Zeman, a rising senior at Scripps College, in California, came on the bus that left Ohio at 3 P.M. with the second group of volunteers a week later. She turned twenty-one the very day of departure (27 June) and took great delight stating that "participating in Freedom Summer became my first act of personal and legal 'emancipation' since I had been able to sign my own papers and to proceed without otherwise-required parental consent."[53] Zeman remembered a fitful night on the southbound bus as volunteers tried to get some rest and quietly contemplated the task they had undertaken, knowing that they might disappear like Goodman and his colleagues, James Chaney and Michael Schwerner. Joe Youngerman, from Illinois, who had just graduated from Yale, sat next to her. Both of their fathers were doctors, and he had plans to go to medical school (he would become a psychiatrist). Years afterward he admitted to Zeman that on the ride, "I was trying to memorize the signposts and the street names of every city we were going through so I could find my way back if they burned the bus."[54]

The bus did not burn, and it arrived at the Clarksdale station intact early on 28 June. Disembarking on a Sunday morning, most local people were at home, eating breakfast, polishing shoes, straightening ties, and fixing hats, preparing for a morning of worship. They were not on the streets, driving to work, or shopping in stores to witness the arrival of the outsiders. Those who had come a week earlier waited to greet them, as did the police. Told by their comrades to hurry out of the bus, their suitcases were thrown into waiting cars and they walked in a single file to the Freedom House. Under surveillance, they moved in an orderly and rapid fashion to avoid arrest for loitering or obstructing the sidewalk. Police cars cruised next to the walking students, calling out at times or just silently staring at each one in turn. Zeman recollected: "We'd been told to keep our eyes to the ground and not respond to them in any way. I remember that it was very hot and humid and that this was a frightening parade."[55]

Zeman probably was not the only fearful one that morning. Local and state authorities also did not know what to expect, so they anticipated the worst and prepared for war. In COFO's prospectus for Freedom Summer, the author wrote, "As the winds of change grow stronger, the threatened political elite of Mississippi becomes more intransigent and fanatical in its support of the status quo."[56] Governor Paul Johnson and the state legislature prepared for Freedom Summer with grit and determination. The onslaught of pre-summer publicity had given the state's white power brokers ample time to write new laws. Enacted in late April and May, these laws curbed activities like marches and other demonstrations and were designed to put as many offenders in jail as possible. Akin to ordinances already in place in Clarksdale, the laws restricted demonstrations and leafleting, extended police authority and jurisdiction, prohibited picketing, and increased penalties for violating city ordinances. The *Clarksdale Press Register* assured its white population worried about the "invasion" that "Mississippi is better prepared today to handle its own problems, through proper law enforcement agencies, than ever before in its history."[57]

Preparedness did not necessarily dissipate concern. Reporter Curtis Wilkie was assigned to the mass meetings and rallies and eventually befriended Aaron Henry and other local activists. As for the summer of 1964, he recalled: "The prospect that a new foreign element was about to be injected into the community troubled Clarksdale's establishment. Already besieged by NAACP lawsuits, street demonstrations, and a civil rights bill gathering strength in Congress, the city sensed the potential for a major disturbance." The young journalist, excited at the prospect of reporting on national news-making activities, wrote sympathetic pieces and tried to position them on the front pages. However, Joseph Ellis, the publisher, laid down a strict policy that relegated civil rights news coverage to the interior, unless major developments warranted front-page treatment.[58]

The local press did, in fact, report on most of the activities during Freedom Summer, but the "major developments" were stories of activists arrested for allegedly breaking laws, or news that did not support any movement progress. Stories about the activists winning in the courts or having good results from campaigns never made the front page. To read the local paper during the summer of 1964, one would not hear of the multiple incidents of reprisals or violence against volunteers or black locals. Instead, editorials encouraged readers to treat the summer's activities with humor and tolerance and not to let workers provoke abuse and any confrontation. Calling the volunteers "immature collegians and over-ripe missionaries" or referring to them as the "pitiful platoons," the tone mocked the entire program in an effort to negate its effects.[59]

Clarksdale hosted four community center workers, seven or eight Freedom School workers, and the same number for voter registration, with other volunteers coming and going throughout the summer.[60] There were three black SNCC staff in Clarksdale all summer, James Jones, Doris Newman, and Lafayette Surney. Freedom Schools constituted a major component of Freedom Summer. Clarksdale, along with Vicksburg and Mileston, opened the first schools on 2 July with thirty students each. In less than two weeks, COFO reported over 1,500 students from ages eight to eighty-two, attending twenty-five schools, with six more planned to teach at least 500 more. Morning courses included leadership development, remedial reading, writing, mathematics, and history, as well as lessons on contemporary issues. Afternoons were less structured, giving students opportunities to work with COFO staff in the other programs, which offered additional enrichment experiences.

Volunteers ran the Freedom Schools, which were designed to teach basic literacy and social tools to facilitate development as critical thinkers and actors. The principal goal for the schools was to challenge students' curiosity about their world and teach basic literacy skills in the process. Instruction used concrete "case studies" like political campaigning, which included lessons in politics and historical legacies, along with exercises such as writing press releases and leaflets. The Freedom Summer prospectus promised that "by using a multi-dimensional, integrated program, the curriculum can be more easily absorbed into the direct experience of the students."[61] Officially open to all who wanted to attend, not just African Americans, volunteers were asked to approach white families and invite them to participate in COFO summer activities. None ever did.

Zoya Zeman (focusing on health and literacy), Margaret (Margie) Hazelton (health and library), Mark Fast (recreation programming and literacy), and David Batzka (center director) were assigned to a community center that did not exist when they had arrived. A run-down building a block from the Freedom House, previously a bar and restaurant, was donated a day or two after they appeared, and they spent the following days cleaning, painting, and fixing up the place before they could actually begin their assigned work. In general, the community centers, also open to all, were designed for adults and housed a library, sewing facilities, child care classes, health programs, and additional classes on black history. Not only were centers to be places for education, training, literacy (with the library and through classes), and health care for those who did not receive state provisions, but they were also to be safe spaces for recreation—movie screenings, sports, drama, and arts and crafts, for example.[62] One of Zeman's and Hazelton's jobs was to engage the community to sign up for classes or to volunteer their time to teach classes, with the goal of creating programming that would sustain itself after the summer's activities.

In reality, Clarksdale's center, much to the disappointment of the workers, functioned more as a child care facility than as a space for adult learning and enrichment, although a well-attended sewing class, run by Etrula Trotter, a black teen from Memphis visiting family in Clarksdale over the summer, generated some excitement, as did a leather-working class run by local Monroe Whitfield. Workers estimated that between thirty and forty youngsters came into the center during the day, but lack of adult response meant that other programs fell "flat." Margie Hazelton noted that they had spent so much time and energy working on the building itself and planning the classes that they had not done the canvassing and educational work in the community to advertise the programming sufficiently. She also wrote with exasperation about the "chaotic" situation: "We're all working with frazzled nerves and hoarse voices—these kids can really get on your nerves—but we keep hoping we're doing something for them in the long run. . . . Even though the adult response is nil . . . if we can just stimulate one little guy or gal—the summer is worthwhile for me."[63]

COFO also planned "special projects" for the summer. These were specific to communities and the resources available. Zoya Zeman was a quiet, petite, and unthreatening blonde, perfect for the role of educating white people in the community. In her assigned role as a community center worker, she would go around town advertising the center's programming to both black and white families. Folks would stop her as she walked on the sidewalk to ask her about why she was in town, but they rarely liked what they heard: "The expressions on their faces through the whole conversation were those I had pictured to myself many times before this; they looked disgusted and amazed at our willingness to degrade ourselves." She was invited by a couple of white families to talk to them—folks were generally trying to understand what all the fuss was about, feeling that they had treated "their" black people well and genuinely

FIG. 4.5. Local children at Clarksdale's COFO community center during Freedom
Summer in 1964. (Photo by Rev. Frazer Thomason, Hazelton Freedom Summer
Collection, McCain Library and Archives, University of Southern Mississippi)

cared about the well-being of those close to their families. One particular interaction around the dining room table of a prominent white family best captures
the confusion and resistance many white people in Clarksdale and around the
state felt toward the young volunteers. Zeman recounted that her hosts included "quite an angry [man], but his wife was very kind, and his son was very
troubled about race relations."[64]

The Freedom Summer prospectus vaguely and briefly described a project
for a few workers to research the white society from the inside, "to survey attitudes and record reactions to summer happenings." The extent of that project
was not publicized, even to volunteers, and most of the researchers are unknown. Californian Stan Boyd was one of the few on this secret mission, and
in Clarksdale. He had volunteered to participate in Freedom Summer, and
during his training in Oxford, Ohio, he expressed his preference for doing research to learn more about white attitudes toward the race issue. His interest
prompted organizers to ask him to do intelligence work, and he created a com-

plicated ruse to successfully infiltrate the tight-knit white community. Completely undercover, posing as a student doing research for a master's thesis on race relations to counter the media's distortion of white southerners, he knew that he "would have no elaborate safeguards and telephone checks, and [would] have to depend on [his] wits and common sense to avoid trouble."[65]

Boyd carefully thought out how to make his entry into Mississippi, contacting the district's congressman in Washington, D.C., Jamie Whitten, whose office (after carefully sizing up the young man clad in a new suit) advised him to contact the mayor of Clarksdale (and mention the D.C. visit) and stay in the main hotel at the center of town, the historic Alcazar on Third Street. Boyd mused, "Here was a Southern contradiction I was to encounter repeatedly in Clarksdale: if you're considered a critical stranger . . . you can expect great hostility, animosity and no cooperation; if you seek to understand and abide by the prevailing customs, you will be treated to some of the finest hospitality in the country, and doors will open wide."[66] He entered Clarksdale just like the other COFO volunteers, by bus, and like them, sat sleeplessly as he contemplated his fate. Ironically, he was on the same bus from Memphis as the second group carrying Zeman, Youngerman, and others to Clarksdale, and he panicked a little that his cover would be blown before he even arrived. Even though the integrated group of volunteers did not recognize him from his brief time in Oxford and he wore a suit, he was a stranger arriving on the same bus. Separating from the crowd, he walked quickly to the hotel a block or two away and did not attract any attention.

Boyd balanced on a knife-edge as he negotiated within the white community, building trust and collecting information but also, as part of his research, traveling into black sections of town and trying to get African Americans to open up to him and give their honest opinions. He introduced himself at the Freedom House and told the volunteers about his undercover work, if nothing else as a safety precaution in case something happened to him. Together, they planned how to make contact every few days to check his whereabouts. While all the white people he talked to were curious about him and continually gauged his reaction to their comments about the "niggers," he had clear access to the top of the social structure. He talked to Mayor W. S. Kincade (the one who had forbidden the black school band from marching at the Christmas Parade in 1961), Joseph Ellis (editor of the *Clarksdale Press Register*), Semmes Luckett (the school board's attorney), and bank president Eddie Peacock Jr. Boyd's infiltration revealed several important insights not visible from the outside. For one, there were many more moderates in Clarksdale and in the rest of the state than there were audible moderate voices in the political discourse. The solid South was never solid. For instance, he considered Ellis to be a more moderate voice—he used the paper to "work quietly for racial harmony and peace," although he did favor segregation.[67]

He spoke to the bank president about the Citizens' Council and was told that with 700 enrolled, they had not met in two years and "was just there in case it were ever needed." However, he learned that a smaller group of men existed, the Committee of Fifteen, who handled problems as they arose. Originating from the Clarksdale Bar Association in 1962, it consulted the police, mayor, and commissioners about issues. Five lawyers, including Semmes Luckett, the two major bank presidents, four or five major planters, and two or three important local industry representatives made up the membership, and they worked "quietly and effectively behind the scenes." Boyd did not name the members in his thesis, he just gave their positions, but he regularly relayed the information in reports to COFO. Boyd did write, however, that "most of the citizens of Clarksdale think they elect their town leaders, but in reality, the crucial decisions are made by this small group of self-appointed men."[68] He also noted that the black community's push for a biracial committee, if granted, would be only symbolic, as they would have no authority unless members of the Committee of Fifteen were included or supported it, and then the committee would be used to delay any further activity such as protesting. This scenario actually occurred later that year as a community action agency brought federal money into Clarksdale and mandated a biracial committee; but the group consisted of many of these conservatives, and its work was stymied as a result.

Boyd was not completely isolated from the other volunteers. The weekly phone calls maintained communication, and as part of his research he could justify going to the Freedom House on occasion to "interview" volunteers. Knowing that Zoya Zeman wanted to have more contact with white people in town, he had invited her to that fateful dinner at the house of a prominent leader.

> I think he asked me if she was a nigger or not but in any case I said she was white so she came and in the course of the dinner he asked her point blank would she marry a nigger and I don't know if she corrected the word "nigger" but I know she said "well which one?" That did not go down too well. Their host got upset, especially when she said "well it would depend on

their character and so on—education, everything." . . . He couldn't stomach the idea that here was a white girl who would actually consider marrying a black man. . . . He was so upset that he had to excuse himself from the table and go and leave and never see us again.[69]

Abandoned at the table, the wife continued her gracious southern hospitality, but neither Boyd nor Zeman ever forgot that interaction.

Many other programs occurred during the summer, tied into the project itself. Of these, several landed in Clarksdale. In New York City, Tom Levin and others established the Medical Committee for Human Rights in June to provide medical and moral support for the summer volunteers. They sent teams of three from the New York area (a doctor, a nurse, and a dentist) to locations for one-week stays. About ninety-eight personnel worked in the state. Clarksdale hosted the Medical Committee for Human Rights staff, one of seven communities to do so. The staff not only attended to volunteers (with ailments ranging from diarrhea and upset stomachs to salt deficiency and heat rashes) but also went around to rural areas to listen to people and offer medical advice. Also, the NCC trained clergy members to provide moral support and to advise and work to bring unity with white Christians.[70]

In many ways, this aspect of the project, outreach to white communities, proved dangerous and ineffective. Lew Sitzer from Los Angeles summed it up early in the summer: "As far as changing the white folks, I've already expressed my doubts about what can be accomplished. These folks have deeply entrenched values about a certain way of life."[71] White students found resistance even when trying to find a place to worship on Sunday. Margie Hazelton noted that she, along with David Batzka and Paul Kendall, tried to enter the First Christian Church on 5 July, only to be read a thirty-minute statement at the door explaining why the church would not admit civil rights workers.[72] Some volunteers did manage to attend a few services in other churches over the summer—the pastor at First Methodist greeted the workers who came to his church, for instance—but overall, church doors closed firmly in their faces.

Volunteers wrote home, not only to kin and friends, but to their church communities, elected representatives, and colleges, to report on their experiences and activities. Hazelton wrote regularly to her congregation at the Woodmere church in Detroit; and Matt Zwerling wrote home with reports, which his father, a well-connected psychiatrist, Israel Zwerling, used to lobby senators, congressmen, and even the president.[73] At least in Clarksdale, Freedom Summer seemed to change the volunteers profoundly. They received a radical education far away from their lives of relative privilege. From their host towns in Mississippi, they shared their education with the people closest to them. Firsthand reports scribbled or typed hastily in letters inspired many parents to become involved, if only to ensure the safe return of their children. Many lobbied local and national lawmakers, like the Zwerlings did, in order to keep the spotlight on their children in danger. Just as black parents became increasingly politicized as their children offered themselves on the front line, movement leaders anticipated similar reactions from white parents—and from their representatives in Washington. Communication with those out of the state was encouraged, anticipated, and welcomed—an explicit goal for the summer was to bring large numbers of students to not only be more effective in the face of police threats but also to educate the government and the public about the dire situation in Mississippi.[74] Most, if not all, of the volunteers returned to their institutions changed and made choices throughout their lives that continued their activism and radical thinking. Some moved into other social movements in the coming years; others changed their professional goals to focus on social justice in one form or another.

Along with the special projects, Freedom Schools, and community centers, voter registration also occupied much of the volunteers' time. Matthew Zwerling spent a lot of time canvassing in Riverton, a black neighborhood in Clarksdale on the other side of the Sunflower River, and was optimistic. Writing home less than two weeks after his arrival, he documented that he had called a meeting at the biggest church in town to "fire up the people a little." He put all his hope in the mass meeting to get his allotted quota of names in one fell swoop, and he wrote earnestly, "A lot hinges on this meeting—if it really works out I'll feel that I've done something direct and important (even if there is a major turnout—I'll feel good—but the real breakthrough is getting the community to do all this on their own)." The meeting did not go as he had hoped. About fifty attended, and due to the lack of ministers, Zwerling himself led the congregation in songs and prayers. However, he still sought a qualitative breakthrough, a spontaneous community movement that would move things faster, but "we're pitifully far from that," he opined.[75]

Student volunteers achieved only mixed success getting African Americans on the rolls. In Clarksdale, the registrar closed the courthouse in July for over a week for a bogus excuse, but the workers' mandate was to minimize hostility and potential conflict with the white community and focus on the independent party registration. Their principal project in this regard was to register voters (Freedom Registration) for the Mississippi Freedom Democratic Party

(MFDP) and then collect affidavits from those excluded from the political process to push the national Democratic Party to be truly democratic. For many,
the MFDP represented the "one bright spot."[76] The Democratic Party delegation from Mississippi was all-white and favored Goldwater, so the integrated
MFDP delegation went to Atlantic City armed with a prepared case and an
alternative Freedom Registration book, to vie for the state's delegate seats on
the convention floor. Aaron Henry remembered the MFDP as an opportunity
to give African Americans a base in a political party through the creation of a
model that the national party could imitate.[77] The MFDP challenge is complex
and important in the broader Mississippi movement, particularly as part of the
history of SNCC. The party did not create crossroads in Clarksdale as it did in
other Mississippi movement centers, despite Henry's visible interactions, so
that story is not prominent here, aside from the volunteers' efforts to register
voters.

In the national arena, the MFDP's mission became a casualty of old-school
politics. MFDP members lobbied everyone they could, from the credentials
committee to other delegates, to force the issue onto the convention floor.
President Johnson, poised to win his first presidential election and unwilling to share the spotlight at his first convention as president, pulled enough
strings and threatened enough members on the credentials committee that the
MFDP was not offered a compromise but had its collective arm twisted, with a
decision made without its input—two seats (out of the state's thirty-four) or
nothing. The MFDP, devastated and betrayed, went home, not quietly but with
resolve.[78] Some in the MFDP delegation were ready to accept the offer, Henry
included. He was one of the two who were handpicked to be delegates and saw
the need to be present rather than take the radical moral high ground. This
decision created some discord with those unwilling to barter and in many ways
signaled the beginning of the end of that fruitful COFO alliance.

The MFDP's push was revolutionary. Despite its failure to get seated on the
delegation floor in Atlantic City, its presence and vocal protest resulted in
major changes in the democratic process, particularly in 1968 with the Committee on Party Structure and Delegation Selection, otherwise known as the
McGovern-Fraser Commission. In Mississippi, the party ran candidates in
local elections and saw African Americans entering the political system and
disrupting the state's Democratic Party. Henry's apparent willingness to settle
for less than the desired and rightful demands did not win him many friends on
Mississippi's radical left, who continued to organize in other parts of the state.
He felt that the MFDP became redundant when the Democratic Party finally

reformed and incorporated many of the revolutionary party's principles and philosophy, and he aligned himself with the Young Democrats in 1965, revitalized by white moderates like Greenville's Hodding Carter III, and later the Loyalists, who would challenge the state's delegation at the 1968 convention.[79]

The presence of the volunteers occurred alongside, rather than replaced, the activities that happened in Clarksdale in the summer of 1964, unlike in most other locations, where COFO dominated all movement organizing. The presence of the northern students intrigued many of the local youth. Charles Stewart recalled that "we had kids swarming all over us from the first day that we got there, continually asking us, 'When are we going to demonstrate?'"[80] Yet the COFO workers could not participate in testing the newly passed Civil Rights Act, as their mandate limited them to voter registration and the summer's programming. The mandate, orders from the central office in Jackson, became the subject of long, heated meetings among the COFO workers in Clarksdale. Some wanted to train local youth to protest nonviolently, to pass on all their skills learned in Ohio that might keep the protesters safer. Others did not want to risk the entire project by bringing even more negative attention on the volunteers, who tried hard to engage with white community members.[81]

So the local NAACP took on that role, testing restaurants, hotels, and other public places, filing suits when they were turned away. By the time the civil rights bill became law on 2 July, the local NAACP had secured enough bond money to test facilities immediately. Wilkie reported: "Clarksdale recoiled in horror. Untouchables would now be loose on the city's cafés and hotels, into the public swimming pools and parks." Between 6 and 11 July, members of the local branch tried to enter the Alcazar Hotel and its dining room, the Holiday Inn and its dining room, the Southern Inn, the Paramount Theatre, the Deluxe Café, and the Elite Café. The public library admitted some NAACP youth on 10 July but removed all the chairs. Rather than desegregate, the Alcazar Hotel closed its doors, as did Clarksdale's public pool.[82] The NAACP noted wryly, "Integration became only vertical." The next day, an unnamed NAACP member tested Jenkins Barber Shop. The owner, George Jenkins, drove him away at gunpoint. The manager was overheard proclaiming that "any 'nigger' that comes in my shop will be carried out feet first." On the second Sunday of July, groups attempted to desegregate the churches but were turned away and told they were not welcome—some white worshippers carried guns with their Bibles. The organization vowed to test every establishment, threatening

FIG. 4.6. Staff meeting of COFO volunteers in Clarksdale's Freedom House, 1964.
(Photo by Rev. Frazer Thomason, Hazelton Freedom Summer Collection,
McCain Library and Archives, University of Southern Mississippi)

costly legal action if thwarted. Aaron Henry boasted, "Within a month, we had tested all of the public facilities in Clarksdale, and all had either integrated or had suits pending against them."[83]

In 1963, the police had brutally suppressed direct action, throwing activists in jail and inflicting suffering on many. By 1964, the violence had lessened somewhat, due in part to the call for calm in order to avoid the negative publicity that the organizers hoped to generate. Nevertheless, the student volunteers noted that "the police played a big part in our lives" by jailing and harassing them constantly with threats.[84] Mat Zwerling had repeatedly marveled at the lack of violence he witnessed in his first weeks, relative to the events he heard about in Greenwood and the explosion of news coverage about the missing workers, which included his New York neighbor: "There has been absolutely no violence . . . but harassment may pick up as the project picks up."[85] He had found the quietness disconcerting, like the calm before a storm, but recognized the terror among local African Americans, who knew what had come before and what might occur again. Volunteers were not allowed to canvass door-to-door on weekend nights—it was too dangerous.

Zwerling had a couple of harrowing experiences himself, as the project settled into July. Returning from Tunica County, just north of Coahoma, an unmarked vehicle trailed his car, which was filled with volunteers. After a brief but heated debate, Zwerling sped up. By this point, no one expected Chaney, Goodman, and Schwerner to be alive, and no one wanted to risk a possible abduction. Immediately, the trailing car turned on its sirens, revealing itself to be an unmarked police vehicle. Zwerling observed with interest that the policemen "made me get out of the car and open the trunk and they were absolutely stunned that there were no weapons." It was evident to him that they really believed the summer would be an "invasion of arms," which was "ironic of course because the movement was entirely non-violent."[86] Zwerling went on automatic pilot, not fearing for his life (the details of the missing three had yet to be exposed), and as they hauled him off in handcuffs to the courthouse, where he paid his fine, his comrades drove back to the Freedom House.

Logs from SNCC and COFO track the almost daily police-related incidents that volunteers reported in Clarksdale and around the state. Two weeks into the Freedom Summer Project in Clarksdale, a driver in his truck tried to run two black workers, Annie Pearl (from Birmingham) and Allen Goodner (from the University of Michigan and Fisk University), off the road, making the volunteers a little skittish for a few days as they walked the streets. Zoya Zeman remembered that they had instructions to keep the blinds down when the lights were on so that they could not be seen through the windows, both at their host families' homes and at the community center or at Freedom House.[87]

Zeman's most-told story occurred at the community center site when the city unexpectedly delivered a huge pile of iron piping in the yard at the side of the building, claiming the commencement of street drainage work, when in fact it stopped the children playing in the yard. The day after that delivery, on 9 July, as the volunteers worked in the center, the lights flickered off. Outside, a "crazy looking" white man stood grinning with the electricity meter in his hand, stating that he was checking the system. He had been circling the center for days in his truck—one well equipped with a mounted gun rack. Zeman, with a few others, including Lafayette Surney and Doris Newman, came out of the center, and Surney confronted the man. An exchange of ugly words and threats resulted in Police Chief Collins's arrival on the scene. Zeman had checked the license plate of the truck and found it on their list of suspicious vehicles. She and Newman sat on the pipes and waited to see what would happen, knowing that other volunteers were returning from lunch. Zeman remembered that Collins, infuriated and flustered that none of the workers moved when ordered, picked up Newman from the pipes and roughly put her back down, cursing her as she tried to engage him in conversation about the reason for his visit. "And then he walked toward me, and he looked so confused, he looked baffled because I was white, but I was in the wrong place; he couldn't sort it out." It took a phone call to the FBI for the lights to be restored.[88]

Charles Stewart singled out Collins as a major culprit in the summer's unrest. He observed the police chief visiting black cafés and threatening closure by the sanitation department if they continued to serve civil rights workers. Only two out of fifteen resisted his threats. Once again, Collins's spectacularly bad behavior reinforced his reputation. The local NAACP leadership that summer asked the question, "Is his name Uncle Ben, Chief Ben Collins, or Chief Bull Collins. Apparently it makes no difference."[89] Many other volunteers had similar complaints. For instance, Lew Sitzer filed a complaint after only a day or two in Clarksdale. After Collins, wielding a billy club, forced Sitzer into the squad car, he was subjected to a barrage of verbal abuse all the way to the city jail, where he was detained without a phone call for six hours. With only $2.75 in his pocket and refusing to leave town immediately, he was charged with vagrancy. Collins warned him that "there are 100 deputized white citizens trained in the use of billy-clubs and just waiting for the signal to split some heads open."[90]

Even in the confines of City Hall, Collins could not control himself. For example, on 9 July, the same day the community center lost its electricity, Marie Gertge, from Greeley, Colorado, leaned against the wall outside the courtroom with her camera around her neck taking a cigarette break, watching Collins spray violet-scented room deodorant directly on black girls in the building. Another volunteer remembered that "before the trial began, we had packed the courtroom. A policeman entered with a can of air deodorant, and sprayed all of us who were in the room. Since most of us were Negroes, it was a subtle reminder that all Negroes are supposed to smell bad. Most of us just chuckled." Gertge had been refused permission to observe Vera Pigee's trial (which stemmed from an arrest over a spurious traffic violation two days earlier). When she tried to photograph the scene and the reactions, Collins arrested her on a $100 bond, claiming she violated a city ordinance against photographing in a courtroom.[91]

The Freedom House was not free from Collins's wrath either. On 24 July, after midnight, three white men threw bottles through the office windows. The police responded the next day when the thugs returned and broke into the building, arresting and fining them only eleven dollars and releasing them immediately. One of his principal targets was Lafayette Surney, at twenty-two a SNCC field secretary and summer director of COFO operations in Clarksdale

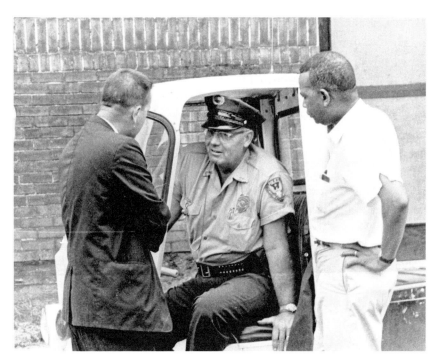

FIG. 4.7. Aaron Henry with Police Chief Ben C. Collins and an
unidentified man during Freedom Summer. (Photo by Rev. Frazer Thomason,
Hazelton Freedom Summer Collection, McCain Library and Archives,
University of Southern Mississippi)

after cutting his organizing teeth in Ruleville in 1962. In his first day back
in town to arrange housing for the impending arrival of volunteers, Collins
snarled at him, "We ain't going to have this shit this year." He taunted Surney
with obscene and abusive language in an effort to start a fight, and if he did
not personally tail Surney every day, Collins assigned an officer to follow him.
Collins even used a child to spy on the volunteers, an open secret among the
workers. One volunteer wrote, "He goes around listening to our talk all day,
finds out where we live, and reports all we do every night. He calls himself
Superman, and rumor has it that he is paid $3 a day for his services. He is only
12 years old."[92]

Collins's reputation had earned him column space in the *New York Times* by
this time. Future Pulitzer Prize–winning reporter David Halberstam titled his
13 July 1964 article "Racial Strife in Clarksdale, Miss., Is Reflected in Incidents
Involving Its Police Chief." Citing some of the incidents involving Collins,

Halberstam stressed, "It is one of the sharpest struggles going on in Mississippi today." Israel Zwerling, father of Mat and actively involved in lobbying the president, encountered Halberstam's piece in his morning paper, carefully clipped the article and enclosed it in his second letter to Johnson. He implored the president to take heed of Halberstam's "unmistakable warnings," pushing again for a more visible federal presence.[93]

Police harassment did affect the summer's fruits. Those working on registering voters for the MFDP noted that fear stopped many local people from following through on their verbal promises to sign up, making the volunteers nervous about the success of Freedom Week, 10–14 August. In correspondence circulating among volunteers, friends, and family, the frustration was palpable. Workers expected arrest, as they planned to picket the county court, but welcomed it if it meant that people attempted to register and responded positively. Volunteer Mark Fast wrote, "Everyone here wants to go to jail, both project workers and local people, so Ben Collins will get his fun."[94]

Volunteers feared Collins because of the power and safety of his position to do to them whatever he wanted. But like the local people who had already faced Collins, they did not respect him. "Poor Ben. He is so stupid and scared. . . . He's getting completely hard up for charges on which [even to] think of arresting us," Zeman wrote in her diary. "John [Suter] . . . said to Ben 'Good morning.' Ben became furious and said something like, 'I don't want any of you sons of bitches speaking to me.' He . . . then said, 'Listen, I don't ever want you speaking to me in public. I don't want anyone to think that I know you damn s.o.b.'s.'"[95]

These young volunteers, full of idealism (and more than a little arrogance), were determined to produce dramatic change during their short sojourn and to leave their mark on the local African American population by breaking through what they saw as universal fear. Zeman likened Freedom Summer to air strikes, helping troops on the ground. She saw herself and the other volunteers as foot soldiers for the "brilliant people in SNCC . . . who had the pure genius to think up these programs and figure out ways to organize such large numbers."[96] In some instances, they did make a difference and took some in the local population one step closer to freedom. They were also slow to realize, as Zeman's words suggest, that without the work accomplished by local leaders beforehand, their efforts, and those of SNCC, would have been for naught. This indifference or lack of foresight resulted in resistance from many local leaders. Indeed, the police were not the only source of antipathy: Vera Pigee displayed her displeasure often.

Mat Zwerling, Lew Sitzer, Charles Stewart, and one other white student stayed with Vera Pigee when they first arrived in Clarksdale. Stewart remembered seeing the bullet hole in Pigee's house: "One of the windows of their house still bears a bullet hole where it was shot into last year. They keep the hole there as a kind of trophy which they proudly display."[97] But Pigee did not extend the same warm welcome to the volunteers who stayed in her home as she did to the local youth council. Writing to his parents, Zwerling described Pigee, who is identified only by her last initial: "She is something else," he wrote. "Busybody—talks incessantly—strong community leader. (I'm sure she is a leader because she can bully people.) We aren't going to see eye to eye much. It should make the summer a little more exciting and be a good course in diplomacy for me. She is a good cook."[98] His comments reveal the not-so-subtle assumed privileges of a young white man. He criticized her vocal self-expression while praising her skills in the domestic, typically female space of the kitchen—a space usually designated for the silent, supportive housewife or domestic. He equated her leadership with bullying and resented her attempts to control his activity.

By 1964, Pigee was not too thrilled with COFO, the organization she had supported with Aaron Henry and Medgar Evers: "We had organized a monster. . . . I was willing to accept my punishment and I was working harder to kill the monster than I did to give it birth."[99] She had never objected to collecting the resources of groups for local needs—indeed, she had taken advantage of SCLC training for Citizenship Schools herself, and then had sent youth out of the state for training sessions, and had worn several institutional hats when organizing campaigns.[100] She hated the monster she could not control. Like youth council member Roy Wright, she felt that the students' presence interfered with already-established local movements and momentum. Protective of her community-based influence and the trust parents had placed in her to protect their children, she saw COFO as too big and unwieldy to manage, recognizing that in terms of numbers on the ground, the NAACP was woefully outnumbered, with only one paid staff member.

From his first days, Zwerling sensed conflict between the NAACP and SNCC, "which sort of stays a little beneath the surface." He noted, "In the city itself NAACP is 'in charge'—as we do county work SNCC (COFO) will do most of the work." A week later, he observed that the local leadership, except for Henry, treated the workers coldly—a situation he did not mind because it gave him the space to take initiative and assume an informal position of leadership.[101] Zwerling, like many of his cohort, assumed that negative black interactions were not reactions to his behavior and arrogance but rather a sign of inactivity and lack of initiative. Henry's sponsorship of COFO's summer volunteers shielded them from much of the wrath that Pigee expressed about their lack of sensitivity to local leadership. She and other NAACP loyalists continued working locally, maintaining ties with the national office while scrapping for control in their communities, their existing leverage they deemed undermined.[102] She managed to maintain activity through the local branch alongside the volunteers' work and interacted with the volunteers minimally, even with those in her house, and definitely not socially. Indeed, Zeman clearly remembered that black locals who were either afraid, or who just did not like them, would react "usually with distancing," maintaining politeness, as is the southern way, but not extending themselves in any other way.[103]

Pigee commented indignantly, "If anyone termed my action or activities as 'power,' it was well-earned power." Indeed, it was power endowed to her by the community through her own personal investment, and she was not about to see her lifelong investment undermined in one summer. Speaking emphatically, she continued: "I didn't like their [activities], and I didn't have to put up with it."[104] She expelled a group of students overnight by calling their hosts, her friends, to turn them out. When Zwerling and Sitzer moved out of Pigee's home, around mid-July, Zwerling gave the excuse that Mary Jane wanted her bedroom back. At first, they had to find their own food, but after a couple of weeks, Zwerling crowed, "we (Lew and I) are eating like kings. She's great [the new host], we really feel like part of a family—a great change from when we stayed with Mrs. P——."[105]

There are two possible reasons why the COFO-led Freedom Summer Project in Clarksdale never received the same attention as it did in other counties. It could be that because of Pigee's perseverance carrying the NAACP banner, and with her personal, palpable influence on the Clarksdale Youth Council and in the community, the volunteers could not crack the local networks effectively. Or it could be that because of the strength of the NAACP, COFO leaders spent resources and energies elsewhere in the state, leaving Clarksdale's volunteers under Henry's wing. In fact, what irked Pigee so much was that the volunteers appropriated the work she had started. She had worked to collect the piles of books through donations before the summer of 1964 that constituted the COFO library, which volunteers claimed as theirs. It was Pigee who organized the Freedom House; yet upon their arrival, David Batzka and Joe Youngerman took to fixing the doors and windows and building a wall to separate COFO staff from Pigee's Welfare and Relief Program headquarters in the back of the building. In no account is there any communication with her concerning these renovations, and all credit for anything positive about local leaders is directed toward Henry.[106]

Similarly, one of the reasons for the lack of interest in the literacy classes at the community center stemmed from the fact that Pigee had successfully run, and trained other teachers to run, similar classes for years under the auspices of the SCLC.[107] Some of the volunteers' programming, therefore, was redundant. Zeman, in her diary, realized this: "One of the things about the community that perhaps is unusual is that there already was such a strong NAACP organization . . . that perhaps we were kind of competing with those groups that were already functioning fine." She continued: "Some of those people were already involved in taking people down to register to vote and in having meetings to discuss these things, and they would have been in NAACP meetings instead of SNCC kind of things. But maybe that is where some of the adults were." Zwerling reached a similar conclusion, although unfortunately not until years later: "I think the fault may have been with SNCC and the COFO people that they didn't give a clear role of what they wanted from her [Pigee] or people who had been around for a decade."[108]

Pigee's heavy-handedness with Freedom Summer volunteers made her few friends in a COFO staffed primarily by SNCC. Zeman recalled a difficult staff meeting called to establish the role of the Freedom Summer Project in Clarksdale. "The strife is coming because the NAACP simply doesn't work like SNCC does. . . . Laf [Lafayette Surney] explained that COFO is actually a SNCC organization and that the other groups hardly do anything. Anyway the conflict here is whether and how to really establish lasting programs."[109] COFO had decided that whoever was on salary in any way would make the decisions, and as most of those making some money were in SNCC, albeit only a few dollars, and all but Charles Evers in the NAACP leadership were volunteers, SNCC had more decision-making powers. So while veterans politely referred to Pigee decades later as a strong local leader, at the time, her lack of enthusiasm resulted in reining in her influence to only the local, contributing to her absence in subsequent narratives of Freedom Summer. Many of the local youth were attracted to the Freedom Summer activities and the energetic volunteers, despite Pigee's protests. This became a defining moment for her in terms of her leadership, where activist mothering relied on community respect and cooperation. In subsequent years, as more legislation protected activists and the environment became less perilous, the need for her brand of community mothering lessened. She had helped to create an environment that ultimately made her role redundant.

However, the opinions of other black leaders in Mississippi toward COFO, and toward SNCC in particular, varied dramatically. Aaron Henry, of course, solicited and welcomed the help, publicity, and resources. He and his wife served as official local sponsors for the volunteers and opened their home every Friday night for backyard parties to help burn off stress and create a space of laughter and relaxation. Mixing college students and parties definitely made him popular. Zwerling stated: "I think SNCC paid a lot of attention ultimately to Aaron Henry," at the expense of navigating the larger picture of internal local politics.

Fannie Lou Hamer in Ruleville, Sunflower County, always contentious when it came to her views about the NAACP, praised the volunteers. She claimed, "They treated us like we were special and we loved 'em." Amzie Moore reasoned, "I found that SNCC was for business, live or die, sink or swim, survive or perish. They were moving, and nobody seemed to worry about whether he was gonna live or die."[110] Differing experiences in other towns and circumstances further complicated the organizational allegiances and loyalties. In Cleveland, SNCC's hands-on approach deeply impressed Moore, who welcomed SNCC volunteers after frustration with national NAACP bureaucracy. In Ruleville, where the NAACP found no anchor, SNCC gave Hamer refuge and a directed sense of purpose as she defied local authority and found her political voice. It is almost impossible to imagine her rise into the national spotlight in 1964 through the hidebound NAACP. For these activists, the raging fire brought energy, passion, and action.

With such positive testimony about SNCC from many local black leaders who recognized the potential of the summer's activities and wanted to harness the youthful energy that poured into the state, perhaps Vera Pigee's animosity (and that of other more conservative local leaders) ran much deeper than cultural differences, loyalty, tradition, and the feeling of being disrespected. Certainly COFO minimized Pigee's influence with the youth in the state, as the organization recruited volunteers she could not control. The NAACP had given her a platform to do her work during the very difficult decade preceding Freedom Summer, but now SNCC and CORE gave other women (like Hamer, Unita Blackwell from Mayersville, and Victoria Gray from Hattiesburg) more autonomy and opportunities for leadership in more democratic organizations that placed them in positions of authority.

COFO encouraged local women to take on leadership roles, and in this way,

Pigee's status as one of the very few women in the regional spotlight was eclipsed. While there is no evidence of interaction between Pigee and Hamer, one can assume that they knew each other, or at least knew about each other, given the proximity of their hometowns. Knowing what they thought of each other's organization, they probably had little to say to one another. That their trajectories became so opposed is ironic, given that Pigee also came from a sharecropper's shack and embodied a story of resilience and quest for self-improvement that enabled her and her husband to move from the fields to work that afforded them property and self-employment. COFO volunteers never experienced Pigee's nurturing ideals; she had no immediate emotional connection or loyalty to them as she did to the local kids she had mothered from the fifties. Hamer, on the other hand, became a confidante and mentor to SNCC and the volunteers—her mothering capacity centered on the group that gave *her* refuge. The history of the movements in Mississippi so far has focused more on SNCC and COFO than on the NAACP, and Hamer's work has thus received more attention, even though Pigee's activism began over a decade earlier.

Aaron Henry represented the best of the NAACP for COFO workers and volunteers, whereas Pigee probably represented the polar opposite. Flexible associations gave Henry opportunities to associate with more people, and he did. The narratives from Clarksdale's Freedom Summer volunteers reveal a deep affection for "Doc," who threw parties and helped open up Mississippi for the summer. One volunteer called Henry's Fourth Street Drugstore "everyone's 2nd Freedom House."[111] Their descriptions of his drugstore evoke images of safety and local refuge from the uncertainty on the streets for the volunteers— just as Pigee's salon, a stone's throw away, had harbored the Youth Council. Henry's willingness to be so flexible and his popularity and resulting publicity at the state and national levels clearly annoyed Pigee.

Despite reservations in Pigee's beauty salon, a discomfort that ultimately marginalized her, the Mississippi NAACP functioned as an integral part of COFO. That the national office held COFO at arm's length has rendered the historical record skewed. Loyal NAACP activists like Pigee remain sidelined in the Mississippi theater because they represented more conservative and traditional positions within the local ranks and were not among the young, vibrant voices capturing the nation's imagination. Henry never worried about the imbalance in COFO that favored SNCC staff, knowing that he would be heard if there was a big problem. He had known the young leaders like Dave Dennis, Bob Moses, and Annell Ponder for years, and mutual respect and complete confidence governed their relationships.

Henry also had access to wider circles that he never shared with other leaders in Clarksdale. Those circles went beyond leading organizations in the state. He was invited to the White House and had Attorney General Robert Kennedy's private phone number. He was on first-name terms with Rev. Martin Luther King and regularly presented Mississippi's movement activity at the SCLC annual conferences, indicating an increased presence in that organization.[112] His position as Mississippi state NAACP conference president and his responsibilities in statewide COFO activities kept him from everyday organizing in Clarksdale by 1964. However, because of his influence, Clarksdale, a movement headquarters for those loyal to the NAACP, also became a site where activists and other allies congregated. Therefore Clarksdale registered the full presence of the multiple personalities and groups that characterized the era, but Henry did not use this access and influence to open up opportunities for local leaders, like Pigee. He would bring visitors and reporters to town through the Freedom House and the community center to see activities and meet volunteers, not something he did often with the faithful NAACP staff who had volunteered their time (and risked their safety) for many years.

The clash of egos in Clarksdale's leadership leaked through the façade of unity that summer. Vera Pigee was no maternal angel. She gave as good as she got and stubbornly stood her ground, taking the moral high road, sometimes when compromise and mediation might have proved to be more effective. In this way, she made enemies in a society still anchored around traditional gender stereotypes, and she was a proud woman who understood the sexism that she encountered and tried to work around it (through her activist mothering), albeit with limits that kept her influence local. In fact, Henry probably took it for granted that she would engage her networks for the cause, and he counted on her to actually run the local NAACP branch effectively in his absence, giving him opportunities to work at the state level, in the wider political and public arena. She carried out her duties, organizing the local youth's direct-action campaigns that summer, but Henry took the credit. That summer, they seemed to work in separate spheres. The mass meetings, the branch meetings, the Citizenship Schools, and the conferences were all spaces where she did her work unnoticed. Indeed, only a couple of photographs of her appear in the local paper in all these years, and apart from the two photographs from SNCC photographer Charles Moore, few published images of her exist. During the summer of 1964, no one ever interviewed Pigee about her years of activism, yet SNCC's presence as the largest component organization of COFO working in the

Delta consumed the nation's imagination. She grumbled loudly about all this in subsequent years.

While such localized bickering probably had only localized effects in draining energy from the movement's possibilities that summer, Pigee's angst provides an exemplary snapshot of statewide ideological and methodological struggles among the organizations in COFO, and among local leaders in Clarksdale, which proved fatal for the coalition's long-term survival. The NAACP, once the premier civil rights organization in the region, had lost its immediate place in the limelight, and the national office eventually intervened to gain back lost ground.

The COFO Coalition Crumbles

Once the summer volunteers had departed to start their new school years, those left behind, who had worked primarily with COFO in the state and had done battle in the MFDP at the Democratic convention in Atlantic City, worked on another Freedom Vote Ballot for that fall, the culmination of most of the summer's voter registration efforts.[113] On the ballot, Aaron Henry stood for senator against John Stennis, and Fannie Lou Hamer ran for Congress (Second District) against Jamie Whitten. The local occurrences of harassment and false charges continued, even with the significantly reduced number of "outsiders" in the state.[114] Despite the concerted and concentrated efforts of the Freedom Summer Project to increase registration on a massive scale, the numbers remained disappointingly small. In Coahoma County, there were 14,404 black people twenty-one years of age and older, but only 2,139 (or 14.85 percent) were "freedom" registered—registered as members of the MFDP. The best numbers from the Second District in northwest Mississippi came from Leflore, Marshall, Panola, Union, and Washington counties, where volunteers had "freedom" registered between one-quarter and one-third of the black voting-age populations. Most of the other counties lagged behind Coahoma County statistically.[115]

While most in Mississippi's larger civil rights community encompassed by COFO could align with many of the goals of Freedom Summer, like the push for social justice, the Freedom Schools, and community work, not as many could swallow the radicalism of the MFDP. The violent resistance prompted by COFO's nonviolent grassroots activism had radicalized many of the younger workers. The nagging worries that many SNCC staffers pushed aside to carry out the Freedom Vote and then Freedom Summer surfaced more frequently, widening the cracks in the integrated group. The MFDP experience in Atlantic City and the "backroom horse-trading" that resulted in a forced compromise and no immediate victory disillusioned most and hastened the demise of SNCC as it once existed.

Registering voters as party members alienated more moderate COFO constituents. The national NAACP's sustained frustration with COFO reached a crossroads, and the NAACP made the first move. As a nonpartisan organization, it did not sanction the political activity of the MFDP, which further exacerbated its differences with COFO. By the November election, the NAACP found itself saddled with pending legal actions and financial difficulty (due to excessive bonds), with very little success to show for it all. Gloster Current campaigned hard for the state NAACP to break ties with COFO, reasoning that white officials would now be more willing to negotiate with the NAACP as the lesser evil. Current and Ruby Hurley made sure to attend the November meeting of the Mississippi State NAACP Conference board of directors, which subsequently recommended withdrawing from COFO. NAACP officers from around the state reported on their experiences with the Summer Project and the COFO staff. Vera Pigee had her say. This was her chance to kill the monster she had helped create. She is quoted as stating, "The grievances come mostly from the volunteer workers. . . . We shared our NAACP office with them. They opened our mail . . . opened packages that were sent to the Emergency Welfare, sat around preaching hate of the NAACP officials."[116] Aaron Henry, who presided over the meeting, had seen the writing on the wall, cut his losses, and now had his mind on the next project—and so conceded to the motion. The Mississippi NAACP formally left COFO before the year ended.

Once the state NAACP pulled out of COFO, the coalition lost its structure. COFO belonged at the grass roots and had filled a basic need for a specific time. In actuality, it was more than an umbrella for the constituent groups—it was the common meeting place in the state that enabled activists to push ahead in the business of securing equality. The NAACP was the glue that had held COFO together—the organizational structure of the veteran group had served to maintain some form of cohesiveness—yet SNCC and CORE had mocked that rigidity as obstructionist. SNCC and CORE staff would continue to work in Mississippi on local projects around the state, but their visibility would never reach the same levels they had had during that long hot summer of 1964.

Henry's next idea was revealed in the new year. Losing the fight to keep the NAACP affiliated with COFO, he and Charles Evers approached Roy Wilkins in the second week of January 1965 with a proposal for the coming summer. The plan consisted of recruiting and assigning at least ten students to work with each branch in Mississippi on voter registration, political organization, and interpreting and implementing the Civil Rights Act and the new War on Poverty legislation on the ground. Allard Lowenstein, who had controversially backpedaled in his support for Freedom Summer as disagreements with SNCC workers over grassroots organizing strategies came to a head, had publicly promoted the NAACP line and had the task of recruiting students of the highest caliber from the North who could contribute a weekly ten dollars for expenses. In this way, they reasoned, the NAACP would be directly involved in civil rights activity in the state and could expand the number of branches established. The NCC had already agreed to train the recruits.[117] While Pigee's reaction to these plans is unknown, they would have suited her desire to have more control over the volunteers under the auspices of local host branches.

After much discussion, Wilkins complied with the proposed plan, and it was approved at the state conference meeting on 7 February in Clarksdale. Sponsoring NAACP units would send 260 NAACP volunteers to Mississippi, to be trained by the NAACP secretary of training, Althea Simmons, with a supervisory task force of four field directors from New York City assigned throughout the state, along with other volunteers. Budgeted to cost at least $20,000, fund-raising began immediately, and Simmons temporarily moved her office from New York City to Jackson. Gloster Current, present at the Clarksdale meeting, wrote to the Executive Committee the very next day requesting its approval in order that the organization could announce the collaboration between the national office and the state conference. The national office, however, made its policy clear: political action and the right to register to vote would remain of primary importance, before the implementation of the Civil Rights Act and the Anti-Poverty Act (both of which had recently passed). This policy minimized direct action and the chances of repeating the activities of Freedom Summer. Indeed, it was a more centralized and structured vision than that of local leaders. This time around, the volunteers would be mainly NAACP members, those cognizant of the organization's strategies and goals and who "are mature enough to understand and accept discipline."[118]

Voting Rights in 1965

Despite Freedom Summer, voter registration had not progressed much in Mississippi. The 1957 and 1960 civil rights legislation had no teeth to make any real change. The Justice Department had tried in Mississippi but lost. In an appeal to the Supreme Court, on 8 March 1965, as the Selma campaign reached a crescendo in Alabama, Justice Hugo Black delivered the opinion that the Justice Department's case against Mississippi's "longstanding, carefully executed plan to keep Negroes . . . from voting" should be heard immediately. A little over a week later, President Johnson introduced the voting rights bill into the House of Representatives. SNCC leaders dismissed the president's action as simply another legislative response to the national coverage of Martin Luther King's march in Alabama.[119]

However, the Civil Rights Commission, relatively silent during the previous two years, spoke out in favor of the bill, requesting provisions to abolish literacy tests and the poll tax. Citing its investigations in 1964, reports by civil rights organizations, and interviews in February 1965, its seventy-four-page report, "Voting in Mississippi," stressed that federal remedies thus far had "proven too slow and cumbersome."[120]

As the voting rights bill made its way through Congress in the late spring and early summer of 1965 and federal poverty programs geared up under Johnson's Great Society, the local NAACP branch in Clarksdale (with Pigee still as secretary and Youth Council advisor) readied itself for another summer. On 5 May, federal representatives from Washington, D.C., the Atlanta SCLC's Rev. Andrew Young, a choir from Higgins High School and Coahoma Junior College, and the revived Youth Council congregated for an antipoverty rally at Higgins High School auditorium. A Freedom Banquet on 6 May ended the branch's fund-raising drive at the First Baptist Church. In keeping with the spirit of the last year, the diners were served "freedom fried chicken with jail going potato salad, bond bailing string beans, door knocking rolls, mass meeting cake and non-violent cakes."[121]

Yale, Harvard, and Radcliffe students came to the Delta that summer to work to increase voter registration in light of the new Voting Rights Act. This time, as planned, volunteers came under the auspices of the NAACP. In Coahoma County, their work resulted in the addition of over 2,000 African Americans to the voting rolls.[122] Largely unreported, events "were keynoted [in] early July by a decision of NAACP officials in Clarksdale *not* to demonstrate." As the Mississippi legislature repealed many of the offending voting laws in anticipation of the Voting Rights Act, national NAACP staffers sought to register voters quietly. In Clarksdale, the ornery J. W. Smith, circuit clerk and registrar, claimed not to have the new registration forms, further antagonizing Aaron Henry, who wanted to march. The new nonprotest tactic proved successful, however. During the four and a half weeks before the bill was signed into law, 800 African Americans registered to vote, almost doubling their numbers, albeit to a still-low 12 percent of potential black voters. The total was nearly the same as the number the 1964 "much publicized, much romanticized" project had registered for the MFDP.[123]

Conservative national columnists Rowland Evans and Robert Novak posited that white segregationists recognized the end of their fight, as "the NAACP's evolutionary technique . . . contrasted with Snick's [SNCC's] revolutionary technique" bore fruit. Reporter Curtis Wilkie observed that with the "new look" voter registration drive, "the sometimes-scruffy looking college students . . . who roamed the city last summer . . . are gone. They have been replaced here by a small staff of imported NAACP workers and volunteers." No doubt these students had more of a dress code to comply with, in keeping with the organization's image of itself. Certainly, the NAACP enjoyed substantial success registering voters in 1965, but African Americans had been politicized through smaller victories desegregating towns and hamlets the year before. SNCC and COFO could take some credit for nurturing local politicization in 1964, laying the groundwork for the NAACP campaign in 1965 facilitated by the Voting Rights Act.[124]

In response, the local Chamber of Commerce launched its own drive to net more white voters. The Coahoma County Citizens' Council sent out a general notice warning of the "shadow of integration and Negro political domination that now loom[ed] over Mississippi in general and Coahoma County in particular." Citing the numbers of potential black voters in the county, the letter informed readers of the civil rights groups working on voter registration, of the money at their disposal, and of the lawsuit against the state. The Chamber of Commerce sought contributions and membership: "We feel that the answer is a strong White organization which can anticipate and counteract the moves by these professional trouble makers." Segregationists clearly sweated. The NAACP quoted one state official as saying: "I'm not too sure what's going to happen. We're caught between the devil and the deep blue sea on this thing. We've opened the doors to Negro voters and they're coming down to register, but apparently the whites don't realize the seriousness of the situation."[125]

They realized it soon enough. The Voting Rights Act passed in August 1965, and an appointed federal registrar arrived in Clarksdale at the end of September. His arrival drew howls of protest from city and state officials, but in the end results were mixed. At the end of October, federal registrars submitted reports from nineteen counties in the states where they worked (Alabama, Mississippi, Louisiana, and Georgia). The figures for Coahoma County ranked among the lowest in the state. The local branch had urged the registrar to stay longer, at least to the end of the cotton-picking season, which kept many in the fields during office hours. As of 1960, 14,604 nonwhites were of voting age, compared to 8,708 whites. However, only 3,328 African Americans were registered by October 1965, as opposed to 6,380 whites. In all, a mere 10.5 percent of the voting population was black, while blacks made up 62.6 percent of those eligible by age to vote. Still, results were better than ever, and by the end of the year, Wilkie reported that nearly 3,000 more African Americans had registered in the county. In the meantime, city hall, the courthouse, and the hospital "quietly desegregated."[126]

Federal officials attributed the decline in black registration following the initial rush to a "lack of political organization and low motivation" but noted that "continued community and governmental activity is necessary so that Negro citizens will learn that the ballot is now available to them." Despite the various tactics employed by the local NAACP branch to motivate potential black voting applicants, the low turnout resulted in a cutback of the federal voter registrar's hours in February 1966 to only Saturdays. Not giving up the fight, the branch announced more fund-raisers and voter registration campaigns and continued to educate and encourage first-time voters.[127] Regardless of the setbacks and continued stubborn resistance, progress was evident.

Multiple frustrations, punctuated by small advances, characterized these years. A series of small local demonstrations by brave women and children to test federal laws in interstate transportation at train and bus stations sparked a chain of events—the boycotts, marches, and protests that dominated the political landscape in Coahoma County. After the murder of Medgar Evers in June 1963, more and more outside activists entered Clarksdale from all directions. Vera Pigee, NAACP stalwart, tried valiantly to retain her leadership of the Youth Council members when the volunteering college students caught their attentions. Her struggle mirrored the frustrations of NAACP leaders in New York City, who realized that the younger generation did not want to patiently let the litigation and federal intervention "trickle down." As COFO harnessed this energy, Aaron Henry found the vehicle through which he could transform Clarksdale and Mississippi. He believed that freedom should be won by any and every means necessary and therefore worked hard to sustain the very loose, and often reluctant, coalition for as long as possible. Once the federal government responded with the Civil Rights Act and the Voting Rights Act, local people could again take the reins to test accommodations and register to vote.

Many locals were becoming empowered to protest for an improvement in their everyday lives and found personal satisfaction in marching, picketing, and registering to vote. Yet so much more was possible. For many, the chase proved more rewarding than the win, particularly when local situations did not change immediately. COFO disintegrated as the organizations battled among themselves and debated internally. Schools still remained segregated, and poverty was still deeply entrenched. Yet there had been some surface changes over the past two years. Many local establishments had relinquished their grip on segregation, usually after boycotts, public demonstrations, and legal action, and now African Americans could enjoy access to an increased number of motels and restaurants in the county.[128] Of course, these changes only affected those who could afford them.

Under COFO, at the pinnacle of the mass direct-action protests, organizations at the state level muted their differences to combat a formidable force. By 1966, with increased numbers of African Americans on the voting rolls and poverty programs in place, not only did new organizations like the Mississippi Voter Registration and Education League and Mississippians United to Elect Negro Candidates emerge, but they joined the older groups in all vying for a piece of the political pie. Notwithstanding those hurdles, black independent candidates won seven elected posts in the 7 November 1967 elections, including a seat in the state House of Representatives, the first in 100 years. A total of twenty-two black officials took office.[129]

Meanwhile, the nation lost a president, became ever more embroiled in an unpopular military engagement in Vietnam, and suffered riots in many major urban areas. Johnson pushed his War on Poverty programs through Congress and opened up a whole new chapter of activism and local political involvement, especially in the South. The mass direct-action component of the movement lessened as immediate demands were met and as federal programs began to address many of the issues affecting the black community. One unresolved issue that threaded throughout these years involved school systems. That fight ran concurrently, but it was after the struggle for voting and employment rights

that education efforts captured the immediate attention of the courts, pushing citizens, particularly the children, back onto the streets. In the fall of 1969,
Clarksdale's African American community marched in waves daily to protest
noncompliance with *Brown*. Still probably the most controversial and fiercely
fought contest, the battle to desegregate the schools continued.

CHAPTER FIVE

Children Should Not Be
Subjected To What Is Going On There

DESEGREGATING SCHOOLS

Yes, a new dimension has been added to the local protest movement.
—Cryer *(1969)*

[There were] no problem[s] with the kids, but they stopped all recesses,
they didn't want them to mix. Whites did all they could to relocate to areas
predominantly white, either to Lee [Academy] or to other parts of town to
avoid sending their kids to black schools. —*Alpha Norphlet (1999)*

CHANGING THE AMERICAN STAGE

America is a stage life land,
All people have parts to learn in hand.
If I were to walk down the street and say,
"I want my freedom this very day,"
I'd raise my fingers and lift my face,
But my people would look at me in disgrace.
"Why should I try to be free?
I already have my liberty."
The people are walking as statues do;
I have no right to look at you.
My face is different, my face is black,
But why should you want to hold me back?

We are a nation, and it is said,
"A Nation when parted is a stage that's dead."
I was once a patriot true.
Now you try to take me with you:
Not to be brothers and to let me be free,
But only to take care of thee.
I still have to play my part;
I am still a slave in my heart.
To look at our flag, and say to thee,
"I am here, but am I free?"
The Nation of America is never to be
Until we have our liberty.

If Khrushchev walked to my hometown,
I'd try my best to show him around,
Even though he is a man in wrong,
I still would try to help him along.
A man is a man, and life is life;
I am a man, and he is in life.

The trail of freedom is all around,
I wish it would come through this sorrowed town.
In this nation, I want you to know,
I am a citizen, and I want to be treated so.
This nation has to get together
And leave it to God to decide who is better.
I am here to testify,
I want my freedom, and that ain't no lie.

So Mr. Charlie, you are the best,
But I am as equal as you and the rest.
I am telling you the earnest truth,
We are people just like you.
So get ready for the fright of your life.
These people are going to get their freedom in height.
Try to be ready, try to be strong,
But you won't hold the black man down for long.

Elnora Fondren wrote this poem seated at one of the donated desks in COFO's community center in Clarksdale during the summer of 1964 as part of the organized activities run by the volunteers. In it, she evoked American history through the imagery of Abraham Lincoln and slavery, which she equated with the world she inhabited one hundred years later. By pointing out the humanity of the nation's number one enemy during the Cold War, Nikita Khrushchev, the rising tenth grader declared her own and asserted her citizenship and equality in the movement to change the American landscape.[1]

More than a year later, on 14 September 1965 to be exact, the school year had already begun and classes were in full swing when now-eleventh-grader Elnora Fondren walked into Clarksdale High School to register for classes for the first time. The admission of the lone black pupil, transferring from Higgins High School, technically desegregated the school. City officials hoped the symbolism would quell any further legal action.[2] On that day, and for many more during that first month, Vera Pigee traveled with Fondren, calming her nerves and shoring up her spirits.

Fondren did not garner the publicity of the Little Rock Nine when they had braved Central High School in neighboring Arkansas eight years earlier. Instead, she shared her daily trials and tribulations with her family and with Pigee, who related news quietly to the rest of the local NAACP branch's leadership. The *Clarksdale Press Register* reported the development in the corner of the front page that day, noting that the school board declined to release her name and that desegregation came "in a totally uneventful way." It is not clear how she was selected or why she was the only one. In fact, the school board minutes omit mentioning her at all. Concerned for her safety, the local NAACP branch publicized her admission minimally but was ecstatic at the turn of events: "We wish her well and pledge her our support in every way. We know that she has the character and the intellect to do well, and we wish her God-speed."[3] Bettie J. Yarborough joined her by the end of September. At the end of 1965, the two were the only black students attending Clarksdale High.

The plight of the students, the local NAACP's responsibility to protect the girls, and the lack of further admissions burdened the activists. Disappointed with the failure of the federal government to fully enforce the law by withholding funds for noncompliance, the branch grimly remarked: "We are in for some rough times."[4] We do not know firsthand what the two girls experienced as they navigated the hallways and classrooms alone. We know, just by the evidence of the poem written in the summer of 1964, that Fondren understood the importance of her actions and that her candidacy as the "first" had strengthened as a result of her politicization, skill, and tenacity. Clearly, however, schools in Clarksdale would never be the same again, and public education across the country would mirror that upheaval.

Unlike the other desegregation struggles that created dramatic images and headlines, the education battle remained localized and connected to the judicial system in Mississippi. Depending on the fortitude of the local black communities and their decisions, efforts to desegregate schools varied widely. For that reason, this chapter shifts in tone, with snapshots of black struggles to desegregate Clarksdale's schools, which ran in parallel to, and had overlapping actors and coalitions with, the more publicized direct-action mass movements and campaigns. It relies heavily on local oral histories and court records. This story is also untidy, with long periods between frenetic action and life-altering changes.

The highly publicized legal battles in the courtrooms had real and serious ramifications in local arenas. Integrating the schools beyond token desegregation meant more than just uniting white students and black students in the same classrooms. The logistics of reassigning and hiring teachers, organizing transportation, agreeing on curricula, creating constructive learning environments, among many details, all had to be worked out amid resentment, anger, and frustration on all sides. The monumental task of overhauling the system took its toll on teachers, parents, and children. Once again, the children are at the center of the story. Lawyers, parents, and teachers, both black and white, battled for years in the courts, conference rooms, and school offices, but the children had to live with these decisions and consequences and still learn and then graduate with enough education to carry them through life. The children themselves are crucial to this struggle, as plaintiffs and students, yet their visibility and their engagement with the process created crossroads for them, made them vulnerable, particularly in a school system controlled by white supremacists.

Yet they did not leave their fate to the adults to fight over. At times they took charge, protesting injustice in the schools and pushing the adults to take on their issues. As those children graduated, however, and the schools settled into a pattern of resegregation, the rigorous activist moment passed, leaving an education system poorer in quality and vigor than ever before. Indeed, the goal of desegregation was imperfect and problematic at the local level. Desegregation through force, although necessary, was not necessarily beneficial to those affected, particularly the children, demonstrating the limits of court-ordered mandates. The journey left many issues unanswered and created an enduring crisis in public education.

The Education Story So Far

Disillusioned with the snail's pace at which school desegregation had taken place in the fifties and frustrated at the deliberate thwarting of justice in the implementation of the "all deliberate speed" ruling in 1955 with *Brown II*, black students had turned their attention to the desegregation of their towns, caught up in the tidal wave of youthful direct-action protests sweeping across the South. Civil rights energies had spun away from schools by 1960, recognizing the futility of fighting against segregationists standing guard over their white boys and girls, particularly when the federal government's activities focused elsewhere.

The Kennedy administration's Department of Justice had released a progress report in the field of civil rights from 20 January to 20 November 1961.[5] Elaborately outlining achievements in policy, voting, employment, and transportation, education barely took up a page. Kennedy applauded the desegregation of schools in Atlanta, Dallas, and Little Rock, as well as the few isolated areas in Florida, Arkansas, Virginia, North Carolina, and Tennessee.

Mississippi's struggle, however, had yet to unfold. Mississippi, Alabama, and South Carolina reported no integration of their schools to the federal government in 1961. The Magnolia State's population ratio was close to fifty-fifty (293,600 white to 283,900 black), unlike the other two states, which had majority white populations. In addition, of all the districts under desegregation orders, Mississippi had none.[6]

Black teachers, on the ground, felt the pain every day as they walked the tightrope. At the local level, frustrated by the lack of resources and the failure to at least "equalize" educational standards, they had to carefully choose their words and affiliations like never before. In 1962, Aaron Henry bemoaned the NAACP's reticence in getting involved in "personal" cases, particularly as he reasoned that inaction would become a big community problem if "we turn[ed] chicken" and did not fight while advising others to risk everything. He continued, obviously exasperated: "Most of the teachers that support our movement are watching to see what we are going to do. All I can tell them is, you just wait, we'll get [the school board]. I hope this optimism will be vindicated." The local NAACP branch attempted to stir action, instigating a telephone and letter campaign to demand reinstatement of fired teachers, like Noelle Henry, but to no avail. All the while, the national office did little in this regard, busy with the multiple other direct-action cases and activities that bombarded them in the early sixties.[7] It is not hard to imagine Aaron Henry's impatience and his subsequent embrace of COFO and the direct action of other groups in Mississippi.

Even black educators without direct ties to civil rights activists suffered indignities. Sara Cannon, for example, moved to Clarksdale in 1954 when she married, after a short spell teaching in the all-black community of Mound Bayou. In 1999, she bitterly recalled her experiences with a vividness that indicated lasting effects on her, forty-five years later:

> When I started teaching up here, the white Superintendent whose name was Mr. [Gycelle] Tynes, had a meeting with the all of us, all the teachers . . . and he talked down to the blacks. He said that we were inferior, our brains were different. And this was . . . when he met with all of us at the beginning of the school session and that was his speech . . . and I wanted to say so bad, 'How do you do this? How do you compare us with our brains, don't we have the same color blood and everything?' But I sat there because I was just getting started up here. I guess everybody would have looked at me as if I was crazy if I had stood, you know, because teachers were really afraid of white people. People were afraid. So I kept my mouth closed and I took it.

Most black teachers, particularly after *Brown v. Board of Education*, did not dare to become members of the NAACP. As part of the state's attempt to eliminate the NAACP, authorities made teachers fill out forms that listed their general affiliations. "They were only looking for one thing—and that was the member of the NAACP," Cannon remembered. "I wasn't active no way then. We all filled it out and we had to have it notarized, that we would not be a member of the NAACP . . . but I knew that they would fire you if they knew that you were connected to any black stuff with your race."[8] For teachers, retaliation and retribution were constant threats, whether they were political or not. If involved, they kept it secret, donating money for campaigns perhaps but not attending meetings. W. A. Higgins, for example, had pushed for the organizing of the local NAACP branch in the early fifties but refused to take any public leadership position. Lillie Neal, a mother in Clarksdale, acknowledged black educators' fears: "Teachers during the civil rights movement . . . were not as active at that time. The Superintendents of the schools were white and they would always threaten our teachers. It was not easy. You did get more of the common people participating."[9]

The federal government would have agreed with Neal's assessment. Six days into 1965, Nicholas Katzenbach, acting attorney general, noted that while the number of black children attending desegregated schools doubled in 1964, that number only represented 2 percent of the group: "There are still 1,900 school districts to be desegregated in the five deep Southern States of Louisiana, Mississippi, Alabama, Georgia and South Carolina." Title IV of the 1964 Civil Rights Act gave the Justice Department some teeth by authorizing federal intervention in legal suits, but the importance of grassroots action came across clearly in Katzenbach's report: "No matter what tensions may occur, local communities do overcome them if permitted to do so."[10]

Prior to the passage of the 1964 Civil Rights Act, on 16 September 1963, twenty-one parents tried to step up the pace of desegregation in Clarksdale's public schools with a petition representing twenty-nine children of the Coahoma County branch of the NAACP. They were still energized from the March on Washington three weeks previously, as well as a full summer of protests, jail-ins, and the local Freedom Vote (the prototype for the statewide campaign). The author of the branch newsletter (probably Pigee) explained: "We regret that these steps, and the methods used have to be done without the consultation, and discussion, with our White Brothers and Sisters." The writer insisted, however, that "we have tried all the methods that we know of to try to bring into being at least a discussion group, composed of both White and Negro Citizens, to study and resolve our problems and the problems of this community." Leaders had written to the mayor and the chief of police and to the school board, requesting a meeting to discuss the region's deepening disquiet. No response was forthcoming. Pigee lamented that "if our White brothers and sisters will not join with the Negro Citizens of this community, then we feel we must 'go it alone' and depend upon the Federal Government, NAACP, and the Almighty God, that made us all, to deliver us from bondage." The petition called for the desegregation of the school system and demanded an answer at the next meeting of the school board.[11] The city refused to budge.

With the city unwilling to act, the next step for Clarksdale's school desegregation was a legal one. On 22 April, Aaron Henry filed suit on behalf of his twelve-year-old daughter, along with other parents, to put an end to Jim Crow in the classroom once and for all. For the next six years, as black parents encouraged their children to learn in the overcrowded segregated schools, *Rebecca Henry et al. v. Clarksdale Municipal Separate School District et al.*, the major desegregation case in Clarksdale, staggered through the courts. The Clarksdale school board fought and disobeyed court orders at every turn.

Unlike the desegregation of public spaces, accommodations, or interstate travel, education required different tactics, because of state control. Two major federal agencies were directly involved with school desegregation: the Department of Health, Education, and Welfare (HEW) and the Department of Justice. On the organizational side, the NAACP remained the leading litigator. Desegregating schools, therefore, involved a smaller constituency than other civil rights campaigns. Other civil rights groups kept relatively silent as this particular battle played out in the courtrooms and the local schoolrooms.

The Clarksdale case was the first filed in the area. New York attorney Derrick A. Bell Jr. represented the plaintiffs. The suit requested that the school board enact a desegregation plan in keeping with the Civil Rights Act of 1964. The plaintiffs preferred the Freedom of Choice plan, which allowed students to choose their schools annually. Another alternative, the Geographic Assignment Plans, purportedly selected pupils based on residence and neighborhood boundaries. Attorney Semmes Luckett, who had represented Police Chief Ben Collins through his legal woes, was employed by the school board in August 1963 "to handle unusual legal problems that may arise from time to time in the school system" and to serve as defense counsel.[12] Curtis Wilkie described Luckett as "polished and cynical . . . blessed with a majestic crown of silky white hair," a man who lived in a big columned house with one of the town's first color television sets near the courthouse. Now Luckett fought the school case with "brazen tactics and artful duplicity."[13] He always filed for more time to prepare desegregation plans and continually stalled the suit's progress. With all deliberate delay, he read the writing on the wall when he addressed Clarksdale's Board of Trustees in June 1964: "In light of several recent decisions by the Supreme Court, and various Circuit Courts of Appeal it appears that the board may be forced to act in a somewhat hasty manner in attempting to come up with a plan for step-by-step de-segregation." Sure enough, a month later U.S. District Court judge Claude F. Clayton ordered the city school district to submit a desegregation plan to the plaintiffs by 24 July 1964, specifying that the plan must desegregate at least one grade throughout the school district by September 1964.[14]

The city scrambled to assemble a plan. In the midst of Freedom Summer activities and up against the deadline, on 21 July a marathon meeting produced four plans, all of which defined zones and boundaries. For white Clarksdalians, the Freedom of Choice Plan was not an option. The Coahoma County school district had adopted this scheme, and the few children who opted for previously all-white schools found their parents fired from their jobs or put off plantations. In the city, however, where the black community was more organized and concentrated, a Freedom of Choice plan, which ultimately placed the burden of desegregation on black students and parents, could not be so easily controlled. White Clarksdalians predicted a huge and unmanageable influx of black applicants to white schools.[15]

At the hearing on 19 August, Judge Clayton considered all options and placed the district under a federal court order requiring desegregation of grades one and two for the first semester of the academic year 1964–65 under a neighborhood school zone attendance plan—in essence, a geographic assignment plan. In a later court appearance, Superintendent Gycelle Tynes described the plan to use school facilities "on a racially nondiscriminatory basis in accordance with sound educational principles." Tynes boasted that a zoning plan that bisected the city along the railroad tracks would afford an optimum teacher-pupil ratio, while maintaining that the board "totally [disregarded] the racial characteristics of the people and [proposed] these zones as being the best for the children and patrons of this school district, and racial considerations [were] just simply out of the window."[16]

The apparently color-blind geographical zoning plan was disingenuous because the railroad tracks, suddenly deemed too dangerous by the school board for children to cross daily, in fact divided the southern black neighborhoods from the white northern sections. Stan Boyd, in his undercover research in 1964, found out from city leaders that in order to exclude the few houses with black families that skirted the white neighborhood, they redrew the city lines to place them outside of the city (and into the county school district). In places where redrawing lines would exclude white people, they slated that area for urban renewal.[17]

NAACP lawyer Derrick Bell returned to court in August 1965, as local activists worked to register voters under the new Voting Rights Act, arguing against several actions taken to retain segregation, including shifting city limit boundaries. Pending the submission of more briefs at the end of October 1965, Judge Clayton further delayed his decision until late spring or early summer of 1966, twelve years after the original *Brown* ruling.[18] The local NAACP branch questioned Judge Clayton's integrity, noting he "continues to permit segregation in Clarksdale Schools. . . . By accepting the zoning lines supplied by the Clarksdale school board, Judge Clayton became a participant in continuing segregation." Claude Feemster Clayton was a son of Mississippi and trained at the University of Mississippi Law School, graduating in 1931. He was nominated to the federal bench by Dwight Eisenhower in February 1958. Known to wear a pistol on his person, Clayton had ample experience in northern Mississippi with his work in segregated private and city practices in his hometown of Tupelo.[19]

Meanwhile, the Johnson administration shepherded the Elementary and Secondary Education Act through Congress, which made federal funds for local school districts contingent on compliance with desegregation orders. As a result, school districts, in Mississippi and in the rest of Dixie, were forced to admit a few black students with relatively minimal violence.[20] The first week's enrollment figures in Clarksdale in the fall of 1965, however, showed that segregationist principles resonated louder than funding motivations.

Against this background, Elnora Fondren entered Clarksdale High School as the first black student, in September 1965, under the court-ordered desegregation plan. She had requested a transfer from Higgins High School to take a subject not offered at the black school, Latin I, and she also enrolled in English III, Chemistry, Shorthand, U.S. History, and Chorus. The school board, under a federal court order imposed that August, had to comply. Judge Clayton had ruled in the *Henry* case that all curricula at all schools should be identical, but school officials claimed the order came too late for them to make the necessary changes. The day before her arrival, Superintendent Tynes assembled the Clarksdale High School students to inform them of her impending registration. He asked the students to "treat her as you might wish to be treated under similar circumstances—civilly and with politeness and courtesy." Despite the official calls for a smooth transition, Cora Hicks, a member of the NAACP Youth Council, remembered the trauma Fondren experienced: "Elnora . . . actually integrated the Clarksdale Public schools by herself. . . . She went through something. . . . They had to take her by taxi everyday and escort her in with policemen for a while."[21]

Vera Pigee took credit, alongside fellow NAACP officer Rev. Rayford, for initiating Fondren's enrollment. A member of the Clarksdale Youth Council, Fondren—and her family—trusted Pigee after years of activist mothering and mentoring. She was their safe haven—their counselor, confidante, and conduit to the local branch officers. Pigee escorted Fondren, with Yarborough later, to school for the first month, and then the local branch established a special finance committee to raise funds to pay a cabdriver to transport them. When costs depleted that fund, Pigee, and a couple of other NAACP officers, paid for the taxis out of their own pockets. Her involvement, as always, came at a price. Intimidation from the police increased, and she carefully logged how they trailed her car during the day or procured a warrant to enter her beauty salon to search for evidence of alleged illegal whiskey selling. She continued her task, however, leaning on her faith: "I sat in my car and read the Bible. . . . See, I'm a Christian and Christians don't hate."[22]

Across the state, those few black students who managed to enter white institutions faced intolerable environments. In the spring of 1966, Kenneth Dean, a member of the Mississippi Council on Human Relations, summarized recent research on the state's desegregation experience after a series of private and group interviews with students and parents, as well as questionnaires, student essays, and conversations with teachers. He presented his findings before the Mississippi Advisory Committee to the Civil Rights Commission in Jackson. He found that black students entering the volatile environment of a once all-white school, usually in tiny numbers, if not alone, faced great discrimination, even beyond the social segregation in the school space. For example, he noted that school boards and principals instructed students and teachers alike to ignore black students in their classrooms and to exclude them from all extracurricular activities, and some faculty openly discussed in faculty lounges giving failing grades to black pupils. As for the Delta, he remarked, "Children should not be subjected to what is going on there." He did see a ray of hope, however, continuing, "There is a backlog of strength and courage in the Negro community. Federal examiners opened the doors to this strength in the area of registration."[23] Referring to the influx of federal registrars to facilitate the provisions of the Voting Rights Act, Dean recognized the potential of the black vote to improve education.

Under oath in the U.S. District Court, Semmes Luckett tried to justify the need for an "escape valve" in the form of private schools to "help areas with a high percentage of Negroes to make a successful transition to desegregated schools."[24] White flight had begun in earnest since the 1964–65 school year in other Mississippi districts, assisted by financial help from the 1964 state legislature. The NAACP branch observed that white, Chinese, and Jewish merchants who had once resided in South Clarksdale with their businesses moved their residences to the Oakhurst area north of the railroad tracks to "avoid Negroes" in schools. In defiance, the *Cryer* read: "Our advice to these unhappy people is to be sure to carry your grocery stores, service stations, theatres or picture shows with you. You will no longer have Negroes spending their hard-earned dollars with you when you so openly say you are too good for us."[25]

Pressure also came from the state in more subtle ways as well. To make sure that black children attended schools in black residential areas, the Mississippi attorney general ordered that legal residence follow that of living parents, with residence of the father taking precedence, except in cases in which the mother had custody after a divorce. This rule explicitly targeted, disregarded, and de-legitimized the widespread practices of extended family structures and cultures in which black children commonly resided with grandparents or aunts and uncles. Insisting on a narrower nuclear family model, the rule had the desired effect of disqualifying many from the school system altogether. It was defended as a color-blind rule to make sure "legal" residents had access to local resources, but the preoccupation with race tainted the purpose and implementation.[26]

Nevertheless, the federal government counted the Freedom of Choice or the Geographic Attendance Zone plans as viable means to achieve desegregation and as "voluntary" plans in cases of compliance. Therefore, despite the dismal attendance figures, most of the southern school districts operated just within the law. Table 3 is a sample of four southern states' 1966 figures. Mississippi, however, continued to stand out. By the end of 1966, only 3.2 percent of black Mississippi children went to schools in which they made up less than 95 percent of the student body.[27]

"And a Child Shall Lead Them" (Isaiah 11:16)

By 1969, frustration with the glacial pace of school desegregation in Clarksdale led youth to bypass the local NAACP and take matters into their own hands. In many ways, this mirrored their initiatives in other direct-action protests. On 22 September, eighty-eight self-organized black pupils arrived at Clarksdale High School to apply for admission. Principal Robert Ellard escorted the group to the cafeteria, where he collected personal information. After he ushered the group off the campus, school officials swiftly screened the applications, rejecting them all because they were not from the school zone. By mid-morning, most of the applicants, who were enrolled at Higgins High School, returned to the Clarksdale High School campus and set up a picket line. Picketing lasted thirty minutes under the watchful eye of the city police and ended peacefully. The adults accompanying the group, including Roberta McCaskill (spokesperson for the Committee of Parents Respecting the Children) and Aaron Henry, tried to talk to Ellard. When he refused, they vowed to return if the students were not accepted. The next day brought more young people and confrontations with the city police. Students marched around the Clarksdale High School campus, despite repeated warnings from the new chief of police, Billy White and about a dozen armed police, and 118 students walked onto the campus and were arrested. The following day, between twenty and twenty-five

TABLE 3. Federal Figures Documenting School Desegregation Compliance in 1966

	Alabama	Georgia	Mississippi	North Carolina
Districts receiving federal funds	118	197	149	169
Districts in litigation	15	10	24	10
Court orders accepted	12	9	20	10
Districts submitting plans	98	180	113	155
Plans accepted	94	180	108	155
Freedom of Choice*	88	165	104	123
Geographic zoning*	1	6	2	16
Closing Negro schools*	0	1	0	4
Ceasing transferring out*	0	0	0	0
Other Plans*	5	8	2	12
1965~	62	128	5	130
1966~	3	15	2	22
1967~	29	37	101	3
Newly desegregated by accepted plan	92	175	97	113
Plans, court orders, and Form 441s accepted	107	194	128	169
% total districts accepted	90	99	85	100
% total accepted by 11 February 1966	88	99	85	100

*denotes type of plan accepted

~ denotes all grades affected by accepted plans

Source: "Elementary and Secondary Education Title VI, Civil Rights Act of 1964, March 1966," *Status of School Desegregation in Southern and Border States under the Civil Rights Act of 1964*, Office of Education, U.S. Commission on Civil Rights (AMP, Box 8, Folder 8, SHSW).

white males gathered on the sidewalk, some armed, to preempt black demonstrations, but local officials dispersed them without incident. Marches lasted well into October.[28]

Unlike the Birmingham Children's Crusade from 1963, in which the Southern Christian Leadership Conference (SCLC) organized children to march for the cameras, these children in Clarksdale initiated their own protests. The adults had to scramble and improvise in order to minimize arrests and unlawful activity. These parents, young adults themselves during *Brown*, had hoped to gain from the ruling. Fifteen years later, their children were tired of waiting. Believing that they had neither the time nor the need to placate white city leaders, many black youth in Clarksdale had sought to rid themselves of segregation once and for all.

The youth did not reserve their impatience just for the ensuing segregation battle in their schools. They had enough energy to take on the adult NAACP branch too. Youth Council members created the Student Committee in Support of Freedom and Justice following the student arrests and petitioned the branch to adopt their seven detailed proposals, designed to increase their presence in branch activities. Two years earlier, Vera Pigee, the organizer of the Clarksdale Youth Council and its longtime advisor, had made the decision to spend most of her time in Detroit, Michigan (that story resumes in the next chapter). However, she left her mark on the students—their tenacity and drive certainly reflected her legacy. Led by Milton Wells, representatives from all the high schools and the Youth Council served on this new Student Committee in Support of Freedom and Justice. The committee called for representation on negotiation committees (particularly on the issue of employment for black youth); support for its projects, like a boycott on Christmas decorations that year; the resumption of the boycott on downtown businesses; and regular Saturday marches until the schools desegregated. The students also wanted the right to attend weekly branch meetings, "as has been done in the past," and full voting power in the branch to ensure that their voices were heard.[29] Clearly Pigee's absence left the branch without the daily bridge between the youth and the adults, and the students demanded that their needs be met.

It is not clear how or if the adults in the local branch responded directly to the students' petitions, but the young people continued to press on with the desegregation struggle. Banking on the public's desire to avoid rioting and dissension, leaders had written to the school board trying to defuse the tension: "The agitation that is now prevalent in the community is partially controllable at this time. To be able to continue to maintain control within the law is difficult to predict at this time." The omnipresent "but . . ." hovered between the neatly typed lines. "Therefore we need your cooperation to ensure the young people and parents of our community that you too can see a plan that has been on trial for 5 years and has not worked, needs changing immediately." They continued to present the options: moderate change or radical revolution. The board did not bite. It maintained its position that the schools ran on a nonracial basis, with no distinction between salaries, pupil-teacher ratios, or per-pupil expenditures: "Every child, teacher, employee — black or white — is treated alike."[30]

A ruling on Derrick Bell's challenges to the zoning plan, promised in 1966 after much wrangling and delay, had finally come in March 1969. The circuit court ruled that the school board's zoning plan did not represent appropriate actions to desegregate.[31] The city's appeal for more time went to the Supreme Court that fall but was sent back to District Judge William Keady in November 1969. Like most of the region's judges, fifty-five-year-old Keady was a product of the South. He was bound by his oath to carry out the letter of the law, yet, like Clayton, he had grown up in a segregated system. He had led a full, active life in his native Greenville, where he served on the school board, which had supported equalization from 1947 to 1951. He maintained memberships in the Chamber of Commerce, the Kiwanis Club, and the Presbyterian Church, and he sat on the local hospital board. When Keady's 1968 confirmation, supported by Senators Eastland and Stennis, highlighted his torn loyalties, he withdrew all his civic and commercial affiliations except his church membership. Once on the bench, he received "blunt letters" from those expressing dismay at the judicial actions of a "son of the Delta."[32]

In an action separate from the zoning challenge, Keady ruled against the Clarksdale school board's October request for an injunction against the black protests, citing the "natural amount of impatience" in the black community. Marches had continued unabated for well over a month, and organized boycotts, named "Black Christmas," threatened to interfere with holiday sales. The local NAACP, using Vera Pigee's proven tactics, nudged the parents to take an active interest in the futures of their children's education. With the children on the front line in the marches, the branch again urged parents to join them on the picket lines in both the city and the county (which was embroiled in controversies over the "intelligence" tests imposed within the county's school system).[33]

Worried about the potential ruling in this defiant atmosphere, Leon Porter, a former city judge and now president of the school board, pointed to the need to "confer informally with [white] parent groups as soon as any definite information is in hand" (that is, make alternative arrangements for their children if necessary). The very next day, Porter and the superintendent received Keady's order mandating HEW to file a report with the court no later than 23 December 1969 for a modified desegregation plan of students and staff. The federal office had kept a keen eye on the court battles, prodded by letters of complaint from the local NAACP. A statement concerning these developments, hurriedly prepared by the board, was released to the two radio stations the day after Thanksgiving.[34]

HEW representatives Jack Simmons and Tom Grant, from Atlanta, visited Clarksdale ten days before Christmas. When the HEW report came, both the plaintiffs and the board flatly rejected it. Even Judge Keady remembered it as a "monstrosity." HEW proposed a consolidation scheme that would transform the two senior high schools into one and the three junior high schools into one; five elementary grades would pair, leaving only one sixth grade elementary school. Plaintiffs predicted that whites would flee and that the sixth grade school would remain all black. The board agreed that the plan, while legally unifying the school system, would start a white exodus, and that when this occurred, it would be beyond its control.[35] Both sides approached Christmas uneasy about the District Court's next move. Clarksdale's case had already outlived the Johnson administration and Rebecca Henry's school years.

Clarksdale's Schools Desegregate

After the Supreme Court's October 1969 ruling on the *Alexander v. Holmes County Board of Education* case, on 9 January 1970 the Fifth Circuit Court rejected the HEW *and* the school board plans and ordered immediate desegregation to begin on 1 February. This was a victory, but an ambiguous one, for the NAACP. The upper five grades were consolidated, and grades ten through twelve utilized the formerly all-white Clarksdale junior and senior high school buildings. Junior high, grades eight and nine, occupied the formerly black Higgins Junior High School and Higgins Senior High School buildings and the Oliver Elementary School building. Withholding an immediate order regarding the elementary schools, the court awaited advice to create a plan to become effective in September 1970.[36]

It was the middle of the school year, and the board worked long hours to interpret the court order and to give the superintendent specific operating instructions. Teachers, pupils, and even schools had to be reassigned, a process that normally would take about half a year "under the best of conditions and circumstances," the board complained. To avoid any possible disruption, Police Chief White assured the board that officers would stand on duty at the two secondary school sites during the first week of February. Many white teachers refused to transfer and resigned rather than comply with the order. The school board noted that "all of the resignations except one for maternity and two for health and financial reasons were brought about by the desegregation of school facilities and school students."[37]

As these teachers protested, white parents also marched against Keady's plan. In response, the local NAACP ruefully acknowledged, "We fully support the right of the white citizens to march. The plan left so much segregation that we don't like it either." Sponsored by a group called the Silent Majority of Coahoma County (borrowing President Richard Nixon's phrase), a crowd of 1,700 white parents, businessmen, housewives, and schoolchildren marched fifteen blocks downtown from the courthouse. Veterinarian Chad Mullins spoke briefly at the end of the march, claiming that the court orders only caused "black to hate white, white to hate black."[38] He echoed the voices of many white parents. At Clarksdale Junior High's Parent-Teacher Association meeting the following week, some parents and white teachers took a "wait and see" stance, reassured by Superintendent Tynes's guarantee that white students, who would be in the minority at desegregated schools, would have extensive supervision. Just as many parents and teachers vowed to remove themselves from the public school system.[39]

Joyce Kendricks vividly remembered the attempts to form alternative private schools for whites. Before desegregation, a highly efficient and active white parents' booster club supported Coahoma County High School's championship football team. That booster club led the grassroots movement to resist integration. Boosters had supported the founding of a private school, which opened in the fall of 1964, when the *Henry* case first entered the courts. With only six pupils in the fall's first-grade class, however, the school was not viable. Given the slowness of the desegregation case in the mid-sixties, the Coahoma Educational Foundation, the organization run by the local men who created the school, decided to end operations. But as one school failed, another rose to take its place. Kendricks recalled the founding of Lee Academy in detail:

Well the way they got Lee Academy was that those good boosters that we had, all those parents at Coahoma County, they were the planners. Good people, they supported us in everything we did. But they put the money where their mouth was and they borrowed money from the bank. . . . They co-signed loans and everything to build that school. . . . So that's where the money came from. The big money came from the county supporters. But they didn't have a place to go to at first, they were going in an old school building out at Lula. . . . They called it Lula-Ridge Academy at first. . . . The parents were going to have an organizational meeting at the courthouse.[40]

Kendricks worked as a secretary for the Chamber of Commerce. Her boss, whose children attended Clarksdale High School, asked her to attend the meeting and take notes. She continued:

I went to the meeting, had all my shorthand stuff ready . . . and Mr. Winter was principal of the Junior High city school at that time and he stood up and everybody clapped. . . . He stood up and said 'Ladies and Gentlemen, you no longer have a school,' everybody got quiet. . . . It put chills all over me, I didn't know whether to cry or throw up, I knew exactly how things would go then. . . . That statement just stunned that whole crowd, and honey, right then before he said another word, people began to stand up and write checks and hand money to build another school—that's where the money started coming for Lee Academy that night. . . . I wrote down everything they had to say, the whole thing. . . . My heart was in my shoes and I didn't sleep much that night. . . . I got up at about 2 A.M. and typed it up, put that in all caps and circled it again and threw it on my boss' desk.[41]

Meanwhile, the first week of comprehensive desegregation in the public schools initiated great changes to the educational landscape in the city. Only one teacher from grades seven and eight of the former white junior high school agreed to serve at the new central school at the Higgins-Oliver site. The rest of the white teachers remained in their original placements. At least 460 pupils in North Clarksdale's formerly all-white schools withdrew from school; some 369 were in grades seven and eight in the junior high school. At least seventy-nine elementary pupils and between twelve and fifteen senior high school students had withdrawn since the close of the first semester. In all, the system experienced at least a 10 percent loss of pupils during the immediate changeover.

The superintendent reported that parents on the whole cooperated but that "instruction had definitely been impaired to some extent in all schools and considerably at the Central Junior High School. . . . The problem of communication between teacher and pupils of dissimilar races would prove to be a serious obstacle to normal teacher-learning activities." At the end of the second week, the superintendent bemoaned the lack of learning since the changeover, complaining that school hours were devoted to "orientation, establishing rapport, developing skills in student-teacher communication and related activities." He continued dramatically: "I have never seen teacher morale at so low an ebb. . . . The specter of death seems to be haunting if not directly stalking the Clarksdale Public Schools. . . . The sins of the well-meaning but erring Court may be visited upon the children of this land to the third and fourth generation."[42]

The woes of the school board continued for some time. Losing a court battle landed the plaintiff's legal bills on its table. With bitter irony, the board now had to pay the NAACP Legal Defense Fund $3,774.79. Many of the teachers and principals obstructed the board's planning process by refusing to sign contracts for the next academic year, 1970–71, without knowledge of the court's ruling. By the end of March, 605 pupils had left the system, "greatly disturbing the pupil enrollment in the various schools." Court bickering over the fate of the elementary schools and the permanency of the high school plans continued through spring and into summer. Then, on 8 May 1970, the Fifth Circuit finally ruled to institute HEW's former elementary school plan while maintaining the district court's order regarding the upper six grades. If the school board had obeyed the ruling in 1964, exercised common sense, and instituted a meaningful, if gradual integration program, it might have avoided the extensive white flight and would not have found itself held hostage by the courts, educators, and parents. Now its only recourse was to wait and see.[43]

Life Desegregated

When school desegregation came to Clarksdale fifteen and a half years after *Brown*, it came swiftly and decisively. Nowhere was it written *how* the community would have to deal with this sudden change. Community reaction revealed the difference between desegregation—the act of mixing students, successfully achieved through the courts—and integration—the acceptance and social interaction with others. How would school administrators react to black students? And why were funds not channeled into the pedagogical training necessary for a smoother transition? Indeed, if the attitudes remained the same, how could integration succeed? These questions were asked at the time, and they remain pertinent today.

Veterans of Clarksdale's segregated school system recounted confusion and bitterness. Alpha Norphlet was one of the teachers selected to teach at the formerly all-white school. The board assigned the best black teachers to teach the white students, sending the lowest performing whites to the formerly all-black institutions, ensuring persistent inequality in standards and resources. Norphlet remembered that children, particularly the black teenage boys, were shuffled around in order to avoid contact with white women teachers. Teaching in once-white schools, she instantly saw how Jim Crow had cheated black children out of resources:

> What really bothered me was that they [the school board] did not want any children above twelve or thirteen years old, especially boys, in the classroom when those white women [teachers] would come over to our classrooms. And they would lift these kids in the middle of the school time and put them in grades two grades higher with 7th or 8th grade kids. And I do believe at that time we lost a lot of children because they could not cope with this and they dropped out of school. . . . I noticed when I was in teaching in the white schools, they had much more materials than we ever got. Right now, we don't get as much even though they have integrated the schools, but basically the white schools will get much more funding than we are getting.[44]

Jean Cauthen, a white woman, ran the local radio station for a time in the seventies and later ran for office on the Democratic ticket. Committed to equal rights, she gave on-air time to black citizens and tried to present balanced reports. She remembered the desegregation order and allowed her son to make a choice:

> My daughter graduated in 1956 and my son in 1971; school integration took place here in 1970—my daughter was already out of school and my son was to be a senior. His junior year they built Lee Academy, and the next year they had a midyear integration. And I gave him a choice. If he wanted to go to the Academy or stay in public school. He said he didn't care—he had friends who were staying and friends who were going. So I said that I wanted him to stay in the public school. At that time, most of the good teachers had stayed, the most experienced. They were riding out pensions and didn't want to leave. So there was not that big a difference. Some black teachers came over. He had an interesting experience that first year of integration. The year before he'd signed up for chemistry, before school was out. During the summer, we decided when talking that he should switch to physics. He went to school the first day and went to the office and told them that he wanted to change. They told him to meet that first-period class, be excused,

and go to the office. And then go into roll call. In the class, it was a black teacher, a man, when he held up his hand and asked to be excused. The teacher said why and he said, "I want to go to the office to change classes." Well, I can imagine what was going through that teacher's head. . . . "I've only been here 10 minutes and he wants out of my class already!" As it happened, the same teacher taught physics. So Doug goes to the office, and physics met 3rd period, so he returned to class. I think he was Professor Battle's pet throughout the year, possibly thinking, "I should learn not to pre-judge too quick!" In fact I saw [him] not too long ago, he's retired. We were talking and he remembered it! Everyone came over with a bit of apprehension—the whites didn't know what to expect, the blacks didn't know what to expect.[45]

Cauthen makes two important points. First, this average white teenager, if asked, did not mind going to school with black children. He was more concerned with maintaining his cohort of friends and graduating with them. The white parents, not their children, were more invested in the segregated system. The parents demanded the restrictions placed on both teachers and students. Second, the court order affected *everyone*—white teachers and students and black teachers and students. Black teachers, teaching white students for the first time, were understandably sensitive to white reactions in the classroom. They assumed that white students and officials lay in wait for an excuse to fire them. Many of the white teachers stayed, not necessarily because they believed in integration, but to wait out their time before retiring with full pensions.

Brenda Luckett grew up in the Clarksdale school system, and her parents were active in the local branch of the NAACP from the mid-sixties. In the late nineties, she taught special needs children in the schools. She recalled her observations in 1970 and echoed Cauthen's conclusion that adults exacerbated the crisis by imposing their prejudice on their children:

I was in Junior High when they integrated. Before that the junior school was our black High School [Higgins]. . . . [Integration] didn't bother me that much because we were in the majority so it wasn't a problem. Even the teachers were in a majority. . . . But the Superintendent and the administration was white, all white. We had had black principals, so it bothered us because they demoted our faculty and put whites over them. The principal of the black high school was taken over to Clarksdale High and made Assistant Principal there, Mr. Joseph Hardy. He sued the city . . . and he won.

They took the black counselor from the black high school and put her up on the third floor in the older building of the high school and she didn't do any counseling—that was Verda Jones. . . . The parents were the ones with the problem; we didn't have no problems! Some of the parents resented the fact that their children had to go to school with us, but they couldn't do anything else. But we did have, for instance, Dr. Bobo—his children came over here to Higgins, [and] they went through the completely integrated system. And he was a doctor, and a lot of blacks started going to him after that. . . . As a matter of fact his wife used to ride the kids over here on horses . . . he was just that down-to-earth; but they were in a minority when it came to whites who came from affluent families—they didn't integrate. A lot of them integrated when they got to High School, and I think that's because a lot of their fathers and mothers went to Clarksdale High, and that was like a stronghold—they refused to let that go. Even in that instance it wasn't bad for us; we didn't have problems—the parents had problems. . . . We had separate proms, separate class parties, the parents had their own. We had nothing at school that was one of the products of integration. Nothing happened after the bell rang to go home. . . . When we had Beta clubs and things like that, they met during school time. . . . One thing that really tickled me was when they integrated they closed the swimming pool. They had a swimming pool at Clarksdale High and they gave swimming classes, but they cemented it in because they did not want blacks and whites swimming in the same pool. . . . A lot of activities that they had, they stopped having it.[46]

Luckett's testimony bemoaned the loss of extracurricular activities, which normally filled out the day in segregated schools. Children of both races could sit together in the classroom, but as the court order did not extend to extracurricular or recreational clubs and activities, neither made attempts to integrate. Children were unable to create or sustain friendships and bonds with each other if separated during leisure time, exacerbating rather than mitigating distrust and prejudice. Of course, that was the point. Denying African Americans access to such facilities, like the swimming pool, cost white children the chance to swim also. Rather than desegregate, both did without.

Some of the prejudice exhibited by parents inevitably trickled down to the children. On both sides, students sometimes demonstrated great hostility toward each other. The school board, however, already bitter about the court order, aggravated the situation by disproportionately disciplining black children over white. The case of Linda Johnson illustrates one of the many problems that desegregation produced.

On 3 April, two months after the court ordered desegregation, tenth-grader Linda Johnson picked up a softball bat in a physical education class, thrust it in the face of fellow student Deidra Ellis, and spoke of using it with words liberally peppered with profanities. Linda (who was black) was suspended immediately for threatening another student, Deidra (who was white). Linda showed no remorse, and neither she nor her mother would pledge against a future reoccurrence. During the subsequent hearing with the school board on 20 April, Linda, flanked by her parents and a lawyer, justified her actions, stating that Deidra had referred to her as black and a "nigger." Linda stood by her actions, although she did not report the incident to any school official, stating emphatically that she would do the same in similar circumstances. The board believed Deidra, who denied the insult. Linda sat out the remainder of the school year.[47]

Her case did not stand alone. The superintendent reported that Clarksdale Junior High School suspended twenty-one students between 21 April and 14 May. Although the students' racial identities did not appear explicitly in the school board minutes, accompanying reports suggest a direct correlation. A month before, the superintendent had complained about the lack of discipline and problems with language from South Clarksdale (the black side of town) among the teachers, pupils, and parents. Furthermore, the board announced the restoration of order to the school, and "teaching and learning conditions improved markedly."[48] Evidently, the board tolerated racial epithets and slurs from whites but proscribed the language of people from South Clarksdale and Johnson's defensive actions.

The local NAACP made sure to see the court order carried out to the letter. On a sweltering mid-July evening, the Clarksdale Neighborhood Center hosted an "enthusiastic gathering of NAACP members, parents, and children" at the weekly branch meeting. The meeting centered around the blatant manipulation from the school board and city administration for black students to attend Agricultural High School (Aggie) rather than the city high school. Many interpreted the "press statements and verbal utterances . . . to be an attempt to circumvent, evade, or get around the Court Orders." By encouraging black student enrollment at Aggie, outside of the city limits, the student population at Clarksdale High would whiten once again, encouraging white parents to leave their children in the public system.

Students stood up assertively and raised other points for the adults to dis-

cuss and act upon during the meeting. As Brenda Luckett described, transferred black instructors were assigned roles as assistants to white teachers,
particularly in the administration, counseling, and athletic departments and
in extracurricular activities. Despite the students' complaints, the demotions
of black teachers continued. They also grumbled about internal segregation
within the building. In order to keep the races separate and to circumvent the
desegregation order, officials put black students with a black teacher in one
room while an identical course took place in another classroom with white
teachers and students. Additionally, students complained indignantly about
acts of harassment and of not being included in awards, extracurricular activities, and busing.[49]

These students represented a new generation. Barely out of puberty when
the Student Nonviolent Coordinating Committee (SNCC) had come to town,
they had observed the power and potential of their generation in molding and
forcing change in their world. They absorbed the fearlessness and tenacity they
had witnessed, and that energy came forth with abundance when the opportunity came for them to lead. In a prime position as the pioneers of a desegregated system, many asserted themselves and commanded the adults to follow their lead. At the end of the meeting, they insisted that the adults in the
branch submit a report the following week outlining progress made in the
issues raised. They would accept nothing less. They declared: "We the students
insist that these problems that we have mentioned be corrected immediately.
Either you adults correct them your way, or you leave us no course but to develop a method of [our] own."[50]

Parents, who had been reared in the post–World War II period and who had
suffered in poor schools under the belligerent rhetoric of segregationists, stood
behind their children. In their lifetimes, they had witnessed the possibilities of
real, substantive change, and many agitated to make sure their children benefited. Mothers, in particular, kept track of their children's daily progress in
their new environments. Brenda Luckett remembered the gendered nature of
oppression and attitudes of resistance:

> Especially those mothers who had boys, they were really active, because
> they did not want their sons to be humiliated the way other men had been
> humiliated. The majority of my students are boys [in special education] be-
> cause they're bad and people don't want to deal with them, but I tell them
> all the time that you all don't realize that you are our leaders. And a black

boy doesn't have to do anything but stand up, that's all. And there's a fear in this community when it comes to black men who will stand up, and I also believe there's always been a conspiracy to destroy them . . . to put them in such a light that other people will not want to deal with them. . . . There are very few men who worked in the civil rights movement that have survived, financially or socially. . . . A lot of them didn't make it because they couldn't handle the pressure . . . but the women could handle it better. Plus a lot of these women worked for these whites. They raised their children and they couldn't really confront them the way they could black men, because they were still working in their kitchens and they were still feeding their children. . . . They couldn't deal with the women, because the women had already infiltrated their families. . . . They would say, "How can you hate me when I nursed your child? . . . I'm good enough to nurse your child but I'm not good enough to sit by you?"[51]

Lillie Neal, a single mother with four children in school, remained very involved in her children's education. Her children had attended Immanuel Conception, the parochial Catholic school for African Americans, and two of them were the first to integrate St. Elizabeth—the white counterpart. She remembered rallies for homecoming queen and the organizing of the black students to choose only one or two candidates from which to vote in order to avoid splitting their majority and rendering the sole white candidate the winner: "It was totally being racial but if they didn't they were not going to have [a black homecoming queen] over there. They had to be taught, you know children have to be trained too. Later on we said it's time for you to get the best person and they understand that now. If someone is qualified, you give it to them regardless of color, but only after things got better. But at first you had to show them." She knew what was at stake. "It was that important to me that my children had a better life than we have," she said.[52]

Not all white parents fled the system or supported the rabid activities of their peers. Joyce Kendricks, note taker during the meeting that organized Lee Academy, raised her children within the city limits and refused to send them to Lee. She recalled her horror to learn of her church's involvement in the resistance against desegregation:

Well, they didn't have their school built yet, so my church, Oakhurst Baptist Church, a couple of the deacons there offered the use of our church as a junior high for the rest of the year. . . . That stunned me—I thought my church would not go along with this. And they absolutely did. That bothered me more than anything, because I began to think that if these people really feel that strongly about it and they wanted to start a private school that's their business, they would put their money in it and make sure their children didn't go to school with anybody they don't want to. . . . There's no such thing as a private church in my view — every church is God's house. . . . I fought and wrestled with that for the longest kind of time.

It was not long before white supremacist rhetoric was overtly preached from the pulpit, affecting this congregation adversely. She continued:

And it began to creep into the sermons in church. I began to notice a difference between the kids in church, my kids were approaching Junior High at the time — the ones who were going to the private school at the church began to shun the kids who were not, that they had been friends with before, and I thought this is happening in my church! And it was discussed in Sunday School . . . and the word got out that . . . a delegation of blacks were going to come on a certain Sunday or whatever. . . . I thought, what's the big deal, they won't like it here anyway. . . . Finally I got my Sunday School teacher off to the side, I respected him so much . . . he was the most gentle person and one of the best Christians I'd ever known. . . . And I asked him . . . "What would you do if you were standing at the door and a black came at the door of the church and wanted to come in," and he said that he wouldn't allow him to come in, and I said, "What if they wanted to come in anyway?" and he said, "I'd have to call the police." And I said, "This is God's house," and he said, "We built this church and we paid for it." . . . But in my view, once you build it it's not yours anymore. . . . That disillusioned me so much.[53]

She was not the only voice of dissent. Charles C. Wiggers, a member of the First United Methodist Church, wrote a letter to the membership and congregation opposing the use of church facilities for private schools, particularly when those schools "are in direct conflict with the teachings of this church and more especially the Gospel of Christ." He requested that each member search his or her heart and soul to make the decision, ending his appeal with a request that respect should govern members' treatment of each other, regardless of decisions made, as "every individual is entitled to the basic freedom of his decision." Even Judge Keady recalled regrettably, "My ruling of massive desegregation in elementary schools caused wholesale white flight to the city's churches until such time as Lee Academy could be enlarged to care for an exploding student body in the private school."[54]

In the meantime, white flight out of residential areas in South Clarksdale continued in droves: "It was apparent that people were re-locating in an effort to have their children attend neighborhood schools in which their culture is the dominant one." The school board, unwilling to save the deteriorating public school system, vowed to continue to "tell the truth of the situation of education in Clarksdale rather than try to persuade people to stay in the system."[55] Clarksdale's ranking in the state for funding fueled the exodus. The district ranked fourth out of the state's 148 districts for revenue from local sources, and ninety-second out of 120 for revenue from the state and from federal sources. Therefore, the school system, unable to receive substantial federal assistance due in part to the violation of Title VI of the Civil Rights Act of 1964, received most of its budget from local taxation. White parents balked at the prospect of paying for the education of the black majority in the new consolidated school system, just as they had for the equalization programs' tab years before. As more students left, the system experienced loss of income from the tax levy and state funds and less affluent parent involvement than it had had, leaving it in dire straits.[56]

Attempts by the black community to collaborate with the school board for a smoother transition encountered hostility and evasion. The Bi-racial Advisory Committee, established and sanctioned by the district court in the winter and spring of 1970 to negotiate the elementary school plan, struggled for board recognition. Securing a thirty-day delay of the deadline to report to the district judge regarding further desegregation, the board flatly refused to meet in December, suggesting that the Bi-racial Advisory Committee's chair, Joseph Wheatley, should contact HEW in Atlanta to help. Two weeks into 1971, the board scheduled to meet with the committee—for one hour.[57]

The board did make history in early 1971, however—1 February marked the day that the first African American, Henry Espy, was appointed to Clarksdale's school board. Born and raised in Yazoo City, Mississippi, he graduated from Southern University in Baton Rouge, Louisiana, in 1964, majoring in business. Involved in civil rights activities on campus and marching in Baton Rouge to desegregate the lunch counters, he was confronted with the prospect of arrest. Knowing that his parents did not have the means to bail him out and deciding that his arrest would not further the cause, he concluded that the best way to beat the system was at the conference table rather than on the streets. Change could be made through negotiation, and he set out to break the numerous glass ceilings above his head. After teaching school for one year in Hammond, Louisiana, he came to Clarksdale in 1965 to direct the Century Funeral Home, one among the family's many funeral homes scattered throughout the area.[58]

Whether regarded as the token "safe," more moderate black member with no seniority rights and no real voice on the majority white board, or as a pioneer in the community, he was the first. Espy served as a conduit between the school board and the black community. During the first summer school session in his tenure, Espy discovered that the plaintiffs in the school desegregation case had complained to the court about the noncompliance of the program, stating that all five of the summer teachers were white. With this information, a special board meeting convened to rectify the situation in order to avert further court orders or penalty. Espy's assigned role was clarified in the next academic year when he was sent to get "his" community's reactions to proposals for a school in southeast Clarksdale near a new housing project. Rather than engaging with the Bi-racial Advisory Committee members themselves, the board specifically sent him to "get the reaction of leading citizens" and to impress "upon them the crucial nature of the problem the children in the Oliver Zone are facing next September and the months following."[59]

Black teachers' lives had changed. Once relatively anonymous in the segregated system unless they were known as NAACP members or sympathizers, now standing before white students made them subject to greater scrutiny. Indeed, Jean Cauthen's testimony about her son's experience with his physics teacher illustrated tensions in the classroom. Teacher Vera Harrell remembered: "They had department heads. . . . They would come in and look to see, I guess they were evaluating what we were doing. . . . They gave us our children, black children. . . . In other words they said take your class over there." Harrell bitterly resented the supervision:

> They would sit in your class as if you didn't know what you were doing. . . . It looked like I saw [the particular observer] every week. . . . It got so they had to tell us what we had to do. . . . If you went about doing what you were meant to do, you wouldn't have any problems with them. . . . When some of the white children got into your classes, they thought you didn't know what you were doing. They would come up, me in a math class, with funny little math problems and say work this for me. I call it silly math — had nothing to do with algebra which is what I was teaching. They did it to test you to see if you knew what you were doing. Once they found out that I knew what I was

doing, they stopped testing me. Some other teachers didn't fare that well. We were evaluated in everything that we did, everything. You are knowing that you are going into a situation where you are unwanted in the first place.

She had to deal with harassment from the white students too:

> I had one boy who called me a black bitch. I wanted to flunk him but I couldn't flunk him. They talked about you. . . . He called me a black bitch — I wanted to hit him. But we knew that you couldn't bother them — there would have been a law suit. . . . One thing that Mr. Stampley [Assistant Superintendent Jerome W. Stampley] always asked us to [do was to] join the Teacher's Association. . . . I can see now why we needed to when we went over there, because you had to be prepared for what you had to do. . . . The children in the classroom went down, I know a lot of them did and told the principal something, and who did the principal believe, the black child, the white child, or the teacher. They'd believe a white child. . . . Some of the other black teachers really caught it.

The administration and the school board undermined the black teachers at every turn, preventing them from gaining promotions:

> When we got to Clarksdale High school, if you were white anyone could be a department head, but when we got there they wrote in that you had to have a master's degree to be a department head. So what happened that all of us who they said were good went to Delta State and got our master's degree. Then . . . there were more blacks in Clarksdale High with master's degrees than whites, they cut them out, didn't have any more department heads. . . . We would have been in the majority as far as being department heads.[60]

Sara Cannon was a mother as well as a teacher. She was transferred to Oakhurst, formerly a white school, and described what life was like for black teachers: "They [white teachers] had breaks. We knew nothing about no breaks, they wouldn't give us breaks! Our principal wouldn't let us go outdoors with children. We didn't have recess with children. . . . We stayed in school all day long. . . . There was so much difference between what their teachers were doing and what our teachers were doing."[61]

Donell Harrell, Vera Harrell's husband, had worked in the school system since 1964. At the time of his reappointment in 1971, a parent complained that in December 1970 he had used "inappropriate" material in a sociology course.

Henry Espy, as the official liaison, checked the material and deemed it suitable but stated "that some criticism continue[d] to come concerning a possible hang up or fixation on controversial matters or racial overtones in Mr. Harrell's sociology classes." Harrell had taught two sociology classes, an elective course, and three American government classes at the high school the previous year. The offending class, sociology, was for one semester for half of a credit. The questionable material consisted of discussions about race and discrimination. After a school board meeting with the parent, Dean Spradling, and city commissioner Billy Garrett (who refused to reveal his sources), the superintendent received instructions to watch the lesson plans, which had purportedly developed into a black history course. Harrell was reappointed only after Sam Kendricks, the principal, observed his class to monitor its content. This caution signaled a growing hesitancy to precipitate legal proceedings. Judge Keady in his memoirs noted the proliferation of employment litigation in the district, the most conventional cases involving black teachers suing school boards for discriminatory behavior based on the equal protection clause and Title VII.[62]

Court decisions affected white school administrations also. Sam Kendricks became principal as a result of the order. Previously employed as a football coach in the Coahoma County public school system, he had resigned because he did not want to be director of athletics and head coach under the court terms, with "the resulting effect upon the pupil population at the high school." His wife, Joyce, recalled the difficult few months. Kendricks coached a highly successful football team in the county school, and when the desegregation order came down, most of the team transferred to Lee Academy, leaving him with no team: "That decimated him. . . . So he resigned and the principal had told him that if he couldn't coach the way he wanted to that he can leave. . . . Lee was recruiting heavily to get teachers." She talked him out of going to Lee, saying it would be run like a country club with the paying parents in his way making his work difficult and frustrating.[63]

Preferring to work in Clarksdale, where his three children attended elementary school, rather than teach at Lee Academy, Kendricks became a social studies teacher, head of the department, and second assistant principal for the high school. He had AA certification in secondary school administration and social studies, with eleven years experience as a teacher and coach. His wife said, "He was already taking classes at Delta State where he had already worked on his master's in administration, and he was working on his specialist [credentials]." When Joseph J. Hardy, the black assistant principal, resigned in June 1971, Kendricks took the position, against his wife's advice. Instead of replacing Hardy with another African American to keep the ratio in school administration comparable to the teaching staff, the board chose to promote Kendricks to ensure that the top two in the school were white. Joyce had warned him that "the pressure is going to be worse when the real integration comes in this fall" and that it would affect his home life. Kendricks was promoted to principal after Superintendent Tynes retired in 1972.[64]

In the midst of all the changes occurring in the teaching faculty and administration of the newly organized schools, the local NAACP monitored the situation and continued to push for improvements in educational services as guaranteed by law. Aaron Henry, prompted by *Swann v. Charlotte-Mecklenburg Board of Education* (1971), wrote a public letter to the board early in the 1971 school year regarding busing. On behalf of the branch and the "Black Community of Clarksdale," he requested adequate modes of transportation for the many small children who walked long distances to desegregated schools: "We are grateful for the plan of desegregation issued by the courts, but we do not feel that the City school board should participate in a punishment effort to make it as difficult as possible for Black Children and Poor White Children to participate in this newly gained freedom."[65] No transportation existed after desegregation, and the letter hinted that if an amicable solution could not be made, a court decision would prevail.

In response to Henry, the board issued a lengthy letter, published in the *Clarksdale Press Register* and read out on-air at the radio station. The board blocked Henry Espy from the deciding vote, with the questionable reasoning that his tenure began *after* the desegregation plan order. The minutes, however, documented that the board "released" Espy from signing his name on the decision. Having excluded Espy, the board swiftly made a decision that was in the interests of segregationists. Cleverly, they silenced Espy with their justifications, citing the "potential" conflict of interest and not letting him compromise his position as the liaison, arguably the only real reason he was a member. The public excuse merely covered up Espy's probable opposition, effectively silencing but not disgracing him. The board blamed the current situation on the plaintiff's persistence in the courts and based their resistance on the idea that "anyone with the slightest degree of intelligence and an acquaintance with the local conditions had to know that such results would follow the imposition of such a plan." The board's counter-letter stressed its preference for neighborhood schools and deplored that students had to walk past perfectly good schools near their homes because of the court order. It claimed it had neither the authority nor the funds to provide transportation: "We can add that if we had the authority to provide pupil transportation out of funds available to us — which we do not have — we would not do so. It could only be done by eliminating necessary educational services and by a drastic cut in teachers' salaries."[66]

Children as Activists and Pawns

On 1 August 1972, a motion was filed to require the district to provide buses for elementary schoolchildren residing more than a mile away from school.[67] In a subsequent hearing, Superintendent Robert Ellard reported the demographics in the seven elementary schools in the district (see table 4). The black, poor areas where Riverton, Washington, and Hall elementary schools were located show significantly more black students than white. Heidelberg and Kirkpatrick schools, located in predominantly white residential areas, reflect more equal racial numbers. Oakhurst, a white area on the cusp of black neighborhoods, saw a flood of black students in and an opposite wave of white students out. All the schools were predominantly black by 1972 — the majority of white students migrating to Lee Academy or to church-based schools.[68]

Ellard argued that trying to move students around to minimize busing would not change the racial composition of the schools. Leon Porter, chair of the Clarksdale Board of Trustees for at least four years, testified that "the white pupil population has diminished sizably. . . . I think we lost over a thousand elementary white pupils. A thousand forty-three, if I recall correctly." Arguing against busing, attorney Semmes Luckett for the school board said: "Why should we have to bus a child to the equivalent of an all black school when he has got one right in his neighborhood that he can walk to the school? What necessity is there for us to do that?" All his pontificating proved fruitless. On 3 October, the district court ruled that the board *had* to work out how to create a transportation system, based on *Swann*, with the three existing buses in the city.[69]

Such tit-for-tat maneuvering between the black community (represented by the NAACP) and white citizens (represented by the school board) continued outside of the courtroom. For example, in the summer of 1972, the board received copies of a student conduct code, along with personal appearance regulations, discipline policy, and administrative procedures, for inclusion in the 1972–73 student handbook. The code came from the Pascagoula public schools, a district entangled in an extensive federal lawsuit due to many of the items

TABLE 4. Racial Demographics in the Seven Clarksdale Elementary Schools in 1972

School	Percentage of Black Students in School	Grade	Number of Black Students	Number of White Students
Heidelberg	60	3rd	39	52
		4th	64	42
Kirkpatrick	57	5th	54	46
		6th	64	44
Oakhurst	94	5th	176	9
		6th	147	11
Riverton	80	1st	128	23
		2nd	33 (24 in S.E.)	19
Washington	95	3rd	158	12
		4th	150 (10 in S.E.)	6
Oliver	99	1st	39	1
		2nd	47	0
		3rd	64	0
		4th	52	0
		5th	108	3
		6th	83	0
Hall	95	1st	146	10
		2nd	15	12
		3rd	60	2
		4th	48	0

S.E. = Special Education

Source: School board figures submitted to the court hearing, Monday, 25 September 1972 in front of Judge Keady, U.S. District Court in *Rebecca E. Henry, et al. v. Clarksdale Municipal Separate School District, et al. (DC 6428-K)*.

included. The city board decided to forge ahead to implement these stricter changes.[70] One of the codes governed student hairstyles—especially the length of boys' hair. In the days of the growing popularity of the Afro, which was encouraged by Black Power rhetoric, many black boys were punished for their stylish dos and sent home.

Sara Cannon recalled the double standard in the dress code that was enforced in the schools in order to expel black boys in particular. Her own son carefully grew his Afro, which she washed and curled for him regularly. One of the school principals took out a ruler to actually measure the length of his hair and threatened to expel him. Rulers never came close to white boys' long hair. To combat these actions, she helped to organize a Parent-Teacher Association at Clarksdale High School. Following in Vera Pigee's activist mothering footsteps, she used her connections as an NAACP member to help the parents of one boy on the football team who was expelled for having "hair on his face," even as white boys grew their hair long. Cannon weighed the risks of her actions but decided that she was so well connected within the community that firing her would be more trouble than it was worth: "The community was going to be with me, so if [the school principal] fought me he would have to fight everybody, and I knew that, because I was going to pull everybody in on him."[71]

The black youth continued to be active and voice opinions, despite tightened discipline targeted directly at them. On 16 February 1973, approximately 125 black students at Clarksdale High simultaneously left their classes at the end of the first period and congregated in the school gymnasium. Protesting Principal Sam Kendrick's denial of Student Council president Jonathan Harris's application to hold a black history assembly program, the students disrupted a scheduled physical education class. Kendricks was placed in a difficult position. His wife, Joyce, recollected: "Sam was told by the administration . . . the central office told him that no, it would stir up a lot of trouble." Court records read: "There is a definite need felt by black students to emphasize black history and to express appropriate tributes to black persons famous in American history. This need is especially felt since these figures, by and large, do not appear and are not discussed in the standard history books used in public school."[72] The school had allowed interested teachers to conduct classes emphasizing black history in eleventh-grade American history classes, but for the student body as a whole a comprehensive program did not exist.

This was a nonviolent demonstration. Arriving at the gymnasium, Kendricks found the students seated in the bleachers listening to Larry Holden, one of the later plaintiffs, reading to the crowd from the Bible. Fellow student Pat Williams sang a solo; Sandra Williams read an excerpt from Julius Lester's *To Be a Slave*; and Jonathan Harris, Holden, and other students read from famous black writers. Kendricks repeatedly ordered the students to return to classes for twenty minutes, to no avail.[73] Gerald Johnson, the third named plaintiff, expressed his dissatisfaction with Kendricks's request by raising his fist skyward in the Black Power salute and encouraging the students to stand fast.

Kendricks returned to his office and reported the incident to the superintendent, who advised the principal to warn the students that they had three options: return to class, go home, or suffer suspension. Within five minutes following his warning in the gym, Kendricks called the city police. Only when Larry Holden was seized by the arm and escorted out of the room by the police did the other students follow. All of the students were suspended—118 for three days and seven indefinitely. Four went to Assistant Superintendent Jerome W. Stampley, who determined that they should be readmitted. The cases of the remaining three went to a special faculty committee "composed of two blacks and one white, plus Mr. Stampley."[74] About 200 black students met at the Clarksdale Neighborhood Center on 20 February to organize a boycott of the city schools after a meeting of black parents with Superintendent Ellard to clarify the meaning of "indefinite suspension." Ellard had reportedly brushed them off, telling parents to meet with the Board of Trustees. The ensuing march was peaceful and orderly, with adult advisors accompanying each group of students to their particular school.[75] The parents and their attorney arranged a hearing before the school board on 27 February. Ruling in the interest of maintaining school discipline, the board upheld the suspensions for the balance of the school year.

Joyce Kendricks recounted the incident as she witnessed her husband's struggle:

The blacks boycotted the school and the businesses and they had marches. . . . And that drove [her husband] nuts—he was scared to death. When this took place, the kids were OK with it, the white kids would've been OK with it if the parents had left them there, because the kids got along—it was new to both of them, but they got along and would have continued to do so. It was the adults who probably had endured more overt racism and bigotry in their long life span than the young ones had. . . . The young ones were little geese like I was, in high school just thinking about boyfriends. . . . If the adults had stayed out of it I think there would have been a different atmosphere. And the look on his [Sam's] face when he came home and when he couldn't sleep at night, he didn't expect people to react to him, because he didn't intend to mistreat anybody, he was just going to run the school. . . . He was a strict disciplinarian. This is a white perspective that this was the first rallying point that they could put their finger on that this was prejudicial and it was, it was OK. But I did not expect it, nor did my husband. It was a scary, miserable time.[76]

Well versed in the social and political situation in Clarksdale by this point, the court acknowledged that "Clarksdale [was] a community having a sophisticated, well organized and extensive black leadership. Its black citizens [were] alert to the issues of the times. This awareness [was] reflected directly in their sons and daughters who attend the Clarksdale public schools."[77] Regardless, the court ruled that the procedural due process used in disciplining the protesters was lawful. The school board had provided a biracial faculty committee, thus cushioning themselves from further accusations of racism. The plaintiffs argued against the unreasonable punishment, given the intelligent leadership of the three young men, but the court would not rule on school board discipline, especially as the students *had* blatantly breached school discipline codes. The court also ruled that the students benefited from equal protection of the law, and that their leadership warranted their different punishments from the others involved. However, the court did agree with the plaintiffs' demand for a black history month program. Keady argued that in Clarksdale it might actually improve relations between the races, and he issued an injunction requiring the Clarksdale school board to institute a week for a Black History Month program during the month of April. Attendance would be optional but open to all. He ended by chastising the students for protesting before seeking court guidance, since the actions had severely disrupted the lives of the three young men.

Members of the local NAACP branch viewed this ruling with mixed emotions. While delighted that Judge Keady realized the necessity of black history in the public school system, they were disappointed that he had nevertheless "sacrificed three Black students for their efforts to bring this action about." Calling the three expelled students martyrs, the branch's report to the national office repeatedly evoked the gender of the teenagers as a principal reason for such stern action against them. "It is a tragedy that Judge Keady, as fair as he tries to be, did not discover the real evil thinking and intent of some member of the Clarksdale city school board and some members of the School Administration, regarding the expulsion of three Black male students with obvious leadership qualities." The report continued: "The evil compounded in the school board's expulsion decision is a manifestation of the racism of some members of that group, who are determined to destroy and subdue 'Black Male Leadership.'

The fact that these three expelled students are Black males, is crucial."[78] The NAACP evoked the images of martyrdom encapsulated by the deaths of Medgar Evers, John and Robert Kennedy, Martin Luther King, and Vernon Dahmer, and the three young men carried upon them the yokes of oppression also suffered by the thousands of lynchings that stained the nation's soil.[79] Theirs was a symbolic lynching—a symbolic castration. Lillie Neal recalled: "They expelled Dr. Jonathan Harris in his senior year. He took his GED [General Educational Development tests] and went on to college in Xavier down in Louisiana and said that is what made him become a doctor."[80] As before, however, the setback only spurred on the young activists.

In the summer of 1973, the local NAACP branch wrote Mayor Joseph Nosef and the city commission, which then included Henry Espy. Unable once again to secure an audience with the Clarksdale school board, the letter listed the grievances still lurking in the school system. The government, the newly elected mayor, and a fresh batch of commissioners inspired hope in the black community. Expecting some positive action, the letter questioned the ratio between black and white teachers and students in the system, the unwarranted and unexplained refusal to renew the contracts of certain black faculty members, and the disparity in salary increases between the races. They also requested the appointment of another black board member after the 18 May resignation of Henry Espy (so he could serve as a city commissioner). Furthermore, they asked for a study of bus routes in the city so that the itineraries could best serve the black community.[81] By January 1974, the branch, exasperated with the city government's indifference in dealing with the problems outlined, voted a motion of "no confidence," and, adding to the list of grievances, the branch noted the discrimination in the police department and city staff promotional systems.[82]

The Story Continues: Illusory Progress?

By 1971, a high percentage of white children had left the public schools to attend alternative institutions, creating a still highly segregated public school system. As per Judge Keady's court order on 25 January 1971, the school board had to submit a report of the enrollment figures for each semester (see table 5). The slightly raised totals from 1987 onward result from "others"—namely Chinese immigrants to the city school system, who attended those schools where the majority of the students were white.[83] Table 6 shows a further breakdown of the figures for the fall semesters of 1977, 1979, and 1980, illustrating

TABLE 5. Ratio of Black Children to White Children from the Spring Semester
Figures for 1977–79, 1982–87, 1993, and 1995–97 in Clarksdale Public Schools

Year	Black Students	White Students	Total Students	Ratio
1977	2,795	541	3,336	5.16
1978	2,769	554	3,323	4.99
1979	2,717	565	3,282	4.8
1982	2,805	549	3,354	5.11
1983	2,817	589	3,406	4.78
1984	2,842	597	3,441	4.76
1985	2,997	753	3,750	3.98
1986	3,045	832	3,877	3.66
1987	3,229	1,267	4,506	2.55
1993	3,460	1,025	4,505	3.376
1995	3,330	937	4,290	3.55
1996	3,333	888	4,242	3.75
1997	3,301	856	4,178	3.856

Source: Figures submitted each semester to the U.S. District Court for the Northern District of
Mississippi, Delta Division, as per the order of 25 January 1971 by Judge William C. Keady,
U.S. District Court Clerk's Office, Oxford, Miss.

the segregated nature of the schools, despite the desegregation order. Note
the reversal in the distribution of black and white students in those schools
located in predominantly white neighborhoods (Heidelberg and Kirkpatrick
elementary schools). There was a far greater imbalance in junior high than in
high school, as many white parents placed their children in parochial schools
during their formative years.

By the mid-eighties, no white children consistently attended Hall, Oliver,
or Booker T. Washington elementary schools; they attended Heidelberg or
Kirkpatrick schools instead. In 1986–87, two new elementary schools opened,
Hall IV and Stampley—built to cope with the burgeoning number of black
students in the school system. Although Stampley elementary school had a

TABLE 6. Desegregation in Clarksdale Public Schools—Fall Semester Figures for 1977, 1979, and 1980

1977	Black Pupils	White Pupils	Total Pupils	Black Teachers	White Teachers	Total Teachers
High School	425	199	624	11	30	41
Junior High	557	24	581	25	4	29
Intermediate	292	42	334	11	10	21
Hall Elementary	243	2	245	6	5	11
Heidelberg Elementary	63	95	158	2	5	7
Kirkpatrick Elementary	83	109	192	2	7	9
Oakhurst Elementary	219	6	225	5	12	17
Oliver Elementary	498	0	498	17	9	26
Riverton Elementary	172	61	233	5	8	13
B. T. Washington Elementary	281	0	281	10	5	15
Total	2,833	538	3,371	94	95	189

1979	Black Pupils	White Pupils	Total Pupils	Black Teachers	White Teachers	Total Teachers
High School	455	238	693	12	14	26
Junior High	521	3	524	26	2	28
Intermediate	270	19	289	12	11	23
Hall Elementary	209	0	209	5	8	13
Heidelberg Elementary	60	123	183	4	8	12
Kirkpatrick Elementary	56	122	178	2	10	12
Oakhurst Elementary	235	7	242	5	10	15
Oliver Elementary	330	1	331	12	7	19
Riverton Elementary	160	57	217	6	9	15
B. T. Washington Elementary	407	0	407	14	6	20
Total	2,703	570	3,273	98	85	183

1980	Black Pupils	White Pupils	Total Pupils	Black Teachers	White Teachers	Total Teachers
High School	471	219	690	16	28	44
Junior High	516	5	521	27	3	30
Riverton Intermediate	247	28	275	12	11	23
Hall Elementary	207	0	207	5	8	13
Heidelberg Elementary	70	138	208	3	5	12
Kirkpatrick Elementary	50	140	190	2	10	12
Oakhurst Elementary	234	3	237	5	10	15
Oliver Elementary	364	1	365	13	7	20
Riverton Elementary	143	55	198	5	7	12
B. T. Washington Elementary	411	2	413	17	4	21
Total	2,713	591	3,304	105	97	202

Source: From the biannual reports to the U.S. District Court for the Northern Division of Mississippi as per the order of 25 January 1974 by Judge William C. Keady, U.S. District Court Clerk's Office, Oxford, Miss.

handful of white pupils in the early years, the numbers dwindled to zero by the fall of 1995; Hall IV elementary school was all-black from the beginning.[84]

In 1984, thirty years after *Brown*, social psychologist Alvis Adair asked: "Has there been real or illusory progress for Black America over the past twenty-five years?" He called for a moratorium on all "forced school desegregation," compiling research on what he labeled "the illusion of black progress," while mourning the loss of black education and black educators to the hostile and estranged environments in which black children now studied. In the push to desegregate schools, he argued, the movement had forfeited African American control and the interests of black students and black education professionals by adhering to the idea that integrated schools were best for all. Indeed, his premise stands on the fact that the move to desegregate schools had done little to "transfer an equitable share of self-determination to Blacks." In fact, desegregation had merely taken money away from black schools and businesses and eliminated black principals and other black education administrators.[85] Had the changes and benefits outweighed the costs? The actions of the courts and black leaders in Clarksdale illustrated his concerns. In the mid-1980s, both parties agreed on a consent order regarding elementary school pupil assignments, to reestablish neighborhood schools. Under this plan, children had the right to transfer to a school of their choice, with immediate steps to improve the quality of education in the black-majority schools and to increase extra-curricular activities.[86] Two steps forward and one back? Or one forward and two in reverse?

Judge Keady, who presided for years over the Clarksdale school desegregation case, also reflected on its effects, concluding that white flight to the academies diminished interest in public schools and made passing bond issues nearly impossible. In hindsight, Keady faulted the Fifth Circuit Court, whose judicial error in taking the lead in desegregation resulted in "unnecessarily strong medicine."[87] This was, and is, of course, a national issue also. Like chemotherapy attacking good cells as well as the cancer, judicial rulings might have also permanently harmed what was promising and good as they sought to eradicate inequality.

Both Adair and Keady would have agreed that desegregation never integrated the schools. Social acceptance of racial equality never replaced the resentment on both sides. It is crucial to keep in mind, however, that in the context of white supremacy and the extent and persistence of inequality and white control over education (by limiting black authority) in the many decades before 1970—before the Civil Rights Act and before *Brown*—school desegregation clearly was limited, but unsurprisingly so. And a related issue—wages for black teachers had always been woefully inadequate. Many, like Bennie Gooden who began teaching in 1960, started on salaries below the poverty line. In order to make ends meet, for a while he held three jobs: teaching in the public school system, teaching privately at night, and driving a school bus.[88] So, despite his position as a schoolteacher, one highly regarded in the black community and considered middle class in those days, he qualified for assistance alongside field hands. By 1965, his situation had not changed much, and given that percentages of base earnings dictate raises, very few black teachers could boast a salary that would reflect their social status.

The last word should be from the students, however. It was their futures at stake. The desegregation of the schools occurred in 1970, but Elnora Fondren had walked those halls alone four and a half years earlier, buoyed by her experiences in Freedom Summer the year before and her community's activism for over a decade. Hope had supported her in Clarksdale High School and in those first classes in 1970, and hope kept young people committed and on fire. One of Fondren's classmates in the community center that summer in 1964 was Allan Goodner, who wrote a battle poem of inspiration, filled with hope.[89]

SEGREGATION WILL NOT BE HERE LONG

Segregation will not be here long
I'll do my best to see it gone

And when it is gone the world will be
So very full of equality.

The people will sing and begin to shout;
And everyone will know what it's all about.

They will leap for joy with a sigh;
Praise the Lord . . . Some will cry.

Glory Hallelujah . . . blessed be;
God is a just God . . . for all eternity.

For we've been buked for such a long time;
Being Black . . . was such a crime.

And when it's over . . . the world will see;
God made us all brothers . . . Even you and me.

On every corner . . . you will hear us say,
We're FREE . . . Free and Free to stay.

Even on the street . . . from every side;
We're free . . . We're free . . . and God was our guide.

They've killed us . . . and hung us from trees so high;
But we knew some of us would have to die.

Dying was not really oh so bad;
We've got equality . . . and we're really glad.

So now it's obvious and plain to see;
God made us all equal . . . You and Me.

CHAPTER SIX

It Was a Peaceful Revolution

JOHNSON'S GREAT SOCIETY AND ECONOMIC JUSTICE IN COAHOMA COUNTY

A large part of the solution to black and white is green.
—Polly Greenberg, The Devil Has Slippery Shoes.

There is something there that we are involved with. There's a place
for me to go to air my grievance. If somebody's mistreated me at the food
stamp department, at the schools, there's another place I can go.
— Troy Catchings (1994)

The presence of the federal government brought great transformations to the southern landscape. Actively enforcing federal legislation and court orders initiated by mass protest muzzled white supremacy, disallowing discrimination on the basis of race. At least that has been standard rhetoric for the sixties and for the mass civil rights movement. But just like the years of Reconstruction, a century earlier, the racist beast still lived and struggled to disentangle itself from its legal bindings. While it tussled with the law in the courts and with people on the streets, many African Americans in Mississippi seized the opportunities now available. They fought to desegregate local public accommodations and schools and to register to vote. By doing so, they welcomed the federal enforcers into the Mississippi Delta and further forced open the "closed society."

President Lyndon B. Johnson, a Texan, acknowledged the extent of southern isolation. He dreamed of a Great Society—one that could take care of its own, one in which all of its citizens could enjoy its freedoms and be the positive contrast to the threatening global spread of Communism. He declared a war on poverty.

Grassroots activists had already expressed Johnson's concerns. For instance, by black Delta standards, Vera Pigee prospered. A woman with her own business, she could afford to be politically active and work for civil rights to help her community. For years, she encouraged children's participation by opening her home to them for food, shelter, and instruction. Twice a week, after closing the beauty shop following a long day on her feet, she taught parents in citizenship classes in her back room. In 1962, she served as the co-chair of the Emergency Welfare and Relief Committee to help alleviate poverty in the Delta, soliciting and organizing national donations of food, clothing, and medicine. She understood that civil rights could only be achieved by recognizing basic human needs, by recognizing a universal humanity.

She was not alone. Civil rights workers and leaders had acknowledged the dire need to correct the economic disparity. The Delta, hauntingly beautiful and rich, perpetuated horrific poverty and degradation within a relatively prosperous post–World War II nation. Some Freedom Summer volunteers were generally skeptical of the small desegregation victories and of federal efforts to alleviate the situation in Mississippi, given what they saw. For example, Charles Stewart stated that the 1964 Civil Rights Act "was important to the leadership group, but for the mass of people, it had no meaning," especially when most could not read and did not have the money to eat in restaurants.[1] Bob Mandel, another volunteer in Clarksdale, wrote to his parents on 3 July 1964: "Thoughts of the thousands of Negroes, hundreds of thousands who will be helped by the bill, and the millions of poor to whom it will give dignity but no bread . . . they will still be in the cotton fields making three dollars a day. They'll still be in white homes working as maids, making three dollars a day. They'll still be starving and afraid. I hurt more than I'm happy. . . . I know these people now, and all I can say to them is vote, organize, starve."[2] Lew Sitzer, in Clarksdale also, wrote to his sister a few days later: "Wherever I go, I see kids without shoes; wherever I go, the air is heavy. . . . There is no escape from the psychological and physical poverty."[3] Working with sharecroppers and laborers, the class differences among African Americans, even in the Delta, became more apparent to the volunteers, particularly as some of the civil rights gains trickled down to elevate the status of a few. Toward the end of August 1964, however, most of the students drifted out of Mississippi as new semesters began in their colleges and universities, beckoning them back.

Nevertheless, the Coahoma County Chamber of Commerce, hoping to attract industry, enthusiastically called the area the "Golden Buckle on the Cotton Belt," referring to the statistic that there were more millionaires per capita than anywhere else in the region. That buckle, and the corresponding bounty of wealth and political power, remained firmly in the hands of a white planter class, while the majority of African Americans continued to lag behind in most areas, despite a growing black professional class. The more things changed in Clarksdale, the more things stayed the same.

Desegregating stores, restaurants, and motels was important in principle, but most black residents could not afford to spend money there. Desegregating schools, always a worthy cause, meant little if parents could not provide sufficient nutrition and clothing for their children. If they could not read or write, how could they vote? Symbolic desegregation only magnified inequality in income and literacy.[4] Forcing apart segregation exposed the underbelly of the American Dream, and the nation had to face the cost of injustice. Johnson's War on Poverty was as innovative as it was controversial. Decades later, political battles continue to rage about its (cost) effectiveness. Community Action Agencies (CAAs) dispensed services provided by the Community Action Programs (CAPs) to the local population, and thus the success of the War on Poverty depended on the efficiency of each agency.

This chapter plots the establishment of poverty programs in Coahoma County as an extension of the struggle to improve the lives of African Americans, by creating spaces for local agency, interracial cooperation, and tangible aid for the poor. Economics and civil rights always went hand in hand as human rights. New Deal policies from over thirty years earlier had failed most African Americans as President Franklin Roosevelt sought to keep his diverse coalition together. President Johnson, watching that same coalition crack further as the black freedom struggle had exposed America's hypocrisy to the world and increased the black vote, responded to grassroots pressure to make this revolution beneficial for African Americans, particularly by forcing the creation of biracial boards at the local level to ensure black participation. Movement activists adopted these policies as part of their overall struggle for racial justice and equal opportunities. Teaching the poor how to navigate the welfare system and to claim their rights and entitlements gave them better access to use the opportunities guaranteed by their civil rights. Local black leaders used the poverty programs to further their civil rights trajectories, seeing them as one and the same, and the programs empowered a larger population of African Americans in new ways.

These poverty programs overlapped with the school desegregation case

taking its place on the federal court docket and with the continued street protests and boycotts. From the battle between city fathers and majority-black organizations to control federal funds, to Project Head Start and adult education
programs, the War on Poverty affected the region by expanding both the federal presence and the black middle class. The investment of federal money in
the local economy ostensibly ended segregation in public places as merchants
and officials reluctantly complied with federal law in order to benefit from the
business generated by the poverty agencies. Also, federal law insisted on interracial boards and management arrangements in newly formed agencies. The
process was never smooth, and while many organizations and programs could
not maintain themselves as politics choked the finances, the legacies survived,
in Coahoma County and in other communities across the nation.[5]

The aim here is not to assess the success of programs in easing poverty—
social scientists lead the way in studying the tangible effects of Great Society
policies.[6] Rather, the goal is to explore what the social implications of these
programs funded by the Office of Economic Opportunity (OEO) are and how
the programs have altered the broader economic and social landscape and affected African Americans in Coahoma County. As this recent history and its
implications continue to unfold, the debates continue to swirl.

The War on Poverty has produced southern and rural stories as well as the
more-often-studied northern and/or urban contexts. In Coahoma County and
Clarksdale, the CAP diversified the movement landscape with its focus on economic equality. While some of the actors on this newer front crossed over from
earlier leadership roles or activities—Aaron Henry in particular—many new
faces and names emerged, causing some friction between activist generations.
A pronounced shift in leadership and the black "elite" occurred in the community. More formal leadership structures took root as a result of increased
federal presence and dollars and decreased danger, structures that reflected
dominant society and displaced leaders with less political clout and those with
less formal qualifications, like Vera Pigee. She found her voice muted in this
arena, despite her continued civil rights work. Subsequently, her authority,
cemented in informal structures of activist mothering through the NAACP, no
longer carried the same weight.

Throughout the Clarksdale story, the recurrent concept of flexible associations surfaces, and this chapter in the narrative explores the testing of locals'
loyalties once again. The NAACP, which had played a central role in the desegregation chronicles thus far, did not play a formal part in this economic dimen-

sion of the struggle, which concentrated more on policy and the distribution of federal funds. The institutional absence, however, did not preclude members' participation. This economic revolution did not appear out of a vacuum, of course. Its roots extend back to the local boycotts, but now federal muscle accelerated and changed the nature of activism, highlighting one of the shifts in the movement as definitions of freedom and institutional loyalty are contested.

The Beginnings of Community Action
Programs in Coahoma County

On 20 August 1964, as preparations for the Democratic National Convention were finalized for the following week, President Johnson signed the Economic Opportunity Act of 1964, launching his War on Poverty. He used more than fifty pens to sign the bill, which provided an initial $947.5 million to fund initiatives. R. Sargent Shriver, the builder of Johnson's vision, a Yale Law graduate, JFK's brother-in-law, and a U.S. Navy veteran, had worked on the new Peace Corps before his appointment to OEO. The federal government could now tender grants directly to community-based organizations, bypassing the state to ensure equal access by minimizing state and local interference. CAPs were designed to give power to the disfranchised. Proponents believed that community members could design tailor-made "prescriptions for ending poverty," allowing for maximum flexibility in local situations.[7]

That same year, Jesse Epps returned to Clarksdale. He called Coahoma County home. Born there in 1936, Epps had left the Delta in his teens when his parents moved to Syracuse, New York, to escape the threat of racial violence against the family in Dublin, Mississippi.[8] He had been heavily involved in school politics, serving as School Council vice president as a freshman at Coahoma County Junior College. Bennie S. Gooden, an old school friend, remembered that "Jesse had a lot of dreams of coming back, and he used to write me long, long letters telling me about what life was like in Syracuse and how he looked forward to coming back to his home county and making a difference."[9] In the Northeast, Epps stepped up his activism, running for public office and joining the International Union of Electrical Workers, serving as chairman of the union's civil rights committee in Syracuse. Noticing that many of the migrant black workers came from rural Mississippi to these northern cities, he realized that with better education, training, and preparation, their improved qualifications for employment would ensure a smoother transition. Finding fertile soil for his idea to create adult education to combat illiteracy in the Delta *before* people migrated from the fields, Epps came back to Clarksdale to pitch his idea.[10]

Activists had experience in trying to help unemployed workers. Coahoma County police often arrested black people on vagrancy charges if they held no employment, a practice at least as old as Jim Crow, so ameliorating their economic situation as part of the struggle against police harassment was key. Youths in Coahoma County were given thirty days on the county road gang, and so the police took "malicious advantage of the high unemployment situation to obtain free penal labor from law abiding citizens." This practice continued the human rights violations against African Americans established in the nineteenth century after emancipation denied the white population a free labor pool. In 1964, Charles Evers and Aaron Henry had requested a Justice Department investigation of police actions, urging the president and Sargent Shriver to consider the unemployment of young adults in the Delta area as part of their developing poverty programming.[11]

Alongside the NAACP efforts to protect the civil rights of the poor, Epps created the Southern Education Recreation Association (SERA) to establish programs impacting education and recreation. In 1964, Coahoma County ranked as one of the top counties in the United States for cotton production, the "Golden Buckle" no less, but in the bottom ten for literacy, in a state where blacks outnumbered whites by two to one.[12] Not knowing much about the new Great Society legislation, Epps envisaged that private foundations would fund the initiative, and he approached several, including the Ford Foundation, which directed him to the fledgling Office of Economic Opportunity.

At OEO, Epps learned about Project Head Start (the first program launched) and asked Gooden to call a leadership meeting in Clarksdale. In January 1965, Sargent Shriver had announced available funds and sought 100,000 children in 300 counties for a pilot project. James C. Gilliam, Benjamin F. McLaurin, Robert L. Drew, Aaron Henry, Charles Stringer, Lillian Rogers Johnson, Cozetta Cooper, and others attended and agreed to work with Epps, who relocated to Clarksdale with his family. Gooden sat with Diane McNutt, a secretary at Coahoma County Junior College, and wrote a proposal for OEO funding. He admitted: "I had never written that type of proposal before, but we did the best we could. I remember we worked all night."[13] The next morning, Epps and Gooden flew to Washington, D.C., clutching freshly typed sheets of paper with their bid for funds.

Not willing to forfeit any control, particularly over money, county and city administrators caught wind of the application and both districts filed their own. In fact, according to a federal report on the Coahoma County projects, "there was some consternation that the SERA venture could have gone so far without the whites in the community knowing about it."[14] *Clarksdale Press Register* reporter Curtis Wilkie noted that the white administrators "had more interest in blocking funds from the likes of Epps than extending aid to the poor."[15] As a result, at least three proposals for Head Start from Coahoma County and Clarksdale sat on a desk in Washington, D.C. Gooden observed that "the government was put in a kind of a quandary, so they decided to fund both the city and SERA. We were funded for the city and the county, but the city school system was funded only for the city."[16] The office, swamped by the response, received 3,300 applications from organizations. In an effort to respond to the demand, OEO organized Head Start as an eight-week program in the summer of 1965, enrolling over half a million six-year-olds.[17] OEO officials were convinced that the need demanded immediate attention and enough work to go around, and authorizing two programs both addressed the crisis and deflected immediate political criticism.

An OEO grant recipient had to have a biracial board for its Community Action Agency (CAA). A biracial meeting was called in the fall of 1964 in Clarksdale. Oscar Carr, a white banker, worked on the white community to agree on an interracial board of directors for SERA, reasoning that the county had the facilities and finances to reinforce the programs. Oscar Carr and his brother Andrew came from a prominent Clarksdale farming family. Oscar, in his negotiations with the Board of Supervisors in Clarksdale, insisted that he had nothing to gain by his actions.[18] He had helped to establish the First National Bank of Clarksdale, known as the "nigger bank" because it did not withhold loans from black farmers and businessmen as others did in retaliation for civil rights actions. Given the Citizens' Council's opinions about such positions, he decided to step back and withdraw his direct involvement rather than jeopardize the poverty programs. Andrew Carr had spent twelve years in the U.S. Navy, returning in 1954, one week before the *Brown v. Board of Education* decision, to work solidly for ten years improving the family farm. When the biracial committee formed, Aaron Henry spoke to him, and he jumped at the chance to participate, shocked by the deterioration of racial relations in the postwar years.[19]

Writer Nicholas Lemann described the Carr brothers as "impeccably respectable Delta planters—long-established, prominent in the cotton industry and social organizations, athletic, and popular—but both of them had spent time in the East and had returned home as civil rights sympathizers."[20] Cushioned by three generations of farming success and encouraged by new federal laws, Andrew Carr stepped forward. He stressed that he was interested in fairness and equal opportunities, not in integration, and the gross injustice he saw disgusted him. He remembered fondly a particular black nurse who had cared for his invalid sister for two decades—she had given him the nickname "the manager" after he refused to allow her to call him "mister," the conventional term she was expected to use once a white boy turned twelve. He never forgot her. And his devotion to Roman Catholicism with the church's inclination toward social justice had fueled his resolve.[21] Bennie Gooden gave him a lot of credit: "He opened doors of the power structure. We couldn't get the board of supervisors or any local officials to meet with us." He added wryly, "He's rich enough, and influential enough, and brave enough not to have to give in to the pressure."[22] Carr borrowed money to lend to Epps as he settled back into Clarksdale, "just to show him that I would do my part if he'd do his part. . . . I was so determined that I was going to not be considered a racist that I went on a limb."[23] Black people unsurprisingly regarded Carr with a degree of distrust initially, particularly as a white, wealthy planter's son he had raised his hand to help those who had once been exploited on his land. Carr understood that he had to earn respect in order to effectively instigate change.

Responding positively to the biracial board of directors, OEO approved the application and pledged approximately $3.5 million to operate the CAA. But the presence of some whites in the organization complicated its function rather than smoothed out problems. When SERA proposed Head Start programs for the summer of 1965, OEO sent Sanford Kravitz, chief of research for the CAP, to Clarksdale. Two meetings on 18 and 20 May 1965 at the Federal Building attracted about 150 people, mostly African Americans; Kravitz emphasized OEO's desire to give aid to the people in the area, and he and his colleagues outlined some of the projects and programs available.[24] Before his arrival, most of the white members had withdrawn from the board, pressured by the Citizens' Council's opposition to federal intervention. This rendered the SERA board racially imbalanced. The Clarksdale Board of Trustees then established its own antipoverty coalition, soliciting some black support for its effort. The Board of Trustees also applied for additional OEO funding.[25] During the Trustees' first meeting, black members, including Charles Stringer and B. F. McLaurin (who had both worked on SERA's initial federal application), requested that Aaron Henry be on the new board. Henry had purposefully stayed in the background, understanding that animosity toward him caused by his on-going civil rights activities might threaten success. The white conservative members fought back bitterly, forcing the black members to repeat the earlier white protest against SERA — that is, they walked out of the meeting. All but Jerome W. Stampley left, who was still employed as the superintendent of black schools in the city. Unfazed, new black members, aligned with the city, were quickly recruited.[26]

In the series of meetings with Sanford Kravitz, OEO made it clear that neither group (SERA or the Board of Trustees) could qualify as a CAP because neither board truly represented the community. As a consolation prize, SERA received $341,313 (a fraction of the initial pledge) for an eight-week Head Start program to serve 1,945 preschoolers.[27] Bennie Gooden was the director for the first Head Start project in the county. The Board of Trustees received $68,932, and it announced the use of black school facilities for its eight-week program.[28] Local district funds totaling $7,795 boosted federal monies, and administration and financial management took place through the city school administrative offices. Rewarding Stampley for his "loyalty," he was named the director of the project, and the local newspaper noted that several of the hired personnel spent a week at the University of Alabama for a six-day orientation program.[29] Additionally, the school cafeterias opened to provide light breakfasts and a full meal at noon, with Coahoma County hospital medical staff coordinating medical examinations for all the children.

The Trustees employed all of their available resources, determined to undermine SERA. They sought to co-opt the program and control and manage the federal funds. But when the county school board prohibited the use of its facilities for SERA's Head Start program, Aaron Henry stepped in and exercised his extensive clout in Washington to focus national publicity and incur an OEO investigation. SERA publicly accused the county of discrimination. County board president C. M. Allen denied the charges, claiming that the board willingly accepted any applications where the greater community good was served "if and when that program is under the direct supervision of a legally constituted board of control that is comprised entirely of Coahoma County citizens."[30] W. E. Young, president of the Board of Supervisors for the county, also defended charges against him by responding to letters with his own missives.[31]

Henry's national influence and authority cannot be underestimated. Federal investigators writing a history of the Coahoma County programs in 1967 explicitly acknowledged Henry as a "powerful force" that both moderates and conservatives recognized. He already had some national notoriety, especially after the August 1964 Democratic National Committee proceedings in Atlantic City, described in chapter 4. To underline the investigators' point about

Henry as a force to be reckoned with, they went so far as to reproduce one of his many letters written to city officials that skillfully, yet politely, accused, exposed, and manipulated in order to encourage negotiations.[32] Henry's interventions brought Jim Draper from the Federal Community Relations Service to Clarksdale to assess the situation. He invited members of both sides back to the table in Washington, D.C. Only Oscar Carr, Harvey Ross, Aaron Henry, and Jesse Epps went, but after a short wavering spell, the county gave in and allowed SERA use of some school facilities.[33] SERA received more money than the other applicants, and with the cooperation of county schools and city churches, SERA established multiple Head Start centers.

All of the Head Start programs began on the blistering hot morning of 21 June 1965. The front page of the *Clarksdale Press Register* printed a photograph of white mothers and their children basking in the morning sun at Clarksdale's segregated country club at 8:56 A.M., juxtaposed next to an image of young black boys and girls excitedly making their way to their Head Start centers.[34] With more than one group administering the program, slight confusion marked the opening day, as both SERA and the city began registering Clarksdale's children. After discussion between both groups, the city ran its program under the direction of Jerome Stampley with its quota of 400, allowing SERA to accommodate its overflow. In the county, SERA and the Coahoma County Board of Education finally formed a directing committee to work together.[35]

By 22 June, SERA was serving 1,558 children in thirteen centers throughout Coahoma County. All children received medical examinations, dental treatment, and two balanced meals; 300 local people were hired as teachers, aides, and social workers. For many who earned livings from farms, this summer income surpassed yearly earnings.[36] SERA also served parts of Tunica County to the north of Coahoma County, based at the all-black Coahoma County Junior College just outside Clarksdale's city limits. Basking in its own success, SERA sought to expand its operations to other programs, continuing to strive to create a CAA for the county.

Establishing Coahoma Opportunities, Inc.

Most studies assessing the creation of CAAs omit rural and southern organizations, yet Clarksdale boasted a highly functional agency with full federal support. Why Clarksdale? During 1965, more radical voices demanded change on the civil rights front, particularly in Mississippi. Spurred on by the slow progress of the movement, the lack of jobs for African Americans, the increasing desperation, and the growing militancy among some activists, some became even more angry. In some urban areas, anger had already turned to violence. For some, the disillusionment derived from bitterness with the realization that much of the benefit from hard-won federal legislation never reached them and that they remained forgotten as mechanization continued to deplete the work supply and as harsh winters endangered many families. Federal official Dudley Morris summarized the situation perfectly: "With the possible exception of Coahoma County, there has been a drastic change in the attitude in the last two years; the reasonableness that used to characterize Mississippi Negroes has been replaced by a militant bitterness that is very similar to the frustrations expressed by people who live in Watts." His observation, mirrored by another federal official who toured the area and saw the desperate situation farmworkers faced, helped to convince OEO to make Mississippi a funding priority as the reputation of federal programs in the state came under close scrutiny.[37]

The experimental program of the CAAs sought to deal with poverty through a range of immediate services and to foster a more long-term "increase in the capacity of individuals, groups, and communities afflicted by poverty to deal effectively with their own problems." The program aimed to redefine welfare by giving the poor the agency and the tools to help themselves by providing access to the larger local community, to "unite the sub-culture of poverty with middle and upper class society on a geographic base." While federal policy preferred to use the county as the basis for community building, in reality more support existed in municipal governments or private agencies, as rural talent and leadership tended to migrate to more populous areas. As such, "the CAP has reacted to the implications of this shallow and evaporating reservoir of rural talent by working to create multi-county units on the assumption that the bigger we make the pond, no matter how stagnant, the more likely we are to find (or be able to pay for the importation of) a few big frogs to run our program."[38]

While SERA was the first to bring Head Start (just one of the programs) to Coahoma County, it was not the only organization of its kind in Mississippi. In the summer of 1965, in association with the Delta Ministry and the Council of Federated Organizations (COFO), the Child Development Group of Mississippi (CDGM) catered to over 6,000 children in eighty-four centers across the state. It was the largest Head Start program in the country that summer.[39] In the national history of Head Start, CDGM is considered a bump in the political road, despite its huge, albeit short-lived, success.[40] As most Project Head Start programs, the organization focused on early education, but it also continued the holistic work done in movement Freedom Schools by centering black culture and politics along with nutrition and health care in the curriculum. Staffed by women and men with direct movement ties, CDGM fell squarely in the sights of Mississippi's white state politicians and bureaucrats, led by Senator John Stennis, who from the group's inception relentlessly sought to undermine the organization and find some way to halt the flow of federal money into the hands of African Americans, in general, and into those of known "agitators," in particular. White officials dug until they found minor financial inaccuracies in the accounts and then used the group's accounting errors to push for an end to the organization's federal funding. Backed against the wall by Stennis's public attacks and political threats, OEO cut CDGM funding. Curtis Wilkie concluded that Shriver "choked on the political pressure" caused by the public brouhaha.[41]

In Mississippi, Clarksdale stood out as one obvious place for an agency, particularly with Aaron Henry's visibility through the NAACP and his predilection for writing frequent letters to the federal government with reports and requests for help.[42] He had also worked with OEO to establish the Mississippi Action for Progress (MAP), serving on the board with Oscar Carr and an influential white moderate Mississippian named Hodding Carter III. Indeed, Stennis had made a deal with Shriver to replace CDGM with this second Head Start program controlled by Mississippi moderates—at the state level, Henry was considered a moderate, despite his position as state NAACP president and all of his past and ongoing civil rights activities.[43] MAP, unlike CDGM, involved prominent whites that Stennis and Eastland could not openly criticize, and Aaron Henry held "civil rights credentials" that could not be denied.

Henry came across as flexible, willing to negotiate and compromise in order to make some gains—a strategy of flexible loyalty he had continuously employed over the years. He also had a strong local cohort around and beside him. Therefore, recognizing the sturdy leadership in the African American community in Clarksdale, a leadership that had withstood over a decade of public struggle and organizational shifting and that was geographically well situated with a relatively urban population, OEO picked the county as the site for a rural demonstration project and invested millions in the resulting private agency. Coahoma County, for many observers, became one of the "show-place programs in the Nation."[44]

The strong local leadership came out of the local NAACP, and even though the organization did not use its letterhead when dealing with issues related to the poverty programs, it *did* work to make sure that Clarksdale and Coahoma County received their share and that the needy would be well informed. For example, the local NAACP branch newsletter, the *Cryer*, advertised a series of meetings for 3 and 4 June 1965 at Haven Methodist Church for farmworkers to learn about new programs to boost their incomes and to give them the opportunity to ask questions of "special representatives" from OEO—100 people attended on 3 June, as Tom Karter explained the program and fielded queries.[45] The poverty programs had to remain bipartisan, but the local branch made sure that the community had information available. In mid-October 1965, responding to the introduction of the food stamp program, black citizens again looked to the local branch for explanations. To expedite the introduction of the program, Bernard Turkla traveled from Washington, D.C., to field local questions about the program's execution at a meeting held at the First Baptist Church.[46] Not surprisingly, given the perpetually malleable boundaries among roles, many of the local branch members served on the board of the resulting CAP or on the organization's staff.

Even with the local NAACP's vigilance, the flow of OEO programs and jobs to the area met resistance at every turn from white city leaders. Realizing the amounts of money invested into the antipoverty programs and the growing African American agency in securing federal grants, white authorities felt their grip slipping and saw the possibility that the very fabric of southern racial society could be changed further. This was in addition to the onslaught they faced in other arenas—an active direct-action movement and a lawsuit to desegregate the schools. In midsummer, the state OEO branch contacted city governments and officials across the state. Bennie Gooden explained bluntly: "If [whites] didn't hurry up and get an organization going—a community action agency—the niggers were going to get the money, and they were going to run it."[47] In Coahoma County and Clarksdale, white officials had worked together against SERA's initiative. Tom Scarbrough, the Sovereignty Commission investigator covering the county, reported that Semmes Luckett (and most of the white leaders) still had no desire to participate in CAPs, but "he learned that unless they did take some hand in administering the affairs of the program that thousands and thousands of dollars would go down the drain by the bungling of incompetent Negroes."[48] This was a common line throughout the South. Knowing that they could get a firmer grip inside the organization rather than outside, they made sure their voices were representative.

How would biracial representation take shape? During the crisis meetings in Washington, D.C., on 1 June 1965, Shriver had again impressed on the

Clarksdale representatives the necessity of a working biracial board of directors for a CAA to be accepted by OEO. If this could be arranged, Shriver promised huge federal grants to the area.[49] Over the following weeks, the Carr brothers bridged both sides to create a board. Andrew Carr made an interesting observation about Clarksdale's white community: "95 per cent of our people here are sheep, 4 per cent are bigots, and one percent are with us. The bigots are cowards, like most gangsters."[50] Bennie Gooden recounted the opinion of William Young (then chairman of the school board): "He made all these nasty statements about [how] he wouldn't sit on a board with Aaron Henry and 'you give a nigger a foot and he wants a yard' and all that kind of thing." Yet again, the intention of the city was not to facilitate the education of the children, but rather "they got on there for the purpose of controlling whatever came down, and they wanted to put applications together that would be minimal, very minimal, more or less for control."[51] Regardless, they met at the Board of Supervisors' chambers in the county courthouse and agreed to apply for a state charter to incorporate a nonprofit organization, to be called Coahoma Opportunities, Inc. (COI). On 23 October 1965, the charter for incorporation was signed by Semmes Luckett, George Maynard Jr., Leon Porter, Harvey Ross, and Vincent Brocato—all known Citizens' Council members still actively fighting civil rights activists. The reluctant coalition remained shaky.[52]

The battles on the COI board continued unabated, and meetings became so ugly that OEO sent in mediators. As OEO released projects, the fledgling organization kept losing bids. The white members of the board strove to block any moves to channel projects toward SERA, which continued to function autonomously: "The board was just against everything. But whatever they were for it was just small, just a little bit to say that they are doing something."[53] They resented federal "interference" in their plans, particularly when Vernon Jordan, a black lawyer working with the Federal Community Relations Service and a friend of Henry's, sat in on the board meetings to mediate.[54] However, the other parties were stronger. African American leaders and sympathetic whites worked with OEO officials to write grant proposals to secure substantial funding for extensive programming.

In the tussle, SERA lost. Unable to be a CAA on its own and dogged by Jesse Epps's colorful personality, which rubbed many people the wrong way, the fledgling organization could not survive. Brenda Luckett, whose father participated actively in the local NAACP branch, remembered that Epps was a target for white supremacists: "They ran him out of town . . . literally ran him out of town. My daddy took him out the back roads out of town, my father and

Bennie Gooden, laid him in the back of the car and got him out of here because it was dangerous and they were threatening to kill him."[55] At the same time, in August 1965, OEO carried out a routine audit of SERA to assess federal expenditure. Epps had lied about his academic qualifications in order to lure backing from the local leadership. He had falsely claimed to have degrees from the University of Chicago and Syracuse University, but he defended his actions, stating that he knew everyone would question his abilities and block his initiatives without a college education. Federal reporters summarized: "He is convinced that [the lie] was instrumental in getting others to accept his leadership and does not believe he could have accomplished what he did without the false credentials."[56] Worsening the situation, he also did not meet the audit deadline, and white opponents pounced on the chance to discredit him and SERA. Andrew Carr, who had backed SERA and served as a board member, struggled to retain his own reputation as the SERA ship sank. Despite all efforts, when the summer Head Start grant expired in August 1965, the organization fell apart. However, SERA's brief existence was not in vain. It planted the seed from which COI could emerge.

And so Johnson's antipoverty crusade roared into Coahoma County via COI. The *Clarksdale Press Register* headline read "'War on Poverty' Grant Announced" on the front page on 21 September 1965. Exactly one week after Elnora Fondren enrolled as the only black student at Clarksdale High School, the article reported that COI would receive $336,666 in federal grants. At that same moment, civil rights activists in Clarksdale were lobbying for federal voter examiners to come into the county. In fact, Aaron Henry was in Washington, D.C., meeting with Attorney General Nicholas Katzenbach, Solicitor General Thurgood Marshall, and Wiley Branton at the Justice Department.[57] Sargent Shriver announced the grant in Washington, D.C., witnessed by COI board chairman Andrew Carr, COI director Gustave Roessler, Harvey Ross, Aaron Henry, and Charles Stringer. The twenty-eight sitting on the COI board consisted of sixteen whites and twelve African Americans, with Bennie Gooden serving as deputy director.[58]

Conservative white board members were horrified at the turn of events. Gooden recalled that "Semmes Luck[ett] said he felt like he was on a railroad train going down a hill and can't put on brakes. He couldn't stop it."[59] Fourteen white members abruptly left en masse on 8 November 1965, desperately trying to sabotage the organization before even a penny had reached the Delta.[60] They argued that OEO wanted COI to be a national showcase and had poured money indiscriminately into the organization, which they perceived as wasteful.[61] Their resignations, printed in the *Clarksdale Press Register*, stated: "Suffice it to say that we are of the opinion that some of the projects which have been proposed, and some which we understand will be proposed are of a nature and size that will prove detrimental to our community and its economy."[62]

Nevertheless, Andrew Carr, the newly appointed chairman, worked frantically once again to convince other white citizens to participate—those not influenced by the city officials. The introduction of more moderate members probably saved the agency. He recalled that he told the *Memphis Commercial Appeal* that he could ensure an interracial board: "And I did. So we got twelve whites to serve in place of the fourteen whites that resigned, and . . . we had a board—rather than fourteen and fourteen, it was twelve and twelve." He did it in a week. Waiting for the grant to arrive, the group set up headquarters on East Second Street, sharing a lone telephone and a few pieces of furniture.[63] White resisters' attempts backfired—without a seat on the board they no longer could directly control the funds.

Coahoma Opportunities, Inc.: Programs and Services

COI was unprecedented. It affected thousands of lives in the early years, through employment and services and because of its holistic approach to combating poverty. COI took over Head Start as its primary program, already established by SERA and the city. Due to its overwhelming popularity in 1966, Head Start had expanded to a year-round initiative (and today operates in fifty states). Mayo D. Wilson, a Korean War veteran educated at Tougaloo College and Jackson State, resigned from his post as a math and science teacher at Coahoma County Junior College to direct the COI Head Start project in 1966, where he stayed until 1971.[64] As part of the program, Wilson managed a staff working in a variety of areas, including special education programs, educational incentives, social services, psychological services, and nutrition and health programs. As Vernon Keys summarized, "They really cared for the whole child."[65] The centers also provided transportation for most of the participants. A fleet of certified car and bus owners in the community were contracted to drive for reimbursement. At the centers, Wilson hired some people without certified training: "Maybe some of them might have had high school and some might have had as much as two years of college training as teachers and lead teachers." Training the teachers on-site, Wilson stressed, "We took people who had no training, who were, again, community-based poor people who needed jobs, to perform the aid and support duties. And we developed programs during that time to help them to upgrade, to get their GEDs . . . to help them to get a two-year certificate in early childhood so that they could be certified by the state to teach early childhood development and education."[66] His hiring patterns reflected his politics. Two generations benefited from Head Start—the small children for whom the program was designed and those workers hired to staff the project.

Most of the personnel at Head Start were women, but some of the coordinators and outreach workers were male: "We did this deliberately, of course, because we wanted that support and image to be there for the family." These projects came only months after Daniel Patrick Moynihan, then assistant secretary for Policy Planning and Research in the Department of Labor, published his study, "The Negro Family: A Case for National Action," otherwise known as the Moynihan Report. In this nationally controversial study, Moynihan utilized government statistics and census information to conclude that a principal problem facing African Americans in the struggle against poverty was grounded in the deterioration of the black family. Critics accused him of blaming the victim, especially black women, but supporters believed that any programs designed to alleviate poverty had to address the family unit. Even the First Lady, Lady Bird Johnson, noted: "The program was insurance for a smaller welfare roll."[67]

The family, the domestic space, dealt with the socialization of the young child. More young men worked with Head Start during the summer, particularly just after school ended, but during the academic year, women dominated. As Vera Pigee had used her position as an activist mother to improve the lives of those around her by working primarily with the children, so too did these women employed by COI. In effect, the poverty program assisted in federalizing a whole fleet of alternate mothers, a community of nurturing designed to give impoverished children the desperately needed "head start" in life. The scope of black women's work expanded exponentially through the poverty programs and the institutionalization of COI. No longer tied to a perpetual life of service to white families, Vernon Keys pointed out, "white women began to have to do their own work. They had to cook, they had to clean their houses, because their women [black women] came out and started working . . . for the Head Start programs and for the Neighborhood Service Centers." Black women, once making minimum wage in private homes, quit domestic service in large numbers to make more money serving their own children and their own people.[68] Women like Hattie Mae Gilmore, fired from their jobs due to their involvement in the local civil rights movement, now had more opportunities. Whether as secretaries, cooks, or teachers' aides, women found a degree of autonomy from the local economy since federal employees in Washington, D.C., signed their paychecks. Now everyone could take part in the race's uplift.

Children received two full meals each day—breakfast and lunch—and a snack. Just feeding the children required the services of a coordinator, cooks, and staff to select and buy and then prepare the food, enough people so that Head Start became one of the most sought-after employers. Not only did the program pay well, but the children were served: "We tried to provide a comprehensive kind of program so that we would not only build on the educational aspect of a child, but we would build on his physical well being, his emotional stability, and a sense of belonging and self-esteem."[69] For children, seeing parents (mostly mothers) or other members of their neighborhood gainfully employed in a job with responsibility, Wilson hoped, would provide a positive socialization. Vernon Keys elaborated: "Head Start dealt with the whole family. They took the child and then they went into the home and they checked out the home to see what else the home needed."[70]

In Clarksdale, as the school board fastidiously refused requests to use school facilities, activities continued to be located in the churches.[71] Basements and auxiliary buildings housed Head Start children, who were also fed on-site. Federal money did not provide buildings, but funds could be used to refurbish existing structures. In this way, some churches benefited, as they underwent renovations to cater to the children.[72] This arrangement continued until the mid-1970s, when COI obtained its own buildings.[73]

Also as part of the OEO provisions, legal services received brief funding in 1965 under the CAPs.[74] Out of the initial $336,666 given in September 1965 for COI, $82,725 was earmarked for legal aid. It was the only legal service program in the state. Designed to be nonprofit and needs-based, offering counseling and legal advice to the poor, it would also represent those who complained about the violation of a federal law, employing part-time research assistants, who were second- and third-year University of Mississippi law students. However, conflict again arose about money.

The Coahoma County Bar Association fought hard against the service, because by representing the poor, outside lawyers would lose money from fee-generating cases. Protests stalled the service for months, before it was finally chartered as Coahoma Legal Aid, Inc., which began operations on 4 April 1966. To pacify the Bar Association, the program rotated nine attorneys weekly for a salary, and the office functioned, according to the *Clarksdale Press Register*, with "a full-time staff of two field investigators, two secretaries, a youth counselor and an assistant attorney to aid the local lawyer." A lawyer would work one day each week in the office for $100 per day, and the office could not handle civil rights cases.[75] Gooden explained what happened: "Later we found out some of those fee-generating cases that were coming through there were referred back to that [attorney's] office, to their offices. . . . We never had a class action at all."[76] In fact, Semmes Luckett, Tom Ross, and Vincent Brocato, three of the most vocal opponents of black civil rights and COI (they had indeed resigned from the board earlier) earned money as lawyers for the legal aid service. These lawyers were not prepared to litigate against the system, nor were they willing to help the poor with cheap legal aid. They protected their livelihoods and only dealt with minor issues like birth certificates, marriages, and a few divorces. Nothing concerning substantial money in fees or damages went through legal aid. The service lasted about five years until the program was shifted to the newly established North Mississippi Rural Legal Services.[77]

COI also managed adult education, benefiting seasonal farmworkers. Providing an educational experience and an income for about 7,000 farmers became one of the programs that activists fought urgently to acquire for the Delta population. In July 1965, Aaron Henry had initiated an investigation into the 3B program under the secretary of agriculture. Spending considerable time in the nation's capital to acquaint himself with the program, Henry had applied to establish a program in Coahoma County, initially under the aegis of SERA. The program's design stalled in Washington, D.C., and activists suspected that Senators John Stennis or James Eastland had had a role to play in the delay. The battle took months, finally ending in March 1966.[78]

Teachers fired from the school system because of their civil rights involvement, like Noelle Henry and R. L. Drew's wife, worked as instructors in the new adult education program.[79] It was the first of its kind in Mississippi, designed to train 1,000 workers over a seven-month period with an overall federal grant of $3.7 million in a dozen Delta counties. Basic adult education taught people how to read and write in order to provide life tools for field laborers to find work during the off-season. The participants received a stipend of about thirty dollars per week as an incentive. In fact, it was the program originally envisioned by Jesse Epps in 1964 when he had returned to Clarksdale with high hopes. White farmers revolted—they had been paying the laborers far less than the stipend and employing workers for only about thirteen weeks per year. Bennie Gooden remembered serious confrontations, not so much in Coahoma County but in other areas like Sunflower County. COI had money and authority to provide adult education in eighteen counties, but because of resistance from farmers, not all received the aid. Joseph Wheatley, educated in the Coahoma County school system, ran the program for COI, later taking the project and developing the Mississippi Delta Council, which worked specifically for farmworkers. By that time, machinery had displaced most of the tenant farmers, so the program worked to retrain those workers. Finding jobs for the newly trained proved to be more difficult in the weak Mississippi economy, and this hampered the success rates for the program overall.[80]

Of the participants in the adult education program, 75 to 80 percent were female. Gooden reasoned, "We don't have as many males, period, and males that could find a job were working otherwise."[81] Male migration and the war in Vietnam took many men out of the area. In fact, the population in the county had dropped dramatically since 1950 and would continue to drop. People left the rural county and never returned. In 1950, 49,361 lived in Coahoma County, dropping to 46,212 in 1960 and 40,447 in 1970. By 2000, the number had plummeted to 30,622 (29 percent white and 69 percent black). Clarksdale's population numbers remained steadier, with families moving in from the fields counter-balancing the out-migration. In 1950, 16,539 people lived in Clarksdale, rising to 21,105 in 1960 (in that year, 53.5 percent were characterized as "nonwhite"). According to the 2000 census, 20,645 people resided within the city limits: 29.95 percent (6,184) were white, and 68.52 percent (14,146) were African American.[82] With the county numbers dipping, a large number of the remaining farmworkers in 1965 were women, who picked and chopped cotton in the heat of the Mississippi Delta fields. Such work, though, became less available with the increase in mechanization.

Like the private domestics in the city, these women took advantage of the choices now available to them. The extra money supplemented families' meager incomes, and while young children were at the Head Start centers mothers had more time to also educate themselves. With more education, women could acquire better-skilled jobs and not only provide more for their families but also become role models for children to finish school.

Neighborhood centers in Clarksdale and the county provided a physical presence and base in the community away from the prominent civil rights hubs like the Freedom House or the bigger churches. Troy Catchings, employed in 1966 as a technical assistant (who would become the COI director in the eighties), asserted that the centers were "the heart of Coahoma Opportunities . . . [which provided] people in the community a voice in their future. It was out of those centers where we set up libraries, we did some community organizations, we received community input." Outreach staff, locals themselves, trained in the benefit programs so that they could easily answer questions and perhaps help individuals apply to the various agencies. Many had only a high school diploma and now had the opportunity to return to school. Outreach was necessary as many citizens did not know of their rights or their entitlements. The elderly, who qualified for government insurance benefits, suffered silently, unaware of available aid. These people had to be sought out, educated, and then helped to apply and fill out the paperwork. The neighborhood center also developed youth activities: movies, presentations, and even a skating rink. Catchings remembered that the neighborhood center "was a place for [the community] to go to sign up for different services that were available at the time. We taught quilting, we bought sewing machines to teach people how to sew. . . . The theme at that time was self-sufficiency. . . . We had even things for young people to do, recreational activities, things to keep them off the streets and to get them more involved in something constructive."[83] It became a space resembling what Zoya Zeman had envisioned for the community center during Freedom Summer a couple of years earlier, only now with federal support.

The Neighborhood Youth Corps program under the COI umbrella began in the summer of 1967 for people between the ages of fourteen and twenty-one. Organized in three phases, the first phase involved an in-school program to provide work for students for the minimum wage; the second phase was the summer program, which enabled young people to acquire summer jobs for eight weeks; and, finally, an out-of-school program was designed to help school dropouts earn money and get their GED or to encourage them to return to school. The work did not involve providing skills for the larger job market, but by keeping youth busy with janitorial and maintenance work, education could be seen as the key to the door out of menial labor and potential trouble. Catchings remembered that the Neighborhood Youth Corps developed self-esteem "to try to teach them the basic work habits." The Neighborhood Youth Corps stayed with COI for about four or five years before the program merged with the college system.[84]

Housing also concerned COI. It was a pressing problem in the Delta, where many families lived in structures unfit for livestock. As OEO sought to secure improvements for the poor, it had partnered with some churches to provide low-income housing in places where no development interest existed in the private sector. In 1970, as a member of Chapel Hill Church in Clarksdale, Bennie Gooden paved the way for the institution to extend its social development ministry. During Governor Ross Barnett's administration (1960–64), the state legislature had changed the statute so that public housing in Mississippi could only occur through a local referendum. Given the racial politics, the provision halted public housing development. With the OEO initiative, Gooden saw a chance to bypass the statute by partnering with nonprofit groups, like his church, which could back a long-term mortgage. The result was the Chapel Hill Heights development, the first low-income housing site in two decades in the city.[85] COI itself worked with existing home structures, initiating housing rehabilitation and home repairs in order to improve housing to give more people "a sense of solidarity for purposes of change and improvement of the way of life and representation."[86]

In addition to these programs, subsidies of more than $30,000 were earmarked to revive the United Order of Friendship of America, a credit union operated in Clarksdale by Robert L. Drew, which provided small loan services to the community. It became the Friendship Federal Credit Union in October 1965 as part of the demonstration grant designed to provide low-cost lending to members (COI employees and participants) while promoting self-help and offering family and personal financial counseling as part of financial education. The credit union helped to offset the effects of loan sharks and the economic retaliation from many banks against those engaged (or thought to be engaged) in civil rights activities.[87]

Effects, Debates, Assessments

Coahoma Opportunities, Inc. enjoyed national recognition, just as federal planners had hoped. The programs provided were ambitious and numerous. Its profile was high enough to elicit a visit from Senators Robert Kennedy (D-N.Y.) and Joseph Clark (D-Pa.) when they toured antipoverty projects in Greenville and Clarksdale on 11 and 12 April 1967 for Senate hearings on hunger. Kennedy visited Clarksdale's neighborhood center for about twenty minutes on his way to the Memphis airport and was besieged by more than 1,000, mostly black, residents. He stood on the hood of a car shaking hands with patrons while advising the children and teenagers to stay in school.[88]

Sergeant Shriver and OEO intended that CAAs facilitate maximum feasible participation by the poor so that they could develop their own solutions. In Coahoma County, participation occurred in multiple ways. As an example, the Parent Volunteers Advisory Committee served on the Head Start program, and the outreach work consisted of trained community members who also conducted home visitations. In the neighborhood centers, sewing classes attracted women, who came to learn to sew and produce clothing from bolts of fabric with an eye to job creation in the future. In a democratic vote during an advertised public meeting, community committee members were chosen. In short, in those first years COI mostly realized OEO's objective to fully incorporate community involvement into its very foundation. The presence and participation of movement workers also ensured spaces for increased community empowerment.

As a result, more and more African Americans became politicized. Despite the public mass movement in Clarksdale from the late fifties, many African Americans had shied away from the sometimes dangerous business of direct involvement. With a federally supported organization devoted to the quality of their lives, coupled with the chance for better-paying jobs, the once disfranchised now had more of a purpose. When the teenagers at Higgins High School marched to Clarksdale High School in 1969 to register at the all-white school, many of the adults picketing with them were COI employees and participants. Meetings relevant to the protest took place in COI buildings. The strong roots to the local movement and leaders shielded them from the same fate that CDGM's activist employees had experienced. Also, the students' protests revolved around compliance with the law, so white supremacists had a much harder time justifying retaliation.

Subtle shifts in race relations embodied the most valuable long-term contribution. "COI opened doors for communication between whites and blacks on an almost equal basis," said Gooden.[89] When the hostile white leadership abruptly abandoned the COI board, they thought the organization would fold without their presence to diversify the management. Instead, coalition building and a dogged determinism, mirrored at the federal level, won out. Within the coalition, races worked together to ensure the smooth running of the programs; the organization gave moderate whites a place to exist away from the grasp of conservative forces. As Mayo Wilson asserted, COI "was a solid nucleus that served as a catalyst for change"[90]—with economic independence came grudging respect. Vernon Keys announced, "It was a peaceful revolution."[91]

COI retained its funding at high levels through 1972 with the sustained tolerance of biracial groups and the boost to the local economy: "From October 1, 1965, to July 1, 1972, COI introduced approximately $18,465,811 into Coahoma County's economy—an average of $2,637,973 annually," employing over 11,000 local people between 1965 and 1972.[92] All the vendors associated with the federally funded programs had to comply with the Civil Rights Act, thereby ensuring that merchants modified their racial comportment. Black patrons were courteously addressed as businesses sought a piece of the federal pie and to benefit from increased black buying power. Whites who once resisted change, Vernon Keys noted, "accepted it because it was their livelihood too. They wanted your money, they wanted your cooperation, they wanted your participation, so they made the changes."[93] The desegregation of businesses happened relatively quietly over time in the late sixties.[94]

A major COI accomplishment was the ability to engage more impoverished and working people. While high school and college graduates benefited, outreach workers came from the grass roots, in constant contact with the wider community, ensuring that the populace remained "somewhat politically active." These key outreach workers—most, if not all, women—"may have been cooks in a cafeteria or they were active, anyway, in the early civil rights movements," Troy Catchings reasoned. "But they didn't have the education to get the few jobs that were available."[95] In this way, Catchings continued, a degree of individual self-sufficiency developed. People, particularly women, who formerly worked in dining rooms or on farms, became teacher's aides and made a decent living and had benefits. Additionally, they played a vital role in educating their children and other adults, and many sought to be further educated themselves, some of them moving from high school to studying at Delta State to becoming teachers in the school system. These workers became politicized and in turn politicized others who may not have otherwise been reached by civil rights organizing.

This had a profound effect on society and the local economy. "Clarksdale really got shook up because all of a sudden people were going to be self-sufficient and people were going to have self-esteem—people were being motivated to move on up to higher heights and that made it inconvenient [for white employers needing janitorial or domestic services]. . . . They were going to get jobs that had titles, that had salaries, that had benefits," stated Keys proudly. Keys herself made about $3,000 more per year when she left Coahoma County Junior College to work for COI. After several years as administrative assistant, she assumed the post of personnel director from 1972 to 1979.[96] This pattern of elevation affected everyone. Raising the black median income "angered the astute or the aristocratic community. It did not affect the poor community of Clarksdale but it did the aristocrats because these women then started trying to bargain with their maid."[97] Mayo Wilson concurred, stating, "We had a lot of freedom to engage and involve people who had not been involved at the table before—to bring them into the structure—get their respectful level of opinions—and to include them as equals. Attitudes . . . about themselves basically changed and so consequently they came more active in their nature."[98]

Although the poor undoubtedly benefited from the poverty programs, as designed, clearly so did the middle classes. When Head Start came to the region, for instance, the salaries for the higher positions were greater than those for public school teachers. As a result, many resigned from the school system to work for COI, and in order to retain teachers the school board had to raise school salaries. The earlier example of Bennie Gooden, a teacher since 1960, is a case in point.[99] In other areas, black people earned higher salaries in COI than in the private sector. As a direct result, the overall wage levels increased in order to compete for quality labor, and the entire community benefited. The agencies' suppliers and local merchants benefited, and banks enjoyed the influx of federal dollars.[100]

Not all African Americans in the Delta approved. More militant civil rights activists working under the slowly disintegrating SNCC disagreed with antipoverty programs. Fannie Lou Hamer had always derided the NAACP for its classism, and although she applauded the concept of the War on Poverty, she opposed a great deal of the implementation. In 1966, she spoke out: "The NAA[CP] is the big wheel in the state of Mississippi and so help me God nothing in the world is so unjust as this poverty program in Mississippi." She continued: "It's a disgrace and it's a shame before God for people to operate this kind of thing and call it a poverty program. . . . They ain't thinking about none of those poor people."[101] Hamer, a spokesperson for the destitute, agreed with claims that the programs benefited only certain blacks, particularly those jumping on the civil rights bandwagon. Her argument, supported by class consciousness, accused the NAACP of bias against the poor. Many shared her sentiments. The history of the ill-fated CDGM reflects the tensions between these one-time allies as COFO crumbled and federal money became available.

The CDGM fight had further divided civil rights activists. Radical voices vigorously criticized moderate Aaron Henry for not supporting CDGM and for colluding with segregationist senators. Fannie Lou Hamer stood firmly at the front of the dissenters, further labeling Henry a sell-out, particularly in light of the Mississippi Freedom Democratic Party delegation fiasco in Atlantic City two years earlier.[102] Yet, Nicholas Lemann stressed, "Henry had decided once again to side with the liberal elements in the federal government instead of the forces of independent black radicalism, and in doing so, he had saved Sargent Shriver's neck."[103] These middle-class moderates did not want to throw out the baby with the bathwater and once again manipulated their associations in order to maintain federal support, suppress opposition as much as possible, and help desperately needy children.[104]

Uniting against radicals during the CDGM controversy, the NAACP and the Sovereignty Commission ironically ended up on the same side in this one case, causing Erle Johnston, one-time commission director, to note: "With the known militancy of some of the groups that had invaded Mississippi, I began to wonder if the NAACP—once the ugliest letters in the language of Mississippi whites—seemed to be the best agency for communication at the national level and could work better with local leadership in providing a smoother path into the future."[105] Both he and Stennis employed a sort of flexible coalition that enabled them to ally with the lesser of two evils in order to minimize militant activity. In the end, no one really got all they wanted, although some with influence got more concessions than others, but the political wheels of compromise continued to turn nevertheless.

Locally, despite the increase in job opportunities, women's roles in these poverty programs rarely surpassed their positions in civil rights organizations, adding yet another layer to the mix. As Vera Pigee experienced national marginalization because she worked with children in the youth councils, yet enjoyed the latitude to exercise her local leadership, Head Start also became feminized, contributing to the perception that the program remained non-political. Women continued to be involved with the education and care of younger children, developing kindergarten, day care, and nursery education, but none of the OEO senior staff were female. Once again, alternative and politicized mothering existed and even thrived, mostly unnoticed. Through Head Start, the federal government sponsored mothering, which was devalued in rank yet potent and successful for its direct contact with children. The federal government utilized and capitalized on parental and familial concern, which motivated the creation of a program to help children generally.[106]

Vera Pigee's movement story in Clarksdale ends during COI's early years. Her exquisite fire and passion buoyed her in the darkest years when very few risked so much to lead movement activity. As economically independent from the plantation system, Pigee utilized her place and type of business to communicate, shelter, and teach, and so her light shone bright in the state. As more civil rights organizations, particularly through COFO and, by extension, SNCC, pried open spaces in the closed society in the sixties, they also dislodged Pigee's authority and status, creating new places and ways to protest louder and with more national impact. Outside volunteers in Clarksdale preferred Henry's counsel and his open style of leadership and, as a result, trod roughly and somewhat rudely over what Pigee had painstakingly built for a decade. A year later, as COI was being established, she found her leadership challenged by local people, now empowered to participate.

She worked for a short while with the poverty programs, but, still entwined with the NAACP, she did not assume a leadership position within COI. While COI dealt with the federal government, the NAACP continued to work in litigation and to enforce the Civil Rights Act and the Voting Rights Act. She partnered with Joseph Wheatley from May 1966 to March 1967 in charge of recruitment for the basic adult education program, continuing her past efforts in teaching citizenship classes. In that post, she remembered the heartbreaking stories of poverty she came across in the county. She recalled the stark contrast of her day: the morning spent qualifying a single mother and her children for welfare when they lived on dirt floors and ate rice out of a pot, and then returning home to her husband for a nourishing lunch. She said: "I couldn't eat. I went to bed. I cried, and prayed and slept all afternoon."[107]

Although Pigee had attained middle-class status as a successful business-woman, it was an uncomfortable fit. In many ways, she stood within the long tradition of black club women, which extends back into the nineteenth century. She sought her own uplift through her volunteer work in her community helping those less fortunate than her but linked to her by race and fate. Yet she did not have the formal education the class usually expected and did not necessarily identify with the welfare rights movement activists. Middle class by wealth and by community standards, she now chose to secure that status more formally.

In the first semester of the 1968–69 school year, Pigee had enrolled at the Detroit campus of the University of Michigan to begin work on a bachelor's degree in sociology and journalism. Whether prompted by the formalizing of qualifications in the public sector or because she now had more time, she decided to go back to school. Her husband, Paul, had landed a good job as a foreman in a factory in Detroit, so they purchased a home there and she commuted back and forth monthly between the Motor City and Clarksdale in order to continue her duties in the local NAACP branch. Even with her studies, she managed to organize some residents in Grosse Pointe, Michigan, to join the NAACP.[108] As a long-time movement veteran—at this time she had been on the front lines for over fifteen years—she was tired, and she resented how more formally educated newcomers had assumed leadership positions in Clarksdale. She felt that they had not paid their communal dues as she had. And, of course, she was right to a large extent. The poverty programs, particularly COI, provided jobs, respectability, and opportunity for a whole cadre of people, and she highlighted teachers particularly, who had not participated in the movement previously. Once the Civil Rights Act and the Voting Rights Act passed in the mid-sixties and the federal presence in the city began to keep segregationist retaliation at bay and money rolling in through COI, it was now safe for individuals to realize their own ambitions economically and politically.

More open conflict now broke out in the NAACP branch, directly connected to the issues in COI. Pigee bitterly announced: "The chances to survive for blacks who participated in the NAACP had increased 100 percent in Mississippi, and the jealousies of some of the active . . . members had begun to surface on all levels. A whispering campaign was in process, saying the branch needed a new secretary who lived in Clarksdale." Yet many members had rejected her offers to resign. A wealth of institutional knowledge would have migrated north with her. So they worked out a system whereby the assistant secretary, E. L. Martin, could take the reins in her absence. He resigned shortly thereafter, citing lack of authority and executive board rivalry. Before the semester had ended, as she transferred to Wayne State University, the visible conflicts broke through the surface. Ironically, given Fannie Lou Hamer's and Vera Pigee's competing organizational affiliations and loyalties, they both wondered whether poverty programs assisted the black middle class in its aspirations for upward mobility more than they helped the poor.[109]

The COI work was similar to the work Pigee had carried out for years in citizenship classes, yet title and rank made a difference now (as noted, Jesse Epps had lied about professional qualifications in order to be taken seriously). This was the double-edged sword of government aid, whereby government money came with strings attached and raised the issue of "who is truly qualified." Blacks and whites worked together, but salaries were set on a sliding scale: "One's degree determined the title and salary scale," which left Pigee, an undergraduate student, at the lower rungs, despite her years of experience and community influence.[110] She found that some of the managers and "experts" who dealt with the poor had no point of reference or empathy. In one position as a teacher's aide at Hull Elementary School in Coahoma County, a "white Washington so-called expert on black folks" entered the classroom and quizzed her on whether she had taught students about the proteins in steak. She incredulously answered no, following up with the statement that she *did* note the nutritional content of dried peas: "I asked him how many steaks he thought a person could buy with $30.00 a week."[111]

Unfortunately, and somewhat ironically, instead of remembering her work with the youth in Clarksdale as the pinnacle of her achievements, at the end of her life Pigee lamented the years in which internal conflicts tore apart the unstable unity within the NAACP and the movement in general. By 1970, "the little clique" had found opposing nominees for the secretarial post, the first time Pigee had ever been seriously challenged. Everyone wanted to be a leader, "particularly the ones who had a little smell of education," she complained. With a membership of over 1,000, fewer than 100 voted. Pigee kept her position, garnering more votes than the other two candidates combined, but she stated, "I was tired of dragging the branch along." Voting fraud and negative publicity marred the NAACP branch elections in 1970 and again in 1972, in an effort to unseat the civil rights veteran. Still commuting between Detroit and Clarksdale, Pigee remained active in the local NAACP branch as an at-large member—but it was never the same. She stated, "I wish they would use that energy to fight their enemies." The conflicts between the old guard and the new spilled into the state conference, where she was eventually nudged aside as youth council advisor there too.[112] Finally, in 1973, Edna Luckett beat Pigee, in a vote of 215 to 67, and became the branch secretary. Vera Pigee was relegated to a position as executive board member at-large.[113]

These turns of events elicit both outrage for and criticism of Pigee. Undoubtedly, she had paid her dues and deserved better treatment and acknowledgment. But egos clashed and her feelings got hurt. Her leadership had relied on community support in the midst of stultifying violence and repercussions. Those with the degrees and certificates were not risking their livelihoods. The cracks in the mask of civility and agreement are visible on paper, oftentimes by their absences. Aaron Henry did not write about Pigee as part of the leadership group in his autobiography. There she is sidelined, and she also disappears in his correspondence and papers. His stories differed from hers—he focused on the roll call of notoriety and successes that he claimed as his own; she focused on the daily toll and community events. Firsthand accounts from Pigee in her last years in Clarksdale—from the very existence of her own autobiography, written and published in 1975 expressly to redress the imbalance in the narrative, and from her daughter decades later—speak to how she felt betrayed, forgotten, and unvalued.

She had real reason to feel vexed. Although she did not need to take a position in COI given her civil rights work, she had wanted to help the organization and offer skills she had gained on the front line. Yet she also wanted a piece of the federal pie too. Those she labeled "Johnny Come Latelys" were the younger generation—like Bennie Gooden, who had been in her Youth Council, or Edna Luckett, who could not voice her support because of her position as a teacher but whose job allowed her husband to participate (he served as an armed guard at Henry's house and had many other jobs, including driving cabs and having various railroad assignments).[114] Witnesses to movement activity for over a decade, they wanted to lead and were in a position to do so. Pigee was in that position herself in the fifties. And while she may have had legitimate complaints about others' interpersonal communications and actions, she also lost opportunities to collaborate and to harness that energy and skill and evolve her work in ways that might have caused her less stress.

This was not to be, however. In Pigee's view, Sargent Shriver's goal to present CAPS as "an enabling device for the movement in its next phase" ultimately failed. She completed her degree in December 1973, and by the mid-seventies, Pigee had moved to Michigan permanently. Her stress-induced stomach ulcers proved to be too much for her to continue on the front lines in the Delta.[115] For her, the movement ended.

Which War? Whose War?

It is hard to track the progress of COI through the decades, once the support for the organization waned as national politics turned to the right. With fewer studies conducted and decreasing federal funds, media reports from the field dried up and the spotlight shifted more firmly to the urban landscape. Records in Clarksdale are scarce and scattered. By tracking the declining earmarked federal money, the shifting of programs from one office to another, and the rhetoric against the poor, it is clear that COI would never regain its heyday of its first five to seven years.

The federal commitment to the War on Poverty always remained in question. Even in the mid-sixties, Andrew Carr noted: "Only when the government becomes truly resolute can we effect change. People in Washington make a lot of pretty plans but they either backtrack on them or they get lost in the bureaucratic struggle."[116] With the Nixon administration aggressively seeking to cut funding and undo the programs laid out by Johnson, funds shrank, as did the programs.[117] One of Nixon's moves was to transfer Head Start from OEO to HEW in 1969. With Donald Rumsfeld appointed as director in July 1969, OEO became more institutionalized and the states were encouraged to participate more in program development, which ultimately decreased poor people's direct access to the federal government. In January 1973, Nixon abolished OEO entirely, scattering its programs among larger federal agencies by 30 June.

Nixon stated: "After more than 7 years of existence, Community Action has had an adequate opportunity to demonstrate its value within the communities it serves, and to build locally based agencies. OEO has taken steps to help Community Action agencies put down local roots through a program of incentives and training. . . . Further Federal spending on behalf of this concept, beyond the $2.8 billion which has been spent on it since 1965, no longer seems necessary or desirable."[118] In short, the president closed the window of opportunity for communities to carve out a path and a plan to overcome economic inequality at the local level, passing the controlling funds to the elected officials rather than to the private agencies.

The original hope, to create programs that could sustain themselves, never materialized, in part because white cooperation was never solid and local African Americans were new to the political process at this level. The programs did not change attitudes or alleviate all racial problems. Many in the white community continued to stand in the way of collaboration between the races, and only a few worked in the organization. By 1967, very little involvement came from the local government, particularly given the virulent opposition of those controlling the purse strings. Only a few vacant buildings had been used, but city and county officials continued to balk at operating school facilities for Head Start and the later Early Childhood Development programs, for instance. "The denial [of requests to use existing public facilities] necessitated the purchase and rental of similar facilities thus increasing per pupil costs." As OEO designated COI one of its "demonstration" programs (which accounted for the huge initial injections of grant money), many white conservatives and some of the COI employees criticized the overmanagement at the federal level that resulted at times in conflicting directives and advice from federal personnel, causing problems for local administrators. The largest single factor for excessive costs in Coahoma County, however, was the local political struggle.[119]

Also, there was an inherent lack of black expertise to support the benefits that COI began to yield. Troy Catchings reasoned: "You had the money coming in, which was never sufficient, but you still didn't [have] the plan and the foresight at that time that the people have now. The people are still learning."[120] COI's programming sought to help as many as possible, as soon as possible, and maintained a necessarily wide base of support that concentrated programs could not. Setting up small businesses in the late sixties, for example, was not the first priority—basic literacy and nutrition were more pressing. Today, the Mississippi Economic Development office provides that service. The Neighborhood Youth Corps and the Manpower Development Training Act (enacted in 1962) sought to train people for work, but soon it was evident that the jobs for which they were trained had diminished in number. In the Delta, despite money injected into training programs, no jobs existed, adding to frustrations and a gross lack of self-sufficiency.

Only the strongest projects, like Head Start, continued to survive and prosper. In Coahoma County, COI continues to run Head Start. CAAs originally established programs, nurtured them to a point of administrative stability, and then released them into the community. Under Joseph Wheatley, adult education successfully left the COI umbrella; so did the Neighborhood Service Center, Legal Aid, the Credit Union, and the Neighborhood Youth Corps. Head Start was another matter. The school board always remained eager to bring the program under its auspices, but COI directors knew that to give the school board control of Head Start would result in the displacement of many of its workers. The school board would have required certain educational standards for employees, which would have disqualified most of the personnel, and as a result, Head Start remained under COI.[121]

Despite their inability to reorder Delta society, poverty programs went further than desegregating bus terminals or fighting for children's educational opportunities. If children could not compete in desegregated schools, they could not earn the money to travel or sit on desegregated stools at lunch counters. The poverty programs, born out of Johnson's War on Poverty, did the most to try to even the political and economic playing field. Curtis Wilkie wrote in the nineties that the legislation "began in a sunburst of noble intentions," but he repeated Martin Luther King's assertion—that the "dream had died, along with thousands of American servicemen in the mire of Vietnam later in the decade." Yet the dream gave critical momentum and empowerment to thousands.[122] Federal programs offered unprecedented opportunities, free from outwardly racist white paternalism and control.

Many more African Americans could live in Coahoma County as autonomous beings, not beholden to local white employers. Some of the participants went into banks, some went into stores, and many sat on boards and commissions that decided the fate of their communities. For instance, Mayo Wilson, once the director of Head Start, became the first black vice president of a bank in the county.[123] Wilkie had also acknowledged that COI suffered from a few bureaucratic problems, but "it elevated salaries in the local job market and encouraged a simple policy—even the poorest supplicant for help had to be addressed as Mr. or Mrs."[124] Catchings recounted: "They've had an impact on getting regulations relieved [particularly at the food stamp and welfare office;]

they've had an influence on getting people to change policies on how they treat people."[125] The organization won many awards between 1968 and 1972 and survived several administrations over the decades that shaved off funds.

In 1974, Congress established the U.S. Community Services Administration, which replaced OEO as an independent agency. This was abolished, in 1981, by Ronald Reagan, who blamed the poor for their situation and saw welfare as counterproductive.[126] As a result, he sought to reduce the national deficit and taxes while increasing military spending by destroying social programs. Intense lobbying by supporters of antipoverty efforts saved the programs from a hostile White House. The Omnibus Budget Reconciliation Act of 1981 created two block grants: the Social Services Block Grant and the Community Services Block Grant. These grants went to the states to distribute to the poverty programs and in effect ended community control, which had been protected by the federal government. Community Services Block Grants gave preference to CAAs as recipients of block grant funds. Head Start did not get incorporated into the block grant, unlike the CAAs; instead, after fierce lobbying by Head Start supporters, it got grant-in-aid status. It remains under the renamed Department of Health and Human Services. Congressional appropriations for Head Start went from $96.4 million in 1965 to $6.2 billion in 2001. During the Reagan years, federal money to the rest of the War on Poverty programming significantly dropped, and the monetary value of the average block grant continued to decline in the 1990s.[127]

In the early nineties, under the directorship of Troy Catchings, COI moved into economic development. Partly due to the changing society and the national economy, the shift acknowledged the reduced resources earmarked for directly helping the poor. In the Clinton administration, money inevitably moved out of one program to fund another.[128] After a decade of conservatism in the White House, the future of COI depended on its aggressiveness and its ability to function like a corporate business and solicit funds and resources in the private sector. Clinton envisaged developing small business initiatives in the Delta to facilitate the growth of black-owned establishments as a way to alleviate poverty. Housing was one area that could yield big results, and Bennie Gooden's success underscored the potential that could ensure COI's survival.

After starting the housing project with COI, building Chapel Hill Heights and Eastgate Gardens developments, Bennie Gooden quit COI to manage the new projects. He continued to build in Clarksdale, a total of six projects (including the Bennie S. Gooden Estates), and by the late 1980s he was managing an empire throughout Mississippi, Arkansas, and Tennessee, with a total of sixty developments through the Southland Management Corporation. He was known as one of the richest black men in Clarksdale. The Clarksdale developments are known for their green areas and good maintenance and for the fact that Gooden knew many of the tenants. He made a point to build near middle-class areas to avoid the ghettoization of the poor, and he lived in one of the biggest houses in Clarksdale, which he built in the 1980s, near Chapel Hill church and the developments.[129]

Most programs continued under the Clinton administration, although they remained scattered throughout the federal departments and agencies. Statistics at the turn of the millennium noted about 31,139,000 persons below the poverty line, or 11.3 percent of the national population. Even given these staggering figures, the numbers reflect a dramatic drop in poverty levels from the 1960s.[130] Programs like Head Start, Job Corps, Legal Services, and VISTA (Volunteer in Service to America) flourished.[131] The census at the end of the twentieth century showed that 24.2 percent of the civilian population in Coahoma County (including Clarksdale) worked in management, professional, and related occupations; 25.1 percent in service occupations; and 27.4 percent in sales and in office occupations. Only 2.4 percent of the working population engaged in farming, fishing, or forestry work. The highest-ranking industry in terms of employment was in the sector of education, health, and social services (23.2 percent). The next closest industry, at 18.7 percent, was in arts, entertainment, recreation, accommodation, and food services. Nearly 20 percent of workers received their paycheck from the federal government (19.6 percent); 73.9 percent earned a private wage or were salaried employees. These statistics mirror the massive changes in the Delta rural economy in the past fifty years, away from agriculture and toward the service industry. The federal government, as a major employer in the county, retained its presence there, although poverty levels remained high. A staggering 25.6 percent of households had incomes of less than $10,000, whereas just over 5 percent earned over $100,000. In terms of official poverty status, 29.8 percent of families lived below the poverty line, and 42.6 percent of those had children under the age of five. In families with a female householder and no husband present, 52.3 percent lived below the line; 63.7 percent of these households had children under the age of five.[132] These figures, however, show small improvements. In 2000, 35.9 percent of the Coahoma County population lived in poverty; in 1989, the figure had been 45.5 percent.[133] Racial and class boundaries have not been greatly transformed by the poverty programs, as hoped, despite individual cases of empowerment and mobility.

COI occupied a prominent position in Coahoma County, but operations at the millennium were smaller than in the seventies: the neighborhood centers closed in the eighties, and about 650 children were funded for Head Start in 2000, compared to about 1,000 in the late sixties. COI still employed community people to work in the programs: between 160 and 170 trained and untrained staff were on the payroll. As for the board, it remained predominantly black, with white board members representing mostly the business sector.[134]

And so the War on Poverty and COI left both positive and negative marks on the national and local landscape. The Vera Pigees saw their leadership power diminished in the professionalization of skills and controlled access to programs. In contrast, Homer Hill, a Clarksdalian himself, declared, "The resultant expansion of African-American representation in the county's economic arena created a situation that put middle class blacks in a position to offer new opportunities to the black underclass and, with opportunity, a new measure of self-respect." By the mid- to late sixties, the black landscape in the Delta had changed. SERA plowed the land for COI and utilized latent black potential. As Hill astutely stated, the black middle class "used COI as a vehicle out of the 'backyards' of their community," and COI "proffered an economically cramped and vulnerable black middle class the opportunity to move toward self-sufficiency."[135] Rather than ending the movement, poverty programs expanded its constituency, pulled in federal muscle, and shifted the tone. But this fracture in the community—between older veterans, who suffered economic reprisals, bombings, imprisonment, and beatings to realize civil rights, and the younger cohort, who were perhaps politicized through the movement as teens or who were former teachers now able to assume leadership without recrimination—reflected not only the generational differences and struggles but also a new educated middle class primed to climb up the sociopolitical ladder.

I Have Not Ended the Story
For There Is No End

CONTINUING HISTORIES OF CLARKSDALE'S
BLACK FREEDOM STRUGGLE

*But the absence of brutality and unregenerate evil is not the
presence of justice. — Martin Luther King Jr. (1967)*

*Despite the symbolic gestures of fairness, decency and respect [that we
are only beginning] to practice in the American South, the quality of life
[in the Mississippi Delta] . . . is still compromised by our racial preoccupation.
It is not sufficient merely to listen and report, but we must think of doing something that will . . . finally . . . resolve what seems to be a historical and endless
problem in this country. — Jerry Ward, chairperson, Mississippi Advisory
Committee to the U.S. Commission on Civil Rights (1997)*

*There will always be a civil rights movement in America.
If you didn't fight the last time, you can fight now, because the battle
rages and we need warriors. — Nelson Rivers III (2003)*

The school day began at 6 A.M. The dusty yellow school bus would start its
long journey from the Lyon subdivision where I lived for a year out in the
county, surrounded by cotton fields. With my Sony Walkman clamped to my
ears, I would climb on that bus before 7 A.M. and stare out of the window as
it chugged around the fields, picking up children from what could only be
termed shacks. Our destination, Coahoma County High School, right on the

town line (and at one time the consolidated school, built in the fifties in an effort to avoid integration), was about a forty-five-minute meander away. As the crow flies, it would take only ten to fifteen minutes to get to school, but my stop was the first on the route, so every morning I got to see those places where "progress" had passed on by. Even with indoor plumbing and electricity, most of these houses from the outside resembled the thirties WPA photographs of the Delta.

Walking into Coahoma County High School in 1991 shocked me. It was not the America I thought I knew from my childhood visits to the Northeast. I had expected the rural landscape, and I anticipated the flat fields of cotton and the accents different from my own, but I did not foresee the stark inequalities marked by race. I was not very conscious of racism in my childhood, in part because of my parents' vigilant protection from the ugliness that they had experienced (I know that now). But parents in Mississippi could not protect their children from the harsh realities. The school, desegregated by court order in 1970, was practically all black. In the graduating class of 1992 of about seventy students, perhaps five were white. On that long school bus ride every morning, we sped by the pristine campus of Lee Academy, where most white students sat at their desks.

I had not expected this—I had not read about this in my world history class. At Coahoma County High School, I learned about race in America very quickly—trial by fire—and I faced my own personal crossroads. Yet my Mississippi history class planted the seed that has produced this book. The teacher, a perfectly decent young white man, taught solely from the textbook without deviation or pause. The War of Aggression and the Lost Cause elicited not a flicker of discomfort as he stood before African American students. Beyond a brief mention of Martin Luther King Jr., it was as if the postwar black freedom struggle had never come to Mississippi, and there was no acknowledgment of the famous local, Aaron Henry, who represented the district in the Mississippi legislature at the time. Black Mississippi history pooled around the few acceptable characters, mostly artists or inventors but none with any political chops. Even with my scarce knowledge of the state's history, I saw the bias and was irked. Now, decades later, with research to draw from, I empathize with those students in 1973 who protested and got expelled for trying to change the curriculum to reflect their histories.

Fast-forward to the end of the decade. In July 1999, President William Jefferson Clinton gathered an entourage that included the secretaries of transportation and labor and agriculture, the small business administrator, and the undersecretary of the treasury, and left Washington, D.C. Billed as an "antipoverty" investigation, the name of the excursion, the "New Markets Tour," belied its real agenda. The Clinton administration had recently enjoyed a healthy run of economic growth, with unemployment dropping from 7.2 percent to 4.3 percent. So he could afford politically to focus on community empowerment and private sector mobilization in areas of the country still suffering economically. In four days, he went to six places nationwide: Annville/Hazard, Kentucky; Clarksdale, Mississippi; East St. Louis, Illinois; Pine Ridge Indian Reservation, South Dakota; Phoenix, Arizona; and Los Angeles/Anaheim, California.[1] On a hot, sultry Delta day, Tuesday, 6 July, Mayor Richard M. Webster Jr. escorted the sweating group through Clarksdale.

Charismatic Clinton, his shirtsleeves rolled up in the heat, pressed palms with the hundreds of black residents who crowded around the entourage as it paused in Clarksdale. During his five and a half hours in town, he visited one of the few stores still open amid the boarded-up properties on Issaquena Avenue, once the liveliest street for black commerce in the county. By that time, most people went to stores and chains in the strip malls flanking Highway 61 (now 161). The president sat and listened intently to the testimonies of many black Clarksdalians unable to find work. Clinton brought brief exposure and a national audience to Clarksdale as he announced his New Markets Initiative, which would give tax breaks and incentives to businesses and industries willing to relocate to the Delta. He committed $15 million in community development grants for the Mississippi Delta—part of a $46.5 million funding package attached to his initiative—and expressed optimism that local poverty indicators, which reported that a startling 40 percent of the population lived below the poverty line, could be improved.[2]

The day before his arrival, the *Clarksdale Press Register* interviewed Ernestine Whitfield, an African American who had invited Clinton to call on her at her dilapidated house on Yazoo Avenue. Barely upright, the house epitomized the region's persistent crisis in housing and poverty. The 1990 census noted that in Coahoma County, 58.5 percent of black families and 7.2 percent of white families lived below the poverty line. County unemployment rates were startling too: 21.9 percent of African Americans and 4.7 percent of white citizens reported being out of work. Whitfield was not ashamed to welcome the president, hoping that his visit would precipitate reform and bring jobs and stable sources of income in order to sustain prosperity and achieve long-term stability. The lack of both economic opportunities and organized social outlets for children left to fend for themselves constituted another chief community concern. It was "easier for a teenager to join a gang than it is a softball team."[3] The community yearned for the youth centers once run by Coahoma Opportunities, Inc. (COI), which had closed in the eighties, a casualty of the Reagan era.

Clinton's trip differed from Robert Kennedy's highly publicized tour in 1968. Then, a huge press corps trailed the senator, and the papers had covered his trip over several days. Clinton grabbed headlines for one day. What was "the most exciting thing to happen in Clarksdale in a long time" quickly faded into memory, and the poor continued to eke out their existence as they had before. The 1999 tour's effect, "like rain in the desert," quickly evaporated. The burst of excitement it generated returned to apathy, as "in Clarksdale, people pay as little attention to Washington politics as Washington politics pays to them."[4] Washington was still far away.

Both snapshots of Clarksdale in the 1990s, two narratives coming from different directions but meeting at the Crossroads, offer insight into how much the city has changed but how it remains deeply mired in problems precipitated by race and power dynamics. Both stories fail to showcase the hope and aspirations of the mass movement; instead, they reveal the tensions and results of political winds shifting to the right. This epilogue tackles two questions. What happened to Clarksdale's mass movement? And a corollary, what are some of the manifestations of the rightward shift? Clearly, the story of Clarksdale has not ended.

Rather than offering a narrative of declension predicated on the assumption that all would be "fixed" by the mass movements, Clarksdale's story reflects a narrative of human struggle. As history swings like a pendulum, with political positions pushing and pulling at weighted issues over time, it creates the ebb and flow that occurs during prolonged struggle. Detailing the fights for civil and economic rights, despite the depressing reality still evident in the region, a history of success, empowerment, and perseverance, rather than one of deterioration, becomes all the more relevant and useful. The story of Clarksdale offers a more critical analysis of the meaning of improvement and its costs and encourages a better understanding of these debates at the national level.

Calculating degrees of success depends on the positions of the goalposts. If steps to address legal standards of equal citizenship by eliminating de jure segregation denote racial advancement, the mass movement succeeded. As a result of the various laws passed and court orders handed down, equality exists—at least on paper. This definition is satisfying for some, convincing many that an equal playing field prevails and that the only things standing in people's way to success are their own personal failings and weaknesses. Although African Americans are still worse off than most whites in the Delta, many would point to the growth in the number of new black middle-class homes and in black prosperity as signs of progress.

If the premise of the mass movement was more complicated, however—if it included the establishment of basic rights (particularly equal access in education and to voting) from which African Americans could work toward political power, if it held that power ought to properly be exercised in fairly drawn districts, and if it dreamt of economic opportunity with equally administered contracting—then the assumptions about the mass movement's successes and failures have proven incorrect. Therefore the myth of the movement, the one that harks back to a perceived golden age in African American history where brave and noble women, men, and children stood shoulder to shoulder against Jim Crow, remembers the legal successes as proof of an improved society. Indeed, the chapter about COI plots the rising black middle class and its new-found confidence and voice.

In Clarksdale, the NAACP branch took center stage in the mass movement years, willing and poised to react to daily events affecting black people. The death of Aaron Henry in 1997 took its toll, and branch membership and activity dwindled significantly as a result. Yet Bertha Blackburn, a long-time Clarksdalian, born in 1924, who had worked in the school system and at COI as a nutritionist, took the mantle of the branch presidency in 2001. She had been an NAACP member "way back before people could pay their dues on the top of the table." As many of her fellow teachers had, she admitted that her civil rights activities were covert: "It could not be in the open because you have to make a living you know." In her role as president, the branch had to be revitalized. Blackburn commented: "After Aaron got sick and passed, so did the branch. It was totally out of existence for a number of years and the national office was about to take the charter [in 2000]."[5]

She empowered her other networks, working with and mentoring local sororities (particularly Zeta Phi Beta) to create a project for the debutantes to collect branch memberships. In this way, her work followed Vera Pigee's activist mothering—utilizing her skills and connections along with hard work to transform and reincarnate the local branch, amid the sexism and lack of enthusiasm she endured from her male counterparts. Indeed, the two women were friends and reunited in 2003 at the branch's fiftieth anniversary. The local paper waxed poetically: "When these two matriarchs meet, the past and the future of the N.A.A.C.P. melds. They are one spirit, struggling toward the same goal: forward for freedom."[6] Blackburn's diligence paid off, particularly in an election year, and 500 signed their names and paid dues. Her success prompted her own election, despite her advanced age.[7]

Through her work and the efforts of mostly women volunteers, the local branch created standing committees to deal with certain issues. Legal redress in the community became vital as cases of civil rights violations continued to increase in number. The volunteers helped to fill out forms and directed the complaints to the correct agencies and departments. Problems with the police persist in Clarksdale, as they do around the country, and these problems are deeply entwined in the prison industry mandates. Blackburn saw her role as a fact-finder—to get to the root of cases and document them correctly to assist attorneys and the national NAACP. Her mission was to expand these operations with more volunteers so that once the organization started winning cases, some of the issues would subside.

Blackburn's volunteers were much younger than she was. Many of those who had literally put their bodies on the front lines in Clarksdale and throughout the Delta during the fifties and sixties tired in the seventies and eighties. Not only were they aging, but many, like Vera Pigee, felt frustrated at the turn of events and turned their attentions elsewhere or settled into their lives at work and at church. Pigee lived in Michigan until her death in August 2007. Her husband had died the year before, and they rest side by side in a cemetery in Detroit. In the last decades of her life, she continued to accept speaking engagements for women's clubs, churches, NAACP branches, and other civic organizations, recounting her life experiences and offering advice where she could. An active member of the significantly larger Detroit NAACP branch, she remained engaged with the organization's local activities.

Personal sacrifices went further than the leaders in the headlights of massive resistance. Behind and beside them, families lived and dealt with the consequences of their loved one's actions. Vera Pigee's daughter, Mary Jane, left Clarksdale for college in Ohio by the mid-sixties and never returned. She is not nostalgic for her place of birth, saying, "I didn't owe Clarksdale anything. I gave what I could when I could."[8] Davis angered when recalling seeing her mother endure abuse from whites and later rejection by her own. She visibly smarted at the insult when the mostly male leaders were remembered and honored with named roadways or buildings, and Vera Pigee received only a little back street on a housing estate bearing someone else's name.[9] So, despite the positive changes she experienced as a result of her mother's work—opportunities once not available — she questioned the personal cost. She walked through her childhood with police officers following her, and in 2005 she mused, when looking at youth today, "I wonder why I gave up my childhood." She said, "Yes — we as a race are retrogressing — so the fact [is] that I am wondering why did I do all this. If it changed things for a moment — but that moment was not long enough for me. And I am to the point now and say Lord, why did I give up my childhood for us to come to this. Most of the civil rights gains that we made — we are slowly but surely losing. Nowadays people don't vote."[10]

Rebecca Henry had two parents affected by civil rights activities. She was in junior high in 1964 when her father, Aaron, filed the lawsuit to desegregate Clarksdale schools on her behalf. He had remained a target for white supremacists throughout his life, and her mother, Noelle, had lost her teaching position as a result of her husband's leadership. Rebecca spent her formative years in her parents' shadows and always under tight security. She missed her father's daily presence, and it affected her deeply. Her bitterness, revealed in later interviews, dominated the memories of her father, who died of heart failure following a stroke in May 1997. She recalled: "I resented that when I was little and still do — big time — always getting somebody else to take us places, and, at my high school graduation, we had marched in and everybody was sitting down and my daddy was not there. . . . I needed a daddy and my mama needed a husband."[11] Rebecca Henry died from diabetes complications in 1999, leaving two sons, who were also ambivalent about their grandfather's legacy.

These stories of personal anguish and the persistent intra-organizational conflict have remained in the background of the movement's histories. However, they illustrate another critical dimension. The black community was never monolithic, and attitudes continually shifted, a fact in Clarksdale's history that became very evident in the mid- to late sixties, exemplified through Vera Pigee's story. Still the premier black organization in the county and allied in membership with the leaders of COI, the NAACP attracted the new black elite, who stood on the shoulders of those who pioneered the local struggle and strove for upward social and economic mobility.

Many of those in that new black elite have mixed feelings also. In the stories of desegregation, and in the sorrows expressed by black teachers who made the transition from segregated to court-mandated integrated schools in 1970, many African Americans expressed their experiences of disruption of community and of the social sense of linked fate that once bound black people together. Writer Anthony Walton noted: "This sense of community was the other half of the black experience in Mississippi, the palliative to the difficulties of Jim Crow, and the unifying glue—the larger, self-contained and self-sustaining bond—that some felt had been lost with the advances of the civil rights age."[12] The conditions that perpetuated the need for the bond, the communal fate of their blackness, transformed. Some African Americans, those able to succeed economically and socially through the destruction of Jim Crow, have moved up the economic ladder, and with individual opportunity comes individual advancement. But this positive change presents challenges. While economic progress brings success and prosperity, it makes coalition building harder. No longer does the rhetoric of group uplift illuminate the path for many middle-class African Americans. While the fight for complete equality continues, a changing community needs to adapt its tools to help more to climb the ladder.

The stagnation of Clarksdale's economy and the paucity of local resourcefulness to enable more to ascend this ladder dominated Clinton's trip to Clarksdale in July 1999, which intended to showcase the region's potential for economic investment. The systematic cauterization of most capillary streams of funding and aid to the poor, which Nixon began, had continued during Clinton's terms in office. For instance, the federal government designated the mid-Delta region as an empowerment zone in 1993, authorized by the Omnibus Budget Reconciliation Act to provide tax incentives to businesses. Designed to empower businesses, not the poor, e-zones did not work.[13] Clinton had also dismantled what was left of the safety net provided by federal social insurance policy with the 1996 Personal Responsibility and Work Opportunity Reconciliation Act. Handing over more of the controlling reins to the states, among other clauses that impacted the poor, this act literally numbered the days that recipients could claim welfare benefits, without requiring that improvements be made in job placement services or system efficiency. By 1999, as a lame duck president with political problems of his own, Clinton's legacy was at stake. The tour became part of his vision for redemption and reconciliation, but in reality it highlighted the extent to which federal policies had shifted since Nixon.[14]

Mississippi's economic and political policies and practices have only exacerbated the rising poverty statistics. The history of Mississippi's economy reflects what happens when the economic base disappears. In Coahoma County and the surrounding locales, COI sought to alleviate the most dire economic situations and it was successful in its early years because it did what it promised and because the Office of Economic Opportunity had worked closely with the local board. COI still exists, albeit as a mere shadow of its former self. As the conservative backlash at the federal level gave block grants to states, the focus changed at the local level. Head Start, the major program offered by COI, received funding directly from the federal government, but state block grants financed the rest of COI's programming.[15] While many of the programs in COI's first years sought to educate and empower poor residents to become politically active, almost five decades later most programs could only afford to provide the most basic assistance in alleviating housing and energy needs. The community centers, youth programs, legal services, and training programs that once caused the offices to bustle with community members of all ages no longer exist. The organization struggled annually to maintain its levels of funding and found that with increased costs of living it was able to help fewer and fewer families. COI—originally the flagship community action organization for federal funds—was reduced to hustling for funds and cutting programs despite evident need. This story again forces a reexamination of the movements' goals and success but acknowledges those still fighting the uphill fight.

COI is no longer the biggest employer in town. Tourism and casinos are among the fastest-growing industries in the Delta—some legislators in the state called the 1990 legalization of gaming along the Mississippi River and the Gulf Coast the "Mississippi Miracle."[16] If casinos and the tourist industry have been touted as a major economic boost to the area, however, they nonetheless continue to perpetuate what scholar Clyde Woods has described as the reality of the plantation legacy: since power and profit remain locked in their racialized places despite the different economic enterprises, they are only a miracle for the already wealthy.[17]

Attracting more visitors should alleviate economic pressure from depressed areas. Yet the burgeoning heritage tourist industry in the Delta repeats the slumming that Harlem attracted in the twenties. The Delta Blues Museum in Clarksdale occupies the now-defunct Illinois Central railroad station that Mary Jane Pigee and two other teens desegregated in the early sixties. Domestic and foreign visitors come to marvel at the blues legacy in the area, perhaps visiting the blues festivals, but after a brief sojourn in the Delta, most turn around on Highway 61 to return to the casinos or to Memphis further north. A cultural tourism based on "ethnic supremacy" allows visitors to dip into prescribed Delta history, which is carefully crafted and disinfected for delicate palates with deep pockets.[18]

Earlier tourism centered on monuments to white supremacy—antebellum homes, reenactments, battlefields, plantations, and collectibles—think *Gone with the Wind*. Today's tourist trails, promoted by the local Chamber of Commerce and tourist boards, follow blues history, and that has become Clarksdale's draw. Ironically, civil rights tours based in Memphis have now become fashionable, although Clarksdale has only just begun to acknowledge the need for civil rights landmarks in the city. In 2010, Highway 161, running through the city—Highway 61 now bypasses the center of town—was named the Dr. Aaron E. Henry Memorial Highway, but no markers dot the town describing civil rights sites and events, as multiple signs depict the haunts and homes of blues legends. However, like the plantation tours of antebellum homes, civil war battlefields, and reenactments that are bereft of any reference to slavery (other than pointing out the refurbished slave quarters from the big house's beautifully restored wrought iron balcony), the memorialization of the recent past continues to sanitize and minimize both black suffering and black contribution to the physical landscape and regional wealth. Such forays into local "folk" areas are planned and coordinated. On the Hopson plantation, the site of the invention of the first production model machine to pick cotton, the commissary now is a restaurant and museum about the family's mechanization inventions, and entrepreneurs have refurbished sharecroppers' shacks at the Shack Inn to rent to tourists hoping for a "real" experience. Local contested African American experience remains censored from the narrative, just as black communities are excluded from the benefits of the fortunes reaped from these new industries.[19]

The arrival of Hollywood actor Morgan Freeman's upscale blues establishment, Ground Zero, near the museum, at zero Blues Alley, allows tourists and better-heeled white Clarksdalians to experience the blues along with their burgers or catfish. In addition, he has a fine dining French restaurant, Madidi, also located in the gentrified downtown area.[20] Freeman's motivations for his Clarksdale investments seem to involve only business. Recognizing a prime location for entrepreneurship, given the blossoming tourist industry, the actor and Delta resident saw a good opportunity and found a willing investment partner in white attorney Bill Luckett. It would be convenient to say that Freeman acted out of financial interest. However, he has quietly contributed to African American interests in the Delta, like funding the first integrated prom in his Delta hometown, at Charleston High School in 2008, after the school board had rejected his 1997 offer. Teaming up with Paul Saltzman, a Canadian filmmaker and a Freedom Summer volunteer, Freeman produced "Prom Night in Mississippi," which documents the rocky journey to that evening of gowns and corsages, acknowledging the racism that exists where he lives but also challenging Mississippi to do better.

He has also publicly campaigned for Luckett's gubernatorial bid as a Democrat, stating in a press release that "holding on to the old politics of race, class and region has starved Mississippi for too long," and that "Bill Luckett will work diligently to see that the rhetoric that has divided us will never again keep us from tackling such problems."[21] This is significant, given that Luckett's great-uncle was Semmes Luckett, the Clarksdale attorney hired to protect segregation in the schools and across the county. Perhaps it is here, where profits from restaurants capitalizing on blues tourism pay for transformative social change, that Morgan Freeman's biggest contributions lie.

Economic incentives also attracted the gaming industry to Mississippi as casinos flocked to the banks of the Mississippi River and to the Gulf Coast to cash in on regional markets. Tunica County, north of Coahoma County and a stone's throw south of Memphis, now hosts a bevy of casinos. The region competes with Atlantic City and Las Vegas in size and attraction.[22] Isle of Capri (formerly Lady Luck) Casino stands alone at the foot of the Helena-Arkansas Bridge in Coahoma County, the nearest river crossing to Clarksdale. Two miles from Helena, it occupies land in rural Coahoma County, twenty miles north of Clarksdale. It is the closest casino to Little Rock, only 110 miles away; Tunica County is forty minutes north. The brightly colored moored vessel is surrounded by fields of soybeans, a new crop introduced as the seventies' economic response to the drop in cotton prices.[23] The county vote for the casino was contentious. In the summer of 1993, unofficial results counted 4,501 votes in favor and 3,121 opposed (59 to 41 percent), with a 45 percent voter turnout. The promise of 600 jobs, tax breaks for the county, and a cut of the revenue convinced voters.[24] In the end, the *Clarksdale Press Register* reported, "the pocketbook proved mightier than the pulpit" in the orchestrated battle between morality and economics.[25]

The casinos in the Delta are a mixed blessing. While they provide much-needed jobs to local Mississippians, the local revenue generated by their presence did not necessarily improve conditions in the surrounding counties. Wealthy landowners increased their profits by leasing or selling land to these industries and to the attendant array of hotels and retail outlets, while local politicians controlled the influx of local money. New jobs existed for many African Americans previously unable to find work, but positions remain restricted to service. Very rarely are black faces seen in managerial posts.[26] More often than not, they are consumers, frequenting the buffets and penny slot machines, with very few other leisure outlets available elsewhere.

The other fast-growing sector in the Delta is the corrections industry. African Americans dominate in this industry, on the wrong side of the cell doors.

The construction of private prisons in the region has proliferated as correctional facilities move to places with more land, a cheaper workforce, and a poor local economy eager for any injection of capital. In 1995, a huge construction program ensued to house the 6,500 prisoners registered in Parchman, the state penitentiary. Many studies from advocate groups and scholars agree that incarceration rates and educational spending are strongly and inversely correlated. In 2002, Grassroots Leadership, a nonprofit dedicated to community organizing since 1980, released a report entitled *Education v. Incarceration: A Mississippi Case Study*. Calling attention to the $45 million allocated to building private prisons in Mississippi at the expense of educational spending, the group argued that African Americans ultimately shoulder the burden of both.[27]

Poor counties have accepted private prison growth because lawmakers promised them local revitalization—and, in particular, jobs. While no new prison compounds are in Coahoma County (yet), many residents work (or are held) in neighboring facilities or have relocated to those counties. Black women, mostly single mothers, make up nearly half of the guards, while the prison population remains 70 percent black. Yet because owners and management are white, like the gaming industry, precious little of the money trickles into the local coffers.[28] In the same way that Jim Crow lined the pockets of planters and industrialists in need of cheap controlled labor, prison industries provide new avenues for revenue at the expense of the same population. Prisons have become the new way in which black bodies are quite literally controlled and fettered. Accordingly, protesters campaigned against the policy to build private prisons to help the Mississippi economy. The 2002 report stated: "Rather than invest in education for the rural workforce and positive economic development for poor communities, the state is undertaking a backwards approach to budgeting in which they . . . shop for inmates to validate these expenditures after the fact." Haley Barbour's 2003 gubernatorial victory, based on his pledge for "safer communities" through stiffer sentencing and the extension of private jails in the state, opened the door to more prisons.

Obviously, the many facets to the economy provide a lot of material with which to analyze changes and challenges, but consider next the trajectory of two other primary areas in Clarksdale. First, education. President Lyndon Baines Johnson once proclaimed that "education is the only valid passport from poverty," acknowledging the link between economics and education. Bertha Blackburn, as a child raised in the Delta in the twenties and thirties, "was taught that education was the escape hatch from poverty's black hole."[29] Yet the last fifty years of federal laws and court orders desegregating schools neither significantly improved most of the public schools in Mississippi nor altered many white Mississippians' feelings about integration.[30] In Clarksdale, integration in schools lasted for barely a school year. Most white students fled the public school system, and parents created Lee Academy, still in existence today, as a private school over whose admissions policies they would have total control. Research has found that where private schools flourish, support for public schools decreases. And, in fact, Delta district schools scored disproportionately lower than the state average by the turn of the century.[31] State-sanctioned neglect of black children of a new kind developed, a neglect harder to challenge or change and a situation that worsened after subsequent court rulings.[32]

Two stories stand as examples of how changes and continued challenges go hand in hand. The first involves the fight to promote an African American to the position of superintendent of Clarksdale's public schools in 1995. The second is the struggle to build a desperately needed new high school building in Clarksdale. Donell Harrell was named superintendent in July 1995. He stepped behind his desk determined to build a new high school in Clarksdale. A well-educated black man, he had received an associate degree in the arts from Natchez Junior College in 1962 and then went on to earn a bachelor's degree from Alcorn State University, a master's degree in education from Delta State University in 1974, and a specialist educational degree in 1980.[33] The *Clarksdale Press Register* summarized his teaching career: "In 1964 he came on board at Higgins Junior High as a teacher and moved to Clarksdale High in 1970. After nine years, he served as principal at Riverton Elementary from 1979 to 1982. From there [he] worked as assistant Superintendent of schools for 13 years, starting in 1982. He then settled into the Superintendent's position in 1995."[34]

His appointment did not happen easily. Since he had served as assistant superintendent since 1982, the promotion seemed logical, but Harrell had acquired a few enemies en route. On 11 January 1992, Robert Ellard had announced his pending retirement, effective 30 June. Harrell applied for the post and became one of the five finalists, two of whom subsequently withdrew their names. The biracial committee, mandated by the U.S. federal district court and the U.S. Department of Justice to be an integral part of the Clarksdale schools operations, was excluded from the initial process.[35] Only after the committee's chair, Bennie Gooden, complained, could the biracial committee review the applications of the three remaining candidates, and it unanimously nominated Harrell.[36] The Mississippi state conference of the NAACP also wrote a formal letter of complaint against the school board to the Civil Rights Department at the Justice Department. Citing the actions of Dr. Ellard in hiring a white consultant from Delta State University, his alma mater, to carry out the search, the organization accused the school board of gross misconduct by ignoring the legal existence of the court-ordered biracial committee.[37]

The Justice Department promptly informed Ellard of the complaints made against him: "Specifically, the complaint alleges that the school district has followed a practice of promoting employees within the school system, but recently when a qualified assistant Superintendent employed in the district, who is black, applied for the position of Superintendent, he was not selected for racial reasons."[38] Initiating a preliminary investigation, the Justice Department asked Ellard to provide all the application materials pertaining to the post by 31 July for its consideration. Only after federal intervention did Harrell gain his promotion.[39]

Then on Friday, 5 September 1997, at 10:00 A.M., the groundbreaking ceremony for the new Clarksdale High School took place. Attended by members of the state legislature and city and county elected officials, as well as students, parents, and community members, the ceremony marked the end of years of struggle to construct a new high school in Clarksdale.[40] The old building should have been condemned years before. In fact, school board minutes reveal that in 1968 discussions to rebuild Clarksdale High School had begun. However, once schools desegregated, spending money on the buildings was no longer a priority. Major structural weaknesses, inadequate, old facilities, and overflowing classrooms had prompted black school board members and community leaders to campaign for new constructions. Several bond issues to raise funds failed in the eighties and finally passed in May 1996. Hard campaigning had paid off. The organization Parents for Public Schools worked diligently to bring out voters and work with parents, teachers, and students. Those against the bond issue fought hard too: "They were concerned about the impact of the higher taxes on Clarksdale and pushed consolidation with the Coahoma County School system as a solution to Clarksdale High's building problems." Tom Shaw, president of the school board, noted: "It wasn't a white thing or a black thing, it was a Clarksdale thing," using often-employed color-blind economic ruses to distract from what was a distinctly racial issue, which had prompted plans for similar solutions in the fifties when attempting to circumvent the *Brown v. Board of Education* decision.[41]

In hindsight, Donell Harrell learned many lessons from these multiple bond attempts: "The first two times, we didn't involve the community. . . . I think that was a mistake."[42] The third time around, campaigning was vigorous and aggressive, reminiscent of mass movement organizing. The *Clarksdale Press Register* experienced such a deluge of letters about the issue that the editor published a note declaring that all letters could not be printed. By coming out in favor of the bond issue, Harrell opened himself to attack and criticism. Seeking to bail from the sinking ship of declining public schools, businessmen and other whites not invested in the system campaigned against it.[43] However, coalition building and the participation of many parents, who used the press to campaign and encourage others, still worked to create momentum for change.

The new Clarksdale High School's modern one-story building, located adjacent to residential and commercial areas on the outskirts of the city, exuded the aura of progress. The old crumbling school stood idle, overgrown with weeds, and every window shattered, while current students enjoyed high-tech and improved facilities a couple of miles away. But only the building has changed. The school remained highly segregated and still overcrowded, and the majority of the students are still African American. The whole school system remains a shadow of its former self—underfunded and undersupported by the community. Although black parents won the court battle, the victory was bittersweet, as schools lost the resources black children needed to compete equally in the workforce.[44]

Compounding the problem at the local level, in hindsight, the closing of the black segregated schools also undermined a sense of community among many African Americans in Clarksdale. Vera Harrell, who taught in the school system with her husband, Donell, preferred working in the segregated system. She lamented:

> I now wish we had stayed over there. . . . I think integration did more harm to the black children. . . . When we first went over to the Clarksdale High School, the white children embraced, kissed everything, smoked, they drank beer . . . and they all had cars. You let a black child go out and drink . . . [and] by the time they got home they were sober because they knew what their parents were going to do to them. . . . They would've got a beating. . . . When they went over there and saw what the white children were doing and got just like [them]. They wanted cars knowing that their parents couldn't afford a car. I didn't know about dope when I went to Tougaloo, I found out about dope when I went to Clarksdale High School.[45]

Like many other black teachers who worked through the transition from segregated to integrated schools, Harrell felt that integration had lowered disciplinary standards and she saw white youth culture as deleterious to black children unaccustomed to and unprotected from the consequences of such antisocial behavior. She turned white fears about the perceived debased black influence on white culture on their head. These points are arguably standard generational complaints: most parents bemoan their children's habits and styles. Yet the lack of historical knowledge black children have of their own culture and their own local heroes exacerbates the problem.

Scholarly research concurs. In the public schools, Black History Month and the Martin Luther King public holiday are often treated as a diversion from the curriculum and the business of *real* learning—the same historical figures are celebrated, with little effort given to acknowledging local heroes or even living heroes. As a result, Debbie Maddux argues that "African American studies in traditional public high schools are set up for failure by a negligent and cruel system that does a poor job of providing adequate skills and political education."[46] Children, young adults, and even teachers are not given adequate opportunities to critically explore their identity, their history, and the context of that history. Uncritical minds accept, rather than challenge, the status quo.[47]

Despite the obvious shortcomings and lack of support, there continue to be firsts. For example, Dr. Wilma Wade was the first (black) female superintendent for the Clarksdale municipal school district. She taught in the newly desegregated system in 1970. In 2004, she recalled her struggles, from facing prejudice as she did graduate work at the University of Mississippi in the mid-seventies, to pushing for higher academic achievement in the schools. As superintendent, one of her goals was to get former students to come back to Clarksdale after completing their teacher training to work and invest in the schools. She recognized that as opportunities to enter the economic mainstream developed, the resulting black brain drain—the exiting of skills and knowledge from black communities and poverty-stricken areas—would leave institutions short of leadership and experience.[48] Yet without viable industries and businesses in Clarksdale to sustain the black community more broadly, what are the prospects for young black adults graduating from the Mississippi public school systems? These questions present challenges that need to be addressed holistically, acknowledging the undeniable connections between economics and education—who has access and who is left out?

The second primary area to consider alongside education is voting and political access, key to facilitating transformations from the top down. The challenges facing activists against the prison industrial complex also include the disfranchisement of black men charged with felonies in Mississippi. Unfortunately, this is not the only site of struggle in the realm of voting rights. White local and state leaders found loopholes to circumvent the 1965 Voting Rights Act, but the legal system also assisted the rollback. As early as 18 February 1971, Justice Orma Smith (U.S. district court judge) ordered the adoption of a redistricting plan to bring Coahoma County in line with federal law. As a result, reregistration was necessary.[49] This meant that all the work undertaken during the decade before to register black voters had to be redone. Twenty counties, including Coahoma, purged their voting registers after the 1970 census. From 1965 to 1970, black registered voters, numbering anywhere from 28,000 to 280,000, had to be reregistered for the 1971 elections.[50] In an effort to recoup their losses, student volunteers again came to Clarksdale in April to help with the reregistration campaign.[51] State and local gerrymandering and redistricting attempts, changing electoral procedures from single to at-large or multimember tickets, purposefully hindered black participation and electoral victory further by diluting black majorities.[52]

Despite these persistent voting problems, the numbers of black elected officials rose steeply, although many social critics, like Clyde Woods, maintain that this rise is "severely overstated."[53] As Lerone Bennett put it: "[African Americans] are still systematically exploited as consumers and citizens. . . . The movement changed, destroyed, wiped out the visible and dramatic signs of racism, but it did not and perhaps could not at that time deal with the subtle forms of institutional racism."[54] The presence of black politicians did not decrease overall poverty or suffering in black communities. Access to the formal political arena has not proved to be the agent for change as once hoped. Those who attained political office could praise the mass civil rights movements for opening doors and providing opportunities, but once part of the system, and if they wished to stay in office, they had to redirect their loyalties toward reelection goals.[55] Furthermore, white majorities in the state legislature continue to stymie any substantial legislating initiated by black politicians, calling into question the extent of power the traditional political system actually has for real change.[56]

Many civil rights activists from the mass movement years chose public office as their next venue for action. Aaron Henry entered the political playing field in Mississippi, running successfully for the state House of Representatives in 1982, a seat he held until his death in 1997. Firmly planted, with his movement legacy and his capacity for coalition building, no one in his district could beat him, and he spent more and more time in Jackson working in the House to secure equal access and equality. His notoriety and influence kept the local

NAACP alive, and he put his name to many initiatives that spoke to his lifelong quest for fairness. After Henry won the suit against Jackson television station WLBT and forced the Federal Communications Commission to act against discrimination on the airwaves, President Jimmy Carter appointed him to the Federal Commission on Aging and to the President's Council. Henry became the chair of the National Caucus and Center on the Black Aged in 1975, serving until he suffered his stroke, in 1996, building the organization into an enterprise with a multimillion-dollar budget.[57] His death marked the end of an era for Clarksdale's mass movement, and his influence on behalf of the needy, now lost, is sorely missed by the thousands he helped.

The scholarship of civil rights histories in the United States continues to unearth and analyze the important local stories of mass civil rights movements. As the many stories of Clarksdale and Coahoma County illustrate, the thousands of local narrative threads together create a ball of knowledge that documents vital moments in the nation's history and gives a sense of the scale of what occurred. This collage of histories shatters the smooth manufactured commercialization of the memory of those years by revealing the unique nuances found in Clarksdale, influenced by the presence of characters like Aaron Henry and Vera Pigee working side by side but not always seeing eye to eye.

The Clarksdale story demonstrates how issues and tensions were negotiated locally, while also acknowledging the sometimes-deep cracks in various coalitions and the range of organizing modes and leadership styles—and the shifting sands on which everything stood over time. These stories in Clarksdale took decades to play out, as issues and crises developed and as the political winds changed direction. The actors evolved as their lives advanced and their loyalties and associations remained flexible. These narratives all come from multiple directions at different speeds (sometimes racing each other), but eventually all meet at the Crossroads.

The black freedom struggle continues even though the mass movement ended. The social values around plantation economies persist and remain regressive in whatever shape they take, and the fundamental question about how to solve the problem lingers unanswered. The struggle for civil rights opened up the system to a certain point, particularly politically and in some social situations, but did not and perhaps could not change an infrastructure embedded in an antilabor free market. The War on Poverty was an impermanent measure to stem the hemorrhaging of black people (literally and figuratively) in the South, but in Clarksdale, COI managed to create some positive change. Jobs programs and employment need protection from the whims of plantation economies and from values that may have originated in field labor but endure in new industries and labor relations. The individuals who do better are those who might already do well, and the lack of education for the majority continues to keep that population noncompetitive and on the margins. The poor and the illiterate continue to be left out. They may be off the plantation and able to attend school year-round, but they are marginalized and blamed for not taking advantage of what are considered openly available opportunities.

Prejudice and inequality persist in driving race relations and political activity, albeit with different casts and implicit language. From continuing federal rollbacks on Great Society programs, to Supreme Court decisions like *Shaw v. Reno* (1993), which affected voting and gerrymandering, to the persistent arguments and misunderstanding around affirmative action, to the rise of neoconservatism, sometimes under the veil of equality—the culminating effects, at every level, are devastating.[58] Despite the deafening rhetoric of meritocracy and color blindness during Barack Obama's presidential campaign and subsequent victory, African Americans of all classes continue to be judged and analyzed as a distinct group that exists parallel to the dominant discourse. In short, race still matters, and continued racial discrimination requires race-conscious remedies supported by coalition building.[59]

In Clarksdale, the appropriation of blues history and the casting of it as the *only* black history is a recent way in which power and control perpetually remain in the same hands. It therefore follows that questions pertaining to African Americans must also accommodate the social, political, and economic changes and strategies. The mass civil rights movement is part of a larger black freedom struggle interminably in motion and continuously changing. In the end, the civil rights movements were a calculated success based on calculated and well-timed political moves. Many African Americans in Clarksdale had the opportunity and were able to raise their standards of living and life chances for their children, even if that meant just a full school year in a heated school building and hot meals there. The goal of equality remains, but in order to be effective, activism needs to evolve—to rethink strategies, the constituency, and goals. Times have changed, but the story has not finished.

Appendix

Black and White Freedom Summer Volunteers in Clarksdale

In parentheses: hometown; college or sponsoring organization. CC = Community Center; FS = Freedom School; MCHR = Medical Committee for Human Rights; VR = Voting Rights; XX = missing information

Annie Pearl Avery (Birmingham, Ala.), CC

David Batzka (Monticello, Ind.; Disciples of Christ), CC

Stan Boyd (Atascadero, Calif.; Antioch-Putney), Community Project

David Bradshaw (Old Greenwich, Conn.; Hartford Art School), CC

Martha Davis (New York, N.Y.), MCHR and CC

Mark Fast (West Orange, N.J.; Princeton University), CC

Marie Gertge (Sterling, Colo.; Colorado State University), FS

Susan Gladstone (West Hartford, Calif.; Pembroke and Brown University), FS

Allen Goodner (Ann Arbor, Mich., and Nashville, Tenn.; University of Michigan and Fisk), FS

Margaret Hazelton (Detroit, Mich.; Wayne State University), CC

Dr. Lee Hoffman (New York, N.Y.; MCHR), MCHR

Les Johnson (Glendora, Calif.; University of California at Berkeley), FS

James Jones (Jackson, Miss.), SNCC staff

Paul Kendall (Dobbs Ferry, N.Y.; Wooster and Union Theological Seminary), FS

Yvonne Klein (Minneapolis, Minn.; XX), Communications Director

Carolyn Lane (New York, N.Y.; MCHR), MCHR

Robert and Lisa Mandel (Berkeley, Calif.; Reed), CC

Robert Newberry (North Hollywood, Calif.; Stanford), CC

Doris Newman (Washington, D.C.; Howard), SNCC staff

Dr. Leo Orris (New York, N.Y.; MCHR), MCHR

Rev. Charles Pendleton (Conn.; National Council of Churches), CC

Kate Quinn (Seattle, Wash.; University of Washington), FS

Sandy Seigel (Culver City, Calif.; University of California at Davis), FS coordinator

Lew (Lewis) Sitzer (Los Angeles, Calif.; University of California at Riverside), VR

Dr. William Sykes (New York, N.Y.; MCHR), MCHR

Jane Steidemann (St. Louis, Mo.; Wellesley), FS

Charles Stewart (Prairie du Chien, Wis.; Stanford), CC

Lafayette Surney (Miss.; Tougaloo), SNCC staff

John Suter (Fairfield, Calif.; Wesleyan), FS

Rev. Frazer and Mrs. Loris Thomason (Des Moines, Iowa; National Council of Churches), CC

Joseph Youngerman (Chicago, Ill.; Yale and Harvard Medical School), FS

Frederick Winyard (La Mesa, Calif.; Reed), CC

Zoya Zeman (Lincoln, Neb.; Scripps College), CC

Matthew Zwerling (New York, N.Y.; University of Rochester and Stanford College of Medicine), VR

Sources: Correspondence to Toby Graham, 17 December 2001, Zoya Zeman Papers, M320, box 1, folder 29, USM; "Addresses," Zoya Zeman Papers, M320, box 1, folder 23, USM; Zeman Senior Thesis. This is a list generated mostly from Zoya Zeman's papers at the University of Southern Mississippi and papers she gave to me from her personal collection. While many of these volunteers arrived in June 1964 and stayed the duration, a few came later in the summer and stayed for shorter periods. Also from Martha Davis Collection, M412, folder 1, USM; "Transcript of the Freedom Summer Pocket Journal of Margaret Hazelton," Hazelton Papers, M359, box 1, folder 10, USM.

Notes

RCNL	Regional Council of Negro Leadership
RFK	Robert F. Kennedy
RG	Record Group
SCLC	Southern Christian Leadership Conference
SCLCP	Southern Christian Leadership Conference Papers
SCP	Sovereignty Commission Papers
SHSW	State Historical Society of Wisconsin
SNCC	Student Nonviolent Coordinating Committee
TC	Coleman Library, Tougaloo College, Tougaloo, Mississippi
USCRC Report	Report of the United States Commission on Civil Rights, *Racial and Ethnic Tensions in American Communities: Poverty, Inequality, and Discrimination, Volume VII: The Mississippi Delta Report*, February 2001
USM	University of Southern Mississippi, Center for Oral History and Cultural Heritage
WHCF	White House Central Files
ZZP	Zoya Zeman Papers

Preface

1. Federal Writers' Project of the Works Progress Administration, *Mississippi*, 318.

2. Ibid.; Dittmer, *Local People*, 10; Lemann, *Promised Land*, 3–5.

3. Wilkie, *Dixie*, 305. Curtis Wilkie graduated from the University of Mississippi in 1963 and worked as a reporter at the *Clarksdale Press Register* through the rest of the sixties. He later wrote a memoir about his experiences reporting the news.

4. Zeman Diary, 4, M320, ZZP, USM.

Introduction

1. See Palmer, *Deep Blues*; Weeks, *Clarksdale and Coahoma County*; and Gioia, *Delta Blues*.

2. See Weeks, *Clarksdale and Coahoma County*.

3. For a range of models of local studies, see Rhonda Y. Williams, *Politics of Public Housing*; Orleck, *Storming Caesar's Palace*; and Chafe, *Civilities and Civil Rights*. Also important is Thornton, *Dividing Lines*. For organizational histories, the following have been useful: Morris, *Origins of the Civil Rights Movement*; Carson, *In Struggle: SNCC and the Black Awakening of the 1960s*; Branch, *Parting the Waters*; and Branch, *Pillar of Fire*. For groundbreaking work on black activism in Mississippi, see McMillen, *Dark Journey*; Payne, *I've Got the Light of Freedom*; and especially Dittmer, *Local People*. Crosby's *A Little Taste of Freedom* focuses on Claiborne County, south of the Mississippi Delta, primarily through the personality of Charles Evers. Moye's *Let the People Decide*, about Sunflower County, builds on the work of SNCC, Mrs. Fannie Lou Hamer, and Mississippi Freedom Democratic Party politics.

4. See Woods, *Development Arrested*, for scholarship that extended the origins of the movement backward in time before *Brown* existed in the 1960s. For example, see Dalfiume,

"'Forgotten Years' of the Negro Revolution." Nikhil Pal Singh wrote extensively about the "long civil rights era" in the 2004 *Black Is a Country*. Recent attention revolves around Jacquelyn Hall's essay "The Long Civil Rights Movement and the Political Uses of the Past." Responses to Hall's essay include Litwack, "Fight the Power! The Legacy of the Civil Rights Movement"; and Arensen, "Reconsidering the Long Civil Rights Movement."

5. Henry, *Fire*, 28.

6. Dittmer, *Local People*, 121.

7. For a full treatment of this concept of flexible associations and loyalties, see Hamlin, "Collision and Collusion."

8. Interview with Septima Clark by Jacquelyn Hall, 25 June 1976, Charleston, S.C., Southern Oral History Program, University of North Carolina, Chapel Hill. For a vivid portrait of Clark, see Charron, *Freedom's Teacher*.

9. See Collins, *Black Feminist Thought*; and Pigee, *Struggle of Struggles, Parts 1 and 2*. For a detailed analysis of Pigee's mothering, see Hamlin, "Vera Mae Pigee (1925–): Mothering the Movement."

10. Thirty-four interviews were conducted by the author for this project. They were supplemented by interviews already transcribed in archives around the country. For a thorough discussion on the inherent problems and the invaluable merits of oral history, see Hamlin, "'The Book Hasn't Closed, The Story Is Not Finished': Coahoma County, Mississippi, Civil Rights and the Recovery of a History."

11. For a selection of biographies on women involved in the movement, see Curry, *Silver Rights*; Kay Mills, *This Little Light of Mine*; Lee, *For Freedom's Sake*; Fleming, *Soon We Will Not Cry*; Grant, *Ella Baker*; Ransby, *Ella Baker and the Black Freedom Movement*; and Charron, *Freedom's Teacher*. For examples of autobiographies by white women, see Belfrage, *Freedom Summer*; and Curry, *Deep in Our Hearts*. For black women, see Moody, *Coming of Age in Mississippi*; and Holland, *From the Mississippi Delta*. Holsaert et al., *Hands on the Freedom Plow*, is a collection of personal accounts by black and white SNCC women.

12. Hall, "The Long Civil Rights Movement and the Political Uses of the Past," 1235.

Chapter 1

1. Many thanks to Mrs. Alpha Norphlet for her copy of a few pages of Aaron Henry's miscellaneous handwritten undated notes.

2. Henry, *Fire*, 96.

3. Aaron Henry interviewed by Dennis O'Brien, second oral interview, Oral History Project Transcripts, 13 May 1969, St. Louis, JFKL.

4. Vera M. Pigee interviewed by author, 25 January 2000.

5. Lemann, *Promised Land*, 45; Aaron Henry interviewed by Dennis O'Brien, second oral interview, Oral History Project Transcripts, 13 May 1969, St. Louis, JFKL; Aaron Henry interview, 1 May 1972, Center for Oral History and Cultural Heritage, USM.

6. For a full description of his life in school, see Henry, *Fire*, 35–39. Coahoma County Agricultural High School would become part of Coahoma County Junior College in 1949.

7. Ibid., 63. See also Aaron Henry interviewed by T. H. Baker, Clarksdale, 12 September 1970, tape one, Oral History Project Transcripts, LBJL; and Aaron Henry interviewed

by John Jones and John Dittmer, Clarksdale, 22 April 1981, Oral Histories, MDAH. Examples come from Aaron Henry conversation with Jerry DeMuth at Henry's home, Clarksdale, 3 August 1964, Jerry DeMuth File, SHSW; and Aaron Henry interviewed by Robert Wright, Clarksdale, 25 September 1968, Ralph Bunche Collection, Moorland-Spingarn Research Center, Howard University, Washington, D.C.

8. For a comprehensive discussion of the lack of benefits afforded African Americans and women despite the huge U.S. economic growth during the Truman years, see William Chafe, "Postwar American Society: Dissent and Social Reform," in Lacey, *Truman Presidency*.

9. See Chafe, *Never Stop Running*; Cummings, *Pied Piper*; and Aaron Henry interviewed by John Jones and John Dittmer, Clarksdale, 22 April 1981, Oral Histories, MDAH.

10. Henry, *Fire*, xiv.

11. Pigee, *Struggles: Part One*, 13–15.

12. Vera M. Pigee interviewed by author, 12–13 October 2001. She did not mention any repercussions for this action.

13. For an excellent argument for those alternative modes of resistance that gave oppressed black people in the grip of Jim Crow some kind of agency and control over their lives, see Kelley, "We Are Not What We Seem."

14. Pigee, *Struggles: Part One*, 18–19.

15. Pigee interviewed by Robert Wright, Masonic Temple, Jackson, 5 July 1968, Ralph Bunche Collection, Moorland-Spingarn Research Center, Howard University, Washington, D.C.

16. Mary Jane Pigee Davis in conversation with author, 1 June 2010; Rebecca Hood-Adams, "Local NAACP Marks 50 Years," *CPR*, 25 October 2003. In the 1980s, Pigee bought property at 417 Yazoo and opened another parlor there.

17. Current to White, memorandum, 10 May 1948, part 18, reel 22, II series A, NAACPMF.

18. Ibid. For further information on the effectiveness of radio, see Savage, *Broadcasting Freedom*.

19. For scholarship linking global politics to the civil rights movement, see Dudziak, *Cold War and Civil Rights*; and Borstelmann, *Cold War and the Color Line*.

20. John Bell Williams, "Civil Rights."

21. For an in-depth and thorough discussion of African American activism in Mississippi before this period, see McMillen, *Dark Journey*; and Woodruff, *American Congo*. Indeed, there are many studies documenting these local and national moments where people stood up to Jim Crow with varying degrees of success. For a cross section of examples, see Sitkoff, *A New Deal for Blacks*; Marable, *Race, Reform, and Rebellion*; Gilmore, *Gender and Jim Crow*; and Daily, Gilmore, and Simon, *Jumpin' Jim Crow*. I also include on this list the historiography of black club women's movements from the turn of the century up to and including this period. A selection should include Giddings, *In Search of Sisterhood*; Deborah Gray White, *Too Heavy a Load*; Hine, *Black Women in White*; and Stephanie Shaw, *What a Woman Ought to Be and to Do*.

22. Murphy, "The South Counterattacks," 373.

23. For a sense of the organization during this time, see NAACP, Annual Reports; Zangrando, *NAACP Crusade against Lynching*; and Sullivan, *Lift Every Voice*. For a comprehensive account of the litigation sponsored by the NAACP, see Greenberg, *Crusaders in the Courts*; and Jonas, *Freedom's Sword*. For a history of the NAACP in one urban area, see Christopher Robert Reed, *Chicago NAACP and the Rise of Black Professional Leadership*.

24. *Smith v. Allwright* questioned the constitutionality of white-only primaries; *Morgan v. Virginia* attacked segregation in interstate travel; *Sweatt v. Painter* and *McLaurin v. Oklahoma* concerned admission to law schools; and *Henderson v. United States* tackled the desegregation of dining cars on interstate trains.

25. These two texts are significant. Truman's committee report signaled a federal concern initiated by the White House regarding civil rights, and Mrydal's highly publicized and often-quoted study remains seminal in the study of American race relations.

26. "German Visits Place Where His Father Was POW," *JDN*, 31 July 1980, 1B; Bubba Burnham, "Between the Goal Posts," *CPR*, 29 October 2010. See also Skates, "German Prisoners of War in Mississippi."

27. Haywood Stephney, quoted by McMillen, "How Mississippi's Black Veterans Remember World War II," in *Remaking Dixie*, 102.

28. Bell, "Negro Warrior's Home Front," 276. For more information on African Americans in the U.S. Army during World War II, see Morehouse, *Fighting in the Jim Crow Army*; and Latty and Tarver, *We Were There*.

29. See Dittmer, *Local People*, 19. For background information on Amzie Moore, see Forman, *Making of Black Revolutionaries*; biography of Amzie Moore in the finding aids of his papers at the State Historical Society of Wisconsin; and Raines, *My Soul Is Rested*. For background information on Medgar Evers, see Vollers, *Ghosts of Mississippi*; and Myrlie B. Evers, *For Us, the Living*.

30. Henry, *Fire*, 70.

31. Ibid., 64.

32. Box 50, IIIC, folder 867, AHP, TC.

33. Henry, *Fire*, 63; *CPR*, 22 September 1953; a Mississippi interview from 8 July 1947, box 9, Alexander Heard Papers, Southern Politics Collection, Vanderbilt University, Nashville.

34. Dittmer, *Local People*, 25.

35. In the 1940s, Ella Jo Baker served as the national director of branches before she resigned in July 1946; Gloster Current took over the post.

36. In 1918, the first branch in Mississippi opened in Vicksburg, site of intense combat during the Civil War. Organized by three black professionals—a dentist, a pharmacist, and an attorney—the branch struggled and died in infancy as the leaders were run out of town. McMillen, documenting this event, suggests convincingly that if it was not their activities that numbered their days, it was their relative prosperity and economic status (McMillen, *Dark Journey*, 31).

37. The NAACP Board of Directors voted on the establishment of the Southeast Regional Office on 10 September 1951. Gloster Current to Roy Wilkins and Walter White, memorandum, 10 January 1952, part 25, reel 4, II, NAACPMF.

38. Gillette, "NAACP in Texas," 135.

39. Gloster Current, memorandum, 21 March 1951, Southeast Regional Conference correspondence, 1951, II C221, NAACPP.

40. Hurley to Current, 18 September 1951, ibid.

41. Ruby Hurley interviewed by John H. Britton, Atlanta, 26 January 1968, Ralph Bunche Collection, Moorland-Spingarn Research Center, Howard University, Washington, D.C.

42. See press release, 25 June 1943, II A587, NAACPP.

43. Ibid.

44. See White to Hastie, 8 March 1943, and Hurley to White, 5 May 1943, II A587, NAACPP.

45. *Jet*, 28 August 1980. She died in 1980 at the age of seventy after retiring from a career in law in 1978. See also obituary in *NYT*, 15 August 1980, D15. Her commitment to personal privacy mirrored Ella Baker's—we know very little about either woman's husband or personal relationships (see Ransby, *Ella Baker and the Black Freedom Movement*). Vollers, writing about Medgar Evers, described Hurley as a "tall, elegant single woman with a taste for good clothes and fine scotch. She smoked long cigarettes. She was utterly fearless and totally devoted to the NAACP" (Vollers, *Ghosts of Mississippi*, 58). Note that in this description, Hurley is single, but there is no indication of why or how.

46. Howard purchased the Magnolia Mutual Life Insurance Company as a commercial venture to sell insurance to African Americans. Many thanks to Professor David T. Beito for sharing his conference paper on T. R. M. Howard, from which most of this information comes. See also Beito and Beito, *Black Maverick*. For further information on African American independent hospitals during this time, see Beito, "Black Fraternal Hospitals in the Mississippi Delta, 1942–1967."

47. Bolivar County Invitational Committee of the Proposed Delta Council of Negro Leadership, letter, 10 December 1951, box 7, folder 2, AMP, SHSW.

48. Ibid.

49. The reach and influence of the organization is remarkable. Novelist William Faulkner spoke at the 1952 annual meeting, as did Governor Hugh White in 1954. Running as a nonprofit organization, in 1985 the annual budget was a quarter of a million dollars. For more information, see Cash and Lewis, *Delta Council*; see also Woods, *Development Arrested*.

50. Henry, *Fire*, 80.

51. Ruby Hurley to Walter White, memorandum, 8 October 1952, II A381, NAACPP. Interestingly, and perhaps not surprisingly, in 1958 the Sovereignty Commission papers labeled the RCNL as an "integration organization." See RCNL folder file, SCP, MDAH; and Zack J. Van Landingham to Director, 9 October 1958, SCP, MDAH.

52. RCNL 6th anniversary meeting announcement, 26 April 1957, RCNL folder file, SCP, MDAH.

53. Ruby Hurley to Walter White, memorandum, 8 October 1952, II A381, NAACPP.

54. Ibid.

55. McMillen, *Dark Journey*, 316.

56. Henry, *Fire*, 79; see also Kelley, "We Are Not What We Seem."

57. Hurston, *Mules and Men*, 2; James C. Scott, *Domination and the Arts of Resistance*, xiii.

58. Vollers, *Ghosts of Mississippi*, 41.

59. *Crisis* 59, no. 8 (October 1952).

60. See Southeast Regional Conference correspondence, 1951, II C221, NAACPP.

61. For example, see Current to Ruby Hurley, 20 May 1955, II C223, NAACPP. Evers even got reprimanded for delegating paperwork to his secretary. Current wrote, "In future, when you are acting under a directive from your immediate superior, please do not delegate any alteration in procedure or policy to a subordinate" (Current to Evers, 18 May 1956, and Smith to Current, 9 May 1956, III C243, NAACPP).

62. See Southeast Regional Office correspondence, 1952, II C222, NAACPP.

63. Gloster Current obituary, *Jet* 92, no. 9 (21 July 1997): 18.

64. Hurley to Black, 16 September 1952, Southeast Regional Office correspondence, 1952, II C222, NAACPP.

65. Lucille Black to Ruby Hurley, 24 April 1952, re: lack of response from Mississippi regarding membership campaigns, and Hurley's reply, 29 April 1952, II C222, NAACPP.

66. Hurley to Current, part 25, reel 4, II C222, NAACPMF.

67. Hurley to Current, memorandum re: report for the June meeting of the board, 27 May 1953, part 25, reel 5, series A, II C224, NAACPMF.

68. Ibid.

69. *CPR*, 23 July 1951.

70. "General and Statistical Information," October 1965, Carnegie Public Library, Clarksdale.

71. Henry, *Fire*, 70, 71. Henry concluded that the Civic Music Association disbanded in 1955 in the wake of the *Brown* decision.

72. Ibid., 69. Walker heard about Henry through a black doctor, O. G. Smith, and had always supported Henry's activities (from Aaron Henry conversation with Jerry DeMuth at Henry's home, Clarksdale, 3 August 1964, Jerry DeMuth File, SHSW). See also Aaron Henry interviewed by John Jones and John Dittmer, Clarksdale, 22 April 1981, Oral Histories, MDAH. By all accounts, it was a relationship based on Walker's financial investment in a black business, which promised large returns because of Henry's community stature.

73. "Two Local Negro Women Charge They Were Criminally Assaulted, One Robbed, Near City Sunday," *CPR*, 14 August 1951; *CPR*, 17 August 1951. For the full trial coverage, see *CPR*, 29 January 1952. Also mentioned in Aaron Henry interview, 1 May 1972, Center for Oral History and Cultural Heritage, USM.

74. Henry, *Fire*, 72. Aaron Henry's autobiography noted that two *girls* aged seventeen and nineteen were raped by *two* white men. Furthermore, he claimed one of the girls was the sister of his close friend. Despite these discrepancies in information, the importance of this case in this chapter remains the same.

75. Henry, *Fire*, 72.

76. Hill, "Coahoma Opportunities, Incorporated," chap. 1, in author's possession; Aaron Henry interviewed by John Jones and John Dittmer, Clarksdale, 22 April 1981, Oral Histories, MDAH.

77. *CPR*, 28, 29, 30 January 1952.

78. For some texts describing the racial and sexual politics of the South, see Feimster, *Southern Horrors*; Gillespie and Gillespie, *Devil's Lane*; Hall, *Revolt against Chivalry*; and Barbara E. Smith, *Neither Separate nor Equal*.

79. Henry *misc.*

80. *CPR*, 30 January 1952.

81. Henry, *Fire*, 75.

82. Ibid., 77. His partner nicknamed Henry "Red" in jest. Henry replied, "It's hell enough being black without being black and red at the same time" (ibid.).

83. Ibid., 73.

84. Ibid.

85. Ibid. The white community did not comment on the possibility of a branch, "so sure were they of the entrenchment of the system of segregation."

86. Ibid.

87. Part 25, reel 19, series A, II C270, NAACPMF. The end-of-the-year report lists Aaron Henry as president, Annie F. Wright as secretary, Miss C. B. Lucas as chairman of the membership committee, Charles Stringer as chairman of the Legal Redress Committee, Medgar Evers as chairman of the Committee on Labor and Industry, Mrs. Cleora Guest as chairman of the Entertainment Committee, Mrs. Noelle Henry as chairman of the Education Committee, Grand Master James Gilliam as chairman of the Press and Publicity Committee, G. J. Thomas as chairman of the Finance Committee, and Rev. Skipper as chairman of the Housing Committee. Indeed, the branch listed the establishment of all the committees on the annual report sheet.

88. Henry *misc*, paper; II A171, NAACPP. The branch's activities were evident in its success in reaching its Freedom Fund quota in 1955 of $150, precipitating a letter from Lucille Black to the branch secretary (Black to Wright, 14 January 1955, II C351, NAACPP).

89. *CPR*, 22 September 1953.

90. *CPR*, 24 March 1954.

91. *CPR*, 30 March 1954.

92. July 1954 newsletter, Southeast Regional Office, II C222, NAACPP.

93. Ibid.

94. *CPR*, 11 March 1954, 9. Page numbers are given for news not on the front page of the local paper.

95. See box 7, folder 2, AMP, SHSW.

96. Henry, *Fire*, 80.

97. "Coleman Urges State Proceed with Its Equalization Program," *CPR*, 2 June 1954. A month later, in response to the NAACP's vow to file suits, Attorney General Coleman publicly asked white lawyers to join him in a united front to work against any efforts to litigate against segregation in public schools. Writing to the Mississippi Bar Association, he asked lawyers to accept appointments as special assistant attorneys general, who would represent any school official in a suit ("State's White Lawyers Asked to Accept Roles in Fighting Integration," *CPR*, 1 July 1954). See also "Mississippi," Desegregation: Schools Branch Action Mississippi, 1955, II A227, NAACPP.

98. For white primary sources on the school districts, see Survey on Clarksdale Separate School District by Associated Consultants in Education, Inc., 1954, 5, Ivy Papers, MDAH; Survey on Coahoma County Public Schools by Associated Consultants in Education, Inc., 1954, 1, Ivy Papers, MDAH; "Clarksdale and Its Resources," published by the University of Mississippi, Clarksdale City Schools, and the Clarksdale Junior Chamber of Commerce,

November 1958, Carnegie Public Library, Clarksdale; and Ellard, "History of Clarksdale, Mississippi, Public Schools."

99. "High Court Expected to Rule against Segregation; Warren Is 'Arch Foe,'" *CPR*, 19 October 1953, 2.

100. "White Adopts Wait-and-See Policy on Equalization of White, Negro Schools," *CPR*, 29 January 1951, 2.

101. *CPR*, 25 October 1951.

102. For a complete history of the equalization program and the Clarksdale/Coahoma County component, see Hamlin, "The Book Hasn't Closed" (dissertation).

103. See Bolton, "Mississippi's School Equalization Program"; Bolton, *The Hardest Deal of All*; and Hamlin, "The Book Hasn't Closed" (dissertation). Reported on the front page of the *CPR*, a black pastor from Columbia, Mississippi, openly instigated a leaflet and handbill campaign for "voluntary segregation." *CPR*, 21 October 1955.

104. *CPR*, 1 July 1954.

105. Bolton, *The Hardest Deal of All*, 53–54.

106. Bartley, *Rise of Massive Resistance*, 76.

107. Dr. T. R. M. Howard's address to the Governor's Conference in Jackson, 30 July 1954, II A227, NAACPP.

108. Ibid.

109. Ibid. The governor, shocked by the deliberate sabotage of his plan to present a united yet segregated front to the press, resolved to hold a special session of the Mississippi state legislature to consider a constitutional amendment to abolish the state's public school system. See news clippings, II A227, NAACPP. This amendment actually got ratified by a solid majority in a December 1954 referendum. Mississippi was the first to enact a pupil assignment law during the 1954 session to be locally administered, an attempt to bypass the law (Bartley, *Rise of Massive Resistance*, 78).

110. Quoted in Johnston, *Mississippi's Defiant Years*, 17.

111. Henry *misc*, paper.

112. Henry, *Fire*, 91.

113. Quoted in Johnston, *Mississippi's Defiant Years*, 14.

114. Quoted in Martin, *Deep South Says "Never,"* 4.

115. *CPR*, 14 September 1954; Martin, *Deep South Says "Never,"* 14. Points of access to the local communities were clubs like Rotary, Kiwanis, Civitans, and Exchange Club.

116. *CPR*, 10 September 1954.

117. *CPR*, 23 August 1954. The decreased number of black voters made a difference in that summer's senatorial race. Incumbent Eastland held onto his seat decisively, with 136,014 votes to Lieutenant Governor Carroll Gartin's 81,908. In Coahoma County, Eastland received 1,812 votes to 707 (*CPR*, 25 August 1954). The paper, reporting on complaints made by the NAACP's Ruby Hurley against threats to Mississippi's members, noted Eastland's promise to run the organization out of Mississippi during his campaign (*CPR*, 4 September 1954).

118. For details of the tactics of the Citizens' Councils, see Bartley, *Rise of Massive Resistance*, especially chap. 12; and McMillen, *Citizens' Council*.

119. *CPR*, 24 September 1954.

120. *CPR*, 27 September 1954, 2.

121. Amzie Moore to Wilkins, June 1955, part 18, reel 12, series C, NAACPMF.

122. NAACP press release, 6 September 1954, Southeast Regional Office correspondence, 1954, II C222, NAACPP. The *Clarksdale Press Register*, reporting on the press release, did not include Hurley's comment about the reduced fear exhibited by blacks. Rather, the paper emphasized the pressure exerted on the NAACP, as if to notify the readers of the strategy's effectiveness (*CPR*, 14 September 1954).

123. Transcript of phone recording of Howard to Current at the 10 December 1954 meeting of the Southeast Regional Advisory Board, Columbus, Mississippi. Included in a letter to Clarence Mitchell, 9 February 1954, part 18, reel 13, series C, IIA422, NAACPMF.

124. Affidavit from Amzie Moore, 29 December 1954, part 18, reel 12, series C, NAACPMF.

125. Copy of affidavit by Lurleaner Johnson found in NAACP-Clarksdale folder file, SCP, MDAH.

126. Ibid. The NAACP used this affidavit in its press release titled "School Petitioners Fired at Federally-Aided Hospital," 9 February 1956. According to the press release, the affidavit, along with another from a hospital employee, was sent to the U.S. Department of Health, Education, and Welfare, because the hospital received federal funds under the Hill-Burton Act (III A229, NAACPP).

127. Current to Staff, memorandum re: staff reorganization, 14 September 1954, II C389, NAACPP.

128. Ibid.

129. This is probably the same speech given in Clarksdale described earlier by Henry.

130. Vollers, *Ghosts of Mississippi*, 48. This technicality apparently was that his references came from his county of residence not from the county of his birth. The University of Mississippi changed the requirements promptly afterward to five alumni recommendations per applicant, thus denying Evers the opportunity to reapply the following year. See also Myrlie B. Evers, *For Us, the Living*.

131. Current to Wilkins, memorandum, 19 November 1954, II A585, NAACPP.

132. Vollers, *Ghosts of Mississippi*, 54, 63.

133. *CPR*, 8 January 1955. Of course, the meeting's results promptly appeared the next day in the paper, paraphrasing Byrd's speech while giving full names and titles of all the new branch officers (*CPR*, 11 January 1955). It is hard to know the demographics of the membership, given that many names remained anonymous on written records for fear of membership rolls falling into the wrong hands.

134. Harry T. Moore was an NAACP coordinator killed when his home was bombed in Mims, Fla., on Christmas Day in 1951. 1955 marked the first year of the award given in his honor (Southeast Regional Office newsletter, March 1955, II C223, NAACPP).

135. Ibid.

136. Hurley to branch officer, 3 June 1955, II C223, NAACPP; Hurley to NAACP Friend, 3 June 1955, II C223, NAACPP.

137. *CPR*, 7 January 1955.

138. "Local NAACP Branch Cites 'Inequalities' in City Schools, Offers Integration Plan," *CPR*, 31 March 1955.

139. Ibid.

140. Henry, *Fire*, 86; see also Bartley, *Rise of Massive Resistance*, 67; and Dittmer, *Local People*, 52.

141. Henry, *Fire*, 80.

142. Howard to Dr. McCoy, president of Mississippi Conferences of NAACP, 13 June 1955, part 17, reel 26, NAACPMF. Howard himself was lukewarm about trying to integrate or equalize schools, noting the economic strain the state already was under (see Beito and Beito, *Black Maverick*, 85–86).

143. Current to regional office staff, memorandum, 9 June 1955, II C389, NAACPP.

144. The Vicksburg petition had 140 signatures; Natchez had 100; Jackson had 53 on two documents (*CPR*, 2 August 1955).

145. *CPR*, 12 August 1955.

146. Henry, *Fire*, 93.

147. Aaron Henry interviewed by John Jones and John Dittmer, Clarksdale, 22 April 1981, Oral Histories, MDAH.

148. For a detailed account of the murder, see Whitfield, *A Death in the Delta*; and Huie in *Look* magazine, 24 January 1956, expanded in *Wolf Whistle*.

149. For an insightful and detailed discussion of the ramifications of the death of Till in history and memory, manifested in cultural productions, see Rubin, "Reflections"; and Metress, *Lynching of Emmett Till*.

150. Moody, *Coming of Age in Mississippi*, 122, 123, 125.

151. Wilkins to staff, memorandum, 27 September 1955, part 18, reel 13, series C, II A422, NAACPMF. Walter White died from heart failure on 21 March 1955.

152. Rubin, "Reflections," 49.

153. In a letter from Hurley to Lucille Black (Hurley to Black, 16 September 1952, South-east Regional Office correspondence, 1952, II C222, NAACPP), Hurley complained about feeling like she was in a foreign land in the South, yearning for the national conference in Oklahoma City that year where she could speak her "native language" for the first time in six months. In Aaron Henry's interview with Dennis O'Brien in 1969, he placed Hurley in the fields with a cotton sack trying to get information from local people about Till's murder. Aaron Henry interviewed by Dennis O'Brien, second oral interview, Oral History Project Transcripts, 13 May 1969, St. Louis, JFKL.

154. Henry, *Fire*, 79.

Chapter 2

1. NAACP pamphlet, part 18, reel 13, series C, II A423, NAACPMF.

2. The four known to have been killed in Mississippi were Rev. George Lee (on 7 May), Lamar Smith (on 13 August), Emmett Till (on 28 August), and Clinton Melton (on 8 December). Quote from Amzie Moore in Forman, *Making of Black Revolutionaries*, 281.

3. Official NAACP statistics, "Total Paid Membership of Branches in Southeast Region," III C174, NAACPP.

4. Vera M. Pigee interviewed by author, 12–13 October 2001. The *Clarksdale Press Register* mentioned Charles Diggs being seated at the black press table with two unidentified com-

panions (*CPR*, 22 September 1955, 7). Aaron Henry interviewed by John Jones and John Dittmer, Clarksdale, 22 April 1981, Oral Histories, MDAH.

5. Coahoma Council's Youth Charter, in Vera Pigee Personal Papers; see also Pigee, *Struggles: Part One*, 26; Southeast Regional Office correspondence, 1960, III C171, NAACPP; and Dittmer, *Local People*, 85.

6. Henry, *Fire*, 97; Martin, *Deep South Says "Never,"* 31; Aaron Henry interviewed by Dennis O'Brien, second oral interview, Oral History Project Transcripts, 13 May 1969, St. Louis, JFKL.

7. Martin, *Deep South Says "Never,"* 30; *CPR*, 5 August 1955.

8. *CPR*, 5 August 1955; *CPR*, 3 August 1955; *CPR*, 15 August 1955; *CPR*, 17 August 1955. Board members were E. P. Peacock Jr., Ralph N. Baltzer (executive vice president of the Coahoma County Bank and Trust Company, who became first vice president), P. F. Williams Sr., W. E. Young, E. Cage Brewer, R. N. Hopson (plantation owner), Crawford S. McGivaren (vice president of the Bank of Clarksdale), and S. Hudson Kyle; *CPR*, 17 August, 22 August 1955, 14 June 1956. E. P. Peacock Jr.'s father was an original stockholder of the Bank of Clarksdale, not very affected by the Great Depression, which destroyed most banks. His son became the vice president in 1937 and then took over from his father in 1949 (Bank of Clarksdale Fiftieth Anniversary, 1900–1950, publication printed by Clarksdale Printing Company, Inc., n.d., MDAH). See also Stan Boyd interviewed by author.

9. "Help End Racial Tyranny in Mississippi," *NYT*, 3 October 1955, 19. See also Fairclough, "Little Rock Crisis," 375; Bartley, *Rise of Massive Resistance*, 194; and *CPR*, 21 March 1956, 13.

10. Johnston, *Mississippi's Defiant Years*, 48. For a brief history of this agency, see the introduction to the file catalog at MDAH. Joe Hopkins from Clarksdale was the representative from the area on the first commission. See also Rowe-Sims, "Mississippi State Sovereignty Commission"; and Katagiri, *Mississippi State Sovereignty Commission*.

11. Bartley, *Rise of Massive Resistance*, 180.

12. *CPR*, 10 March 1956; Murphy, *The South Counterattacks*, 379. For information on the NAACP in other states, see Current, "Significance of the NAACP."

13. Hurley's tour, which included investigations in Yazoo City, Belzoni, and Clarksdale, was reported in *CPR*, 13 October 1955.

14. NAACP, Annual Reports, 1955, 28.

15. Nossiter, *Of Long Memory*, 45.

16. Vera M. Pigee interviewed by author, 25 January 2000.

17. Mary Jane Pigee folder file, SCP, MDAH.

18. The *Clarksdale Press Register* published full details of the names and roles played on the program, including the fact that Mary Jane attended Higgins High School (*CPR*, 3 January 1956, 8). See also Mary Jane Pigee folder file, SCP, MDAH.

19. *CPR*, 3 January 1956, 1, 8. Culberston had been connected with the United Mine Workers, the CIO, the AFL, and the Brotherhood of Railroad Trainmen.

20. Mary Jane Pigee folder file, SCP, MDAH.

21. Aaron Henry folder file, SCP, MDAH.

22. "Local NAACP Asks Exchange of Viewpoints," *CPR*, 28 June 1956.

23. Ibid. See *CPR*, 1 September 1956, 5; 10 September 1956, 8; and 2 November 1956, 5.

24. Evers and Bond to Current, report, 23 January 1956, III A230, NAACPP; NAACP, Annual Reports, 1956, 21.

25. The United Order of Friendship was a credit union/ fraternal organization that provided services to the black community to rival the Knights and Daughters of Tabor. See section on T. R. M. Howard in chap. 1. Although little is known about this particular organization, McMillen identifies several others that thrived in Mississippi as the strongest black businesses in the interwar years, many of which dissolved into social organizations (McMillen, *Dark Journey*, 182–83). See also Beito, *From Mutual Aid to the Welfare State*.

26. For further harassment directed toward Drew, see *CPR*, 13 February 1956; and Charles C. Stringer Files, report dated 5 June 1956, SCP, MDAH.

27. Reel 7, group V, series B, box 10, NAACPMF.

28. Current to Wilkins, memorandum, 11 January 1956, Mississippi Pressures: Special Relief Fund, III A230, NAACPP.

29. Evers and Bond report, 23 January 1956, III A230, NAACPP.

30. Mississippi Pressures: Special Relief fund, III A230, NAACPP.

31. First quote from Nossiter, *Of Long Memory*, 39; second quote from Dittmer, *Local People*, 52.

32. Russell Johnson, Peace Education secretary of the American Friends Service Committee, to Amzie Moore, 12 February 1957, box 1, folder 3, AMP, SHSW. Ella Baker was introduced to the RCNL meeting held 14 January 1957 by Moore (box 74, VIA, folder 1411, RCNL meeting minutes, AHP, TC). See also correspondence from Ella Baker to Ruth Moore, 25 February 1957, and F. E. Hutchens, American Friends Service Committee, Southwest Regional Office, to Amzie Moore, 28 February 1957, box 1, folder 3, AMP, SHSW.

33. Thanks to writer and former SNCC staffer Charles Cobb for this precise information.

34. Howard Suttle, "J.P. Says Rights Bills Aims Will Worsen Race Relations," *JDN*, 7 February 1957; Civil Rights Act of 1957, Public Law 85–315, passed in the 85th Congress, H.R. 6127, 9 September 1957.

35. Quoted in "Council Blasts CR Measure," *JDN*, 30 August 1957. The article made reference to the first Force Bill, otherwise known as the Lodge Bill, named after Henry Cabot Lodge, who sought to enact federal government provisions to make elections fair for all voters. The bill was defeated in 1890 after a successful filibuster.

36. See Johnston, *Mississippi's Defiant Years*, 69. For firsthand accounts of the experiences of those involved in Little Rock, see Beals, *Warriors Don't Cry*; and Bates, *Long Shadow of Little Rock*.

37. "Kickoff of Drive to Get Negroes to Vote Scheduled in Clarksdale Sunday Afternoon," *CPR*, 6 December 1957, in RCNL folder file, SCP, MDAH.

38. Special report from the Mississippi field secretary, 11 December 1957, II C244, NAACPP. Underlined by Evers.

39. Ruby Hurley to Medgar Evers, memorandum, 14 January 1958, Southeastern Regional Office correspondence, II C172, NAACPP; Medgar Evers's Monthly Report, March 1957, Medgar Evers Files, III C244, NAACPP.

40. Gloster Current, Report and Recommendations on Membership and Staff, 1958, Membership Campaign Losses, 1957, II C279, NAACPP. Region V had 44,447 members in

1956, dropping to 26,775 in 1957, a loss of 17,672. Branches outside the South did not show a numerical increase to make up the losses. Louisiana lost 11,000 and Texas lost 9,000, bringing the South's losses to 37,672. This was the first year since 1949 the NAACP had suffered a membership loss (Membership Campaign, III C279, NAACPP).

41. Dittmer, *Local People*, 78; Evers to Wilkins, 11 March 1957, III C244, NAACPP.

42. Henry interviewed by Robert Wright; Aaron Henry interviewed by T. H. Baker, Clarksdale, 12 September 1970, tape one, Oral History Project Transcripts, LBJL; Henry, *Fire*, 101. See also Watson, "Assessing the Role of the NAACP," 453; and Stanford University's online Martin Luther King Papers archive, vol. 4: Martin Luther King Jr. to Aaron Henry, 29 May 1958, http://www.stanford.edu/group/King/mlkpapers/.

43. Martin Luther King Jr. to membership, 20 January 1958, box 7, folder 7, AMP, SHSW.

44. Medgar Evers to Ruby Hurley, 24 January 1958, Medgar Evers Files, 1958, III C244, NAACPP.

45. Medgar Evers to Robert Carter, 24 February 1958, part 22, reel 20, group V, series B, box 24, NAACPMF.

46. "Negroes Bone Up on Constitution," *JDN*, 4 March 1958; Sovereignty Commission clipping. Citizenship classes also came under the purview of SCLC, of which Henry was also a member. The infiltration of state NAACP members in the RCNL did not go unnoticed. In a report by Van Landingham to the director, 6 May 1959, he made it explicitly clear that this was the case and that any correspondence on RCNL letterhead should be regarded as NAACP correspondence (NAACP-Clarksdale folder file, SCP, MDAH).

47. Stanford University's online Martin Luther King Papers archive, vol. 4: SCLC to Dwight Eisenhower, telegram, 29 May 1958, http://www.stanford.edu/group/King/mlkpapers/. Medgar Evers's June 1958 Monthly Report noted the SCLC Clarksdale meeting (Medgar Evers Files, 1958, III C244, NAACPP). Stanford University's online Martin Luther King Papers archive, Martin Luther King Jr. to Aaron Henry, 29 May 1958. In the summer, Dr. John L. Tilley, executive director of SCLC, and Ella Baker visited the area following the Clarksdale conference, further nourishing the roots and links (Amzie Moore to Tilley, 26 September 1958, box 1, folder 3, AMP, SHSW). No evidence suggests conflict between Evers and Henry, who were friends, over SCLC involvement.

48. Program, NAACP meeting, Haven Methodist Church, Sunday, 5 October 1958, box 6, folder 1, AMP, SHSW. For examples of state-sanctioned harassment, see Johnston, *Mississippi's Defiant Years*, 80–81; and Medgar Evers to Roy Wilkins, 2 May 1958, part 22, reel 2, group V, series B, Administration File, NAACPMF.

49. Van Landingham's report to the director of the Sovereignty Commission, 7 November 1958, NAACP-Clarksdale folder file, SCP, MDAH.

50. Both Andrew Carr, a prominent white farmer who aided in the founding of the poverty program in Clarksdale in 1965 (see chap. 6), and Robert Birdsong, a firefighter and tour guide in Clarksdale, stated independently of each other that the Ku Klux Klan never was strong in the Delta but had more leverage in the state's hill counties (Andrew Carr interviewed by author; informal conversations with Robert Birdsong, September 2010).

51. She gave a sworn affidavit on 12 May 1959 to the federal government, a copy of which is in Commission on Civil Rights Microfilm, reel 44, JFKL. Aaron Henry appealed to the

Justice Department on her behalf also, and John Doar encouraged Henry to call the local FBI agent, Hopkins, for help (ibid., reel 45).

52. See "Clarksdale NAACP Urged FBI to Investigate Slaying of Negro," *Jackson Advocate*, 23 May 1959; Police Department report, 10 May 1959, NAACP-Clarksdale folder file, SCP, MDAH.

53. *Jackson Advocate*, 23 May 1959.

54. Aaron Henry's testimony noted in Edgar Brown and Norman Kurland report, 28 August 1962, Commission on Civil Rights Microfilm, reel 45, JFKL.

55. *CPR*, 14 December 1955.

56. In October 1962, Noelle Henry sued the Coahoma County school board, which claimed the legal right to fire her, further claiming that it did not have to furnish its reasons. She had taught for eleven years at McCloud School near Farrell ("County School Board Denies Teacher's Charge," *CPR*, 13 December 1962).

57. See Van Landingham to the director, report, 22 October 1959, NAACP-Clarksdale folder file, SCP, MDAH.

58. For a detailed overview of the Coahoma County and Clarksdale school systems, see chap. 3 of Hamlin, "The Book Hasn't Closed" (dissertation). See also Bolton, "Mississippi's School Equalization Program"; and Bolton, *The Hardest Deal of All*.

59. Henry, *Fire*, 85.

60. For insight into the Little Rock Crisis, see Beals, *Warriors Don't Cry*; and Bates, *Long Shadow of Little Rock*.

61. Fairclough, "Little Rock Crisis," 371–74.

62. Ibid., 374.

63. Cora Lee Hicks interviewed by author.

64. Current to Hurley, 17 November 1958, Southeast Regional Conference, 1958, III C172, NAACPP.

65. Evers to officers and members, 19 February 1959, box 6, folder 1, AMP, SHSW.

66. Quoted in Feldstein, *Motherhood in Black and White*, 74.

67. B. L. Bell, Report, 27 April 1959, RCNL folder file, SCP, MDAH; flyer, box 7, folder 2, AMP, SHSW; *MCA*, "Negro Civil Rights Theme of Meeting," 3 April 1959. During a meeting of the RCNL on 24 January 1960, Aaron Henry openly accused Bell of passing information, as his presence in meetings roused suspicion because no other schoolteacher would attend meetings, fearful of losing their jobs. Bell vehemently denied a connection, stating that as a black man these meetings were open to him (RCNL folder file, SCP, MDAH).

68. By February 1960, there were only twenty-five members. In a handwritten list submitted to the national Youth Department, Pigee named eleven teenagers and their addresses, the remaining fourteen identified as "John Doe" with no specific addresses (III E23, NAACPP).

69. The Clarksdale/Coahoma County youth council was behind Laurel (192); Meridian (51); and Greenville (18). As a state, Mississippi had 223 members in youth councils in 1958 and 366 in 1959—behind all other states in the region, except South Carolina, which had only 170 in 1959 (Correspondence File, 1960, III C171, NAACPP).

70. Membership Campaigns, 1960, III C280, NAACPP.

71. Gillette, "NAACP in Texas," 146.

72. Pigee, *Struggles: Part One*, 31; Vera M. Pigee interviewed by author, 12–13 October 2001.

73. Ransby, *Ella Baker and the Black Freedom Movement*, 136.

74. Historians of African American history recorded the many ways men and women have continued to adopt strategies and redefine their social positions in order to survive and maintain their civic presence. For a handful of examples, consider the work of Hunter, *To 'Joy My Freedom*; Evelyn Brooks Higginbotham, *Righteous Discontent*; Litwack, *Been in the Storm So Long*; Gilmore, *Gender and Jim Crow*; Kelley, *Race Rebels*; and Morris, *Origins of the Civil Rights Movement*.

75. Quote from Naples, "Activist Mothering," 450.

76. Pigee, *Struggles: Part Two*, 24.

77. For literature on other mothering, start with Stack, *All Our Kin*; and James, "Mothering: A Possible Black Feminist Link to Social Transformation," in *Theorizing Black Feminisms*, ed. James and Busia. African American women's mothering techniques for resistance are a part of a tradition carried forth from slavery and beyond, rooted in some African family structures. For a good introduction to this subject, see Deborah Gray White, *Ar'n't I a Woman*; Deborah Gray White, *Too Heavy a Load*; Robnett, *How Long? How Long*, 45; Boris, "The Power of Motherhood," in Michel and Koven, *Mothers of a New World*, 213–45; and McDonald, "Black Activist Mothering."

78. McDonald, "Black Activist Mothering," 776; Naples, "Activist Mothering," 448. Emphasis in original.

79. The exact date of the demonstration is unknown; the *Clarksdale Press Register* did not report the incident.

80. This was despite the claim that the NAACP wanted to heed the voices of the youth and had in fact arranged regional leadership training conferences. The Southeast Regional session was held in Memphis on 20–21 February, attracting 198 youth, in order to lay the groundwork for sit-down protest demonstrations (Reports, 1960–62, III E50, NAACPP).

81. Pigee, *Struggles: Part One*, 45–47.

82. Ibid., 46; see also "Miss Mary Jayne Pigee," Coahoma County, 1964–65, III C73, NAACPP.

83. Pigee, *Struggles: Part One*, 45–47.

84. Sheila Shiki y Michaels, "Freedom Is a Constant Struggle: Overcoming Reticence, Denial, Shame, and Pain," presented at Oral History Association Meeting, St. Louis, October 2001 (in author's possession). See also Julie Willett's *Permanent Waves*, for her discussion on the history of beauty salons and the different political roles that black and white salons have played.

85. For more information on Highlander, see Highlander Research and Education Center Papers, 1917–78, and finding aid description, SHSW.

86. Myles Horton quoted in Morris, *Origins of the Civil Rights Movement*, 145.

87. Septima Clark quoted from a report of the beauticians workshop held at Highlander, 15–17 January 1961. The fifty-two participants came from Tennessee, Alabama, and Georgia, with the workshop repeated in October 1962. See Highlander Research and Education Center Papers, 1917–78, box 80, folder 10, SHSW.

88. Guinier, *Lift Every Voice*, 303.

89. Pigee, *Struggles: Part One*, 63; Payne, *I've Got the Light of Freedom*, 142; "Report of the Citizenship School—Workshop and Other Activities," 11 December 1961, box 136, folder 28, Citizenship Education Program Papers, SCLCP, MLKC; letter to Myles and Aimee Horton, 29 November 1961, box 136, folder 10, SCLCP, MLKC; Young, *An Easy Burden*, 141–43.

90. Clark quote from Charron, *Freedom's Teacher*, 324.

91. Coahoma County NAACP Annual Report for 1961, Annual Report: Mississippi, 1956–65, III C190, NAACPP.

92. Citizenship School Report, July 1964–June 1965, subgroup E, series 3, box 155, folder 2, SCLCP, MLKC.

93. Rebecca Hood-Adams, "Local NAACP Marks 50 Years," *CPR*, 25 October 2003.

94. For extended dialogue on the boundaries of private and public households, see Evelyn Nakano Glenn, "Social Constructions of Mothering: A Thematic Overview," in Glenn, Change, and Forcey, *Mothering*.

95. For an excellent treatment of black women's working-class activism, see Hunter, *To 'Joy My Freedom*.

96. Vera M. Pigee interviewed by author, 25 January 2000.

97. Vera M. Pigee interviewed by author, 12–13 October 2001.

98. Cora Lee Hicks interviewed by author.

99. See Roy Wilkins to Jane Stembridge, SNCC secretary, 14 July 1960, SNCC, 1960–65, III A212, NAACPP.

100. Gloster Current to Herbert Wright, memorandum, 28 October 1960, and Wright to Current, memorandum, 1 November 1960, Herbert Wright Memos and Reports, 1958–62, III E53, NAACPP; Annual Report, Branch Department, 1960, III C219, NAACPP.

101. Southeast Regional Office correspondence, 1960, III C171, NAACPP.

102. Raines, *My Soul Is Rested*, 234.

103. Ibid., 236.

Chapter 3

1. "God Has Always Had a Time, a Place, and a People: Mrs. Vera Mae Pigee," Coahoma County Files, 1964–65, III C73, NAACPP.

2. Pigee, *Struggles: Part One*, 50.

3. Ibid., 51. As the incident passed calmly, it is unclear exactly when it took place. Given that Pigee was buying a ticket for her child returning for the holidays, we can assume that she made the purchase in late November or early December. Rev. J. D. Rayford provided quiet leadership through these years. Affiliated with the Century Burial Association, the Knights and Daughters of Tabor, and the United Order of Friendship of America, he also was the pastor of a chapel. See open letter from Henry and Pigee, 25 May 1964, box 6, folder 2, AMP, SHSW.

4. Pigee, *Struggles: Part One*, 53.

5. See Arsenault, *Freedom Riders*.

6. *CPR*, 1 November, 27 December 1961. H. Ray, U.S. attorney for the northern district

of Mississippi, reported to Burke Marshall on 3 January 1962 that the segregation signs had been removed (memo for the attorney general, Wednesday report, 3 January 1962, box 16, Monday and Wednesday Reports, Burke Marshall Papers, JFKL).

7. Herbert Wright to Gloster Current, memorandum, 5 December 1960, Herbert Wright Memos and Reports, 1958–62, III E53, NAACPP.

8. Annual Reports, 1940–51, Youth File, II E2, NAACPP. In 1939, there were 122 youth councils and 15 college chapters, including 14 surviving organization committees of the 42 formed, making 137 youth groups in the association. Herbert Wright, youth director, Annual Report of the Youth Division for Year Ending 31 December 1952, Annual Reports, 1952, II E2, NAACPP. By 1953, there were 245 youth councils and 60 college chapters.

9. Bartley, *Rise of Massive Resistance*, 288, 181.

10. Johnston, *Mississippi's Defiant Years*, 99. In July 1960, Medgar Evers voiced his concern that $20,000 of public funds would be given to the Citizens' Councils from the Sovereignty Commission, urging each branch to voice its protests. By the time of the report, mass protest meetings had taken place in Clarksdale, Greenville, and Jackson (Medgar Evers Files, III C244, NAACPP).

11. Katagiri, *Mississippi State Sovereignty Commission*, 69.

12. Scarbrough Report, 11 October 1960, Coahoma County folder file, SCP, MDAH.

13. See chap. 1; and Henry, *Fire*, 26.

14. Details of this incident are from a four-page report by Judge Leon Porter to all the members of the executive committee of the Coahoma County Citizens' Council, 26 July 1960, NAACP-Clarksdale folder file, SCP, MDAH. From the report, it is unclear who called the police.

15. Wilkie, *Dixie*, 134. It is unclear how these women were related, but they were probably cousins.

16. Governor Ross Barnett actively campaigned for unpledged electors to hold the parties for ransom in order to influence the selection of the president and vice president during the election campaign. It worked in the primaries. Mississippi's unpledged voters for the first and only time in history won the election, winning 116,248 votes against the Democrats' 108,362 and the Republican's 73,561 (Johnston, *Mississippi's Defiant Years*, 126).

17. Task Force Reports, Harris Wofford, memorandum re: civil rights, 30 December 1960, Pre-presidential Papers, box 1071, JFKL.

18. Patterson, *Brown v. Board of Education*, 123.

19. Task Force Reports, Harris Wofford, memorandum re: civil rights, 30 December 1960, Pre-presidential Papers, box 1071, JFKL.

20. Aaron Henry to JFK (on national office NAACP letterhead), 22 January 1961, Aaron Henry Name File, box 1192, WHCF, JFKL. For information about Henry's election, see Henry, *Fire*, 101; and Ruby Hurley to Roy Wilkins, memorandum, 9 November 1960, Mississippi State, III C75, NAACPP.

21. *Student Voice* 2, no. 3 (March 1961), in Community Relations Department, series 5, box 26, folder 4, CORE Papers, SHSW. Henry wrote a similar letter of encouragement to the president on 19 February 1961 as the secretary of the Regional Council of Negro Leadership, of which Rev. Theodore Trammell, pastor of Haven Methodist Church, was now presi-

dent (attached to White House office route slip to Harris Wofford, 25 July 1961, Aaron Henry Name File, box 1192, WHCF, JFKL).

22. Coahoma County NAACP Annual Report, 1961, Annual Report: Mississippi, 1956–65, III C190, NAACPP. Vera Pigee touted the event as the first "integrated state presentation in Mississippi" ("Miss Mary Jayne Pigee," Coahoma County, 1964–65, III C73, NAACPP); Candi and Guy Carawan interviewed by author.

23. Pigee, *Struggles: Part One*, 32; Coahoma County NAACP Annual Report, 1961, Annual Report: Mississippi, 1956–65, III C190, NAACPP.

24. Candi and Guy Carawan interviewed by author.

25. Wilkie, *Dixie*, 118; Coahoma County NAACP Annual Report, 1961, Annual Report: Mississippi, 1956–65, III C190, NAACPP.

26. "Program: Operation Mississippi," Mississippi State, III C75, NAACPP.

27. Letter from Current to Henry, 6 October 1961, Mississippi State, III C75, NAACPP.

28. Johnston, *Mississippi's Defiant Years*, 129; Medgar Evers, 1961, III C245, NAACPP; *News from the NAACP* release, 8 April 1961, III A229, NAACPP; Mississippi Pressures: Aaron Henry, III A229, NAACPP.

29. White House office route slip to Harris Wofford, 25 July 1961, Aaron Henry Name File, box 1192, WHCF, JFKL; John Doar interviewed by author.

30. Henry, *Fire*, 105. John Doar's aversion to publicity renders him enigmatic in civil rights history, yet his presence in the South during these years is unmistakable. He was born on 3 December 1921 in Minneapolis, attended Princeton University, and served as a second lieutenant in the Army Air Corps during World War II. After the war, he graduated from law school at the University of California at Berkeley before returning to New Richmond, Wisconsin. Called to the Civil Rights Division in the waning month of the Eisenhower administration as first assistant to the attorney general, he stayed on when the Kennedys entered the White House (biographical information from "Ubiquitous Rights Aide: John Michael Doar," *NYT*, 3 September 1963, 27); see also John Doar interviewed by author; and Robert Kennedy to John Doar, 22 July 1961, Attorney General's Files, 1961–63, box 8, Burke Marshall Papers, JFKL.

31. For Henry on Doar, see Henry, *Fire*, 104, 105, 106; and Aaron Henry interviewed by T. H. Baker, Clarksdale, 12 September 1970, tape one, 16, Oral History Project Transcripts, LBJL. Henry remembers incorrectly that Doar was present. Doar was in another part of Mississippi at that time but states that he had many dealings with Henry in the time he worked in the state but few trips to Clarksdale, although he had been there a few times in earlier years visiting friends (Doar interviewed by author).

32. Aaron Henry interviewed by T. H. Baker, Clarksdale, 12 September 1970, tape one, 5–6, Oral History Project Transcripts, LBJL; Henry, *Fire*, 107.

33. Monthly Report from Julie Wright, Southeast Regional field youth secretary, 6 September 1961, Reports, 1961–62, III E55, NAACPP.

34. "Negro Youths Charged Here," *CPR*, 24 August 1961; Jack Young to Robert Carter, 13 September 1961, part 22, reel 6, group V, series B, NAACPMF; Pigee, *Struggles: Part One*, 48; Current to Henry Moon, NAACP public relations director, memorandum, 24 August 1961, Mississippi NAACP, III E9, NAACPP; Henry to Current, 28 August 1961, III C75,

NAACPP; *Mary Jane Pigee et al. v. State of Mississippi*, brief for appellants on appeal from the County Court of Coahoma County, September 1961; Scarbrough Report, 5 September 1961, Vera Pigee folder file, SCP, MDAH; Monthly Report from Julie Wright, Southeast Regional field youth secretary, 6 September 1961, Reports 1961–62, III E55, NAACPP.

35. Coahoma County NAACP Annual Report for 1961, Annual Report: Mississippi, 1956–65, III C190, NAACPP; *Mary Jane Pigee et al. v. State of Mississippi*, brief for appellants on appeal from the County Court of Coahoma County, September 1961. Attorney Jack Young for the NAACP cited that the juveniles received $100 fines and thirty-day suspended sentences and that Mary Jane was fined $200 and received a sixty-day suspended sentence (Young to Robert Carter, 13 September 1961, part 22, reel 6, group V, series B, NAACPMF). The station closed by the end of the decade as it merged with Amtrak, which closed smaller stations on the line.

36. Pigee, *Struggles: Part One*, 49; see also Coahoma County NAACP Branch Annual Report, 1961, written by secretary Vera Pigee, Annual Reports: Mississippi, 1956–65, III C190, NAACPP.

37. Pigee, *Struggles: Part One*, 55. Here she addressed the arresting officer in Clarksdale, December 1961.

38. Report, 5 September 1961, Vera Pigee folder file, SCP, MDAH. Mary sang at the NAACP's fund drives from the age of eight and later attended the Highlander Folk School for two weeks in 1960 and for a week at Dorchester, Georgia, for further civil rights training ("Miss Mary Jayne Pigee," Coahoma County, 1964–65, III C73, NAACPP).

39. Roy Wright to Laplois Ashford, 1 July 1964, Mississippi State, III E9, NAACPP. In this letter, written on behalf of the Clarksdale Youth Council, Wright complained about the lack of recognition awarded to Vera Pigee.

40. Pigee, *Struggles: Part Two*, 83; Vera M. Pigee interviewed by author, 12–13 October 2001.

41. "God Has Always Had a Time, a Place, and a People: Mrs. Vera Mae Pigee," 15 May 1964, Coahoma County, 1964–65, III C73, NAACPP.

42. Ibid.

43. Feldstein, *Motherhood in Black and White*, 89.

44. Dear Editor, from Larry Graham, "Leadership Vacuum to Blame for Economic Woes," *CPR*, 8 August 2003.

45. Long conversations with Mary Jane Pigee Davis reveal that the façade of unity masked deep conflicts, which had to be sidelined in the face of opposition from local whites. Long conversations with John Dittmer facilitated the process of speculating on these relationships.

46. Monthly Report from Julie Wright, Southeast Regional field youth secretary, 6 September 1961, Reports 1961–62, III E55, NAACPP; Calvin D. Banks to Roy Wilkins, 1963 memorandum, Coahoma County, 1956–63, III C73, NAACPP. In recognition of her efficiency, at the NAACP annual convention in July 1963, Pigee received the first-prize Advisor's Award from Laplois Ashford, national youth director (Pigee, *Struggles: Part One*, 44).

47. Coahoma County NAACP Annual Report, 1961, Annual Reports: Mississippi, 1956–65, III C190, NAACPP; Pigee, *Struggles: Part One*, 29. She misdates the incident as 1963.

See also "The Clarksdale Story," box 66, IVE, folder 1142, n.d. (estimated end of September 1963), AHP, TC; Henry, *Fire*, 111.

48. The officers in 1961 were Wilma Jean Jones (president), Jerry Wilson (vice president), Susie Wilson (secretary), and Rebecca Henry (treasurer). Installation of Officers Program held Sunday, 5 March 1961, at Centennial Baptist Church; Vera Pigee folder file, SCP, MDAH.

49. Pigee, *Struggles: Part One*, 29.

50. Henry to Current, 25 November 1961, Mississippi Pressures: Clarksdale, 1956–63, III A229, NAACPP; Coahoma County NAACP Annual Report, 1961, Annual Reports: Mississippi, 1956–65, III C190, NAACPP.

51. Henry to Current, 25 November 1961, Mississippi Pressures: Clarksdale, 1956–63, III A229, NAACPP; letter from Rev. Rayford, 20 February 1962, Coahoma County folder file, SCP, MDAH; Annual Reports: Mississippi, 1956–65, III C190, NAACPP.

52. Henry to Current, 25 November 1961, Mississippi Pressures: Clarksdale, 1956–63, III A229, NAACPP.

53. Southeast Regional Office, Misc., 1957–64, III C173, NAACPP; Annual Reports, Branch Department, 1961–64, III C219, NAACPP.

54. CCFCO flyers, n.d. (probably December 1961), part 23, series A, reel 21, NAACPMF; Report from Current to Wilkins, memorandum, 7 December 1961, Mississippi Pressures: Aaron Henry, III A229, NAACPP.

55. Scarbrough Report, 9 January 1962, Coahoma County folder file, SCP, MDAH. They were charged under Section 26, Subsection 6, Book 2A, Mississippi Code of 1942. See also "The Clarksdale Story," box 66, IVE, folder 1142, n.d. (estimated end of September 1963), 2, AHP, TC; Report from Henry in a memo to Wilkins from Current, 7 December 1961, Mississippi Pressures: Aaron Henry, III A229, NAACPP; and Coahoma County NAACP Annual Report, 1961, Annual Reports: Mississippi, 1956–65, III C190, NAACPP.

56. Pigee, *Struggles: Part One*, 53, 55. Roy Wilkins responded by sending a telegram to Robert Kennedy, mentioning the use of handcuffs and requesting an investigation by the Department of Justice (Mississippi Pressures: Aaron Henry, 1961–65, and Clarksdale, 1956–64, both III A229, NAACPP).

57. Medgar Evers 1962 Report, III C245, NAACPP. Evers noted that on that particular night, 500 attended the weekly mass meeting at Haven Methodist Church. Scarbrough's Report noted that the county courthouse was filled to capacity before ten in the morning, the time for the trial: "In fact, two deputy sheriffs turned back quite a few Negroes after the Negro section was filled." A busload of students and teachers came from Rust College in Holly Springs to witness the event (Scarbrough Report, 9 January 1962, Coahoma County folder file, SCP, MDAH).

58. Scarbrough Report, 9 January 1962, Coahoma County folder file, SCP, MDAH.

59. Medgar Evers 1962 Report, III C245, NAACPP. Aaron Henry documented that the circuit court ruled that the petition should be amended. But without an amendment, they were neither acquitted nor found guilty and their bond money was held, rendering them unsure of their legal status. The boycott itself was called off after the passage of the Civil Rights Act of 1964 (Henry, *Fire*, 114).

60. Information taken from the affidavit of Bessie Turner, 1962. Also in box 1, folder 21, Howard Zinn Papers, SHSW. In *Struggles: Part One*, Pigee named the officers (38), but the names are not included in the affidavit.

61. "FBI Investigates Brutality in Clarksdale," *Mississippi Free Press*, 10 February 1962, MFSPC, MDAH.

62. Pigee, *Struggles: Part One*, 38.

63. Forman, *Making of Black Revolutionaries*, 242. In his autobiography, Forman reprinted the affidavit in full, only omitting the names of the officers involved. See also Henry, *Fire*, 107.

64. Emphasis in the original. Flier in Coahoma County folder file, SCP, MDAH.

65. Henry, *Fire*, 124.

66. Howard, *Men Like That*, 99–103, 161.

67. Two excellent examples of scholarship that demonstrate how black health was linked to disease are Hunter, *To 'Joy My Freedom*; and Roberts, *Killing the Black Body*. See also Howard, *Men Like That*, 143–44.

68. See Johnson, *Sweet Tea*, 109, 546.

69. Howard, *Men Like That*, 153–58.

70. According to a press release sent to Henry Moon by Gloster Current, Robert L. Carter and Jess Brown counseled Henry (Mississippi Pressures: Aaron Henry, III A229, NAACPP). See also Medgar Evers 1962 Report, III C245, NAACPP; and Current to Wilkins, Morsell, Moon, Carter, and Black, memorandum, 30 April 1962, Mississippi State, III C75, NAACPP. For the Sovereignty Commission's account, see Scarbrough Report, 13 June 1962, Aaron Henry folder file, SCP, MDAH. For Aaron Henry's account, read the chapter titled "Diabolical Plot," in Henry, *Fire*. See also NAACP Press Release, "Miss. Supreme Court Frees NAACP Leader," 7 June 1963, Mississippi State, 1964–65, III C75, NAACPP; "Negro Leader Fails in Libel Case Plea," *NYT*, 3 December 1963, 36; and "Negro's Conviction Upheld," *NYT*, 13 July 1963, 7. Thanks to John Howard for additional sources on the case. The Southern Conference Education Fund Inc. sent out an action memo to "Friends and Organizations everywhere" detailing the case and urging readers to write to the Justice Department and the Commission on Civil Rights to reverse the Mississippi court decision. The quote from Henry is from this memo (23 July 1963, box 4, folder 46, Papers of Fred L. Shuttlesworth, MLKC).

71. Bertha Blackburn interviewed by author.

72. Daniel, *Standing at the Crossroads*, 66.

73. Howard, *Men Like That*, 142. In conversations with Mary Pigee Davis, she revealed that she and most of the youth counselors suspected that Henry was bisexual, noting that he had hired a flamboyant and unmistakably gay man, "Tommie," to work in the NAACP office located right next to his drugstore.

74. Leslie McLemore interviewed by author.

75. Johnson, *Sweet Tea*, 4.

76. Leslie McLemore interviewed by author.

77. Howard, *Men Like That*, xi.

78. Ibid., xvii.

79. Leslie McLemore interviewed by author; Howard, *Men Like That*, 171.

80. Henry, *Fire*, 128.

81. Coahoma County Branch NAACP newsletter, n.d. (estimated 1–5 August), Coahoma County, 1956–63, III C73, NAACPP.

82. Henry, *Fire*, 107.

83. Ibid., 109. Henry as COFO president to the White House, telegram, 29 August 1962, box 1192, WHCF, JFKL.

84. Henry, *Fire*, 115.

85. Mississippi Field Secretary Special Report to Roy Wilkins, 12 October 1961, and Gloster Current and Ruby Hurley, re: operation of other civil rights organizations in the state of Mississippi, Mississippi State, III C75, NAACPP; see also Dittmer, *Local People*, 116. Lewis quoted in Raines, *My Soul Is Rested*, 98; and Morris, *Origins of the Civil Rights Movement*, 174–75. For the most comprehensive study of the Freedom Rides movement, see Arsenault, *Freedom Riders*. For more information on Woman Power Unlimited, see Tiyi Morris, "Local Women and the Civil Rights Movement in Mississippi: Re-visioning Womanpower Unlimited," in Theoharis and Woodard, *Groundwork*, 193–214. The SCLC had a presence in the Delta, although not so much in Coahoma County. Rev. James Bevel served as a SCLC field secretary in Mississippi for about a year from October 1962, recruiting for training, talking in churches, and bailing out ministers. Weekly progress reports in 1962 and 1963 detail his activities throughout the Delta. See box 141, folders 4–8: Mississippi, SCLCP, MLKC.

86. Wilkins to Edward King, 1 September 1961, SNCC, 1960–65, III A212, NAACPP.

87. Letter, 8 September 1961, ibid.

88. Report by Ruby Hurley, November 1961, ibid.

89. In June 1962, SNCC received $5,000 from the Voter Education Program and organized voter registration drives in six counties, including Coahoma (Payne, *I've Got the Light of Freedom*, 141). Henry, *Fire*, 130; Coahoma County Branch NAACP newsletter, n.d. (but estimated 12–19 July 1962), Coahoma County, 1956–63, III C73, NAACPP; "The Clarksdale Story," box 66, IVE, folder 1142, n.d. (estimated end of September 1963), 3, AHP, TC. Idessa Johnson had accompanied Vera Pigee when they desegregated the Greyhound bus terminal in 1961. In the SCLC Records, Johnson is mentioned in a 1965 survey of citizenship teachers who by then had conducted a citizenship school; having done door-to-door canvassing, she had successfully registered "quite a few" voters. See "Teacher Surveys–MS, 1965," box 155, folder 20, SCLCP, MLKC.

90. Henry, *Fire*, 132; box 1, folder 21, n.d., Howard Zinn Papers, SHSW; Community Relations Department, series 5, box 14, folder 9, CORE Papers, SHSW.

91. Report to Mississippi State Conference, Memberships and FFF Contributions Received to Date, 29 October 1962, III C75l, NAACPP; Mississippi State and Conference Statement, box 6, folder 1, AMP, SHSW; CORE, III A199, NAACPP; SCLC, 1963–65, III A212, NAACPP.

92. "Dear Friends," Aaron Henry, Christmas Day 1962, Coahoma County, 1956–63, III C73, NAACPP; David Dennis, Community Relations Department, series 5, box 14, folder 9, CORE Papers, SHSW; Holland, *From the Mississippi Delta*, 202.

93. David Dennis, CORE Report, February 1963, Community Relations Department, series 5, box 14, folder 9, CORE Papers, SHSW. See also "Economic Pressure against 5,000 Negro Families Affects 22,000 People," *Jet*, 21 February 1963, 18.

94. Donaldson quoted in Raines, *My Soul Is Rested*, 257.

95. Ivanhoe Donaldson interviewed by author.

96. Ibid.

97. "Two Accused of Violating Narcotics Act," *CPR*, 28 December 1962; "Shipments to Negroes Were Result of Appeal," *CPR*, 29 December 1962; "2 Ex-Students Held in Barbiturate Case," *MCA*, 29 December 1962; "Narcotics Suspects Held to Grand Jury," *MCA*, 30 December 1962; "The Clarksdale Story," box 66, IVE, folder 1142, n.d. (estimated end of September 1963), 4, AHP, TC; Scarbrough Report, 4 January 1963, Coahoma County folder file, SCP, MDAH; memo to attorney general, Monday Report, 3 January 1963, Civil Rights Division Report, box 16, Burke Marshall Papers, JFKL; Raines, *My Soul Is Rested*, 258; Coahoma County Branch NAACP, n.d. (probably late January 1963), Coahoma County, 1956–63, III C73, NAACPP.

98. Raines, *My Soul Is Rested*, 257.

99. Gregory and Lipsyte, *Nigger*, 172, 174.

100. Ibid., 176. Dick Gregory Day was advertised in Coahoma County Branch NAACP newsletter, n.d., Coahoma County, 1956–63, III C73, NAACPP.

101. Morsell to Wilkins, memorandum, "The Mississippi Relief Operation," 7 March 1963, Mississippi Special Relief Fund, 1956–65, III A230, NAACPP. Monetary contributions had also been sent, deposited in an account managed by Pigee and Henry. Following the conversation, Morsell pledged $1,000 from the NAACP to assist with the effort (ibid.). See also Press Releases, 14 March 1963, Mississippi Special Relief Fund, 1956–65, III A230, NAACPP; and 15 March 1963, Mississippi Pressures: Clarksdale, 1956–63, III A229, NAACPP.

102. Aaron Henry interviewed by T. H. Baker, Clarksdale, 12 September 1970, tape two, 2, Oral History Project Transcripts, LBJL; Johnston, *Mississippi's Defiant Years*, 95–96; Attorney General's General Correspondence, 15 December 1962, box 11, RFK Papers, JFKL; "Resolution of the United States Commission on Civil Rights," April 1963, box 10, Commission on Civil Rights, Berl Bernard Papers, JFKL.

103. Ibid.; Reports, box 10, Berl Bernhard Papers, JFKL. Bernhard served as the executive director of the Civil Rights Commission.

104. "The Clarksdale Story," box 66, IVE, folder 1142, n.d. (estimated end of September 1963), 4, AHP, TC; Aaron Henry to Robert Kennedy, 6 April 1963, Mississippi Pressures: Clarksdale, 1956–63, III A229, NAACPP.

105. Wilkie, *Dixie*, 21.

106. Gregory and Lipsyte, *Nigger*, 189; Henry, *Fire*, 140. On 15 September 1963, a bomb tore through the basement of the Sixteenth Street Baptist Church in Birmingham, killing four black girls (Addie Mae Collins, Denise McNair, Carole Robertson, and Cynthia Wesley), who were preparing for Bible School.

107. Aaron Henry interviewed by Jerry DeMuth at Henry's home, 3 August 1964, Jerry DeMuth File, SHSW.

108. "Two White Men Indicted in Coahoma Firebombing," *Clarion-Ledger*, 11 July 1963.

109. "Negro Congressman Is Unhurt in Clarksdale, Miss., Bombing," *NYT*, 13 April 1963, 35; "Let There Be No Compromise Here," *Vicksburg Evening Post*, April 1963; Henry, *Fire*, 143–44; Coahoma County Branch NAACP newsletters, 27 July 1963 and about 24 April 1963, Branch Coahoma County, Mississippi, 1956–63, III C73, NAACPP. See also Crespino, *In Search of Another Country*.

110. "Mississippi Blast Rips NAACP Aide's Store," *NYT*, 5 May 1963, 82; "Mississippi Blast Laid to Lightning," *NYT*, 6 May 1963, 22.

111. "The Clarksdale Story," box 66, IVE, folder 1142, n.d. (estimated end of September 1963), 4, AHP, TC. See also affidavit, signed 24 May 1964, COFO Records, MDAH; "Clarksdale Lady Beaten—Then Convicted of Disturbing the Peace," *Mississippi Free Press*, 4 May 1963, cited in Pigee, *Struggles: Part One*, 60; Pigee's handwritten statement, Coahoma County Branch, 1956–63, III C73, NAACPP; and *MCA*, 26 April 1963.

112. "Clarksdale Lady Beaten—Then Convicted of Disturbing the Peace," *Mississippi Free Press*, 4 May 1963, cited in Pigee, *Struggles: Part One*, 61. Quote from Coahoma County Branch NAACP newsletter, 27 April 1963, Coahoma County, 1956–63, III C73, NAACPP. See also "The Clarksdale Story," box 66, IVE, folder 1142, n.d. (estimated end of September 1963), 4, AHP, TC.

113. Coahoma County Branch NAACP newsletter, 27 April 1963, Coahoma County, 1956–63, III C73, NAACPP. Underlining in original.

114. Brenda Renee Luckett interviewed by author.

115. "God Has Always Had a Time, a Place, and a People: Mrs. Vera Mae Pigee," 15 May 1964, Coahoma County, 1964–65, III C73, NAACPP; affidavit signed 24 May 1964, COFO Records, MDAH; Pigee, *Struggles: Part One*, 38.

116. Pigee quoted in Rebecca Hood-Adams, "Local NAACP Marks 50 Years," *CPR*, 25 October 2003. See also Vera M. Pigee interviewed by author, 12–13 October 2001; Coahoma County Branch NAACP, 8 June 1963, Coahoma County NAACP, box 31, Social Action Vertical File, SHSW; and Scarbrough Report, 5 September 1961, Vera Mae Pigee folder, SCP, MDAH.

117. Testimony of Aaron Henry, 13 June 1963, Coahoma County, 1956–63, III C73, NAACPP.

118. "The Economic Impact of Racial Unrest," Report, Civil Rights—General, box 97, President's Office Files, JFKL. Arthur Schlesinger Jr., special assistant to the president, wrote to Robert Kennedy that in 1958 Mississippi paid $385 million to the federal government in revenue but received $668 million in federal benefits (Civil Rights—Mississippi, 27 September 1962, ibid.). See also Mississippi, box 20, Burke Marshall Papers, JFKL; Subject File, 17 October 1962, WHCF, JFKL; RFK to JFK, n.d., Attorney General's General Correspondence, box 11, RFK Papers, JFKL; "Resolution of the United States Commission on Civil Rights," April 1963, Commission on Civil Rights, box 10, Berl Bernard Papers, JFKL; and Crespino, *In Search of Another Country*.

119. "Clarksdale Joins NAACP Mississippi Protests," Press Release, 22 June 1963, Mississippi Branches: Clarksdale, 1956–63, III A229, NAACPP. The church picketing initiated eight arrests, with fines set at $100 and thirty-day sentences given ("The Clarksdale Story,"

box 66, IVE, folder 1142, n.d. [estimated end of September 1963], AHP, TC). See affidavit by Hattie Mae Gilmore, 24 May 1964, COFO Records, MDAH. She received a thirty-day jail sentence and a $100 fine at her 20 June trial. All the defendants were represented by Jess Brown (Press Release, "Clarksdale Joins NAACP Mississippi Protests," 22 June 1963, Mississippi Pressures: Clarksdale, 1956–63, III A229, NAACPP). She did odd jobs before settling in as a cook for Head Start, where she remained until her retirement (Hattie Mae Gilmore interviewed by author). Also see Brenda Luckett interviewed by author.

Chapter 4

1. President Kennedy's television and radio address to the nation, 11 June 1963, Civil Rights—General, box 97, President's Office Files, JFKL. Clarksdale was one of seven Mississippi cities listed as places of the least possible progress. Clarksdale and Greenwood represented Mississippi in the list of southern cities most likely to have black demonstrations (memorandum, RFK to JFK, 4 June 1963, President's Office Files, box 97, JFKL). Hundreds of protests had occurred nationwide from May 1963, as the Justice Department documented the summer's events. From 20 May to 25 September, 1,580 demonstrations took place in thirty-eight states, in Washington, D.C., and in 263 other cities (Demonstrations, boxes 31 and 32, Burke Marshall Papers, JFKL).

2. Current to Wilkins, memorandum, 5 November 1964, COFO, III A200, NAACPP.

3. "The Clarksdale Story," box 66, IVE, folder 1142, n.d. (estimated end of September 1963), 5, AHP, TC. Several clergymen were invited, including Bishop Charles Golden and Rev. M. Lindsey; several were from the National Council of Churches, including Rev. A. D. Ward and Rev. Arthur Walmsley; also included were Charles Evers, Martin Luther King Jr., Abernathy, and Rev. Wyatt T. Walker (ibid., 6).

4. For a list of the fifty-nine names, see Enclosures for "The Clarksdale Story," box 66, IVE, folder 1142, n.d. (estimated end of September 1963), AHP, TC; Pigee, *Struggles: Part One*, 70–71; "Injunction Granted: Chancellor Bars Integration Demonstrations," *CPR*, 9 July 1963; *City of Clarksdale v. Aaron Henry et al.*, "Bill for Injunction," in part 23, series A, reel 21, NAACPMF; "Two White Men Indicted in Coahoma Firebombing," *Clarion-Ledger*, 11 July 1963.

5. "The Clarksdale Story," box 66, IVE, folder 1142, n.d. (estimated end of September 1963), 6, AHP, TC. Charles Evers spoke that night, tearing up his injunction at the pulpit and declaring his defiance to the audience. King was served his papers immediately on his arrival, and a meeting of all the organizational leaders made the agreement to comply with the injunction (Scarbrough Report, 12 July 1963, Coahoma County folder file, SCP, MDAH).

6. Henry to Roy Wilkins, "Dear Boss Man," 18 July 1963, Coahoma County, 1956–63, III C73, NAACPP. On 19 August 1963, H. Y. Hackett, Coahoma County Branch NAACP treasurer, wrote to Wilkins to thank him for the $25,000 contribution (Coahoma County, 1956–63, III C73, NAACPP).

7. In an agreement made between attorney R. Jess Brown and Clarksdale city attorney Charles Brocato, the only adult case that came before the court was Aaron Henry's, in which

he was fined $101 and sentenced to thirty days in jail (COFO Press Release to the attention of Thomas Gaither, 1 August 1963, "Clarksdale Arrest Total Mounts to Eighty-one," box 16, Social Action Vertical File, COFO Papers, SHSW). See also SNCC News Release, August 1963, "5 Jailed in Clarksdale Sit-In, NAACP Head Made to Haul Garbage," SNCC, box 47, Social Action Vertical File, SHSW; and "The Clarksdale Story," box 66, IVE, folder 1142, n.d. (estimated end of September 1963), 7, AHP, TC. On 30 July, fifty-two were arrested; fifteen were arrested on 31 July; fourteen were arrested on 1 August; and five were arrested on 2 August (Enclosures for "Clarksdale Story"); see also "Clarksdale Jails NAACP Leader," *NYT*, 31 July 1963, 13.

8. Coahoma County Branch NAACP newsletter, 14 September 1963, stated that the mayor and at least twenty more citizens had received sworn affidavits, doctors' reports, and photographs of African Americans badly treated at the hands of the police (Coahoma County NAACP, box 31, Social Action Vertical File, SHSW). In a letter dated 6 October 1963 to Burke Marshall at the Justice Department, Aaron Henry enclosed copies of the affidavits, which also circulated to Roy Wilkins, NAACP attorney Jack Young, and Clarence Mitchell at the NAACP Washington Bureau (Coahoma County, 1956–63, III C73, NAACPP).

9. Many archives now house multiple copies of affidavits and other statements—the local NAACP branch and COFO made sure to circulate these atrocities. For examples, see Coahoma County NAACP, box 31, Social Action Vertical File, SHSW; COFO Records, MDAH; testimony presented publicly in a July 1964 mass meeting in Clarksdale, Board of Directors, Special Mississippi Investigating Committee, 1963–64, part 22, reel 10, group V, series B, box 14, NAACPMF; "Report from Lafayette Surney," Clarksdale, box 1, folder 21, Howard Zinn Papers, SHSW; Community Relations Department, series 5, box 14, folder 9, CORE Papers, SHSW; CORE Southern Regional Office Papers, Reports on Mississippi Summer 1964, box 7, folder 12, CORE Papers, SHSW; and Civil Rights Reports, 25 June 1962, to Attorney General, box 16, Burke Marshall Papers, JFKL.

10. Coahoma County Branch NAACP newsletter, 6 July 1963, Coahoma County NAACP, box 31, Social Action Vertical File, SHSW. See Hamlin, "The Book Hasn't Closed" (dissertation), for details from the affidavits.

11. Affidavit of Odessa Brooks, 14 August 1963, Mississippi Freedom Movement, box 29, Social Action Vertical File, SHSW.

12. Ibid.; COFO press release 8/2/63, "Five Clarksdale Sit-Inners Arrested," box 16, Social Action Vertical File, COFO Papers, SHSW; COFO Records, MDAH; and Enclosures for "The Clarksdale Story," box 66, IVE, folder 1142, n.d. (estimated end of September 1963), AHP, TC.

13. Book 16, 133, Minutes of the Board of the Mayor and Commissioners, Clarksdale. In 1965, Random House published a collection of fifty-seven affidavits from black and white activists and citizens given to COFO in evidence against Sheriff Rainey, in conjunction with the murders of the three civil rights workers in the summer of 1964. See Misseduc Foundation, Inc., *Mississippi Black Paper*. Fifteen were from Coahoma County and specifically detail brutality inflicted by Police Chief Ben Collins. See Henry, *Fire*, 116; Stan Boyd interviewed by author; Wilkie, *Dixie*, 123; Coahoma County Branch NAACP newsletter, n.d.

(but estimated mid-June 1962), Coahoma County, 1956–63, III C73, NAACPP; and book 16, 431, 432, 452, 456, 485, Minutes of the Board of the Mayor and Commissioners, Clarksdale.

14. "The Clarksdale Story," box 66, IVE, folder 1142, n.d. (estimated end of September 1963), 7, AHP, TC.

15. Pigee, *Struggles: Part One*, 93. Story comes from Coahoma County Branch NAACP newsletter, n.d., in Enclosures for "Clarksdale Story"; and Charles Evers's Monthly Report as Mississippi field secretary, 25 September 1963, Charles Evers, 1963, III C243, NAACPP.

16. Coahoma County Branch NAACP newsletter, 5 October 1963, part 23, series A, reel 21, NAACPMF.

17. See Fairclough, "The Preachers and the People," 405.

18. Henry, *Fire*, 54, 55; see also Charles Payne, in Crawford et al., *Women in the Civil Rights Movement*, 5–6.

19. Pigee, *Struggles: Part One*, 62, 64.

20. "The Clarksdale Story," box 66, IVE, folder 1142, n.d. (estimated end of September 1963), AHP, TC.

21. Greene, *Praying for Sheetrock*, 28.

22. Jenkins, *Mississippi United Methodist Churches*, 85. Many thanks to the former pastor of Haven, Rev. Jon McCoy, for kindly providing a printout of the church's history (in author's possession).

23. For in-depth discussion of the National Council of Churches, see Findlay, *Church People in the Struggle*; and Newman, *Divine Agitators*.

24. Henry, *Fire*, 167; Newman, *Divine Agitators*, 7; "Leaders of Local White Churches Rebuke Visitors Invited Here by NAACP," *CPR*, 9 July 1963; "Mayor Asked to Discuss Racial Issue," *CPR*, 30 July 1963.

25. *CPR*, 6 August 1963. Thirty-six ministers are listed in the local NAACP's document, "The Clarksdale Story," box 66, IVE, folder 1142, n.d. (estimated end of September 1963), AHP, TC. See Findlay, *Church People in the Struggle*, 79; testimony presented publicly in a July 1964 mass meeting in Clarksdale, Board of Directors, Special Mississippi Investigating Committee, 1963–64, part 22, reel 10, group V, series B, box 14, NAACPMF; affidavit of Charles L. Pendleton, sworn 7 July, COFO Records, MDAH; Community Relations Department, 3 August 1964, series 5, box 22, folder 3, CORE Papers, SHSW.

26. Findlay, *Church People in the Struggle*, 89, 91, 94, 99, 111–12. The NCC gave training and ministerial counseling by sponsoring the two week-long sessions at Oxford, Ohio, on 13–27 June 1964. The organization worked extensively in Hattiesburg with SNCC and had a base in Jackson during the summer of 1964, training church volunteers in nonviolent resistance and self-protection.

27. "General Board Action Concerning a Ministry among the Residents of the Delta Area of the State of Mississippi—Feb. 26, 1964," in folder 4, Daniel Wacker File, SHSW. See also Findlay, *Church People in the Struggle*; and Newman, *Divine Agitators*.

28. "The Clarksdale Story," box 66, IVE, folder 1142, n.d. (estimated end of September 1963), AHP, TC.

29. *U.S. v. State of Mississippi et al.*, civil action no. 3312, Case Documents Statistics on voting registration, box 24, Burke Marshall Papers, JFKL.

30. Chafe, *Never Stop Running*, 166, 180–82; Cummings, *Pied Piper*, 229–36. For a comprehensive study of the Yale students, see Wilgoren, "Black and Blue."

31. "SCLC Man 'Winner' in Mississippi Mock Vote," SCLC newsletter, September 1963, vol. 12, box 17, Berl Bernhard Papers, JFKL. The same press release is found in Mississippi Freedom Movement, box 29, Social Action Vertical File, SHSW. In Clarksdale's actual Democratic primary, 4,517 votes were cast: Coleman received 2,671 and Johnson received 1,796.

32. See Coahoma County Branch NAACP newsletter, 31 August 1963, Coahoma County NAACP, box 31, Social Action Vertical File, SHSW.

33. Coahoma County Branch NAACP newsletter, 12 October 1963, box 66, IVE, folder 1142, AHP, TC; Joan Bowman, SNCC field secretary, Report, 23 October 1963, box 1, folder 20, 1956–70, Howard Zinn Papers, SHSW; Chafe, *Never Stop Running*, 182; Cummings, *Pied Piper*, 233, 236; Hogan, *Many Minds, One Heart*, 144–46; Aaron Henry interviewed by John Jones and John Dittmer, Clarksdale, 22 April 1981, Oral Histories, MDAH.

34. Hogan, *Many Minds, One Heart*, 147–50; Cummings, *Pied Piper*, 240; Chafe, *Never Stop Running*, 185. See also Sinsheimer, "Freedom Vote of 1963"; "50 Yale Men Aid Mississippi Negro," *NYT*, 30 October 1963, 24; "Vote Drive Planned to Register 80,000 Negroes in Mississippi," *NYT*, 7 November 1963, 30; and "Prospectus for the Mississippi Freedom Summer," box 1, MFSPC, MDAH.

35. Chafe, *Never Stop Running*, 184–85; Wilgoren, "Black and Blue"; email correspondence between Steve Bingham and author, September 2010; Steve Bingham interviewed by author. The curfew, in place for years, by 1964 stated that African Americans could not drive after 10 P.M. and no one could be on foot from midnight until 4:30 A.M., unless catching the truck to go chop cotton in someone's field (Elizabeth Smith, "Events of '03 Stirred Memories of Yesteryear," *CPR*, 16 January 2004).

36. Joan Bowman, SNCC Field Secretary Report, 23 October 1963, box 1, folder 20, 1956–70, Howard Zinn Papers, SHSW; Cummings, *Pied Piper*, 234.

37. Aaron Henry interviewed by John Jones and John Dittmer, Clarksdale, 22 April 1981, Oral Histories, MDAH. Henry later served on the station's board after its license was restored.

38. Task Force Reports, Harris Wofford, memorandum re: civil rights, 30 December 1960, box 1071, Pre-presidential Papers, JFKL.

39. Thanks to Charles Cobb for this detail. He also stressed that organizational labels helped identify workers outside of Mississippi, but for the most part, local people referred to the young activists as "freedom riders" or "non-violents."

40. Charles Evers, 1964, III C243, NAACPP.

41. COFO, 1964–65, III A200, NAACPP. For more on Annell Ponder, see her records and field reports, box 155, SCLCP, MLKC.

42. Gloster Current to Aaron Henry, 28 February 1964, and Henry to Current, 8 March 1964, Mississippi State, 1964–65, III C75, NAACPP; Current to Charles Evers, 1 April 1964, Charles Evers, 1964, III C243, NAACPP; Gloster Current to Roy Wilkins, memorandum, 20 May 1964, COFO, III A200, NAACPP; Charles Evers, 1964, III C243, NAACPP; Dittmer, *Local People*, 178, 355.

43. Henry was commenting on why he never took Evers's job after the assassination

(Aaron Henry interviewed by T. H. Baker, Clarksdale, 12 September 1970, tape one, Oral History Project Transcripts, LBJL).

44. Current to Evers, July 1964, Charles Evers, 1964, III C243, NAACPP.

45. Donaldson quoted in Raines, *My Soul Is Rested*, 257.

46. Wilkie described the scene: "Shelves stocked with pomades, hair straighteners, and laxatives lined the aisles, and in the back, Aaron filled prescriptions and offered advice on the telephone" (Wilkie, *Dixie*, 120). Jerry DeMuth, writing for SNCC in 1964 during the Freedom Summer Project, described the store in detail (Jerry DeMuth File, SHSW).

47. Pigee, *Struggles: Part One*, 35.

48. Wright to Laplois Ashford, 1 July 1964, Mississippi State, III E9, NAACPP; Vera Pigee, "Task Force Recommendations," n.d., Coahoma County, 1964–65, III C73, NAACPP; Pigee, *Struggles: Part Two*, 25.

49. Aaron Henry interviewed by John Jones and John Dittmer, Clarksdale, 22 April 1981, Oral Histories, MDAH.

50. Zwerling to Christopher Hexter and Alicia Kaplow, 24 August 1966, Matthew Zwerling File, SHSW; Mat Zwerling interviewed by author.

51. Mat Zwerling interviewed by author; Zwerling to parents and Sara, 23 June 1964, Matthew Zwerling File, SHSW.

52. Report on Mississippi Summer Project, 1964, by Charles Stewart (written September 1964), Charles Stewart File, SHSW.

53. "Transfer and Arrival," Diary Addendum, M320, box 1, folder 20, ZZP, USM.

54. Zeman interviewed by John Rachal, 18 April 1996, Oral History Project, USM.

55. "Transfer and Arrival," Diary Addendum, M320, box 1, folder 20, ZZP, USM; Zeman Senior Thesis, Scripps College, M320, box 1, folder 24, ZZP, USM.

56. "Prospectus for the Mississippi Freedom Summer," box 1, MFSPC, MDAH.

57. SNCC News release, 30 April 1964, "Mississippi Readies Laws for 'Freedom Summer,'" and "Mississippi Introduces More Laws to Curb Freedom Summer," 6 May 1964, box 1, folder 22, Howard Zinn Papers, SHSW. See also Rachal, "Long, Hot Summer"; and "Mississippi Is Prepared," *CPR*, 22 June 1964.

58. Wilkie, *Dixie*, 136, 137.

59. "With Dignity and Restraint," *CPR*, 20 June 1964, 1; "City and County in Readiness," *CPR*, 23 June 1964, 3; "Civil Rights Worker Tells Why He's Here," *CPR*, 27 June 1964, 1; see also Weill, *In a Madhouse's Din*, 127–29.

60. See appendix for list of volunteers in Clarksdale.

61. *Student Voice* 5, no. 16 (15 July 1964), in M336, box 1, folder 11, Matthew Zwerling Papers, USM; "Prospectus for the Mississippi Freedom Summer," box 1, MFSPC, MDAH.

62. Zeman interviewed by John Rachal, 18 April 1996, Oral History Project, USM; Zeman Diary, 4, M320, ZZP, USM; Zeman Senior Thesis, Scripps College, M320, box 1, folder 24, ZZP, USM; "Transcript of the Freedom Summer Pocket Journal of Margaret Hazelton," Hazelton Papers, M359, box 1, folder 10, USM; *Student Voice* 5, no. 16 (15 July 1964), in M336, box 1, folder 11, Matthew Zwerling Papers, USM; "Prospectus for the Mississippi Freedom Summer," box 1, MFSPC, MDAH.

63. Zeman Diary, 4, M320, ZZP, USM; letter, Margie Hazelton to Zoya Zeman, 29 July 1964, M320, box 1, folder 2, ZZP, USM. See also "Transcript of the Freedom Summer

Pocket Journal of Margaret Hazelton," Hazelton Papers, M359, box 1, folder 10, USM; and Stanley Boyd's master's thesis, "Mississippi on Trial."

64. Zeman Diary, 4, M320, ZZP, USM; "Two Meetings with White Clarksdale Families in Summer '64," Diary Addendum, M320, box 1, folder 20, ZZP, USM; Zeman interviewed by John Rachal, 18 April 1996, Oral History Project, USM.

65. Boyd, "Destination Clarksdale," a chapter version from his thesis, "Mississippi on Trial," 4 (in author's possession).

66. Ibid., 9; Stan Boyd interviewed by author.

67. Boyd, "Mississippi on Trial," 15–16, 23.

68. Ibid., 30–32.

69. Stan Boyd interviewed by author.

70. Zeman Senior Thesis, Scripps College, M320, box 1, folder 24, ZZP, USM. Zeman listed four of the staff: Dr. Leo Orris, Dr. William Sykes, Carolyn Lane (R.N.), and Martha Ann Davis (Ph.D.). M320, box 1, folder 23, ZZP, USM. For more information on the Medical Committee for Human Rights, see Dittmer, *Good Doctors*. See also "Recollections of the Medical Committee for Human Rights and the Summer of 1964," Martha Davis Collection, M412, folder 1, USM. A partial list from a log of treatment given to students over a three-day period in August, from Charles R. Drew's report on medical aid to Mississippi from the Medical Committee for Human Rights, Henry Papers, box 85, IVA, folder 1141.

71. Lew Sitzer letter, 29 June, in Martínez, *Letters from Mississippi*, 23.

72. "Transcript of the Freedom Summer Pocket Journal of Margaret Hazelton," Hazelton Papers, M359, box 1, folder 10, USM.

73. "Dear People of Woodmere," Hazelton Papers, M359, box 1, folder 6, USM; M336, Matthew Zwerling Papers, USM; Matthew Zwerling File, SHSW.

74. "Prospectus for the Mississippi Freedom Summer," box 1, MFSPC, MDAH.

75. Zwerling to parents and Sara, 30 June 1964, and Zwerling to parents, 3 July 1964, Matthew Zwerling File, SHSW; see also Zwerling to Zeman, postmarked 24 July 1964, M320, box 1, folder 2, Matthew Zwerling Papers, USM.

76. Martínez, *Letters from Mississippi*, 239; "Prospectus for the Mississippi Freedom Summer," box 1, MFSPC, MDAH.

77. Aaron Henry interviewed by John Jones and John Dittmer, Clarksdale, 22 April 1981, Oral Histories, MDAH.

78. For a comprehensive examination of the challenge and its controversies, see Hogan, *Many Minds, One Heart*, chaps. 7–9. Hogan states that the Mississippi Freedom Democratic Party was the most successful popular party of the twentieth century, organized in the most difficult state of the union. See also Chafe, *Never Stop Running*, 196–200; Payne, *I've Got the Light of Freedom*, 340; and Dittmer, *Local People*, 272–302.

79. Aaron Henry interviewed by John Jones and John Dittmer, Clarksdale, 22 April 1981, Oral Histories, MDAH; see also Hamlin, "Collision and Collusion."

80. Report on Mississippi Summer Project, 1964, by Charles Stewart, Charles Stewart File, 4, 5, SHSW.

81. Zeman Diary, 4, M320, ZZP, 5, 10, USM.

82. Wilkie, *Dixie*, 139; Coahoma County Branch NAACP, *Cryer*, 11 July 1964, Coahoma County, 1964–65, III C73, NAACPP. See also SNCC Files, 6–9 July, box 47, Social Action

Vertical Files, SHSW; and Wilkie, *Dixie*, 139–41, for accounts of integration attempts. See WATS Line Digest, 9–11 July 1964, Community Relations Department, series 5, box 14, folder 9, CORE Papers, SHSW. Wilkie, *Dixie*, 140, reported that the library board wanted to close the library, so removing the chairs so that black people could not sit with whites was the concession. The Carnegie Public Library in Clarksdale had allowed black patrons to use a segregated basement room. A "colored" branch opened in 1930, mainly through black fund-raising efforts (McMillen, *Dark Journey*, 11).

83. Coahoma County Branch NAACP, *Cryer*, 11 July 1964, Coahoma County, 1964–65, III C73, NAACPP; Wilkie, *Dixie*, 141; Henry, *Fire*, 173.

84. For example, see WATS line digest, 21 July 1964, Community Relations Department, series 5, box 14, folder 9, COFO Papers, SHSW.

85. Zwerling to parents and Sara, 29 June 1964, Matthew Zwerling File, SHSW.

86. Mat Zwerling interviewed by author.

87. Zeman Diary, 4, M320, ZZP, USM; Zeman interviewed by John Rachal, 18 April 1996, Oral History Project, USM.

88. Ibid.

89. Coahoma County Branch NAACP, *Cryer*, 11 July 1964, Coahoma County, 1964–65, III C73, NAACPP; "Transcript of the Freedom Summer Pocket Journal of Margaret Hazelton," Hazelton Papers, M359, box 1, folder 10, USM.

90. Affidavit of Lewis R. Sitzer, COFO Records, MDAH; Lew Sitzer interviewed by author; testimony from John Suter presented publicly in a July 1964 mass meeting in Clarksdale, Board of Directors, Special Mississippi Investigating Committee, 1963–64, part 22, reel 10, group V, series B, box 14, NAACPMF; affidavit of John Suter, sworn 27 June, affidavit of Robert Mandel, sworn 26 July, and affidavit of Frederick W. Winyard, all COFO Records, MDAH.

91. Martínez, *Letters from Mississippi*, 155; Federal Removal and Habeas Corpus cases, box 16, Social Action Vertical File, COFO Papers, SHSW; WATS Line Digest, 9–11 July 1964, Community Relations Department, series 5, box 14, folder 9, CORE Papers, SHSW; *CPR*, 10 July 1964. For examples of further violence, see affidavit by J. D. Rayford, sworn on 30 June, COFO Records, MDAH; WATS line digest, 21 July 1964, Community Relations Department, series 5, box 14, folder 9, COFO Papers, SHSW; testimony presented publicly in a July 1964 mass meeting in Clarksdale, Board of Directors, Special Mississippi Investigating Committee, 1963–64, part 22, reel 10, group V, series B, box 14, NAACPMF; affidavit of James A. Campbell, sworn on the same day, COFO Records, MDAH; WATS Line Digest, 13 and 14 July, box 16, folder 5, Social Action Vertical File, COFO Papers, SHSW; and Zeman Diary, 4, M320, ZZP, USM.

92. Affidavit of Lafayette Surney, sworn 29 July, COFO Records, MDAH. See also WATS Line Digest, 9–11 July 1964, Community Relations Department, series 5, box 14, folder 9, CORE Papers, SHSW; letter, Hazelton to Zeman, 29 July 1964, M320, box 1, folder 2, ZZP, USM; anonymous entry dated 9 July, in Martínez, *Letters from Mississippi*, 83.

93. Israel Zwerling to LBJ, 13 July 1964, HU box 38, Gen HU2/ST24, 7/18/64–8/9/64, WHCF, LBJL. He also sent this letter to Attorney General Robert Kennedy. For a sample of the many letters Dr. Zwerling sent, see open letter by Donald Zwerling, 1 July 1964, Matthew Zwerling File, SHSW; Israel Zwerling to LBJ, 8 July 1964, HU box 38, Gen HU2/

ST24 7/1/64-7/17/64, WHCF, LBJL; Israel Zwerling to LBJ, 10 August 1964, HU box 39, HU2/ST 24, 8/10/64, WHCF, LBJL; and Zwerling to parents, 20 July 1964, Zwerling to parents and Sara, 30 June 1964, and Zwerling to parents, 3 July 1964, Matthew Zwerling File, SHSW.

94. Letter, Hazelton to Zeman, 29 July 1964, M320, box 1, folder 2, ZZP, USM; letter, Mark Fast to Robert Popkin, 30 July 1964, M320, box 1, folder 2, ZZP, USM.

95. Zeman Diary, 4, M320, ZZP, USM.

96. Zeman in conversation with author on the telephone, 27 January 2010.

97. Report on Mississippi Summer Project, 1964, by Charles Stewart (written September 1964), Charles Stewart File, SHSW.

98. Zwerling to parents, 30 June 1964, Matthew Zwerling File, SHSW.

99. Pigee, *Struggles: Part One*, 35, 72, 77.

100. A workshop report for 18-22 June (whether 1963 or 1964 is unclear) lists participants, including Cedonia Bonnabel Davis and Barbara Jean Gates—and Willie Griffin, Clara B. Harris, and Claudette Evone Wilder from Clarksdale; see box 155, folder 20, teacher training worship reports, 1963-64, SCLCP, MLKC.

101. Zwerling to parents and Sara, 23 June and 30 June 1964, Matthew Zwerling File, SHSW.

102. Coahoma County Branch NAACP newsletter, 12 January 1964, Coahoma County NAACP, box 31, Social Action Vertical File, SHSW.

103. Zeman interviewed by John Rachal, 18 April 1996, Oral History Project, USM.

104. Pigee, *Struggles: Part One*, 70; Vera M. Pigee interviewed by author, 12-13 October 2001.

105. This news came from Hazelton's letter to Zeman, 20 July 1964, M320, box 1, folder 2, ZZP, USM; and "Dear Folks," from Zwerling, 20 July and 3 August, M336, box 1, folder 1, Matthew Zwerling Papers, USM.

106. Zeman Diary, 4, M320, ZZP, 5, USM.

107. See "Teacher Surveys—MS 1965," box 155, folders 2 and 3, SCLCP, MLKC. Annell Ponder reported at the 1963 SCLC annual convention that in Coahoma County a good citizenship training program thrived. In the same folder, Ponder acknowledged, "The first classes were held in Clarksdale in 1961 under the direction of Mrs. Vera Mae Pigee and other NAACP leaders." She also noted the assistance of the local NAACP chapter in the SCLC's endeavor to create and sustain schools. See box 155, folder 26, field reports, 1962-65, Records of Annell Ponder, SCLCP, MLKC.

108. Zeman interview with John Rachal, 18 April 1996, Oral History Project, USM; Mat Zwerling interviewed by author.

109. Zeman Diary, M320, ZZP, USM.

110. Hamer and Moore quoted by Raines, *My Soul Is Rested*, 233, 236.

111. Zeman Diary, M320, ZZP, USM.

112. Aaron Henry interviewed by John Jones and John Dittmer, Clarksdale, 22 April 1981, Oral Histories, MDAH. See also box 130, folder 2, program for 1963, SCLCP, MLKC; box 130, folder 8, program for 1964, SCLCP, MLKC; box 130, folder 13, agenda for 1965, SCLCP, MLKC; and box 12, folder 37, Aaron Henry, March 1962-September 1966, MLK Papers, MLKC. Mary Jane Pigee Davis noted years later that calls would often come to

Henry's Fourth Street Drugstore to invite Vera Pigee to speak but that she would not get the messages and would find out later that Henry had taken the engagements—and the honoraria (conversations with Davis, 2009 and 2010).

113. Dittmer, *Local People*, 322; see also Matthew Zwerling File, SHSW.

114. For example, many Yale University students were harassed in October 1964 in Clarksdale; see Community Relations File, series 5, box 14, folder 9, CORE Papers, SHSW.

115. Freedom Registration Statistics for Second District, (northwest) Mississippi, 16 August 1964, box 8, folder 9, AMP, SHSW.

116. Current to Wilkins and Bishop Stephen G. Spottswood and the Members of the Board, memorandum, 29 December 1964, part 22, reel 11, group V, series B, box 14, NAACPMF; Current to Wilkins, memorandum, 9 November 1964, COFO, III A200, NAACPP.

117. See Chafe, *Never Stop Running*, 188–96; Cummings, *Pied Piper*, 257–63, 279–80; Henry and Evers to Wilkins, 13 January 1965, Mississippi State, 1964–65, III C75, NAACPP; and Aaron Henry interviewed by John Jones and John Dittmer, Clarksdale, 22 April 1981, Oral Histories, MDAH.

118. The Director of Branches to the Executive Committee, memorandum, 8 February 1965, part 22, reel 11, group V, series B, box 14, NAACPMF; see also memo to Wilkins from Current, n.d., box 72, IVH, folder 1230, AHP, TC.

119. Year-End Report, 6 January 1965, box 16, Burke Marshall Papers, JFKL, 4; *United States v. Mississippi* 380 U.S. 128, argued before the Supreme Court on 26 January 1965 and decided on 8 March 1965; see also Special Report from Student Nonviolent Coordinating Committee, 21 and 23 March 1965, box 3, folder 14, Howard Zinn Papers, SHSW.

120. Press Release by the U.S. Commission on Civil Rights, 20 May 1965, box 57, HU 2-7/ST EX, WHCF, LBJL. The commission held a hearing in Jackson beginning on 10 February 1965 to gather testimony on the denial of voting rights (see Press Release, U.S. Commission on Civil Rights, 7 January 1965, box 3, Lee C. White Papers, LBJL). On 21 May 1966, federal judges finally struck down Mississippi laws requiring literacy tests for voting ("3,800 Added to County's Voting Rolls," *CPR*, 23 May 1966).

121. Coahoma County Branch NAACP, *Cryer*, 1 May 1965, Coahoma County, 1964–65, III C73, NAACPP. The gathering raised $200, $150 of which went to the State Conference. See also Branch Activity Report, filed 17 May 1965, Annual Report: Mississippi, 1956–65, II C190, NAACPP. At this event, organizers suggested a Man of the Year Contest based on a membership drive. There is no evidence to suggest that this idea ever got off the ground.

122. Coahoma County Branch NAACP, *Cryer*, 30 August 1965, Coahoma County, 1964–65, III C73, NAACPP.

123. Rowland Evans and Robert Novak, "Inside Report: Mississippi Summer 1965," *New York Herald Tribune*, 26 August 1965. The reporters stressed that this reflected the state's numbers. The NAACP project registered 12,218 blacks, increasing registration by nearly 50 percent in less than five weeks, before the passage of the Voting Rights Act.

124. Ibid.; "Voter Registration Drive in Area Takes on 'New Look' for Summer," *CPR*, 16 July 1965, 10; "NAACP Summer Projects in Voter Registration—1965," box 69, IVF, folder 1185, AHP, TC.

125. See "NAACP Summer Projects in Voter Registration—1965," box 69, IVF, folder 1185, AHP, TC; "Illiterates on Roles Pose New Mississippi Problems," *MCA*, 20 September 1965; Coahoma County Branch NAACP, *Cryer*, 18 January 1966, IV C17, NAACPP; Coahoma County Citizens' Council to "Friends," n.d., III C73, Coahoma County 1964–65, NAACPP; and "NAACP Summer Projects in Voter Registration—1965," box 69, IVF, folder 1185, AHP, TC.

126. The Civil Rights Commission recommended sending registrars to counties with large numbers of unregistered African Americans and with active civil rights organizations. According to the lists from 14 July, eight Mississippi counties hosted federal examiners, including Coahoma, LeFlore, Madison, Yazoo, Jones, Bolivar, Holmes, and Pike counties, with others listed as possibilities (John Doar to Stephen Pollack, memorandum, 14 July 1965, Administrative History of the Department of Justice, box 6, vol. VII, Civil Rights Part Xa, Civil Rights Division Documentary Supplement, LBJL; Coahoma County Branch NAACP, *Cryer*, 27 September and 18 October 1965, Coahoma County, 1964–65, III C73, NAACPP). The commission also urged the community to go and vote, warning that once the registrar left, getting on the books might prove more difficult (Coahoma County Branch NAACP, *Cryer*, 3 November 1965, ibid.). See also "Summary of Voting Rights Participation as of 31 October 1965, in the Nineteen Counties Certified," box 3, Lee C. White Papers, LBJL; and Wilkie, *Dixie*, 162.

127. "Cumulative Totals on Voting Rights Examining," *Voting Rights Act: The First Months*, 35, box 375, Commission on Civil Rights, 11/23/65–12/4/65, WHCF, LBJL; Coahoma County Branch NAACP, *Cryer*, 11 February 1966, IV C17, NAACPP.

128. During the Mississippi State Conference meeting (held at the once-segregated Holiday Inn) in Clarksdale on 7 February, outside visitors stayed there and also at the Southern Inn and Plantation Court (Branch Activity Report filed 17 May 1965, Annual Reports: Mississippi, 1956–65, II C190, NAACPP).

129. The Mississippians United to Elect Negro Candidates, headquartered in Greenville and representing fourteen counties, was established by a few known SNCC workers: Lawrence Guyot, Joseph Harris, Charles McLaurin, Hollis Watkins, and Owen Brooks (director of the Delta Ministry, headquartered in Greenville). Unlike the Mississippi Voter Registration and Education League, which considered candidates from both races, the Mississippians United to Elect Negro Candidates concentrated on the 100 black Mississippians running for public office that year. See open letter from the leaders listed above, n.d., and 11 July 1967, box 1, folder 7, AMP, SHSW; and "Delta Ministry Reports," November 1967 newsletter, box 102, folder 14, Highlander Research and Education Center Papers, 1917–78, SHSW.

Chapter 5

1. Poem reprinted in Martínez, *Letters from Mississippi*, 312–13.

2. Coahoma County Branch NAACP, *Cryer*, 27 September 1965, Coahoma County, 1964–65, III C73, NAACPP.

3. "Desegregation at CHS Comes Quietly under Court's 'Transfer' Provision," *CPR*, 15 September 1965.

4. Coahoma County Branch NAACP, *Cryer*, 20 December 1965, Coahoma County, 1964–65, III C73, NAACPP; see also Aaron Henry to Peter Labassi, Department of Health, Education, and Welfare, 25 September 1967, Coahoma County, IV C17, NAACPP.

5. Department of Justice, Progress in the Field of Civil Rights: A Summary, 20 January to 20 November 1961, Year-End Report, box 16, Burke Marshall Papers, JFKL.

6. See "Status of Segregation-Desegregation," in *Statistical Summary of School Segregation-Desegregation in the Southern and Border States.* Lee C. White updated the figures so that the information is correct as of 15 March 1962 (Lee C. White Files, box 19, White House Staff Files, JFKL).

7. Roy Wilkins, 19 August 1962, Registration and Vote, Mississippi, 1956–65, III A270, NAACPP. See also open letter from the branch to members, hand-dated 1 January 1962, box 66, IVE, folder 1142, AHP, TC; and *USA v. State of Mississippi* civil action no. 3312, plaintiff's list of exhibits—supplemental in case documents, box 24, Burke Marshall Papers, JFKL.

8. Sara Cannon interviewed by author.

9. See chapter 1 for more on Higgins; Lillie Neal interviewed by author.

10. Katzenbach to LBJ, 6 January 1965, box 16, Year-End Report, 1, 6–8, Burke Marshall Papers, JFKL.

11. Medgar Evers's Monthly Report, 25 September 1963, 3, Charles Evers, 1963, III C243, NAACPP; Coahoma County Branch NAACP newsletter, n.d. (probably September/October 1963), box 66, IVE, folder 1138, AHP, TC; open letter from Vera Pigee, 18 September 1963, and open memo from R. L. Drew, chairman of Executive Committee of Coahoma County's NAACP branch, 16 September 1963, Coahoma County NAACP, box 31, Social Action Vertical Files, SHSW. The document also notes that the petition had the full backing of the state and national NAACP offices. See also letter to mayor and commissioners, 4 June 1963, box 66, IVE, folder 1140, AHP, TC.

12. Book X, 14 May 1964, 206, CBTM; *Rebecca E. Henry et al. v. Clarksdale Municipal Separate School District et al.* (DC 6428-K), ruling by Judge Keady, 10 November 1975, 2; Community Relations Department, series 5, box 25, folder 4, CORE Papers, SHSW; book X, 29 August 1963, 107, CBTM.

13. Wilkie, *Dixie*, 134.

14. 24 June 1964, 331, ConBTM; book X, 25 June 1964, 225, CBTM; book X, 21 July 1964, 250, CBTM; 13 July 1964, 361, ConBTM.

15. Book X, 21 July 1964, 250, CBTM; *Rebecca E. Henry et al. v. Clarksdale Municipal Separate School District et al.* (DC 6428-K), 10 November 1975, 18; Coahoma County Branch NAACP, *Cryer*, 1 October 1966, IV C17, NAACPP. See also Crespino, *In Search of Another Country*, 180–81.

16. Book X, 11 March 1965, 370–72, CBTM; *Rebecca Henry et al. v. Clarksdale Municipal Separate School District et al.* (DC 6428-K), 15 November 1965, proceedings before Judge Claude Clayton in Clarksdale, U.S. District Court for the Northern District of Mississippi, Delta Division, Court Clerk's Office, Oxford, Mississippi. The Geographic Attendance Zone Plan assigned students to schools in relation to their residence "on the sole basis of geography and with no regard for race, color or national origin" ("Federal Rights under

School Desegregation Law"). For information on Tynes, see Ellard, "History of Clarksdale, Mississippi, Public Schools," 95–96.

17. Stan Boyd interviewed by author; Boyd, "Mississippi on Trial."

18. "Judge Hears Local School Issue Argued," *CPR*, 4 August 1965; book XI, 20 August 1965, 49, CBTM; "Local School Desegregation Ruling Delayed," *CPR*, 4 October 1965, 1.

19. Coahoma County Branch NAACP, *Cryer*, 30 August 1965, Coahoma County, 1964–65, III C73, NAACPP. Clayton was born in Tupelo in 1909 and worked in a private practice there and as a county attorney in the 1930s, resuming this work after serving in World War II. Keady, *All Rise*, 56–57.

20. Kluger, *Simple Justice*, 760; "Most of Dixie's School Districts Desegregated This Year, Survey Shows," *CPR*, 20 September 1965.

21. "Desegregation at CHS Comes Quietly under Court's 'Transfer' Provision," *CPR*, 15 September 1965. Cora Lee Hicks interviewed by author.

22. Pigee, *Struggles: Part One*, 40, 42; quote about Christians from Rebecca Hood-Adams, "Local NAACP Marks 50 Years," *CPR*, 25 October 2003.

23. For an example of intolerable circumstances, see Curry, *Silver Rights*. See also "An Evaluation of School Desegregation in Mississippi," by Kenneth L. Dean, box 1, folder 7, Mississippi Council on Human Relations Collection, SHSW. The Advisory Committee met on 16 April 1966 at the Heidelberg Hotel in Jackson to discuss the state's desegregation efforts to date. See program for the Conference on Education Desegregation, box 7, folder 9, AMP, SHSW.

24. "Judge Hears Local School Issue Argued," *CPR*, 4 August 1965; Johnston, *Mississippi's Defiant Years*, 308. The Citizens' Council produced a magazine called *How to Start a Private School*. Around the state in 1964 and 1965, private schools opened—either in old buildings constructed during the 1950s' consolidation program or in churches and private homes (ibid., 309). In January 1968, the representatives of sixty schools met in Jackson at an organizational meeting of the Mississippi Private School Association.

25. Coahoma County Branch NAACP, *Cryer*, 27 September 1965, Coahoma County, 1964–65, III C73, NAACPP; Coahoma County Branch NAACP, *Cryer*, 18 January 1966, IV C17, NAACPP. For studies on other minority groups in Mississippi, see Quan, *Lotus among the Magnolias*; and Loewen, *Mississippi Chinese*.

26. Book XI, 16 August 1966, 287, CBTM; book XII, 12 October 1967, 152, CBTM.

27. Health, Education, and Welfare Report, "Enrollment of Negro Pupils in Southern and Border States," December 1966, box 53, Gen HU2-5, 5/16/66–12/8/66, WHCF, LBJL; Health, Education, and Welfare release, 17 May 1968, box 52, HU2-5, 1/1/68–6/19/68, WHCF, LBJL.

28. *CPR*, 1 September, 22 September, 23 September 1969. See James M. Mohead, weekly report, 9/22/69–9/26/69, Coahoma County folder file, SCP, MDAH. James Mohead had previously worked for five years with the Washington, D.C., police department and for four years with the Clarksdale police before working for the Sovereignty Commission (Johnston, *Mississippi's Defiant Years*, 353). The Committee of Parents Respecting the Children consisted of parents concerned about the integration transition and subsequent treatment of their children. It is unclear if it served as a subgroup within the local NAACP branch,

but it is likely. See "Negro Youths Jailed after March at School," *CPR*, 23 September 1969; "Negro Youths Freed in City," *CPR*, 24 September 1969; "For Blacks Only," *CPR*, 24 September 1969; "Negroes Map New Marches," *CPR*, 26 September 1969; "Dissident Negroes March to Spotlight Grievances," *CPR*, 27 September 1969; "Negroes March to City Hall Again Monday"; an editorial, "The Marches," *CPR*, 30 September 1969; and James Mohead, weekly report, 9/29/69–10/3/69, Roberta McCaskill files, SCP, MDAH. See also *Rebecca E. Henry et al. v. Clarksdale Municipal Separate School District et al.* (DC 6428-K), petition for injunction, filed 1 October 1969 (copy in box 66, IVE, folder 1145, AHP, TC); and *CPR*, 18 October 1969. Ben C. Collins was fired from his position as chief of police earlier that year for "unbecoming" conduct, which included public drunkenness, improper use of a police car, some shady side business deals conducted while in uniform, and undue brutality in the jails. See Wilkie, *Dixie*, 191–92.

29. Petition from the Student Committee in Support of Freedom and Justice to the Coahoma County Branch of the NAACP, 21 December 1969, box 66, IVE, folder 1147, AHP, TC.

30. Book XIV, 27 September, 30 September 1969, 35–37, CBTM.

31. *Henry v. Clarksdale Municipal Separate School District 409F. 2d. 682 (Clarksdale I)*, Fifth Circuit Court of Appeals, New Orleans; *Rebecca E. Henry et al. v. Clarksdale Municipal Separate School District et al.* (DC 6428-K), 10 November 1975, 3.

32. Keady, *All Rise*, 59, 63, 93–98, 106.

33. "City School Status Reviewed at Hearing," *CPR*, 4 October 1969; "NAACP Calls for Boycott in Clarksdale and Coahoma County," n.d., in box 66, IVE, folder 1147, AHP, TC; Coahoma County Branch NAACP, *Cryer*, 15 November 1969, box 66, IVE, folder 1147, AHP, TC; Coahoma County Branch NAACP, *Cryer*, n.d. (around 20 October 1969), box 66, IVE, folder 1147, AHP, TC; *CPR*, 7 November 1969; flyer from Coahoma County Parent and Teacher Association and Coahoma County Branch NAACP, IV C17, NAACPP.

34. Book XIV, 25 November 1969, 81, and 26 November 1969, 85, CBTM.

35. *Rebecca E. Henry et al. v. Clarksdale Municipal Separate School District et al.* (DC 6428-K), 10 November 1975, 4; book XIV, special meeting, 17 December 1969, 97–98, CBTM; Keady, *All Rise*, 107.

36. See *Alexander v. Holmes County Board of Education* 396 U.S. 1218 (1969). The crux of this decision stated, "Continued operation of racially segregated schools under the standard of 'all deliberate speed' is no longer constitutionally permissible. School districts must immediately terminate dual school systems based on race and operate only unitary school systems." See *Rebecca E. Henry et al. v. Clarksdale Municipal Separate School District et al.* (DC 6428-K), 10 November 1975, 6. The *Clarksdale Press Register* printed large portions of the decision on the front page on 15 January 1970 under the headline "Clarksdale City Schools Receive Court Directions."

37. Book XIV, 15 January and 29 January 1970, 105–7, CBTM.

38. Coahoma County Branch NAACP, *Cryer*, 12 January 1970, box 67, IVE, folder 1149, AHP, TC; "March against School Ruling Staged by Clarksdale Whites," *MCA*, 17 January 1970.

39. "Clarksdale Reaction to School Decision Varies," *MCA*, 24 January 1970, 3.

40. Joyce Kendricks interviewed by author. See "875 Children in County Attend Non-

public Schools," *CPR*, 21 September 1965. For a retrospective history on private schools in the county, see *CPR*, 6 April 2008, special edition, "Leadership and Education," 4c, 5c.

41. Joyce Kendricks interviewed by author.

42. Book XIV, 5 February 1970, 113, and 12 February 1970, 123, CBTM.

43. Book XIV, special meeting, 26 March 1970, 154–55, 9 April 1970, 162, 14 May 1970, 188, 17 August 1970, 263, 17 September 1970, 301, 1 October 1970, 306, and 12 November 1970, 334, all CBTM.

44. Alpha Norphlet interviewed by author.

45. Jean Cauthen interviewed by author.

46. Brenda Renee Luckett interviewed by author.

47. Book XIV, 27 April 1970, 178, 25 August 1970, 271, and 3 September 1970, 275–76, all CBTM.

48. Book XIV, 14 May 1970, 183, 11 June 1970, 197, and 8 October 1970, 317, all CBTM.

49. "Statement from Meeting of Thursday night, July 17, 1970," from Coahoma County Branch NAACP, box 67, IVE, folder 1150, AHP, TC. This document was distributed widely to the plaintiff's attorney, the national NAACP office, the Department of Justice, the superintendents of the city and county schools, the mayor, the black assistant superintendent (Jerome Stampley), the president of Coahoma Junior College, and the head of Aggie High School.

50. Ibid. The students continued to complain in a later meeting on 24 September. Principal Ellard refused to let the seniors choose their class rings, allowing only one design. The election of cheerleaders was staged in a way that prevented black students from voting, resulting in an all-white squad ("NAACP Youths Discuss Drug Abuse, Problems Arising from Desegregation of Schools," *CPR*, 25 September 1970).

51. Brenda Renee Luckett interviewed by author.

52. Lillie Neal interviewed by author.

53. Joyce Kendricks interviewed by author.

54. Letter to the members and congregation of First United Methodist Church, Clarksdale, n.d., box 66, IVE, folder 1137, AHP, TC; Keady, *All Rise*, 107.

55. Book XIV, 19 November 1970, 337, and 7 February 1971, 381, both CBTM.

56. Book XIV, 8 April 1971, 440, CBTM. Only 1.15 percent of the 1969–70 budget came from federal funds. Book XV, August 1971, 89, CBTM.

57. Book XIV, 10 December 1970, 351, and January 14, 1971, 370, both CBTM.

58. Book XIV, 11 February 1971, 384, CBTM; book 20, 1 February 1971, 510, Minutes of the Board of the Mayor and Commissioners, Clarksdale; see also Pigee, *Struggles: Part Two*, 53. The Espy family owned the largest black business in Mississippi, the Century Funeral Home, which was a chain throughout the Delta. Henry's brother Mike would become U.S. representative for Mississippi's Second District and secretary of agriculture in the Clinton administration. See Nash and Taggart, *Mississippi Politics*.

59. Book XV, 23 June 1971, 46, and 14 October 1971, 218, CBTM. Espy's role is further cemented in the minutes when in February 1972 the headline was "Mr. Espy Speaks for His Community" (book XV, 10 February 1972, 228, CBTM).

60. Vera Harrell interviewed by author.

61. Sara Cannon interviewed by author.

62. Book XV, 10 August 1971, 100, and 12 August 1971, 114, CBTM; Vera Harrell interviewed by author; Keady, *All Rise*, 127.

63. Book XIV, 21 July 1970, 243, CBTM; Joyce Kendricks interviewed by author.

64. Joyce Kendricks interviewed by author; book XV, 10 June 1971, 30, CBTM.

65. *Swann v. Charlotte-Mecklenberg Board of Education* (1971) ruled on busing as a particular desegregation technique. The Supreme Court ruled that "the preservation of neighborhood schools was not sacrosanct" (Kluger, *Simple Justice*, 768); book XV, 23 September 1971, 142, CBTM. The letter was dated 9 September.

66. Book XV, 23 September 1971, 142, CBTM.

67. See *Rebecca Henry v. Clarksdale Municipal Separate School District et al.*, U.S. 5th Circuit Court of Appeals, 22 June 1973 (480 F.2d 583).

68. School board figures submitted to the court hearing, 25 September 1972, before Judge Keady, U.S. District Court, ibid.

69. Hearing before Judge Keady, U.S. District Court, *Henry* case, ibid., 25 September 1972, 31; book XV, 3 August 1972, 370, CBTM. See also *Rebecca E. Henry et al. v. Clarksdale Municipal Separate School District et al.* (DC 6428-K), 10 November 1975, 9.

70. Book XV, 22 June 1972, 349, CBTM.

71. Sara Cannon interviewed by author.

72. Court record of *Jonathan Harris et al. v. Board of Trustees of the Clarksdale Municipal Separate School District et al.* (DC-73-29-K), before District Court Judge William Keady at Greenville, Mississippi, copy in DHP; book XVI, 1 March 1973 (special meeting), CBTM; Joyce Kendricks interviewed by author.

73. Book XVI, 1 March 1973, 41, CBTM.

74. Court record of *Jonathan Harris et al. v. Board of Trustees of the Clarksdale Municipal Separate School District et al.* (DC-73-29-K). Jerome Stampley was hired as superintendent of the segregated black schools in 1962 after the resignation of W. A. Higgins. The board did not promote the equally qualified Frank B. McCune, the registrar at Coahoma Junior College, because it hoped that Stampley would be unhindered by community pressure to allow him to execute his job to their satisfaction (see book IX, 9 August 1962, 481, CBTM).

75. "Black Pupils Protest, Boycott City Schools," *CPR*, 20 February 1973, 1.

76. Joyce Kendricks interviewed by author.

77. *Jonathan Harris et al. v. Board of Trustees of the Clarksdale Municipal Separate School District et al.* (DC-73-29-K).

78. "A Report on the Black History Week Episode, Clarksdale High School Officials and Black Student Confrontation, February and March 1973," 27 March 1973, by Aaron Henry, in his capacity as Mississippi State Conference president, box 67, IVE, folder 1157, AHP, TC.

79. Vernon Dahmer was a businessman and an active president of the Forrest County chapter of the NAACP. His house was firebombed in January 1966; his wife and children escaped, but Dahmer stayed to protect his property and died from his wounds a day later.

80. Lillie Neal interviewed by author. It is unclear what happened to the other two boys.

81. 6 August 1973, box 67, IVE, folder 1158, AHP, TC.

82. Document dated 4 January 1974, box 67, IVE, folder 1160, AHP, TC; "NAACP, City Break," *CPR*, 12 February 1974; letter to Mayor Joseph Nosef Jr. and Commissioners,

1 January 1974, box 67, IVE, folder 1160, AHP, TC; open letter to the Citizens of Clarksdale, 12 April 1974, box 67, IVE, folder 1161, AHP, TC.

83. Figures submitted each semester to the U.S. District Court for the Northern District of Mississippi, Delta Division, as per the order of 25 January 1971 by Judge William C. Keady, U.S. District Court Clerk's Office, Oxford, Mississippi.

84. All of these statistics, including the information in Table 6, is taken from the biannual reports to the U.S. District Court for the Northern Division of Mississippi as per the order of 25 January 1974 by Judge William C. Keady, U.S. District Court Clerk's Office, Oxford, Mississippi. Many thanks to Mrs. Nancy Smith, daughter-in-law of the late District Judge Orma Smith and employee in the court clerk's office for her assistance.

85. Adair, *Desegregation*, 1, 3, 4, 11.

86. "Consent Order Regarding Elementary School Pupil Assignments and Other Matters," *Rebecca E. Henry et al. v. Clarksdale Municipal Separate School District et al.*, before Judge Keady, 30 April 1984.

87. Keady, *All Rise*, 109–10, 113, 114.

88. Gooden interviewed by Homer Hill.

89. Reprinted in Martínez, *Letters from Mississippi*, 296–97.

Chapter 6

1. Report on Mississippi Summer Project, 1964, by Charles Stewart (written September 1964), Charles Stewart File, SHSW.

2. Martínez, *Letters from Mississippi*, 70.

3. Letter, 7 July 1964, in ibid., 228.

4. Catherine Ross, "Early Skirmishes with Poverty: The Historical Roots of Head Start," in Zigler and Valentine, *Project Head Start*, 37; Robert F. Clark, *War on Poverty*, vii.

5. For more in this vital new field, see Germany, *New Orleans after the Promises*; Kiffmeyer, *Reformers to Radicals*; de Jong, *Invisible Enemy*; Ashmore, *Carry It On*; Greene, *Our Separate Ways*; Rhonda Y. Williams, *Politics of Public Housing*; and Orleck, *Storming Caesar's Palace*.

6. For a detailed study of Coahoma County's program, see Donald C. Mosley and D. C. Williams Jr., "An Analysis and Evaluation of A Community Action Anti-Poverty Program in the Mississippi Delta," July 1967, RG 381, OEO Community Services Administration Office of Operations, Migrant Division, Box 50, Grant Files 1966–1971, NARA (hereinafter referred to as Mosley and Williams). For more general information, see Ellsworth and Ames, *Critical Perspectives*; Ames and Ellsworth, *Women Reformed, Women Empowered*; Zigler and Styfco, *Head Start and Beyond*; Zigler and Muenchow, *Head Start*; Sissel, *Staff, Parents, and Politics in Head Start*; Zigler and Valentine, *Project Head Start*; and Polly Greenberg, *Devil Has Slippery Shoes*.

7. "Anti-poverty Bill Signed by President," *CPR*, 20 August, 1964, 7; Ellsworth and Ames, *Critical Perspectives*, xii.

8. Bennie Gooden interviewed by Homer Hill; "I Am a Man," in Juan Williams, *My Soul Looks Back in Wonder*.

9. Gooden interviewed by Homer Hill.

10. Mosley and Williams, "An Analysis and Evaluation," 3–4.

11. Charles Evers, report to national office, 29 February 1964, III C243, NAACPP.

12. Another source on the Community Action Agency in Coahoma County is Hill, "Coahoma Opportunities, Incorporated."

13. Gooden interviewed by Homer Hill; see also Vernon Keys interviewed by Homer Hill; and Ellsworth and Ames, *Critical Perspectives*, 148, 151.

14. Mosley and Williams, "An Analysis and Evaluation," 7.

15. Wilkie, *Dixie*, 165, 167.

16. Gooden interviewed by Homer Hill.

17. Ellsworth and Ames, *Critical Perspectives*, 148, 151.

18. Mosley and Williams, "An Analysis and Evaluation," 7–11, 17.

19. Carr interviewed by Homer Hill; Andrew Carr interviewed by author.

20. Lemann, *Promised Land*, 314.

21. Andrew Carr interviewed by author.

22. Quoted in Nick Kotz, "Wealthy White Aids Negro Cause," n.d., clipping from Andrew Carr's collection in author's possession.

23. Carr interviewed by Homer Hill.

24. "'Anti-poverty' Goals Outlined in City Today," *CPR*, 18 May 1965.

25. Box X, 23 April 1965, 405, CBTM.

26. Hill, "Coahoma Opportunities, Incorporated"; "Federal Official Notes Capital Hopes to Make Area Anti-poverty Showcase," *CPR*, 2 May 1965. Six whites and six blacks were on this board.

27. "OEO Official Gives Details of Aid Plan," *CPR*, 4 June 964; Coahoma County Branch NAACP, *Cryer*, 31 May 1965, Coahoma County, 1964–65, III C73, NAACPP.

28. Hill, "Coahoma Opportunities, Incorporated"; "Board of Education Denies Refusal of Buildings for 'Head Start' Projects," *CPR*, 12 June 1965.

29. "'Head Start' Projects to Begin Here Monday," *CPR*, 18 June 1965; box X, 28 June 1965, 435, CBTM.

30. *CPR*, 12 June 1965; book X, 13 May 1965, 415–16, CBTM.

31. Letters included in Mosley and Williams, "An Analysis and Evaluation," 12–15.

32. Ibid., 18–22.

33. Hill, "Coahoma Opportunities, Incorporated," 39; *CPR*, 22 June 1965.

34. *CPR*, 21 June 1965.

35. "'Head Start' Projects Kicked Off Here," *CPR*, 22 June 1965.

36. Hill, "Coahoma Opportunities, Incorporated."

37. Dudley Morris to Theodore Berry, memorandum, 18 February 1966, and Thomas Karter, Chief of Migrant Branch, report, 21 February 1966, RG381, Community Services Administration, OEO, Community Action Program Office, Records of the Director (Theodore Berry), Subject Files, 1965–69, box 28, Mississippi Food Demonstration Project, NARA. See also Gene Roberts, "Delta Area of Mississippi in Turmoil," *NYT*, 7 February 1966, 1.

38. William Drayton and Eric Gold, "Structure for Action and Communities: An Analysis of Community Action Agencies" (Drayton Report), 1965, RG381, Community Services

Administration, OEO, Community Action Program Office: Records of the Director, Subject Files, 1965–69, box 27, 1966, NARA.

39. CDGM did not operate in Coahoma County but did in Bolivar, Tallahatchie, and Sunflower counties, all of which border it, as well as in nineteen other counties.

40. Sargent Shriver noted in the 1970s: "The CDGM was an outstanding success in the history of the War on Poverty, [and] I do not think we could have had Head Start operating effectively in Mississippi without it" (Zigler and Valentine, *Project Head Start*, 61).

41. Robert F. Clark, *War on Poverty*, 153; Johnston, *Mississippi's Defiant Years*, 286–88; Ellsworth and Ames, *Critical Perspectives*, xii; Zigler and Valentine, *Project Head Start*, 62, 63; "'Head Start' Audit Indicates Irregularities," *CPR*, 3 September 1965; Wilkie, *Dixie*, 165.

42. For example, see Robert C. Weaver, secretary of Housing and Urban Development, to Sargent Shriver, 8 April 1966, RG381, Community Services Administration, OEO, Community Action Program Office: Records of the Director (Theodore Berry), Subject Files, 1965–69, box 28, Mississippi Housing, 1966, NARA.

43. Johnston, *Mississippi's Defiant Years*, 290. For an overview of the messy history of CDGM and MAP, see Dittmer, *Local People*, 369–88; and Payne, *I've Got the Light of Freedom*, 342–45.

44. Mosley and Williams, "An Analysis and Evaluation," i.

45. Coahoma County Branch NAACP, *Cryer*, 31 May 1965, Coahoma County, 1964–65, III C73, NAACPP; *CPR*, 4 June 1965.

46. Coahoma County Branch NAACP, *Cryer*, 18 October 1965, Coahoma County, 1964–65, III C73, NAACPP. The Food Stamp Act was passed in 1964 as part of the War on Poverty.

47. Gooden interviewed by Homer Hill.

48. Scarbrough Report, 27 July 1965, Coahoma County folder file, SCP, MDAH.

49. Hill, "Coahoma Opportunities, Incorporated," 51; Coahoma County Branch NAACP, *Cryer*, 27 September 1965, NAACPP III C73, Coahoma County, 1964–65; Lemann, *Promised Land*, 314.

50. Quoted in Nick Kotz, "Wealthy White Aids Negro Cause," n.d., clipping from Andrew Carr's collection in author's possession.

51. Gooden interviewed by Homer Hill.

52. Incorporation, RG381, Community Services Administration, OEO, Office of Operations, Migrant Division, Grant Files, 1966–71, box 148, NARA; "Reorganized Anti-poverty Program Due," *CPR*, 26 October 1965; Mosley and Williams, "An Analysis and Evaluation," 23.

53. Gooden interviewed by Homer Hill.

54. Hill, "Coahoma Opportunities, Incorporated," 53. Vernon Jordan continued to work in civil rights and later served as a close advisor to President Bill Clinton.

55. Brenda Renee Luckett interviewed by author.

56. Mosley and Williams, "An Analysis and Evaluation," 10–11. The Sovereignty Commission spearheaded the investigation; see Scarbrough Report, 13 August 1965, Coahoma County folder file, SCP, MDAH; Lemann, *Promised Land*, 313; Carr interviewed by Homer

Hill; and Keys interviewed by Homer Hill. Epps later moved his activism to Memphis, where he played a role in the sanitation workers' strike in 1968.

57. "Civil Rights Group Asks More Registrars in Mississippi," *CPR*, 29 September 1965.

58. "'War on Poverty' Grant Announced," *CPR*, 21 September 1965. Roessler, a local investment worker, took home a salary of $13,500 from COI for his services as director. Roessler was a stockbroker from Pennsylvania who served in the U.S. Air Force in World War II before marrying a farmer's daughter in Clarksdale. He actually served as president of the Citizens' Council but "proved to be a superb administrator whose business acumen and rapport with COI's employees, contract agencies, participant leadership, and regional, state, and local officials, bridged an important gap between the agency and the community" (Hill, "Coahoma Opportunities, Incorporated," 73). See also Lemann, *Promised Land*, 316; RG381, Community Services Administration, OEO, Office of Operations, Migrant Division, Grant Files, 1966–71, box 149, NARA; and Mosley and Williams, "An Analysis and Evaluation," 87. For a list of all the board members, see Scarbrough Report, 15 October 1965, Charles Stringer folder file, SCP, MDAH.

59. Gooden interviewed by Homer Hill.

60. *CPR*, 26 October 1965; Keys interviewed by Homer Hill; Mosley and Williams, "An Analysis and Evaluation," 25–33.

61. For another brief narrative of these events, see Lemann, *Promised Land*, 317.

62. *CPR*, 26 October 1965. The paper listed resignations from Ed Jenkins, Vincent Brocato, Joseph Ellis, Joel Williams, Charles Wells, Semmes Luckett, Pete Williams Jr., Charles Moore, Joe Weeks, Leon Bramlett, Chester Brewer, Leon Porter, D. H. Bailey, and Marvin Sigmon Jr.

63. Carr interviewed by Homer Hill. Ten whites and two black members came to the board: Montyne Fox (director of the Coahoma County Welfare Department); Pauline Clark (with farming interests in the county); Rev. Charles Chambers Jr. (pastor of St. George's Episcopal Church); Rev. W. A. Pennington (pastor of Lyon Methodist Church); Dr. Frank Marascalo; Dr. W. N. Crowson; Carter Stovall (planter); Julian Bloom (scrap metal dealer); Haywood Pickel (machinist); T. J. Perry (contractor); James Gilliam (black retired post office employee); and J. C. Pettis (black farmer) ("Anti-poverty Board Filled," *CPR*, 5 November 1965). See also "Anti-poverty Program Gradually Shaping Up Here," *CPR*, 3 November 1965; and Carr interviewed by author.

64. Wilson interviewed by Homer Hill; Mayo Wilson interviewed by author. When he left Head Start in 1971, Wilson became the first black vice president of a bank in Coahoma County (Catchings interviewed by Homer Hill). Mrs. Daugherty then took over as director (Keys interviewed by Homer Hill).

65. Keys interviewed by Homer Hill.

66. Wilson interviewed by Homer Hill.

67. Ibid.; interview with Moynihan on PBS, http://www.pbs.org/fmc/interviews/moynihan.htm; Zigler and Valentine, *Project Head Start*, 46.

68. Keys interviewed by Homer Hill.

69. Wilson interviewed by Homer Hill.

70. Keys interviewed by Homer Hill.

71. Book XI, 10 March 1966, 168, CBTM.

72. Keys interviewed by Homer Hill.

73. See book 22, 29 August 1974, 567, and book 23, 7 April and 1 May 1975, 142, 160, Minutes of the Board of the Mayor and Commissioners, Clarksdale.

74. Robert F. Clark, *War on Poverty*, 179.

75. Keys interviewed by Homer Hill; "Anti-poverty Effort Pushed," *CPR*, 3 November 1965, 18; "Legal Aid Program for County Approved," *CPR*, 12 March 1966; "'War on Poverty' Grant Announced," *CPR*, 21 September 1965; *CPR*, 12 March 1966; Mosley and Williams, "An Analysis and Evaluation," 52–55.

76. Gooden interviewed by Homer Hill.

77. Wilson interviewed by Homer Hill. In 1969, Donald Rumsfeld, OEO director, elevated legal services to an independent operating division (Robert F. Clark, *War on Poverty*, 186).

78. Scarbrough Report, 27 July and 13 August 1965, Coahoma County folder File, SCP, MDAH; Coahoma County Branch NAACP, *Cryer*, 20 December 1965 and 7 March 1966, Coahoma County, 1964–65, III C73, NAACPP.

79. Keys interviewed by Homer Hill.

80. Gooden interviewed by Homer Hill; see also Lemann, *Promised Land*. Curtis Wilkie wrote a series of articles in the *Clarksdale Press Register* over six days in March 1966 about the changing nature of farm labor. See "Various Factors Changing Farm Labor," *CPR*, 7 March 1966, 10, and 8 and 9 March 1966, and "Workers-Aid Program Devised," 10 and 11 March 1966.

81. Gooden interviewed by Homer Hill; Mosley and Williams, "An Analysis and Evaluation," 67–70.

82. "General and Statistical Information," October 1965, Carnegie Public Library, Clarksdale; 1994 County and City Data Book, Population, Total, and by Race for Clarksdale, Mississippi, Census 2000 analyzed by the Social Science Data Analysis Network; Richard L. Forstall, U.S. Bureau of the Census, "Population of Counties by Decennial Census: 1900 to 1990." The Coahoma County numbers include the population of Clarksdale in the calculation.

83. Gooden interviewed by Homer Hill; Mosley and Williams, "An Analysis and Evaluation," 42; Keys interviewed by Homer Hill; Catchings interviewed by Homer Hill.

84. Catchings interviewed by Homer Hill; Keys interviewed by Homer Hill; *CPR*, 3 November 1965, 18.

85. Box 67, IVE, folder 1150, AHP, TC; Gooden interviewed by Homer Hill.

86. Wilson interviewed by Homer Hill.

87. Mosley and Williams, "An Analysis and Evaluation," 45.

88. "Wild Welcome Here Ends Kennedy-Clark Delta Tour," *CPR*, 12 April 1967; Wilkie, *Dixie*, 169.

89. Gooden interviewed by Homer Hill.

90. Wilson interviewed by Homer Hill.

91. Keys interviewed by Homer Hill.

92. *CPR*, 1 July 1972.

93. Ibid. See Weems, *Desegregating the Dollar*, for a full discussion about the power of money to change white attitudes.

94. There were a few victories. In mid-July 1968, Robert L. Adams, operator of the Picnic-Er drive-in, was fined $2,000 for contempt of a court order, violating the Civil Rights Act of 1964. Curtis Wilkie described Adams as "obviously shaken by the decision," which was handed down by Judge Keady in the U.S. District Court ("Drive-In Operator Fined $2,000 for Contempt in Civil Rights Case," *CPR*, 18 July 1968).

95. Catchings interviewed by Homer Hill.

96. Vernon Keys interviewed by Homer Hill.

97. Ibid.

98. Mayo Wilson interviewed by author.

99. See chap. 5.

100. Wilson interviewed by Homer Hill.

101. Fannie Lou Hamer interviewed by Anne and Howard Romaine, 1966, Anne Romaine File, SHSW.

102. Johnston, *Mississippi's Defiant Years*, 291; Wilkie, *Dixie*, 165, and see especially chap. 4.

103. Lemann, *Promised Land*, 326.

104. Coahoma County Branch NAACP, *Cryer*, 1 October 1966, IV C17, NAACPP; Aaron Henry to Ted Barry, OEO, 27 August 1966, box 66, IVE, folder 1142, AHP, TC.

105. Johnston, *Mississippi's Defiant Years*, 291.

106. Polly Greenberg, *Devil Has Slippery Shoes*, 64; Ellsworth and Ames, *Critical Perspectives*, 336.

107. Pigee, *Struggles: Part One*, 94–96.

108. John Morsell to Lucille Black, memorandum, 10 July 1969, IV C17, NAACPP.

109. Pigee, *Struggles: Part One*, 109, 105–7; Pigee, *Struggles: Part Two*, 67.

110. Pigee, *Struggles: Part One*, 95.

111. Ibid., 97. Pigee's reactions reflected a new mood of distrust toward the government and the leadership it spawned, "a diffuse and instantaneous one with little chance to build strength and unity over time," as Lemann noted (Lemann, *Promised Land*, 164).

112. Pigee, *Struggles: Part One*, 110, 115, 122. Pigee was secretary of the branch in 1972, according to a letter to Roy Wilkins from Aaron Henry (box 72, IVH, folder 1230, AHP, TC).

113. Box 67, IVE, folder 1158, AHP, TC. According to Mary Jane Pigee Davis, Henry nominated Luckett to the post to run against Pigee (conversations with author, 2010).

114. Brenda Renee Luckett interviewed by author.

115. "Announcement for Freedom Fund Banquet," 21 April 1970, box 67, IVE, folder 1150, AHP, TC; Coahoma County, 1964–65, III C73, NAACPP; James Brown Jr., National Youth Director, to Vera Pigee, 13 November 1973, IVE, 10, NAACPP.

116. Quoted in Nick Kotz, "Wealthy White Aids Negro Cause," n.d., clipping from Andrew Carr's collection, in author's possession.

117. Mayo Wilson recalled having to go to Atlanta and Washington, D.C., on numerous occasions around 1968 to 1970 with others to lobby President Nixon, who intended to cut programs (Wilson interviewed by Homer Hill).

118. OEO General Correspondence, 1967–69, RG381, Community Service Administration, OEO, Executive Secretariat, box 13, NARA; "History of OEO during the Nixon Ad-

ministration, 1973," by Kenneth Munden, RG381, Records of the Community Service Administration, OEO, Records of the Office of Planning Research and Evaluation, box 107, NARA; "Weekly Compilation of Presidential Documents 9:9:196–211 (5 March 1973), box 107, NARA.

119. Mosley and Williams, "An Analysis and Evaluation," 76, 80, 90, 91.

120. Catchings interviewed by Homer Hill.

121. See Keys interviewed by Homer Hill. The Mississippi Delta Council for Farm Workers' Opportunities, Inc., organized in 1971 as a nonprofit, now operates programs to assist migrants and seasonal farmworkers in Mississippi. Headquartered in Clarksdale, it is a private organization (http://www.mdcfwoi.org).

122. Curtis Wilkie, "When Races Came Together in Mississippi," n.d. (probably 1995), in Kellogg Cross Group Seminar: Mississippi: Conflict and Change, 8–12 October 1994, MDAH. See Martin Luther King Jr.'s speech delivered at Riverside Church in New York City, 4 April 1967, "Beyond Vietnam: A Time to Break Silence," widely available on the internet.

123. Catchings interviewed by Homer Hill.

124. Wilkie, *Dixie*, 168.

125. Catchings interviewed by Homer Hill.

126. Trattner, *From Poor Law to Welfare State*, 370.

127. Robert F. Clark, *War on Poverty*, 166.

128. In 1997, Community Action Agencies served 20 percent of the poor in forty-four states, totaling about 7 million poor. With the block grants, the federal role in poverty alleviation is minimal at best (Robert F. Clark, *War on Poverty*, 71–74, 148).

129. Lemann, *Promised Land*, 329. Gooden died on 19 February 2009; see obituary, *CPR*, 26 February 2009.

130. Robert F. Clark, *War on Poverty*, 3. In 2000, 21,291,000 whites lived below the poverty line (9.4 percent of the white population); 7,901,000 African Americans lived below the line (22.1 percent of the black population); and 7,155,000 Hispanics lived below the line (11.3 percent of the Hispanic population).

131. Robert F. Clark, *War on Poverty*, 5.

132. "Profile of Selected Economic Characteristics for Coahoma County, Mississippi, 2000." These figures are not broken down by racial characteristics, but 29.6 percent of households received their income through social security income; 12.6 percent received supplementary social security; and 13.3 percent had retirement income.

133. Information on U.S. counties in 1996, http://www.census.gov/statab/USA98/28/0.27.tx. Statewide, Coahoma County still languishes, along with its Delta neighbors, at the bottom rungs of Mississippi's statistics. Coahoma County's median income in 1998 was $21,072, the ninth lowest in the state out of eighty-two counties. In terms of poverty, about 8,896 people, or 28.7 percent of people of all ages, were in poverty, the seventh lowest in the state.

134. Mayo Wilson interviewed by author, 14 January 2004.

135. Hill, "Coahoma Opportunities, Incorporated," 48, 49, 50.

Epilogue

1. "An Overview of President Clinton's Trip to America's New Markets"; "President Did His Job: It's Up to Clarksdale Now," *CPR*, 7 July 1999. Epilogue title quote from Lillian Smith, *Our Faces, Our Words*, 127.

2. "Clinton Visit Leaves City Optimistic," *CPR*, 7 July 1999. Coahoma County had been chosen by the state to be an enterprise zone in 1984 as one of the poorest counties. State tax deductions were used as bait to attract new industry to take advantage of the stagnant labor force. With unemployment close to 14 percent, a million-dollar grant developed an industrial park through the Economic Development Administration on U.S. Highway 49, south of Clarksdale (*MCA*, 24 May and 28 September 1984). The booster campaigns staged in Clarksdale attracted attention briefly. The Big Frog slogan sought a "big frog" for "our small pond." Brochures selling the advantages of the county boasted lower wages and overheads with close proximity to hubs like Memphis and Little Rock. A huge billboard near the Memphis airport called for "overtaxed and overcrowded" industries to relocate to Clarksdale (Chamber of Commerce, Vertical File, Carnegie Public Library, Clarksdale).

3. USCRC Report, 2; "Ernestine Whitfield Invites Clinton to See House," *CPR*, 5 July 1999.

4. "Forget Washington: A Year after Clinton Tour, Poor Cope Alone," *NYT*, 26 September 2000, A1, A18.

5. Bertha Blackburn interviewed by author.

6. Rebecca Hood-Adams, "Local NAACP Marks 50 Years," *CPR*, 25 October 2003.

7. Bertha Blackburn interviewed by author; Rebecca Hood-Adams, "Blackburn Finds a Place with the NAACP," *CPR*, 27 October 2003.

8. Mary Jane Pigee Davis, conversation with author, 7 April 2009.

9. Mary Jane Pigee Davis interviewed by author, 19 July 2005; untaped conversations between author and Davis, 2007–9.

10. Mary Jane Pigee Davis interviewed by author, 19 July 2005.

11. Henry, *Fire*, 208, 209; Rebecca Henry interviewed by author.

12. Anthony Walton, *Mississippi*, 55. Desegregation permanently altered the landscape for black institutions. The assumption that white schools were the best for all led to the cessation of demands for equal funding for black schools and colleges. Desegregation increased different sets of inequalities. Scholar Alvis Adair, writing in 1984, argued that desegregation took tax dollars from black schools, shifted black dollars to white businesses, and became a one-way process that amplified inequity (Adair, *Desegregation*, 3, 4).

13. USCRC Report, 13.

14. The president's proposals for tax incentives for capital investments passed in the Republican-majority Senate in December 2000 but did not include any new spending.

15. Information on the state of COI in 2004 comes from Mayo Wilson interviewed by author, 9 November 2004.

16. See Nash and Taggart, *Mississippi Politics*, 211.

17. See Woods, *Development Arrested*.

18. For details on the museum, see "Clarksdale's Blues Museum," *JDN*, 4 October 1983.

19. David Lush, "Innovation Changed Delta," *Clarion-Ledger*, 1 October 1994, 6B; *Here's*

Clarksdale! September–October 1980, 11, Clarksdale Vertical File, MDAH; Jay Strasner, "Civil Rights Leader Memorialized by Highway Marker," *CPR*, 1 September 2010.

20. See Woods, *Development Arrested*, 259. See also "Our Town 2008 Profile: A *Clarksdale Press Register* Special Edition," *CPR*, 27 April 2008. The entire eight-page pullout highlighted tourist attractions and featured the director of tourism, a Lee Academy graduate.

21. "Morgan Freeman Campaigns for Bill Luckett in Mississippi Governor Race," 13 October 2009, Associated Press.

22. Baruffalo, *Local Politics/Outside Interests*, 16.

23. "Coahoma County Casino Still a Best Bet for Wins," *Starkville Daily News*, 16 July 1995.

24. *Clarion-Ledger*, 25 August 1993. In June 1993, the unemployment rate was 12.8 percent, double the state average. For details on the referendum and the campaigns, see Baruffalo, *Local Politics/Outside Interests*, chap. 6. See also Nash and Taggart, *Mississippi Politics*.

25. *CPR*, 25 August 1993.

26. The USCRC Report cites employment discrimination in the gaming industry, which is primarily located in black-majority counties in the Delta. Commissioners found that the Mississippi Gaming Commission was not required to maintain data on salaries by race and gender and that this was problematic, but they found that whites made up 72.9 percent of casino officials and managers, whereas blacks were 71.2 percent of the laborers. Only 0.8 percent of the gross revenues were allocated to cities and counties (ibid., 6–9).

27. Grassroots Leadership Report, *Education v. Incarceration*; see also Charles Shaw, "War on Drugs Unfairly Targets African-Americans."

28. The organization also questioned the connection between private prison companies and campaign financing, noting that the figures have linked millions of dollars to political campaigns promoting the construction of private prisons (Grassroots Leadership Report, *Education v. Incarceration*). The number of incarcerated black women has also dramatically increased in the past years. In 1996, 807 inmates were housed at the state's only female prison, Central Mississippi Correctional Facility, in Rankin County in the Delta. In 2001, the number was 1,455 in a facility built in 1987 to hold only 1,000. With these numbers, the state's response has been to build another jail or convert a male facility to house the women. See Sherri Williams, "More Women Doing Hard Time in Miss." One of the largest private prison companies operating extensively in Mississippi is the Corrections Corporation of America. See also USCRC Report, 95.

29. President Johnson quoted in James T. Patterson, *Brown v. Board of Education*, 138; Rebecca Hood-Adams, "Blackburn Finds a Place with the NAACP," *CPR*, 27 October 2003.

30. The Citizens' Councils, once a dominant voice of fury in the state, in 1982 maintained a low profile—the Jackson offices operated mainly as an information clearinghouse. But the fire still smolders. William Simmons, the director of the organization, stated: "Time has not blurred the Council's objective. . . . And if the Council is quieter, it's reflective of a silent majority." Furthermore, he claimed that the silent majority believes that "blacks are getting special treatment, not just equality because of the civil rights movement" (Rheta Johnson, "Times Change, but Whites' Fight Goes On," *Delta Democrat Times*, 24 February 1982).

31. Coahoma County public schools scored only a 1.1 in the performance-based accredi-

tation system to evaluate districts. Level 1 means probation and level 5 is excellent. Only one district in Mississippi scored a 5; see USCRC Report, 38–39, 45–50.

32. For examples, see *Milliken v. Bradley* 418 U.S. 717 (1974), *Swann v. Charlotte-Mecklenburg Board of Education* 402 U.S. 1 (1971), and *Board of Education of Oklahoma City v. Dowell* 198 U.S. 237 (1991). See also Orfield et al., *Deepening Segregation in American Public Schools*.

33. "Harrell Named Superintendent," *Columbian-Progress*, 20 July 1995, 3.

34. "City's Top Educator to Retire," *CPR*, 17 July 1999.

35. Donell Harrell to Nathaniel Douglas, section chief, Department of Justice Civil Rights Department, 10 July 1992, in Donell Harrell personal papers, in author's possession.

36. Bennie S. Gooden, chair of Biracial Committee, to Thomas Shaw, president of the school board, 28 May 1992, in DHP.

37. Aaron Henry and Morris Kinsey, Mississippi conference chairman on education, to Nathaniel Douglas, Justice Department, 14 June 1992, in DHP.

38. Ellard from John R. Dunne, assistant attorney general, Civil Rights Division, and Nathaniel Douglas, 14 July 1992, in DHP.

39. On 16 July 1999, Donell Harrell used these principles of promoting from within when he retired on 30 June 2000 after thirty-six years of service in Clarksdale's municipal school district. Strategically executed, his retirement was designed to begin a search for a new superintendent while a black majority held the board. Dr. Wilma Wade, a black woman who had served as Harrell's assistant superintendent, took the top post.

40. "City Breaks Ground on New School," *CPR*, 6 September 1997.

41. "School Bond Vote Set Again for May," *CPR*, 21 October 1988; "City Voters Turn Down School Bond Issue," *CPR*, 18 May 1988; School Bond Issue Killed," *CPR*, 3 May 1989, 1; "Bond Issue Passes!" *Spotlight* (Clarksdale public school paper printed in *CPR*) 69, no. 2 (15 May 1996): 1, DHP.

42. "Harrell Reflects on Tenure at Helm of City Schools," *CPR*, 20 April 2000, 14C.

43. Ibid.

44. See Crespino, *In Search of Another Country*, for his detailed discussion of how white conservatives ultimately won the war.

45. Vera Harrell interviewed by author. Brenda Luckett, who was in junior high when her mother became NAACP branch secretary in 1973, attended the city's desegregated school. She remembered: "We had separate proms, separate class parties, the parents had their own. We had nothing at school, that was one of the products of integration. Nothing happened after the bell rang to go home. When we had Beta clubs and things like that, they met during school time. . . . A lot of activities that they had, they stopped having" (Brenda Renee Luckett interviewed by author). A teacher herself, she noted that the prevailing attitude among black students was that white was better because "[whites] are not taught anything about black history, [and black students] . . . don't deal with white people."

46. Debbie Maddux, "The Miseducation of African Americans in Public High Schools," in Lomotey, *Sailing against the Wind*, 64.

47. See J. E. King, "Dysconscious Racism."

48. Roy L. Brooks, *Integration or Separation*, 106.

49. *CPR*, 9 March 1971; Wilma Wade interviewed by author.

50. Mississippi State Democratic Committee, memorandum, 18 April 1971, "Black Mississippians," box 1, William Minor Papers, MSU Manuscript Collection, Mississippi State, Mississippi.

51. Similar to a decade earlier, African Americans hosted the volunteers, who received ten dollars a week for their room and board. In 1975, there were 22,202 in the voting-age population in Coahoma County. Whites made up 43 percent, at 9,626; 57 percent were black, at 12,576. In 1971, out of a total of 17,030, 44 percent were white and 56 percent were black (Report, *Institute of Politics in Mississippi*).

52. See Foster, "A Time of Challenge." Additionally, behind-the-scenes harassment and improper procedures took place to hinder black participation. In Mississippi in 1983, over 200,000 eligible voters did not register, one reason being the voter registration laws, which required registration at the county courthouse and also in the municipality in order to vote in city elections. Hindered by misinformation or no information given before election day, "many Mississippians have been denied voter registration so long that they have given up altogether." The Justice Department's investigation was nothing more than window dressing, with community organizations not even notified that registrars were in the Delta ("Voter Registration Moving Ahead, but Barriers Remain," *Clarion-Ledger*, 26 June 1983. In fact, several authors cite the Justice Department's unwillingness to enforce the Voting Rights Act as a major problem. Once a friend, the department became a foe, a legacy from Ronald Reagan's administration (Nixon, "Turning Back the Clock on Voting Rights"). See also Nash and Taggart, *Mississippi Politics*.

53. Woods, *Development Arrested*, 215. See also Salamon, "Leadership and Modernization," 624–25; and Harrell R. Rodgers, "Civil Rights and the Myth of Popular Sovereignty," 67. Very little fundamental change has occurred as a result of more black elected officials, who occupied predominantly local or county, not statewide, positions and who were elected primarily from black constituencies. In 1983, the state representative from Bolton, Mississippi, Bennie Thompson, noted that despite Mississippi's 35 percent black population, the group held only 21 of the state's 410 county supervisor positions, only 15 seats in the 122-seat House of Representatives, and only two seats in the 52-member Senate ("Restraints on Blacks Decried," *Clarion-Ledger*, 16 June 1983). Robert Clarke was elected in 1967 to the House of Representatives, the first black since Reconstruction, joined twelve years later by Aaron Henry.

54. Bennett, "Have We Overcome," in Namorato, *Have We Overcome*, 196.

55. Sociologist Kenneth Andrews maintains that "professionalization and moderation are the necessary steps to winning new advantages as groups make the transition from outsiders to insiders," although he fails to consider those left out ("Impact of Social Movements on the Political Process," 3).

56. Orey, "African-American Committee Chairs in the U.S. State Legislatures."

57. Henry, *Fire*, 243.

58. See Spinner, *Boundaries of Citizenship*, 9, 10. This author criticizes liberals for their assumptions that minorities would want to become members of the dominant culture and to cheerfully abandon their own cultural, social, and political identities in order to conform.

59. See Bernard Grofman, "Civil Rights, the Constitution, Common Decency, and Commonsense," in Grofman, *Legacies of the 1964 Civil Rights Act*.

Bibliography

Manuscript and Archive Collections

Atlanta, Ga.
    Martin Luther King Jr. Center for Nonviolent Social Change
        Papers of Fred L. Shuttlesworth
        Papers of Martin Luther King Jr.
        Records of the Southern Christian Leadership Conference
Austin, Tex.
    Lyndon Baines Johnson Presidential Library
        Administrative History of the Department of Justice
        Lee C. White Papers
        Oral History Project Transcripts
        White House Central Files
Boston, Mass.
    John F. Kennedy Presidential Library
        Berl Bernard Papers
        Commission on Civil Rights Microfilm
        Robert F. Kennedy Papers
        Burke Marshall Papers
        Oral History Project Transcripts
        Pre-presidential Papers
        President's Office Files
        White House Staff Files
Chapel Hill, N.C.
    Southern Oral History Program, University of North Carolina, Chapel Hill
Clarksdale, Miss.
    Carnegie Public Library
        Mississippi Room Collection and Vertical Files
        Clarksdale Press Register
    Minutes of the Board of the Mayor and Commissioners
    Minutes of the Board of Trustees of the Clarksdale Municipal Separate School District

Minutes of the Consolidated Board of Trustees of Clarksdale-Coahoma Junior-Senior
    High Schools
College Park, Md.
  National Archives and Records Administration
    Records of the Community Services Administration (RG381)
Hattiesburg, Miss.
  University of Southern Mississippi
    Center for Oral History and Cultural Heritage Archive
    Margaret Hazelton Papers
    Zoya Zeman Papers
    Matthew Zwerling Papers
Jackson, Miss.
  Mississippi Department of Archives and History
    Council of Federated Organizations Records
    Ivy Papers
    Mississippi Freedom Summer Project Collection
    Oral Histories
    Sovereignty Commission Papers
    Vertical Files
Madison, Wis.
  State Historical Society of Wisconsin
    Ella Baker File
    Council of Federated Organizations Papers
    Congress of Racial Equality Papers
    Jerry DeMuth File
    Highlander Research and Education Center Papers, 1917–78
    Mississippi Council on Human Relations Collection
    Amzie Moore Papers
    Anne Romaine File
    Social Action Vertical Files Collection
    Charles Stewart File
    Student Nonviolent Coordinating Committee Papers
    Daniel Wacker File
    Howard Zinn Papers
    Matthew Zwerling File
Mississippi State, Miss.
  Mississippi State University Manuscript Collection
    Civil Rights Vertical Files
    William Minor Papers
Nashville, Tenn.
  Jean and Alexander Heard Library, Vanderbilt University
    Southern Politics Collection
New Haven, Conn.
  Yale University Library

Clarksdale Press Register, 1950–70, on microfilm
    National Advancement for the Advancement of Colored People Papers on microfilm
Oxford, Miss.
   U.S. Federal Court Records
Tougaloo, Miss.
   Coleman Library, Tougaloo College
      Aaron Henry Papers
      Edwin King Papers
      Oral History Collections
Washington, D.C.
   Moorland-Spingarn Research Center, Howard University
      Ralph Bunche Collection
   Library of Congress
      National Association for the Advancement of Colored People Papers

Interviews by Author

Myltree Adams. Clarksdale, 27 August 1999
Josephine Anthony. Clarksdale, 24 August 1999
Stephen Bingham. By telephone, 5 October 2010
Bertha Blackburn. Clarksdale, 9 November 2004
Stan Boyd. Silver Spring, Md., 21 May 2010
Sara Cannon. Clarksdale, 9 March 1999
Candie and Guy Carawan. By telephone, 5 February 2002
Andrew Carr. Clarksdale, 22 September 2010
Jean Cauthen. Clarksdale, 15 February 1999
Marian Cummings. Clarksdale, 21 March 2002
Mary Jane Pigee Davis. Detroit, Mich., 19 July 2005; ongoing phone conversations,
    1 June 2010
John Doar. New York, N.Y., 2 June 2010
Ivanhoe Donaldson. By telephone, 17 August 2010
Vickie Fortenberry. Clarksdale, 15 February 1999
Hattie Mae Gilmore. Clarksdale, 12 March 1999
Bennie S. Gooden. Clarksdale, 8 November 2004
Donald Green. Clarksdale, 25 October 2002
Clara Grey. Clarksdale, 30 March 1999
Herdicine Hardy. Clarksdale, 27 August 1999
Donell Harrell. Clarksdale, 23 October 2002
Vera Harrell. Clarksdale, 23 August 1999
Myrtis Harris. Clarksdale, 9 March 1999
Margaret Hazelton. Trenton, Mich., 20 July 2005
Rebecca Henry. Clarksdale, 11 March 1999
Cora Lee Hicks. Clarksdale, 9 March 1999
Joyce Kendricks. Oxford, 13 February 1999

Brenda Renee Luckett. Clarksdale, 8 March 1999
Joyce McAlexander. Clarksdale, 16 February 1999
Hellen McCray. Clarksdale, 28 October 2002
Leslie McLemore. Jackson, 17 September 2010
Annie Morris. Clarksdale, 14 February 1999
Derrick Neal. Clarksdale, 21 March 2002
Lillie Neal. Clarksdale, 8 March 1999
Alva Norphlet. Clarksdale, 11 March 1999
Vera M. Pigee. By telephone, 25 January 2000; Detroit, Mich., 12–13 October 2001;
    by telephone, 20 February 2003; Detroit, Mich., 4 March 2005
Lew Sitzer. By telephone, 27 September 2010
Yvonne Stanford. Clarksdale, 23 August 1999
Thydosia Thomas. Clarksdale, 27 August 1999
Wilma Wade. Clarksdale, 4 November 2004
Leroy Wadlington. Clarksdale, 21 March 2002
Joseph Wheatley. Clarksdale, 25 October 2002
Elijah Wilson. Clarksdale, 25 October 2002
Mayo Wilson. By telephone, 14 January 2004; Clarksdale, 9 November 2004
Patsy Wilson. Clarksdale, 14 February 1999
Zoya Zeman. Oxford, Ohio, 10 October 2009; ongoing phone conversations,
    27 January 2010
Mat Zwerling. By telephone, 24 September 2010

Newspapers and Journals

Clarion-Ledger	*Jet*
Clarksdale Press Register	*Memphis Commercial Appeal*
Crisis	*New York Times*
Ebony	*Starkville Daily News*
Jackson Advocate	*Vicksburg Evening Post*
Jackson Daily News	

Reports

"Creating a 21st Century Head Start." Final Report of the Advisory Committee on Head
    Start Quality and Expansion. Washington, D.C.: U.S. Department of Health and
    Human Services, December 1993.
"Federal Rights under School Desegregation Law." Washington, D.C.: U.S. Commission
    on Civil Rights, June 1966.
Misseduc Foundation, Inc. *Mississippi Black Paper*. New York: Random House, 1965.
Mississippi: Official and Statistical Register, 1956–60. Jackson, Miss.: Herber Ladner,
    Secretary of State, 1961.
NAACP. Annual Reports.

Orfield, Gary, et al. *Deepening Segregation in American Public Schools*. Harvard Project on
    School Desegregation, 5 April 1997.
Report. *Institute of Politics in Mississippi* 4, no. 1 (July 1975).
Report of the United States Commission on Civil Rights. *Racial and Ethnic Tensions
    in American Communities: Poverty, Inequality, and Discrimination, Volume VII: The
    Mississippi Delta Report*, February 2001.
Statistical Summary of School Segregation-Desegregation in the Southern and Border States.
    Nashville: Southern Education Reporting Service, November 1961.

Unpublished Papers and Manuscripts in Author's Possession

Beito, David T. "T. R. M. Howard." Conference paper.
Boyd, Stanley. "Mississippi on Trial: A Study of Leadership and Racial Attitudes in
    Clarksdale, Mississippi." Master's thesis, Antioch College, 1965.
Germany, Kent B. "Federalizing the Local, Localizing the Federal: The Civil Rights
    Movement, the Great Society, and the Origins of a New Liberalism in New Orleans,
    1965–1968." Paper presented at the annual meeting of the Southern Historical
    Association, Baltimore, November 2002.
Hamlin, Françoise N. "Clarksdale, Mississippi, the Civil Rights Era, and Oral History."
    Paper presented at the annual meeting of the Organization of American Historians,
    Los Angeles, April 2001.
Harrell, Donell. Personal papers.
Henry, Aaron. Miscellaneous undated handwritten notes.
Hill, Homer D. "Coahoma Opportunities, Incorporated." Master's thesis, University of
    Southern Mississippi, n.d.
Michaels, Sheila Shiki y. "Freedom Is a Constant Struggle: Overcoming Reticence,
    Denial, Shame, and Pain." Paper presented at the Oral History Association meeting,
    St. Louis, October 2001.
Pigee, Vera. Personal papers.
Wilgoren, Jodi Lynne. "Black and Blue: Yale Volunteers in the Mississippi Civil Rights
    Movement, 1963–1965." Senior essay, Yale University, 1992.

Online Sources

CENSUS.GOV

Forstall, Richard L. U.S. Bureau of the Census. "Population of Counties by Decennial
    Census: 1900 to 1990." http://www.census.gov/population/cencounts/ms190090.txt.
    Accessed 25 February 2011.
"Profile of Selected Economic Characteristics for Coahoma County, Mississippi, 2000."
    http://factfinder.census.gov/servlet/QTTable?_bm=y&-geo_id=05000US28027&-
    qr_name=DEC_2000_SF3_U_DP3&-ds_name=DEC_2000_SF3_U&-_lang=en&-_
    sse=on. Accessed 7 November 2007.
U.S. Counties in 1996, http://www.census.gov/statab/USA98/28/0.27.tx and http://www

.census.gov/hhes/www/saipe/stcty/c98_28.htm and http://www.census.gov/hhes/ www/saipe/stcty/a98_28.htm. Accessed 7 November 2007.

CENSUS.ORG

Census 2000 Analyzed by the Social Science Data Analysis Network (SSDAN). http:// www.censusscope.org/us/s28/c27/chart_popl.html and http://www.censusscope.org/ us/s28/c27/print_chart_race.html. Accessed 25 February 2011.

GRASSROOTSLEADERSHIP.ORG

Education v. Incarceration. www.grassrootsleadership.org/Articles/MSEdvIn.pdf. Accessed 30 May 2011.

MISSISSIPPI ORAL HISTORY PROGRAM OF THE UNIVERSITY OF SOUTHERN MISSISSIPPI, CENTER FOR ORAL HISTORY AND CULTURAL HERITAGE

Andrew Carr interviewed by Homer Hill, 14 March 1994. http://anna.lib.usm.edu/ ~spcol/crda/oh/ohcarrab.html. Accessed 30 October 2007.
Bennie Gooden interviewed by Homer Hill, 15 March 1994. http://www.lib.usm.edu/ ~spcol/crda/oh/gooden.htm. Accessed 30 October 2007.
Aaron Henry interviewed by Neil McMillen, 1 May 1972. http://digilib.usm.edu/cdm/ compoundobject/collection/coh/id/3292/rec/2. Accessed 27 September 2011.
Vernon Keys interviewed by Homer Hill, 19 March 1994. http://www.lib.usm.edu/ ~spcol/crda/oh/keys.htm. Accessed 30 October 2007.
Mayo Wilson interviewed by Homer Hill, 15 March 1994. http://www.lib.usm.edu/ ~spcol/coh/cohwilsonmb.htm. Accessed 30 October 2007.

NARA.GOV

"An Overview of President Clinton's Trip to America's New Markets." http://clinton2 .nara.gov/WH/New/New_Markets/tripoverview.html. Accessed 14 May 2009.
"Tapping America's Potential." http://clinton2.nara.gov/WH/New/New_Markets/ cities/clarksdale_facts.html. Accessed 30 May 2011.

PBS.ORG

Interview with Daniel Patrick Moynihan. http://www.pbs.org/fmc/interviews/moynihan .htm. Accessed 30 October 2007.

REBECCA HENRY V. THE CLARKSDALE MUNICIPAL SEPARATE SCHOOL DISTRICT ET AL., U.S. 5TH CIRCUIT COURT OF APPEALS

22 June 1973 (480 F.2d 583). http://altlaw.org/v1/cases/517650. Accessed 9 April 2009.

Martin Luther King Jr. to Aaron Henry, 29 May 1958, http://www.stanford.edu/group/King/mlkpapers/. Accessed 7 August 2007.

SCLC to Dwight Eisenhower, telegram, 29 May 1958, http://www.stanford.edu/group/King/mlkpapers/. Accessed 7 August 2007.

UNITED STATES V. MISSISSIPPI 380 U.S. 128.

http://supcourt.ntis.gov/get_case.html?casename=Case Name: UNITED STATES V. MISSISSIPPI 380 U.S. 128 &searchstring=mode=casename&cn_words1=United States v. Mississippi 380 U.S. 128 &cn_words2=. Accessed 31 May 2011.

Books, Articles, Dissertations, and Theses

Adair, Alvis V. *Desegregation: The Illusion of Black Progress*. Lanham, Md.: University Press of America, 1984.

Adams, David Wallace. *Education for Extinction: American Indians and the Boarding School Experience, 1875–1928*. Lawrence: University Press of Kansas, 1995.

Akin, Edward N. *Mississippi: An Illustrated History*. Northridge, Calif.: Windsor Publications, 1987.

Alexander, Michelle. *The New Jim Crow: Mass Incarceration in the Age of Colorblindness*. New York: New Press, 2010.

Ames, Lynda J., and Jeanne Ellsworth. *Women Reformed, Women Empowered: Poor Mothers and the Endangered Promise of Head Start*. Philadelphia: Temple University Press, 1997.

Andrews, Kenneth T. "The Impact of Social Movements on the Political Process: The Civil Rights Movement and Black Electoral Politics in Mississippi." *American Sociological Review* 62, no. 5 (1997): 800–820.

Andrews, William L., ed. *African American Autobiography: A Collection of Critical Essays*. Englewood Cliffs, N.J.: Prentice Hall, 1993.

Applebome, Peter. *Dixie Rising: How the South Is Shaping American Values, Politics, and Culture*. New York: Times Books, 1996.

Aptheker, Bettina. *Woman's Legacy: Essays on Race, Sex, and Class in American History*. Amherst: University of Massachusetts Press, 1982.

Arensen, Eric. "Reconsidering the Long Civil Rights Movement." *Historically Speaking* (April 2009): 31–34.

Arsenault, Raymond. *Freedom Riders: 1961 and the Struggle for Racial Justice*. New York: Oxford University Press, 2007.

Ashmore, Susan Youngblood. *Carry It On: The War on Poverty and the Civil Rights Movement in Alabama, 1964–1972*. Athens: University of Georgia Press, 2008.

Ayers, Edward L. *The Promise of the New South: Life after Reconstruction*. New York: Oxford University Press, 1992.

Ayers, H. Brandt, and Thomas H. Naylor, eds. *You Can't Eat Magnolias*. New York: McGraw-Hill, 1972.

Ayers, William. "'We Who Believe in Freedom Cannot Rest until It's Done': Two Dauntless Women of the Civil Rights Movement and the Education of a People." *Harvard Educational Review* 59 (1989): 520–28.

Baker, Paula. "The Domestication of Politics: Women and American Political Society, 1780–1920." *American Historical Review* 889 (June 1984): 620–47.

Barber, James David, and Barbara Kellerman, eds. *Women Leaders in American Politics.* Englewood Cliffs, N.J.: Prentice-Hall, 1986.

Barnett, Bernice McNair. "Invisible Southern Black Women Leaders in the Movement: The Triple Constraints of Gender, Race, and Class." *Gender and Society* 7, no. 2 (1993): 162–82.

Bartley, Numan. *The New South, 1945–1980.* Baton Rouge: Louisiana State University Press, 1995.

———. *The Rise of Massive Resistance: Race and Politics in the South during the 1950s.* Baton Rouge: Louisiana State University Press, 1969.

Baruffalo, Raymond P. "Local Politics/Outside Interests: An Analysis of Gambling Proposals, Referendums, and Economic Development in Three Mississippi Counties." Ph.D. diss., University of Kentucky, 2000.

Bates, Daisy. *The Long Shadow of Little Rock.* New York: David McKay, 1962.

Bay, Mia. *The White Image in the Black Mind: African American Ideas about White People, 1830–1925.* New York: Oxford University Press, 1999.

Beals, Melba Pattillo. *Warriors Don't Cry.* New York: Simon and Schuster, 1994.

Bederman, Gail. *Manliness and Civilization: A Cultural History of Gender and Race in the United States, 1880–1917.* Chicago: University of Chicago Press, 1995.

Beito, David T. "Black Fraternal Hospitals in the Mississippi Delta, 1942–1967." *Journal of Southern History* 65, no. 1 (February 1999): 109–40.

———. *From Mutual Aid to the Welfare State: Fraternal Societies and Social Services, 1890–1967.* Chapel Hill: University of North Carolina Press, 2000.

Beito, David T., and Linda Royster Beito. *Black Maverick: T. R. M. Howard's Fight for Civil Rights and Economic Power.* Urbana: University of Illinois Press, 2009.

Belfrage, Sally. *Freedom Summer.* New York: Viking Books, 1965.

Bell, W. Y., Jr. "The Negro Warrior's Home Front." *Phylon* 5, no. 3 (1944): 271–78.

Bernhard, Virginia, et al., eds. *Hidden Histories of Women in the New South.* Columbia: University of Missouri Press, 1994.

Bettis, Pamela J., Helen C. Cooks, and David A. Bergin. "'It's Not Steps Anymore, but More Like Shuffling': Student Perceptions of the Civil Rights Movement and Ethnic Identity." *Journal of Negro Education* 63, no. 2 (Spring 1994): 197–211.

Birnbaum, Jonathan, and Clarence Taylor, eds. *Civil Rights since 1787: A Reader On the Black Struggle.* New York: New York University Press, 2000.

Blumberg, Rhoda. *Civil Rights: The 1960s Freedom Struggle.* Boston: Twayne Publishers, 1984.

Bolton, Charles C. *The Hardest Deal of All: The Battle over School Integration in Mississippi, 1870–1980.* Jackson: University Press of Mississippi, 2005.

———. "Mississippi's School Equalization Program, 1945–1954: 'A Last Gasp to Try to

Maintain a Segregated Educational System.'" *Journal of Southern History* 66, no. 4 (November 2000): 781–814.

Bookman, Ann, and Sandra Morgen, eds. *Women and the Politics of Empowerment.* Philadelphia: Temple University Press, 1988.

Borstelmann, Thomas. *The Cold War and the Color Line: American Race Relations in the Global Arena.* Cambridge, Mass.: Harvard University Press, 2003.

Bouvard, Marguerite G. *Women Reshaping Human Rights: How Extraordinary Activists Are Changing the World.* Wilmington, Del.: Scholarly Resources, 1996.

Branch, Taylor. *Parting the Waters: America in the King Years, 1954–1963.* New York: Simon and Schuster, 1988.

———. *Pillar of Fire: America in the King Years, 1963–1965.* New York: Simon and Schuster, 1998.

Braxton, Joanne M. *Black Women Writing Autobiography: A Tradition within a Tradition.* Philadelphia: Temple University Press, 1989.

Brearley, H. C. "The Negro's New Belligerency." *Phylon* 5, no. 4 (1944): 339–45.

Breen, William J. "Black Women and the Great War: Mobilization and Reform." *Journal of Southern History* 44 (August 1974): 421–40.

Brooks, Roy L. *Integration or Separation? A Strategy for Racial Equality.* Cambridge, Mass.: Harvard University Press, 1996.

Brooks, Thomas. *Walls Come Tumbling Down.* Englewood Cliffs, N.J.: Prentice-Hall, 1974.

Brown, Cynthia Stokes. "Literacy as Power." *Radical Teacher* 8 (May 1978): 10.

Brown, Elsa Barkley. "Negotiating and Transforming the Public Sphere: African American Political Life in the Transition from Slavery to Freedom." *Public Culture* 7 (1994): 107–46.

———. "Polyrhythms and Improvisation: Lessons for Women's History." *History Workshop Journal* 31 (1991): 85–90.

———. "'What Has Happened Here': The Politics of Difference in Women's History and Feminist Politics." *Feminist Studies* 18 (Summer 1992): 295–312.

Butler, Judith, and Joan W. Scott. *Feminists Theorize the Political.* New York: Routledge, 1992.

Cade, Toni. *The Black Woman: An Anthology.* New York: Penguin, 1970.

Cagin, Seth, and Philip Dray. *We Are Not Afraid: The Story of Goodman, Schwerner, and Chaney and the Civil Rights Campaign for Mississippi.* New York: Macmillan, 1988.

Callejo-Pérez, David. *Southern Hospitality: Identity, Schools, and the Civil Rights Movement in Mississippi, 1964–1972.* New York: Peter Lang, 2001.

Campbell, Clarice T. *Civil Rights Chronicle: Letters from the South.* Jackson: University Press of Mississippi, 1997.

Carby, Hazel V. *Reconstructing Womanhood: The Emergence of the Afro-American Woman Novelist.* New York: Oxford University Press, 1987.

Carson, Clayborne. *In Struggle: SNCC and the Black Awakening of the 1960s.* Cambridge, Mass.: Harvard University Press, 1995.

Carson, Clayborne, David J. Garrow, Gerald Gill, Vincent Harding, and Darlene Clark

Hine, eds. *The Eyes on the Prize Civil Rights Reader: Documents, Speeches, and Firsthand Accounts from the Black Freedom Struggle, 1954–1990*. New York: Penguin, 1991.

Carter, Dan T. *The Politics of Rage: George Wallace, the Origins of the New Conservatism, and the Transformation of American Politics*. Baton Rouge: Louisiana State University Press, 1995.

Cash, William M., and R. Daryl Lewis. *The Delta Council: Fifty Years of Service to the Mississippi Delta*. Stoneville: Delta Council, 1986.

Cash, W. J. *The Mind of the South*. New York: Vintage Books, 1941.

Chafe, William H. *Civilities and Civil Rights: Greensboro, North Carolina, and the Black Struggle for Freedom*. New York: Oxford University Press, 1981.

———. *Never Stop Running: Allard Lowenstein and the Struggle to Save American Liberalism*. Princeton: Princeton University Press, 1998.

———. *The Paradox of Change: American Women in the Twentieth Century*. New York: Oxford University Press, 1986.

———. *Women and Equality*. New York: Oxford University Press, 1977.

Chan, Wendy, and Kiran Mirchandani. *Crimes of Colour: Racialization and the Criminal Justice System in Canada*. Ontario: Broadview Press, 2002.

Charron, Katherine Mellen. *Freedom's Teacher: The Life of Septima Clark*. Chapel Hill: University of North Carolina Press, 2009.

Chong, Dennis. *Collective Action and the Civil Rights Movement*. Chicago: University of Chicago Press, 1991.

Clark, James C. "Civil Rights Leader Harry T. Moore and the Ku Klux Klan in Florida." *Florida Historical Quarterly* 72 (October 1995): 166–83.

Clark, Robert F. *The War on Poverty: History, Selected Programs, and Ongoing Impact*. Lanham, Md.: University Press of America, 2002.

Cobb, James C. *The Most Southern Place on Earth: The Mississippi Delta and the Roots of Regional Identity*. New York: Oxford University Press, 1992.

———. "Somebody Done Nailed Us on the Cross: Federal Farm and Welfare Policy and the Civil Rights Movement in the Mississippi Delta." *Journal of American History* 77, no. 3 (December 1990): 912–36.

Cobb, James C., and Michael V. Namorato, eds. *The New Deal and the South*. Jackson: University Press of Mississippi, 1984.

Cohen, Cathy J., Kathleen B. Jones, and Joan C. Tronto, eds. *Women Transforming Politics: An Alternative Reader*. New York: New York University Press, 1997.

Cohen, Lizabeth. *A Consumer's Republic: The Politics of Mass Consumption in Postwar America*. New York: Knopf, 2003.

Cohodas, Nadine. *Strom Thurmond and the Politics of Southern Change*. New York: Simon and Schuster, 1993.

Cole, David. *No Equal Justice: Race and Class in the American Criminal Justice System*. New York: New Press, 1999.

Collins, Patricia Hill. *Black Feminist Thought: Knowledge, Consciousness, and the Politics of Empowerment*. New York: Routledge, 1991.

———. "The Meaning of Motherhood in Black Culture and Black Mother/Daughter Relationships." *Sage* 4, no. 2 (1987): 2–10.

Couto, Richard A. *Ain't Gonna Let Nobody Turn Me Round: The Pursuit of Racial Justice in the Rural South.* Philadelphia: Temple University Press, 1991.

Crawford, Vicki, Jacqueline Anne Rouse, and Barbara Woods, eds. *Women in the Civil Rights Movement: Trailblazers and Torchbearers, 1941–1965.* Bloomington: Indiana University Press, 1993.

Crespino, Joseph. *In Search of Another Country: Mississippi and the Conservative Counterrevolution.* Princeton: Princeton University Press, 2007.

Crosby, Emilye. *A Little Taste of Freedom: The Black Freedom Struggle in Claiborne County, Mississippi.* Chapel Hill: University of North Carolina Press, 2005.

Cummings, Richard. *The Pied Piper: Allard K. Lowenstein and the Liberal Dream.* New York: Grove Press, 1985.

Current, Gloster B. "The Significance of the NAACP and Its Impact in the 1960s." *Black Scholar* 19, no. 1 (January/February 1988): 9–18.

Curry, Constance. *Silver Rights.* New York: Harcourt Brace, 1995.

———, ed. *Deep in Our Hearts: Nine White Women in the Freedom Movement.* Athens: University of Georgia Press, 2000.

Dailey, Jane, Glenda Gilmore, and Bryant Simon, eds. *Jumpin' Jim Crow: Southern Politics from Civil War to Civil Rights.* Princeton: Princeton University Press, 2001.

Dalfiume, Richard M. "The 'Forgotten Years' of the Negro Revolution." *Journal of American History* 55, no. 1 (June 1968): 90–106.

Daniel, Pete. *Lost Revolutions: The South in the 1950s.* Chapel Hill: University of North Carolina Press, 2000.

———. *Standing at the Crossroads: Southern Life in the Twentieth Century.* Baltimore: Johns Hopkins University Press, 1996.

Davis, Angela. *Women, Race, and Class.* New York: Vintage Books, 1983.

Davis, Dernoral. "When Youth Protest: The Mississippi Civil Rights Movement, 1955–1970." *Mississippi: History Now.* Online Publication of the Mississippi Historical Society. http://mshistory.k12.ms.us/articles/60/the-mississippi-civil-rights-movement-1955-1970-when-youth-protest. 8 December 2010.

Davis, Vanessa Lynn. "'Sisters and Brothers All': The Mississippi Freedom Democratic Party and the Struggle for Political Equality." Ph.D. diss., Vanderbilt University, 1996.

de Jong, Greta. *Invisible Enemy: The African American Freedom Struggle after 1965.* Chichester, U.K.: John Wiley, 2010.

Denning, Michael. *The Cultural Front: The Laboring of American Culture in the Twentieth Century.* New York: Verso, 1997.

Dent, Tom. *Southern Journey: A Return to the Civil Rights Movement.* New York: William Morrow, 1997.

Denvir, John. *Democracy's Constitution: Claiming the Privileges of American Citizenship.* Urbana: University of Illinois Press, 2001.

Dill, Bonnie Thornton. "The Dialectics of Black Womanhood." *Signs* 4 (Spring 1979): 543–55.

Dittmer, John. *Good Doctors: The Medical Committee for Human Rights and the Struggle for Social Justice in Health Care.* New York: Bloomsbury, 2009.

————. *Local People: The Struggle for Civil Rights in Mississippi*. Chicago: University of Illinois Press, 1995.

Draper, Alan. *Conflict of Interests: Organized Labor and the Civil Rights Movement in the South, 1954–1968*. Ithaca: Cornell University Press, 1994.

Du Bois, W. E. B. *The Souls of Black Folk*. New York: Signet Classic, 1982.

Dudziak, Mary L. *Cold War and Civil Rights: Race and the Image of American Democracy*. Princeton: Princeton University Press, 2000.

————. "Desegregation as a Cold War Imperative." *Stanford Law Review* 41, no. 1 (November 1988): 61–120.

Eagles, Charles W., ed. *The Civil Rights Movement in America*. Jackson: University Press of Mississippi, 1981.

Eckardt, A. R. *Black-Woman-Jew: Three Wars for Human Liberation*. Bloomington: Indiana University Press, 1989.

Edwards, Laura. "Sexual Violence, Gender, Reconstruction, and the Extension of Patriarchy in Granville County, North Carolina." *North Carolina Historical Review* 68 (July 1991): 237–60.

Egerton, John. *Speak Now against the Day: The Generation before the Civil Rights Movement in the South*. Chapel Hill: University of North Carolina Press, 1994.

Ellard, Robert Miller. "A History of Clarksdale, Mississippi, Public Schools from 1905–1975." Ed.D. diss., University of Mississippi, 1977.

Ellsworth, Jeanne, and Lynda J. Ames, eds. *Critical Perspectives on Project Head Start: Revising the Hope and Challenge*. Albany: State University of New York Press, 1998.

Epstein, Cynthia Fuchs. "Positive Effects of the Multiple Negative: Explaining the Success of Black Professional Women." *American Journal of Sociology* 78, no. 4 (January 1973): 913–35.

Erenrich, Susie, ed. *Freedom Is a Constant Struggle: An Anthology of the Mississippi Civil Rights Movement*. Washington, D.C.: Cultural Center for Social Change, 1999.

Eskew, Glenn T. *But for Birmingham: The Local and National Movements in the Civil Rights Struggle*. Chapel Hill: University of North Carolina Press, 1997.

Etter-Lewis, G. *My Soul Is My Own: Oral Narratives of African American Women in the Professions*. New York: Routledge, 1993.

Evans, Sara. *Personal Politics: The Roots of the Women's Liberation in the Civil Rights Movement and the New Left*. New York: Vintage Books, 1979.

Evers, Charles, and Andrew Szanton. *Have No Fear: The Charles Evers Story*. New York: John Wiley, 1997.

Evers, Myrlie B. *For Us, the Living*. Jackson: University Press of Mississippi, 1996.

Fairclough, Adam. "History and the Civil Rights Movement." *Journal of American Studies* 24 (December 1990): 394.

————. "The Little Rock Crisis: Success or Failure for the NAACP?" *Arkansas Historical Quarterly* 56, no. 3 (Autumn 1997): 371–75.

————. "The Preachers and the People: The Origins of the Early Years of the Southern Christian Leadership Conference, 1955–1959." *Journal of Southern History* 52, no. 3 (August 1986): 403–40.

————. *Race and Democracy: The Civil Rights Struggle in Louisiana, 1915–1972*. Athens: University of Georgia Press, 1995.

————. *To Redeem the Soul of America: The Southern Christian Leadership Conference and Martin Luther King Jr*. Athens: University of Georgia Press, 1987.

Farmer, James. *Lay Bare the Heart: An Autobiography of the Civil Rights Movement*. New York: Arbor House, 1985.

Federal Writers' Project of the Works Progress Administration. *Mississippi: A Guide to the Magnolia State*. New York: Hastings House, 1949.

Feimster, Crystal. *Southern Horrors: Women and the Politics of Rape and Lynching*. Cambridge, Mass.: Harvard University Press, 2009.

Feldstein, Ruth. *Motherhood in Black and White: Race and Sex in American Liberalism, 1930–1965*. Ithaca: Cornell University Press, 2000.

Fendrich, James. *Ideal Citizens: The Legacy of the Civil Rights Movement*. Albany: State University of New York Press, 1993.

Fields, Barbara J. "Ideology and Race in American History." In *Region, Race, and Reconstruction: Essays in Honor of C. Vann Woodward*, edited by J. Morgan Kousser and James M. McPherson, 143–77. New York: Oxford University Press, 1982.

Findlay, James F. *Church People in the Struggle: The National Council of Churches and the Black Freedom Movement, 1950–1970*. New York: Oxford University Press, 1993.

Fitzgerald, Tracey A. *The National Council of Negro Women and the Feminist Movement, 1935–75*. Washington, D.C.: Georgetown University Press, 1985.

Fleming, Cynthia. *Soon We Will Not Cry: The Liberation of Ruby Doris Smith Robinson*. Lanham, Md.: Rowman and Littlefield, 1998.

Foner, Eric. *Nothing but Freedom: Emancipation and Its Legacy*. Baton Rouge: Louisiana State University Press, 1993.

Foreman, Christopher H., Jr., ed. *The African American Predicament*. Washington, D.C.: Brookings Institution Press, 1999.

Forman, James. *The Making of Black Revolutionaries*. New York: Macmillan, 1972.

Foster, E. C. "A Time of Challenge: Afro-Mississippi Political Developments since 1965." *Journal of Negro History* 68, no. 2 (Spring 1983): 185–200.

Franck, Thomas M. *The Empowered Self: Law and Society in the Age of Individualism*. New York: Oxford University Press, 1999.

Fraser, Nancy. *Unruly Practices: Power, Discourse, and Gender in Contemporary Social Theory*. Minneapolis: University of Minnesota Press, 1989.

Frederickson, Kari. "A Family Affair: Race, Gender, and the Familial Metaphor in the Dixiecrat Movement, 1938–1950." *Proceedings of the South Carolina Historical Association* (1996): 25–36.

Garner, Roberta, and John Tenuto. *Social Movement Theory and Research: An Annotated Bibliographical Guide*. Lanham, Md.: Scarecrow Press, 1997.

Garrow, David. *Bearing the Cross: Martin Luther King Jr. and the Southern Christian Leadership Conference*. New York: William Morrow, 1986.

————, ed. *The Montgomery Bus Boycott and the Women Who Started It: The Memoir of Jo Ann Gibson Robinson*. Knoxville: University of Tennessee Press, 1987.

Germany, Kent B. *New Orleans after the Promises: Poverty, Citizenship, and the Search for the Great Society*. Athens: University of Georgia Press, 2007.

Giddings, Paula. *In Search of Sisterhood: Delta Sigma Theta and the Challenge of the Black Sorority Movement*. New York: Morrow, 1988.

———. *When and Where I Enter: The Impact of Black Women on Race and Sex in America*. New York: William Morrow, 1984.

Gilkes, Cheryl. "'Holding Back the Ocean with a Broom': Black Women and Community Work." In *The Black Woman*, edited by LaFrances Rodgers-Rose, 217–32. Beverly Hills, Calif.: Sage, 1980.

———. "Together and in Harness: Women's Traditions in the Sanctified Church." *Signs* 10 (Summer 1985): 678–99.

Gillespie, Clinton, and Michele Gillespie, eds. *The Devil's Lane: Sex and Race in the Early South*. New York: Oxford University Press, 1997.

Gillette, Michael. "The NAACP in Texas, 1937–1957." Ph.D. diss., University of Texas at Austin, 1984.

Gilmore, Glenda Elizabeth. *Gender and Jim Crow: Women and the Politics of White Supremacy in North Carolina, 1896–1920*. Chapel Hill: University of North Carolina Press, 1996.

Gilroy, Paul. *The Black Atlantic: Modernity and Double Consciousness*. Cambridge, Mass.: Harvard University Press, 1993.

Gioia, Ted. *Delta Blues: The Life and Times of the Mississippi Masters Who Revolutionized American Music*. New York: W. W. Norton, 2008.

Giroux, Henry A., and Susan Searls Giroux. *Take Back Higher Education: Race, Youth, and the Crisis of Democracy in the Post–Civil Rights Era*. New York: Palgrave Macmillan, 2004.

Glen, John M. *Highlander: No Ordinary School, 1932–1962*. Louisville: University Press of Kentucky, 1988.

Glenn, Evelyn Nakano, Grace Change, and Linda Rennie Forcey, eds. *Mothering: Ideology, Experience, and Agency*. New York: Routledge, 1994.

Glissant, Edouard. *Faulkner in Mississippi*. New York: Farrar, Strauss and Giroux, 1999.

Goings, Kenneth. *The NAACP Comes of Age: The Defeat of Judge John J. Parker*. Bloomington: Indiana University Press, 1990.

———, ed. *The New African American Urban History*. Thousand Oaks, Calif.: Sage Publishers, 1996.

Good, Paul. *The Trouble I've Seen: White Journalist / Black Movement*. Washington, D.C.: Howard University Press, 1975.

Gordon, B. "Toward Emancipation in Citizenship Education: The Cases of African American Cultural Knowledge." *Theory and Research in Social Education* 12 (1985): 1–23.

Gordon, Jacob U., ed. *The Black Male in White America*. New York: Nova Science Publishers, 2002.

Gosse, Van, and Richard Moser, eds. *The World the Sixties Made: Politics and Culture in Recent America*. Philadelphia: Temple University Press, 2003.

Graham, Maryemma. *On Being Female, Black, and Free*. Knoxville: University of Tennessee Press, 1997.

Grant, Joanne. *Ella Baker: Freedom Bound*. New York: John Wiley, 1998.

Greenberg, Cheryl, ed. *A Circle of Trust: Remembering SNCC*. New Brunswick, N.J.: Rutgers University Press, 1998.

Greenberg, Jack. *Crusaders in the Courts: How a Dedicated Band of Lawyers Fought for the Civil Rights Revolution*. New York: HarperCollins, 1994.

Greenberg, Polly. *The Devil Has Slippery Shoes: A Biased Biography of the Child Development Group of Mississippi*. London: Macmillan, 1969.

Greene, Christina. *Our Separate Ways: Women and the Black Freedom Movement in Durham, North Carolina*. Chapel Hill: University of North Carolina Press, 2005.

Greene, Melissa Fay. *Praying for Sheetrock: A Work of Nonfiction*. Reading, Mass.: Addison-Wesley, 1991.

Gregory, Dick, and Robert Lipsyte. *Nigger*. New York: E. P. Dutton, 1964.

Griffin, Farah Jasmine. *"Who Set You Flowin'?" The African-American Migration Narrative*. New York: Oxford University Press, 1995.

Grofman, Bernard, ed. *Legacies of the 1964 Civil Rights Act*. Charlottesville: University Press of Virginia, 2000.

Grossman, James R. *Land of Hope: Chicago, Black Southerners, and the Great Migration*. Chicago: University of Chicago Press, 1989.

Guinier, Lani. *Lift Every Voice: Turning a Civil Rights Setback into a Strong New Vision of Social Justice*. New York: Simon and Schuster, 1998.

Gullet, Gayle. "A Contest over Meaning: Finding Gender, Class, and Race in Progressivism." *History of Education Quarterly* 33, no. 2 (1993): 233–39.

Haines, Herbert. *Black Radicals and the Civil Rights Mainstream*. Knoxville: University of Tennessee Press, 1988.

Halberstam, David. *The Children*. New York: Random House, 1998.

Hale, Grace Elizabeth. *Making Whiteness: The Culture of Segregation in the South, 1890–1940*. New York: Pantheon Books, 1998.

Haley, Alex, and Malcolm X. *The Autobiography of Malcolm X*. New York: Ballantine Books, 1965.

Hall, Jacquelyn Dowd. "The Long Civil Rights Movement and the Political Uses of the Past." *Journal of American History* 91, no. 4 (March 2005): 1233–63.

———. "Mobilizing Memory: Broadening Our View of the Civil-Rights Movement." *Chronicle Review*, 27 July 2001, B10.

———. *Revolt against Chivalry: Jessie Daniel Ames and the Women's Campaign against Lynching*. New York: Columbia University Press, 1993.

Hamilton, Dona Cooper. "The National Association for the Advancement of Colored People and New Deal Reform Legislation: A Dual Agenda." *Social Service Review* 68, no. 4 (1994): 488–502.

Hamlin, Françoise N. "'The Book Hasn't Closed, the Story Is Not Finished': Coahoma County, Mississippi, Civil Rights, and the Recovery of a History." *Sound Historian: Journal of the Texas Oral History Association* 8 (2002): 37–60.

————. "'The Book Hasn't Closed, the Story Isn't Finished': Continuing Histories of the Civil Rights Movement." Ph.D. diss., Yale University, 2004.

————. "Collision and Collusion: Local Activism, Local Agency, and Flexible Alliances." In *Civil Rights Movement in Mississippi*, edited by Ted Ownby. Jackson: University Press of Mississippi, 2012.

————. "Vera Mae Pigee (1925–): Mothering the Movement." In *Mississippi Women: Their Histories, Their Lives*, edited by Martha H. Swain, Elizabeth A. Payne, and Marjorie J. Spruill, 281–98. Athens: University of Georgia Press, 2003.

————. "Vera Mae Pigee (1925–): Mothering the Movement." *Proteus: A Journal of Ideas* 22, no. 1 (Spring 2005): 19–27.

Hampton, Henry, and Steven Fayer, eds. *Voices of Freedom: An Oral History of the Civil Rights Movement from the 1950s through the 1980s*. New York: Bantam Books, 1990.

Harding, Vincent. *There Is a River: The Black Struggle for Freedom in America*. New York: Harcourt Brace Jovanovich, 1981.

Hardy, Gayle J. *American Women Civil Rights Activists: Biobibliographies of 68 Leaders, 1825–1992*. Jefferson, N.C.: McFarland, 1993.

Harris, Frederick C. "Something Within: Religion as a Mobilizer of African American Political Activism." *Journal of Politics* 56 (February 1994): 42–68.

————. *Something Within: Religion in African American Political Activism*. New York: Oxford University Press, 1999.

Hartmann, S. *From Margin to Mainstream: American Women and Politics since 1960*. New York: Knopf, 1989.

Hawkins, Denise. "Mississippi's Crusading Gadfly." *Black Issues in Higher Education* 19, no. 24 (January 2003): 18–22.

Haygood, Wil. "The NAACP Honors Its Heroes: A Report on the 1997 Convention." *Journal of Blacks in Higher Education* 17 (Autumn 1997): 126–27.

Heard, Alexander. *Southern Primaries and Elections, 1920–1949*. Tuscaloosa: University of Alabama Press, 1950.

Henry, Aaron. *The Fire Ever Burning*. Jackson: University Press of Mississippi, 2000.

Hewitt, Nancy A., and Suzanne Lebsock. *Visible Women: New Essays on American Activism*. Urbana: University of Illinois Press, 1993.

Higginbotham, Elizabeth. *Too Much to Ask: Black Women In the Era of Integration*. Chapel Hill: University of North Carolina Press, 2001.

Higginbotham, Evelyn Brooks. "African-American Women's History and the Metalanguage of Race." *Signs* 17 (Winter 1992): 251–74.

————. *Righteous Discontent: The Women's Movement in the Black Baptist Church, 1880–1920*. Cambridge, Mass.: Harvard University Press, 1993.

Hightower, Sheree, Cathie Stanga, and Carol Cox, eds. *Mississippi Observed: Photographs from the Photography Collection of the Mississippi Department of Archives and History with Selections from Literary Works by Mississippians*. Oxford: University Press of Mississippi, 1994.

Hill, Herbert. "The Problem of Race in American Labor History." *Reviews in American History* 24 (1996): 189–208.

Hine, Darlene Clark. *Black Women in White*. Bloomington: Indiana University Press, 1989.

————, ed. *Black Women In United States History*. New York: Carlson Publishers, 1990.

Hodes, Martha. "The Sexualization of Reconstruction Politics: White Women and Black Men in the South after the Civil War." *Journal of the History of Sexuality* 3 (1993): 402–17.

————. *White Women, Black Men: Illicit Sex in the Nineteenth-Century South*. New Haven: Yale University Press, 1997.

Hogan, Wesley C. *Many Minds, One Heart: SNCC's Dream for a New America*. Chapel Hill: University of North Carolina Press, 2007.

Holland, Endesha Ida Mae. *From the Mississippi Delta: A Memoir*. New York: Simon and Schuster, 1997.

Holsaert, Faith S., et al., eds. *Hands on the Freedom Plow: Personal Accounts by Women in SNCC*. Urbana: University of Illinois Press, 2010.

Holt, Len. *The Summer That Didn't End*. New York: Morrow, 1965.

Holtzclaw, Robert Fulton. *Black Magnolias: A Brief History of the Afro-Mississippian, 1865–1980*. Shaker Heights, Ohio: Keeble Press, 1984.

Honey, Maureen. *Bitter Fruit: African American Women in World War II*. Columbia: University of Missouri Press, 1999.

Honey, Michael. *Black Workers Remember: An Oral History of Segregation, Unionism, and the Freedom Struggle*. Berkeley: University of California Press, 1999.

————. *Southern Labor and Black Civil Rights: Organizing Memphis Workers*. Urbana: University of Illinois Press, 1993.

Honigsberg, Peter Jan. *Crossing Border Street: A Civil Rights Memoir*. Berkeley: University of California Press, 2000.

hooks, bell. *Talking Back*. Boston: South End Press, 1989.

Horton, Miles. *The Long Haul*. New York: Doubleday, 1990.

Howard, John. *Men Like That: A Southern Queer History*. Chicago: University of Chicago Press, 1999.

Howell, Leon. *Freedom City*. Richmond, Va.: John Knox, 1969.

Huie, William Bradford. *Three Lives for Mississippi*. New York: WCC Books, 1965.

————. *Wolf Whistle*. New York: Signet, 1959.

Hunter, Tera W. *To 'Joy My Freedom: Southern Black Women's Lives and Labors after the Civil War*. Cambridge, Mass.: Harvard University Press, 1997.

Hurston, Zora Neale. *Mules and Men*. 1935. Reprint, New York: HarperCollins, 1990.

Irons, Jenny. "The Shaping of Activist Recruitment and Participation: A Study of Women in the Mississippi Civil Rights Movement." *Gender and Society* 12, no. 6 (December 1988): 692–709.

Isserman, Maurice, and Michael Kazin. *America Divided: The Civil War of the 1960s*. New York: Oxford University Press, 2000.

Jacobson, Matthew F. *Whiteness of a Different Color: European Immigrants and the Alchemy of Race*. Cambridge, Mass.: Harvard University Press, 1998.

James, Joy, ed. *Imprisoned Intellectuals: America's Political Prisoners Write on Life, Liberation, and Rebellion*. Lanham, Md.: Rowman and Littlefield, 2003.

James, Stanlie M., and Abena P. A. Busia, eds. *Theorizing Black Feminisms: The Visionary Pragmatism of Black Women*. New York: Routledge, 1993.

Janiewski, Dolores E. *Sisterhood Denied: Race, Gender, and Class in a New South Community*. Philadelphia: Temple University Press, 1985.

Jenkins, William L. *Mississippi United Methodist Churches: Two Hundred Years of Heritage and Hope*. Franklin, Tenn.: Providence House, 1998.

Johnston, Erle. *Mississippi's Defiant Years, 1953–1973*. Forest, Miss.: Lake Harbor Publishers, 1990.

Jonas, Gilbert. *Freedom's Sword: The NAACP and the Struggle against Racism in America, 1909–1969*. New York: Routledge, 2005.

Jones, Jacqueline. *Labor of Love, Labor of Sorrow: Black Women, Work, and the Family from Slavery to the Present*. New York: Basic Books, 1985.

Jones, Leroi. *Blues People: Negro Music in White America*. New York: William Morrow, 1969.

Jordan, June. *Affirmative Acts: Political Essays*. New York: Anchor Books, 1998.

———. *Civil Wars*. Boston: Beacon Press, 1981.

Jordan, Winthrop. *White over Black: American Attitudes toward the Negro, 1550–1812*. New York: Pelican, 1969.

Kalodoner, Howard I., and James J. Fishman, eds. *Limits of Justice: The Courts' Role in School Desegregation*. Cambridge, Mass.: Ballinger, 1978.

Katagiri, Yasuhiro. *The Mississippi State Sovereignty Commission: Civil Rights and States' Rights*. Jackson: University Press of Mississippi, 2001.

Katz, Michael B. *The Undeserving Poor: From the War on Poverty to the War on Welfare*. New York: Pantheon Books, 1989.

Keady, William C. *All Rise: Memoirs of a Mississippi Federal Judge*. Boston: Recollections Bound, 1988.

Keating, Bern, and Franke Keating. *Mississippi*. Jackson: University Press of Mississippi, 1982.

Kelley, Robin D. G. *Race Rebels: Culture, Politics and the Black Working Class*. New York: Free Press, 1994.

———. "We Are Not What We Seem: Rethinking Black Working-Class Opposition in the Jim Crow South." *Journal of American History* 80, no. 1 (June 1993): 75–112.

Kessler-Harris, Alice. *Out to Work: A History of Wage-Earning Women in the United States*. New York: Oxford University Press, 1982.

Key, V. O., Jr. *Southern Politics in State and Nation*. New York: Alfred A. Knopf, 1949.

King, J. E. "Dysconscious Racism: Ideology, Identity, and the Miseducation of Teachers." *Journal of Negro Education* 60, no. 2 (1991): 113–46.

King, Martin Luther, Jr. *Where Do We Go from Here: Chaos or Community?* New York: Harper and Row, 1967.

King, Mary. *Freedom Song: A Personal Story of the 1960s Civil Rights Movement*. New York: Simon and Schuster, 1964.

Kirby, Jack Temple. *Rural Worlds Lost: The American South, 1920–1960*. Baton Rouge: Louisiana State University Press, 1987.

Kluger, Richard. *Simple Justice: The History of Brown v. Board of Education and Black America's Struggle for Equality*. New York: Alfred A. Knopf, 1976.

Korstad, Robert, and Nelson Lichtenstein. "Opportunities Found and Lost: Labor,

Radicals, and the Early Civil Rights Movement." *Journal of American History* 75, no. 3 (December 1988): 787–811.

Kousser, J. Morgan. *Colorblind Injustice: Minority Voting Rights and the Undoing of the Second Reconstruction.* Chapel Hill: University of North Carolina Press, 1999.

Kushnick, Louis, and James Jennings, eds. *A New Introduction to Poverty: The Role of Race, Power, and Politics.* New York: New York University Press, 1999.

Kymlicka, Will. *Multicultural Citizenship: A Liberal Theory of Minority Rights.* Oxford: Clarendon Press, 1995.

———. *Politics in the Vernacular: Nationalism, Multiculturalism, and Citizenship.* New York: Oxford University Press, 2001.

Lacey, Michael J., ed. *The Truman Presidency.* New York: Cambridge University Press, 1989.

Ladd-Taylor, Molly. *Mother-Work: Women, Child Welfare, and the State, 1890–1930.* Urbana: University of Illinois Press, 1994.

———. "Toward Defining Maternalism in U.S. History." *Journal of Women's History* 5, no. 2 (1993): 110–14.

Lamis, Alexander P. *Southern Politics in the 1990s.* Baton Rouge: Louisiana State University Press, 1999.

Lasch-Quinn, Elizabeth. *Black Neighbors: Race and the Limits of Reform in the American Settlement House Movement, 1890–1945.* Chapel Hill: University of North Carolina Press, 1993.

Latty, Yvonne, and Ron Tarver, eds. *We Were There: Voices of African American Veterans from World War II to the War in Iraq.* New York: HarperCollins, 2004.

Lawson, Steven F. *Black Ballots: Voting Rights in the South, 1944–1966.* New York: Columbia University Press, 1985.

———. "Freedom Then, Freedom Now: The Historiography of the Civil Rights Movement." *American Historical Review* 96 (April 1991): 456–71.

———. *Running for Freedom: Civil Rights and Black Politics in America since 1941.* Philadelphia: Temple University Press, 1991.

Lawson, Steven, and Charles M. Payne. *Debating the Civil Rights Movement, 1945–1968.* New York: Rowman and Littlefield, 1998.

Lears, T. J. Jackson. "The Concept of Cultural Hegemony: Problems and Possibilities." *American Historical Review* 90 (June 1985): 567–93.

Lee, Chana Kai. *For Freedom's Sake: The Life of Fannie Lou Hamer.* Urbana: University of Illinois Press, 1999.

Lemann, Nicholas. *The Promised Land: The Great Black Migration and How It Changed America.* New York: A. A. Knopf, 1991.

Lerner, Gerda, ed. *Black Women in White America: A Documentary History.* New York: Vintage Books, 1992.

Leuchtenburg, William E. *The FDR Years: On Roosevelt and His Legacy.* New York: Columbia University Press, 1995.

———. *Franklin D. Roosevelt and the New Deal, 1934–1940.* New York: Harper and Row, 1963.

Levine, Lawrence. *Black Culture and Black Consciousness: Afro-American Folk Thought from Slavery to Freedom*. New York: Oxford University Press, 1977.

Lewis, John, and Michael D'Orso. *Walking in the Wind: A Memoir of the Movement*. New York: Simon and Schuster, 1998.

Ling, Peter J., and Sharon Monteith, eds. *Gender in the Civil Rights Movement*. New York: Garland, 1999.

Link, William A. *The Paradox of Southern Progressivism, 1880–1930*. Chapel Hill: University of North Carolina Press, 1992.

Lisio, Donald J. *Hoover, Blacks, and Lily-Whites: A Study of Southern Strategies*. Chapel Hill: University of North Carolina Press, 1985.

Litwack, Leon F. *Been in the Storm So Long: The Aftermath of Slavery*. New York: Alfred A. Knopf, 1979.

———. "Fight the Power! The Legacy of the Civil Rights Movement." *Journal of Southern History* 75, no. 1 (February 2009): 3–28.

———. *Trouble in Mind: Black Southerners in the Age of Jim Crow*. New York: Alfred A. Knopf, 1998.

Locke, Alain LeRoy. *The New Negro: An Interpretation*. New York: Albert Charles, 1925.

Loewen, James W. *The Mississippi Chinese*. Cambridge, Mass.: Harvard University Press, 1971.

Logan, Rayford, ed. *What the Negro Wants*. Chapel Hill: University of North Carolina Press, 1944.

Lomotey, Kofi, ed. *Sailing against the Wind: African Americans and Women in U.S. Education*. Albany: State University of New York Press, 1997.

Lorde, Audre. *Sister Outsider*. Freedom, Calif.: Crossing Press, 1984.

Louis, Debbie. *And We Are Not Yet Saved: A History of the Movement as People*. New York: Doubleday, 1970.

Lyon, Danny. *Memories of the Southern Civil Rights Movement*. Chapel Hill: University of North Carolina Press, 1992.

Machan, Timor. *Private Rights and Public Illusions*. New Brunswick, N.J.: Transaction Publishers, 1995.

MacLean, Nancy. *Behind the Mask of Chivalry: The Making of the Second Ku Klux Klan*. New York: Oxford University Press, 1994.

Marable, Manning. *Black Leadership: Four Great American Leaders and the Struggle for Civil Rights*. New York: Penguin, 1998.

———. *Race, Reform, and Rebellion: The Second Reconstruction and Beyond in Black America, 1945–2006*. 3rd ed. Jackson: University Press of Mississippi, 2007.

Markowitz, Michael W., and Delores D. Jones-Brown, eds. *The System in Black and White: Exploring the Connections between Race, Crime, and Justice*. Westport, Conn.: Praeger, 2000.

Marsh, Charles. *God's Long Summer: Stories of Faith and Civil Rights*. Princeton: Princeton University Press, 1997.

Martin, John Bartlow. *The Deep South Says "Never."* New York: Ballantine, 1957.

Martínez, Corinne, Zeus Leonardo, and Carlos Tejeda, eds. *Charting New Terrains of Chicana(o)/Latina(o) Education*. Cresskill, N.J.: Hampton Press, 2000.

Martínez, Elizabeth, ed. *Letters from Mississippi: Reports from Civil Rights Volunteers and Poetry of the 1964 Freedom Summer*. Brookline, Mass.: Zephyr Press, 2007.

Marwick, Arthur. *The Sixties: Social and Cultural Transformation in Britain, France, Italy, and the United States, 1958–1974*. New York: Oxford University Press, 1998.

Mays, Benjamin. *Born to Rebel*. New York: Scribner's, 1971.

McAdam, Doug. *Freedom Summer*. New York: Oxford University Press, 1988.

———. "Gender as a Mediator of the Activist Experience: The Case of Freedom Summer." *American Journal of Sociology* 97, no. 5 (March 1992): 1211–40.

———. *Political Process and the Development of Black Insurgency, 1930–1970*. Chicago: University of Chicago Press, 1982.

McCourt, Kathleen. *Working-Class Women and Grass Roots Politics*. Bloomington: Indiana University Press, 1977.

McDonald, Katrina Bell. "Black Activist Mothering: A Historical Intersection of Race, Gender, and Class." *Gender and Society* 11, no. 6 (December 1997): 773–95.

McLemore, Leslie Burl. "The Mississippi Freedom Democratic Party: A Case Study of Grass-Roots Politics." Ph.D. diss., University of Massachusetts, 1971.

McMillen, Neil. "Black Enfranchisement in Mississippi: Federal Enforcement and Black Protest in the 1960s." *Journal of Southern History* 43 (August 1977): 351–72.

———. *The Citizens' Council: Organized Resistance to the Second Reconstruction, 1954–1964*. Urbana: University of Illinois Press, 1971.

———. *Dark Journey: Black Mississippians in the Age of Jim Crow*. Urbana: University of Illinois Press, 1989.

———, ed. *Remaking Dixie: The Impact of World War II on the American South*. Jackson: University Press of Mississippi, 1997.

McNair Barnett, Bernice. "Invisible Southern Black Women Leaders in the Civil Rights Movement: The Triple Constraints of Gender, Race, and Class." *Signs* 7, no. 2 (1993): 162–82.

Meacham, Jon, ed. *Voices in Our Blood: America's Best on the Civil Rights Movement*. New York: Random House, 2001.

Meredith, James. *Three Years in Mississippi*. Bloomington: Indiana University Press, 1966.

Metress, Christopher. *The Lynching of Emmett Till: A Documentary Narrative*. Charlottesville: University Press of Virginia, 2002.

Michel, Sonia, and Seth Koven, eds. *Mothers of a New World: Maternalist Politics and the Origins of the Welfare State*. New York: Routledge, 1993.

Milkman, Ruth. *Gender at Work: The Dynamics of Job Segregation by Sex during World War II*. Urbana: University of Illinois Press, 1987.

Mills, Kay. *This Little Light of Mine: The Life of Fannie Lou Hamer*. New York: Dutton, 1993.

Mills, Nicolaus. *Like a Holy Crusade: Mississippi 1964—The Turning of the Civil Rights Movement in America*. Chicago: Ivan R. Dee, 1992.

Mirza, H. *Young, Female, and Black*. New York: Routledge, 1992.

Mississippi Folklife: Folklife and the Civil Rights Movement (special edition) 31, no. 1 (Fall 1998).

Moody, Anne. *Coming of Age in Mississippi*. New York: Dell, 1968.

Moore, Charles. *Powerful Days: The Civil Rights Photography of Charles Moore*. Tuscaloosa: University of Alabama Press, 1991.

Moore, Winfred B., Jr., Joseph F. Tripp, and Lyon G. Tyler, eds. *Developing Dixie: Modernization in a Traditional Society*. Westport, Conn.: Greenwood Press, 1988.

Morehouse, Maggi M. *Fighting in the Jim Crow Army: Black Men and Women Remember World War II*. Lanham, Md.: Rowman and Littlefield, 2000.

Morris, Aldon. *The Origins of the Civil Rights Movement: Black Communities Organizing for Change*. New York: Free Press, 1984.

Morrison, Minion K. C. *Black Political Mobilization: Leadership, Power, and Mass Behavior*. Albany: State University of New York Press, 1987.

Morton, Patricia. *Disfigured Images: The Historical Assault on Afro-American Women*. Westport, Conn.: Greenwood Press, 1991.

Moses, Robert P., and Charles E. Cobb, Jr. *Racial Equations: Math Literacy and Civil Rights*. Boston, Mass.: Beacon Press, 2001.

Moye, Todd. *Let the People Decide: Black Freedom and White Resistance Movements in Sunflower County, Mississippi, 1945–1986*. Chapel Hill: University of North Carolina Press, 2004.

Moynihan, Daniel Patrick. *The Negro Family: The Case for National Action*. Washington, D.C.: Department of Labor, 1965.

Murphy, Walter F. "The South Counterattacks: The Anti-NAACP Laws." *Western Political Quarterly* 12, no. 2 (1959): 371–90.

Myers, Martha A. *Race, Labor, Punishment in the New South*. Columbus: Ohio State University Press, 1998.

Namorato, Michael V., ed. *Have We Overcome? Race Relations since Brown*. Jackson: University Press of Mississippi, 1979.

Naples, Nancy. "Activist Mothering: Cross-generational Continuity in the Community Work of Women from Low-Income Urban Neighborhoods." *Gender and Society* 6, no. 3 (September 1992): 441–63.

———. "Contradictions in the Gender Subtext of the War on Poverty: The Community Work and Resistance of Women from Low-Income Communities." *Social Problems* 38, no. 3 (August 1991): 316–32.

———. *Grassroots Warriors*. New York: Routledge, 1998.

Nash, Jere, and Andy Taggart. *Mississippi Politics: The Struggle for Power, 1976–2006*. Jackson: University Press of Mississippi, 2006.

Nasstrom, Kathryn L. "Beginnings and Endings: Life Stories and the Periodization of the Civil Rights Movement." *Journal of American History* 86, no. 2 (September 1999): 700–711.

Neilson, Melany. *Even Mississippi*. Tuscaloosa: University of Alabama Press, 1989.

Neverton-Morton, Cynthia. "Self Help Programs as Educative Activities for Black Women in the South, 1895–1925." *Journal of Negro Education* 51 (Summer 1982): 207–21.

Newman, Mark. *Divine Agitators: The Delta Ministry and Civil Rights in Mississippi*. Athens: University of Georgia Press, 2004.

Nietzsche, Friedrich. *Beyond Good and Evil: Prelude to a Philosophy of the Future.* Translated by Helen Zimmern. London: George Allen and Unwin, 1967.

Nixon, Ron. "Turning Back the Clock on Voting Rights." *Nation*, 15 November 1999, 11–17.

Norrell, Robert J. *Reaping the Whirlwind: The Civil Rights Movement in Tuskegee.* New York: Alfred A. Knopf, 1985.

Nossiter, Adam. *Of Long Memory: Mississippi and the Murder of Medgar Evers.* Reading, Mass.: Addison-Wesley, 1994.

O'Brien, Gail Williams. *The Color of the Law: Race, Violence, and Justice in the Post–World War II South.* Chapel Hill: University of North Carolina Press, 1999.

Olson, Lynne. *Freedom's Daughter: The Unsung Heroines of the Civil Rights Movement from 1830 to 1970.* New York: Scribner, 2001.

Orey, Byron D. "African-American Committee Chairs in the U.S. State Legislatures." *Social Science Quarterly* 88, no. 3 (September 2007): 619–39.

Orfield, Gary, and Susan E. Eaton. *Dismantling Desegregation: The Quiet Reversal of Brown v. Board of Education.* New York: New Press, 1996.

Orleck, Annelise. *Storming Caesar's Palace: How Black Mothers Fought Their Own War on Poverty.* Boston: Beacon Press, 2006.

Oshinsky, David M. *A Conspiracy So Immense: The World of Joe McCarthy.* New York: Free Press, 1983.

———. *"Worse Than Slavery": Parchman Farm and the Ordeal of Jim Crow Justice.* New York: Free Press, 1996.

Painter, Nell Irvin. "'Social Equality,' Miscegenation, and the Maintenance of Power." In *The Evolution of Southern Culture*, edited by Numan B. Bartley, 47–67. Athens: University of Georgia Press, 1988.

Palmer, Robert. *Deep Blues: A Musical and Cultural History, from the Mississippi Delta to Chicago's South Side to the World.* New York: Penguin, 1981.

Parker, Frank R. *Black Votes Count: Political Empowerment in Mississippi after 1965.* Chapel Hill: University of Chapel Hill Press, 1990.

Parks, Rosa. *Rosa Parks: My Story.* New York: Dial Books, 1992.

Patterson, James. *Brown v. Board of Education: A Civil Rights Milestone and Its Troubling Legacy.* New York: Oxford University Press, 2001.

Payne, Charles. *I've Got the Light of Freedom: The Organizing Tradition and the Mississippi Freedom Struggle.* Los Angeles: University of California Press, 1995.

Peltason, J. W. *Fifty-eight Lonely Men: Southern Federal Judges and School Desegregation.* New York: Harcourt, Brace and World, 1961.

Perkinson, Robert. *Texas Tough: The Rise of America's Prison Empire.* New York: Picador, 2010.

Pigee, Vera M. *Struggle of Struggles: Part One* and *Struggle of Struggles: Part Two.* Detroit: Harlo Press, 1975.

Pitre, Merline. *In Struggle against Jim Crow.* College Station: Texas A&M University Press, 1999.

Piven, Frances Fox, and Richard A. Cloward. *Poor People's Movements: Why They Succeed, How They Fail.* New York: Vintage Books, 1979.

Plummer, Brenda Gayle. *Rising Wind: Black Americans and U.S. Foreign Affairs, 1935–1960*. Chapel Hill: University of North Carolina Press, 1996.

Powdermaker, Hortense. *After Freedom: A Cultural Study of the Deep South*. New York: Viking, 1939.

Prendergast, Catherine. *Literacy and Racial Justice: The Politics of Learning after Brown v. Board of Education*. Carbondale: Southern Illinois University Press, 2003.

Quadagno, Jill. "Unfinished Democracy." In *A New Introduction to Poverty: The Role of Race, Power, and Politics*, edited by James Jennings and Louis Kushnick, 77–84. New York: New York University Press, 1999.

Quan, Robert Seto. *Lotus among the Magnolias: The Mississippi Chinese*. Jackson: University Press of Mississippi, 1982.

Rachal, John R. "'The Long, Hot Summer': The Mississippi Response to Freedom Summer, 1964." *Journal of Negro History* 84, no. 4 (Autumn 1999): 315–39.

Raiford, Leigh R. *Imprisoned in a Luminous Glare: Photography and the African American Freedom Struggle*. Chapel Hill: University of North Carolina Press, 2011.

Raines, Howell. *My Soul Is Rested*. New York: Putnam, 1977.

Ransby, Barbara. *Ella Baker and the Black Freedom Movement: A Radical Democratic Vision*. Chapel Hill: University of North Carolina Press, 2003.

Reddick, Lawrence. "Contrast: 1965 Versus 1975." *Black Scholar* 19, no. 1 (January/February 1988): 4–8.

Reed, Christopher Robert. *The Chicago NAACP and the Rise of Black Professional Leadership, 1910–1966*. Bloomington: Indiana University Press, 1997.

Reed, Linda. *Simple Decency and Common Sense: The Southern Conference Movement, 1938–1963*. Bloomington: Indiana University Press, 1991.

Ritterhouse, Jennifer. *Growing Up Jim Crow: How Black and White Southern Children Learned Race*. Chapel Hill: University of North Carolina Press, 2006.

Robinson, Armstead L., and Patricia Sullivan, eds. *New Directions in Civil Rights Studies*. Charlottesville: University Press of Virginia, 1991.

Robinson, Cedric J. *Black Movements in America*. New York: Routledge, 1997.

Robnett, Belinda. "African American Women in the Civil Rights Movement: Gender, Leadership, and Micromobilization." *American Journal of Sociology* 101, no. 6 (May 1996): 1661–93.

———. *How Long? How Long? African American Women in the Struggle for Civil Rights*. New York: Oxford University Press, 1997.

Rodgers, Daniel T. *Atlantic Crossings: Social Politics in a Progressive Age*. Cambridge, Mass.: Harvard University Press, 1998.

Rodgers, Harrell R., Jr. "Civil Rights and the Myth of Popular Sovereignty." *Journal of Black Studies* 12, no. 1 (September 1981): 53–70.

Roediger, David R., ed. *Black on White: Black Writers on What It Means to Be White*. New York: Schocken Books, 1998.

———. *The Wages of Whiteness: Race and the Making of the American Working Class*. London: Verso, 1991.

Rogers, Kim Lacy. "Oral History and the History of the Civil Rights Movement." *Journal of American History* 75 (1988): 567–76.

Rose, Willie Lee. *Rehearsal for Reconstruction: The Port Royal Experiment*. New York: Vintage Books, 1967.

Rosenberg, Gerald R. *The Hollow Hope: Can Courts Bring About Social Change?* Chicago: University of Chicago Press, 1991.

Ross, Bonnie Lou. "Interpretations of the Black Civil Rights Movement in the Black and White Press." Ph.D. diss., University of California at Irvine, 1985.

Rowan, Carl T. *South of Freedom*. Baton Rouge: Louisiana State University Press, 1997.

Rowe-Sims, Sarah. "The Mississippi State Sovereignty Commission: An Agency History." *Journal of Mississippi History* 61, no. 1 (Spring 1999): 29–58.

Rubin, Anne Sarah. "Reflections on the Death of Emmett Till." *Southern Cultures* 2, no. 1 (1995): 45–66.

Saddler, Valerie Stephanie. "A Content Analysis of *Ebony*'s and *Life*'s 1955–1965 Reporting on Black Civil Rights Movement Issues." Ph.D. diss., Ohio University, 1984.

Salamon, Lester M. "Leadership and Modernization: The Emerging Black Political Elite in the American South." *Journal of Politics* 35, no. 3 (August 1973): 615–46.

Savage, Barbara Dianne. *Broadcasting Freedom: Radio, War, and the Politics of Race, 1938–48*. Chapel Hill: University of North Carolina Press, 1999.

Schulman, Bruce J. *From Cotton Belt to Sunbelt: Federal Policy, Economic Development, and the Transformation of the South, 1938–1980*. New York: Oxford University Press, 1991.

Scott, James C. *Domination and the Arts of Resistance: Hidden Transcripts*. New Haven: Yale University Press, 1990.

Scott, K. *The Habit of Surviving: Black Women's Strategies for Life*. New Brunswick, N.J.: Rutgers University Press, 1991.

Sellers, Cleveland, and Robert Terrell. *The River of No Return: The Autobiography of a Black Militant and the Life and Death of SNCC*. Jackson: University Press of Mississippi, 1990.

Shaw, Charles. "War on Drugs Unfairly Targets African-Americans." *St. Louis Post-Dispatch*, 12 April 2000, http://www.commondreams.org/cgi-bin/print.cgi?file=/views/041200-104.htm. 7 November 2007.

Shaw, Stephanie. *What a Woman Ought to Be and to Do: Black Professional Women Workers during the Jim Crow Era*. Chicago: University of Chicago Press, 1996.

Silver, James W. *Mississippi: The Closed Society*. New York: Harcourt, Brace & World, 1963.

Singh, Nikhil Pal. *Black Is a Country: Race and the Unfinished Struggle for Democracy*. Cambridge, Mass.: Harvard University Press, 2004.

Sinsheimer, Joseph A. "The Freedom Vote of 1963: New Strategies of Racial Protest in Mississippi." *Journal of Southern History* 55, no. 2 (May 1989): 217–44.

Sissel, Peggy A. *Staff, Parents, and Politics in Head Start: A Case Study in Unequal Power, Knowledge, and Material Resources*. New York: Palmer Press, 2000.

Sitkoff, Harvard. *A New Deal for Blacks: The Emergence of Civil Rights as a National Issue*. New York: Oxford University Press, 1978.

———. "Racial Militancy and Interracial Violence in the Second World War." *Journal of American History* 58, no. 3 (June 1971): 663–730.

———. *The Struggle for Black Equality, 1954–1980*. New York: Hill and Wang, 1981.

Skates, John Ray. "German Prisoners of War in Mississippi, 1943–1946." *Mississippi History Now*, http://mshistory.k12.ms.us/index.php?id=233. 22 November 2010.

Skrentny, John D. "The Effect of the Cold War on African American Civil Rights: America and the World Audience, 1945–1968." *Theory and Society* 27 (1998): 237–85.

Smith, Barbara E., ed. *Neither Separate Nor Equal: Women, Race, and Class in the South*. Philadelphia: Temple University Press, 1999.

Smith, Lillian. *Killers of the Dream*. 1949. Reprint, New York: W. W. Norton, 1961.

———. *Our Faces, Our Words*. New York: W. W. Norton, 1964.

Smith, Rogers. *Civic Ideals: Conflicting Visions of Citizenship in United States History*. New Haven: Yale University Press, 1997.

Solomon, Irvin D. *Feminism and Black Activism in Contemporary America: An Ideological Assessment*. New York: Greenwood Press, 1989.

Spinner, Jeff. *The Boundaries of Citizenship: Race, Ethnicity, and Nationality in the Liberal State*. Baltimore: Johns Hopkins University Press, 1994.

Stack, Carol. *All Our Kin: Strategies for Survival in a Black Community*. New York: Harper and Row, 1974.

———. *Call to Home: African Americans Reclaim the Rural South*. New York: Basic Books, 1996.

Stanton, Mary. *From Selma to Sorrow*. Athens: University of Georgia Press, 1998.

Steele, Shelby. *A Dream Deferred: The Second Betrayal of Black Freedom in America*. New York: HarperCollins, 1998.

Sterling, Dorothy, ed. *We Are Your Sisters: Black Women in the Nineteenth Century*. New York: W. W. Norton, 1984.

Stern, Mark. *Calculating Visions: Kennedy, Johnson, and Civil Rights*. New Brunswick, N.J.: Rutgers University Press, 1992.

Sugarman, Tracy. *Stranger at the Gates: A Summer in Mississippi*. New York: Hill and Wang, 1966.

Sullivan, Patricia. *Days of Hope: Race and Democracy in the New Deal Era*. Chapel Hill: University of North Carolina Press, 1996.

———. *Lift Every Voice: The NAACP and the Making of the Civil Rights Movement*. New York: New Press, 2010.

Swain, Martha. "The Mississippi Delta Goes to War, 1941–1942." *Journal of Mississippi History* 57, no. 4 (1995): 341.

Taylor, Verta. "Social Movement Continuity: The Women's Movement in Abeyance." *American Sociological Review* 54, no. 5 (October 1989): 761–75.

Thelen, David. "Memory and American History." *Journal of American History* 75 (March 1989): 1117–29.

Theoharis, Jeanne, and Komozi Woodard, eds. *Groundwork: Local Black Freedom Movements in America*. New York: New York University Press, 2005.

Thornton, J. Mills, III. *Dividing Lines: Municipal Politics and the Struggle for Civil Rights in Montgomery, Birmingham, and Selma*. Tuscaloosa: University of Alabama Press, 2002.

Tilley, Louise, and Patricia Gurin. *Women, Politics, and Change*. New York: Russell Sage Foundation, 1990.

Tolnay, Stewart E. *The Bottom Rung: African American Family Life on Southern Farms*. Urbana: University of Illinois Press, 1999.

Trattner, Walter I. *From Poor Law to Welfare State: A History of Social Welfare in America*. 6th ed. New York: Free Press, 1999.

Tucker, Sterling. "Black Strategies for Change in America." *Journal of Negro Education* 40, no. 3 (Summer 1971): 297–311.

Tyson, Timothy B. *Radio Free Dixie: Robert F. Williams and the Roots of Black Power*. Chapel Hill: University of North Carolina Press, 1999.

Umoja, Akinyele O. "The Ballot and the Bullet: A Comparative Analysis of Armed Resistance in the Civil Rights Movement." *Journal of Black Studies* 29, no. 4 (March 1999): 558–78.

Van Deburg, William L. *New Day in Babylon: The Black Power Movement and American Culture, 1965–1975*. Chicago: University of Chicago Press, 1992.

Vollers, Maryanne. *Ghosts of Mississippi: The Murder of Medgar Evers*. Boston: Little, Brown, 1995.

Von Eschen, Penny M. *Race against Empire: Black Americans and Anticolonialism, 1937–1957*. Ithaca: Cornell University Press, 1997.

Walton, Anthony. *Mississippi: An American Journey*. New York: Alfred A. Knopf, 1996.

Walton, Hanes, Jr. *When the Marching Stopped: The Politics of Civil Rights Regulatory Agencies*. Albany: State University of New York Press, 1988.

Ward, Brian, and Tony Badger, eds. *The Making of Martin Luther King Jr. and the Civil Rights Movement*. New York: New York University Press, 1997.

Ware, Gilbert. "The National Association for the Advancement of Colored People and the Civil Rights Act of 1957." Ph.D. diss., Princeton University, 1962.

Watson, Denton L. "Assessing the Role of the NAACP in the Civil Rights Movement." *Historian* 55, no. 3 (1993): 453–68.

Watters, Pat, and Reese Cleghorn. *Climbing Jacob's Ladder*. New York: Harcourt, Brace and World, 1986.

Weeks, Linton. *Clarksdale and Coahoma County: A History*. Clarksdale, Miss.: Carnegie Public Library, 1982.

Weems, Robert E., Jr. *Desegregating the Dollar: African American Consumerism in the Twentieth Century*. New York: New York University Press, 1998.

Weill, Susan. *In a Madhouse's Din: Civil Rights Coverage by Mississippi's Daily Press, 1948–1968*. Westport, Conn.: Praeger, 2002.

Weinberg, Meyer, and Gertrude Martin, eds. *Covering the Desegregation Story: Current Experiences and Issues*. Evanston, Ill.: Center for Equal Education, 1976.

Weisbrot, Richard. *Freedom Bound: A History of America's Civil Rights Movement*. New York: Norton, 1990.

Welty, Eudora. *On Writing*. New York: Random House, 2002.

Whitaker, Hugh Stephen. "A New Day: The Effects of Negro Enfranchisement in Selected Mississippi." Ph.D. diss., Florida State University, 1965.

White, Deborah Gray. *Ar'n't I a Woman? Female Slaves in the Plantation South*. New York: W. W. Norton, 1985.

———. *Too Heavy a Load: Black Women in Defense of Themselves, 1894–1994*. New York: W. W. Norton, 1999.

White, Walter. *A Man Called White*. Athens: University of Georgia Press, 1995.

———. *Rope and Faggot*. New York: A. A. Knopf, 1929.

Whitfield, Stephen J. *A Death in the Delta: The Story of Emmett Till*. Baltimore: Johns Hopkins University Press, 1991.

Wilhoit, Francis M. *The Politics of Massive Resistance*. New York: G. Braziller, 1973.

Wilkie, Curtis. *Dixie: A Personal Odyssey through Events That Shaped the Modern South*. New York: Scribner, 2001.

Wilkins, Roy. *Standing Fast: The Autobiography of Roy Wilkins*. New York: Penguin, 1982.

Willett, Julie A. *Permanent Waves: The Making of the American Beauty Shop*. New York: New York University Press, 2000.

Williams, Cecil J. *Freedom and Justice: Four Decades of the Civil Rights Struggle as Seen by a Black Photographer of the Deep South*. Macon, Ga.: Mercer University Press, 1995.

Williams, Heather A. "Self-Taught: The Role of African Americans in Educating the Freedpeople, 1861–1871." Ph.D. diss., Yale University, 2002.

Williams, John Bell. "Civil Rights." *Speakers Magazine* (March 1949): 8–10.

Williams, Juan. *Thurgood Marshall: American Revolutionary*. New York: Random House, 1998.

———, ed. *My Soul Looks Back in Wonder: Voices of the Civil Rights Experience*. New York: Sterling, 2004.

Williams, Kenneth H. "Mississippi and Civil Rights, 1945–1954." Ph.D. diss., Mississippi State University, 1985.

Williams, Lea E. *Servants of the People: The 1960s Legacy of African American Leadership*. New York: St. Martin's Griffin, 1996.

Williams, Rhonda Y. *The Politics of Public Housing: Black Women's Struggles against Urban Inequality*. New York: Oxford University Press, 2005.

Williams, Robert F. *Negroes with Guns*. New York: Marzani and Munsell, 1962.

Williams, Sherri. "More Women Doing Hard Time in Miss." *Advocate* (Baton Rouge), 19 February 2002.

Williamson, Joel. *The Crucible of Race: Black-White Relations in the American South since Emancipation*. New York: Oxford University Press, 1984.

Willis, John. *Forgotten Time: The Yazoo-Mississippi Delta after the Civil War*. Charlottesville: University Press of Virginia, 2000.

Wilson, Sondra Kathryn, ed. *In Search of Democracy: The NAACP Writings of James Weldon Johnson, Walter White, and Roy Wilkins (1920–1977)*. New York: Oxford University Press, 1999.

Wing, Adriene Katherine. *Critical Race Feminism: A Reader*. New York: New York University Press, 1997.

Winkler, K. J. "Scholars Reproached for Rejecting Women of Color in U.S. History." *Chronicle of Higher Education* 32 (April 1986): 8.

Wolters, Raymond. "Personal Connections and the Growth of the NAACP." *Reviews in American History* 2 (March 1974): 138–45.

Woodruff, Nan Elizabeth. *American Congo: The African American Freedom Struggle in the Delta*. Cambridge, Mass.: Harvard University Press, 2003.

Woods, Clyde. *Development Arrested: The Blues and Plantation Power in the Mississippi Delta*. London: Verso, 1998.

Woodward, C. Vann. *Origins of the New South, 1877–1913*. Baton Rouge: Louisiana State University Press, 1971.

————. *The Strange Career of Jim Crow*. New York: Oxford University Press, 1955.

Yamamoto, Eric K. *Interracial Justice: Conflict and Reconciliation in Post–Civil Rights America*. New York: New York University Press, 1999.

Young, Andrew. *An Easy Burden: The Civil Rights Movement and the Transformation of America*. New York: HarperCollins, 1996.

Younge, Gary. *No Place Like Home: A Black Briton's Journey through the American South*. Jackson: University Press of Mississippi, 2002.

Youth of the Rural Organizing and Cultural Center. *Minds Stayed on Freedom: The Civil Rights Struggle in the Rural South*. Boulder, Colo.: Westview Press, 1991.

Zangrando, Joanna Schneider, and Robert L. Zangrando. "Black Protest: A Rejection of the American Dream." *Journal of Black Studies* 1, no. 2 (December 1970): 141–59.

Zangrando, Robert. *The NAACP Crusade against Lynching, 1909–1950*. Philadelphia: Temple University Press, 1980.

Zigler, Edward, and Susan Muenchow, eds. *Head Start: The Inside Story of America's Most Successful Educational Experiment*. New York: Basic Books, 1992.

Zigler, Edward, and Sally J. Styfco, eds. *Head Start and Beyond: A National Plan for Extended Childhood Intervention*. New Haven: Yale University Press, 1993.

Zigler, Edward, and Jeanette Valentine, eds. *Project Head Start: A Legacy of the War on Poverty*. New York: Free Press, 1979.

Zinn, Howard. *The New Abolitionists*. Boston: Beacon Press, 1974.

————, ed. *New Deal Thought*. Indianapolis: Bobbs-Merrill, 1966.

Acknowledgments

I have truly been blessed. Just as characters and organizations enter and leave Clarksdale's story at various points, many colleagues and friends have played a part in this project's long voyage from Clarksdale to this book. Here I thank only a few. Hugh Brogan, Larry Barth, and particularly Gary McDowell showed me the possibilities. This book would not exist if I had not had their encouragement and confidence during my formative years at the University of Essex and the University of London.

Early versions of this project benefited from the intellectual generosity extended by peers and mentors. These include Glenda Gilmore and Hazel Carby, and with them Matthew Jacobson, Jonathan Holloway, Alicia Schmidt Camacho, and the late Susan Porter Benson, who all read and commented on the text. Also, I especially thank Leigh Raiford, Andrea Becksvoort, Christopher Geissler, Kat Charron, Claire Nelson, Qiana Robinson Whitted, and Heather Williams, who took the time to read or discuss early portions of the work. Out of those interactions came early articles, one on Vera Pigee and another on the process of conducting oral histories.

The evolution of the book happened in many places. As a DuBois-Mandela-Rodney Fellow at the Center for African and African American Studies at the University of Michigan, there was a lot of conversation and reconceptualizing. Thanks to Kevin Gaines and Penny Von Eschen for those opportunities. Also thanks to Lori Brooks, Kris Peterson, Monamie Bhadra, and Eric Battjes for making that Michigan winter pleasant, memorable, and productive. At the University of Massachusetts at Amherst, colleagues became friends, particularly Laura Lovett, Joye Bowman, and John Higginson. All new junior faculty should be so lucky as to experience mentorship as I did (and do) from these three amazing senior colleagues. In a manuscript workshop, Laura, Dayo Gore, and Rick Lopez gave invaluable feedback on what became the epilogue, and Eve Darian-Smith initiated many a conversation that she will recognize in these pages.

At Harvard University, with the Charles Warren Center Fellowship around themes of politics and social movements, I received careful manuscript readings from two fellows, Daniel Kryder and Susan Ware. I also presented the first chapter to a graduate seminar and my colleagues two weeks before the birth of my son. The Warren Center, and the wonderful home of Judy Silvan in Cambridge, provided quiet and stress-free environments in which to write. Most of the heavy editing work took place during that year.

At Brown University, I have continued the winning streak of finding supportive colleagues who have taken the time to read and comment on this work. Corey D. B. Walker, Charlie Cobb, Naoko Shibusawa, Paget Henry, Karen Baxter, and Robert Self all read the entire manuscript in earlier drafts, providing specific and vital feedback. I have had lively conversations about Clarksdale and the memory of the mass movement with Caroline Castiglione, Nancy Jacobs, Tricia Rose, Tony Bogues, Lundy Braun, Catherine Bliss, Catherine Lutz, and Karl Jacoby. The Department of Africana Studies ran a manuscript workshop that invited outside scholars (Emilye Crosby, Jonathan Holloway, and Annelise Orleck) and Brown colleagues to sit around a conference table for a day and shred the book. They were merciful and gentle, yet brutally honest and totally intimidating. I wholeheartedly recommend the exercise to all authors. Annelise looked me in the eye and instructed me to "write the hell out of these stories." I hope I did.

I had the privilege of meeting John Dittmer when he agreed to participate in a panel I organized for an American Historical Association conference over a decade ago. I now know him as a generous scholar and superb mentor who has supported this project from that first conference paper to the final manuscript. I have had opportunities to share my stories and receive critical feedback at numerous other conferences and invited lectures. These include annual meetings at the Organization of American Historians, the American Historical Association, the Southern Association for Women Historians, the Oral History Association, the American Studies Association, the British Association of American Studies, and the Association for the Study of African American Life and History, as well as at universities across the country. I roped in friends and honest critics to reread sections in the final stretch. Heartfelt thanks to Leigh Raiford, Naoko Shibusawa, Daryl Black, Andrea Becksvoort, Robin Bernstein, and Christopher Geissler for their generosity and candor. I must also thank

Chuck Grench and the staff at the University of North Carolina Press for their work in the final production of the book.

Researching Clarksdale's various crossroads enabled me to see America. I have traveled to Wisconsin, New York, Washington, D.C., Texas, Massachusetts, Michigan, Georgia, North Carolina, Tennessee, and every corner of Mississippi to find sources to tell this story. The Lyndon Baines Johnson and the John F. Kennedy Foundations provided research grants to work in these presidential libraries. The Huggins-Quarles Award from the Organization of American Historians and the American Historical Association's Albert J. Beveridge Research Grant enabled me to carry out much of the research. I was honored to receive the 2005 C. Vann Woodward prize (given by the Southern Historical Association) and the Franklin L. Riley 2006 prize (from the Mississippi Historical Society), which funded more research for the book. I have also received financial support from the University of Michigan and the UMASS Amherst Department of History and from various funding sources at Brown University. Leave time also came from fellowships awarded by the Charles Warren Center for Studies in American History at Harvard University and the Woodrow Wilson National Fellowship Foundation.

Many individuals literally opened doors for me to gather these stories. Archivist Alma Fisher worked at the Special Collections at the Tougaloo College Library in Jackson, Mississippi, when I visited in 1999. She sat with me as we tried to make sense of the then half-organized Aaron Henry Collection, which is currently undergoing reorganization. Nancy Godleski at the Sterling Memorial Library at Yale acquired twenty years of the *Clarksdale Press Register* on microfilm. Apart from the Carnegie Library in Clarksdale, this existed nowhere else. Jean Cauthen in Clarksdale introduced me to Vera Mae Pigee, whose story reshaped how I think about women's activism and Clarksdale's movement. Zoya Zeman, a Freedom Summer volunteer in Clarksdale in 1964, gave me information about (and connected me to) the other workers, whose stories bring that summer to life. Charlie Cobb also introduced me to some of his comrades on the front lines who generously answered my questions. Peggy Jeanes at the Mississippi Historical Society in Jackson and Christina Streets in Clarksdale made it easier to secure some of the key images in this book. Archivists and image reproduction specialists at the University of Southern Mississippi and Emory University went beyond the call of duty to process my requests. Nancy Smith in Oxford, Mississippi, daughter-in-law of the late Judge

Orma Smith, shared her memorabilia, while Homer Hill generously shared his work on Coahoma Opportunities, Inc., and Clarksdale school superintendent Wilma Wade left me alone with ledgers of school board minutes in the headquarters' back room. There are many more souls (professional librarians and activists alike) who led me down paths to uncover information.

Archival research is only one layer to this work. This project began as an oral history assignment, and I sincerely thank all my interviewees for letting me into their lives, sometimes to unearth painful memories. Their words bring life to the project. It is crucial that this book be accessible to those who did the real work of creating change in Clarksdale and that the people whose stories I borrowed can recognize themselves in the end product. Jargon has no place here. When I face the tensions between satisfying the activists' vision of their histories and the academy's penchant for grand theories and abstractions, I stay close to my sources so that those voices can be heard and their knowledge of their experiences can remain at the forefront. At the end of this writing journey, I asked Mary Jane Pigee Davis, daughter of Vera Pigee, to read through the entire piece. I have been blessed by my friendship with her. She is her mother's daughter and a formidable force who read through the manuscript in one sitting and gave me her blessings with enthusiasm. She recognized what she read, which meant I had done my job properly. I thank her for her generosity, her encouragement, her corrections, and for letting me use her precious photographs—and I am grateful for her grace and tenacity, which keeps her mother's spirit and values alive.

Finally, I want to thank my family. Brigitte and Catherine Hamlin are my roots, even though I matured an ocean apart from them. I am indebted to the many caregivers who help me raise my child during the day with humor and kindness so I can juggle my life's many hats somewhat successfully. To Delphain Demosthenes, who saw me through this project from its beginnings, our story began at the point where this book ends, in the summer of 1999. It continues, and I am so grateful for it. Thank you for your love and support. To Elijah Malik Demosthenes, your story has just started. Your presence makes me more accountable for the work that I do, the life that I live, and the legacy that I leave, and in you I see the future. You have made me prioritize my work better than any professionalization seminar or book ever did, and watching you grow and learn is a constant reminder of why it is so important to get this history right so that your future has a firm foundation. I love you.

Index

Italic page numbers refer to illustrations and tables.

Coahoma County High School, xvi, xvii, 2, 183, 244–45
Coahoma County Junior College, 3, 78, 162, 213, 214, 218, 224, 232, 303 (n. 49), 304 (n. 74); Christmas parade ban on, 91, *94*
Coahoma County (Negro) Citizens Association, 37, 47–48
Coahoma County Opportunities, Inc. (COI): African American women and, 225–26, 227–28, 232; community involvement and, 230–31, 232, 235–36; establishment of, 222, 223, 224, 235, 308 (nn. 58, 63); funding of, 231, 238–39, 252, 310 (n. 117); Head Start and, 224–26, 230, 234, 240; housing and, 229–30, 241–42; impact of, 243, 262; legal aid, 226–27; local political involvement, 239; middle class benefit from, 243, 248; national recognition of, 230, 241; Vera Pigee and, 235, 237; white business acceptance of, 231–32; white resignations from board of, 223–24, 231, 308 (n. 62); women and men employed by, 224–26, 240–41
—programs and services of, 224–30, 252; 1990s to 2000s, 241–43, 251–52; adult education, 227–29, 235, 240; buildings for, 226, 228–29, 239; Neighborhood Youth Corps, 229, 239; released into community, 240
Coahoma County school district, 175, 228, 257, 279 (n. 56), 313 (n. 31); desegregation and, 174, 196; Head Start and, 217, 240; segregation before *Brown* and, 30
Coahoma Educational Foundation, 183
Coahoma Legal Aid, Inc., 226
Cold War, 14, 169
Coleman, James P., 33, 35, 45–46, 50, 77, 130, 292–93 (n. 31)
Collins, Ben C., 84, 94, 174, 291 (n. 13), 301–2 (n. 28); disrespect to black activists and, 85, 92, 96–97, 111, 114, 123–24,

128; Freedom Summer and, 149–52, *151. See also* Clarksdale Police Department
Collins, Joe, 84
Commander, Gerald, 84
Commission on Religion and Race, 127
Committee of Fifteen, 143. *See also* Clarksdale Citizens' Council
Committee of Parents Respecting the Children, 178, 301–2 (n. 28)
Committee on Emergency Aid to Farmers in Mississippi (NAACP), 49
Committee on Party Structure and Delegation Selection, 146
Communism, 21, 22, 27, 46, 210, 272 (n. 82)
Community Action Agencies (CAAS), 211, 240, 241, 311 (n. 128); biracial boards for, 143, 215–16, 221–22, 223–24, 231, 308 (n. 63); Coahoma County and, 215–16, 218–19, 222, 230. *See also* Office of Economic Opportunity
Community Action Programs (CAPS), 211, 213; abolition of OEO and, 238–39; in Clarksdale, 212, 216–17, 218, 219, 221, 226. *See also* Child Development Group of Mississippi; Coahoma County Opportunities, Inc.; Head Start; Southern Education Recreation Association
Community Services Block Grant, 241
Congress of Racial Equality (CORE), 4, 71, 156; in Coahoma County, 104, 119, 120, 122, 135; Freedom Riders and, 74, 82, 103; in Mississippi, 102, 103, 105, 114, 160; nonviolent direct action and, 70, 102, 120
Connor, Eugene "Bull," 123
Cooper, Cozetta, 214
Cotton. *See* Plantation system
Council of Federated Organizations (COFO): Clarksdale civil rights and, 104, 116, 119, 122, 135, 164–65, 234, 291 (n. 13); collapse of, 159–61, 233; Emergency-Welfare and Relief Com-

World War II years, 14–15, 17–19, 269 (n. 35); youth councils, 4, 37, 42, 43, 58, 70, 71, 73, 75, 279 (n. 69), 282 (n. 8), 284 (n. 46)

—in Mississippi: 1960s, 4, 100, 112–13, 114, 116, 132, 160, 299 (n. 128), 304 (n. 79); early footholds of, 3, 9, 13–14, 16, 18, 19, 21, 22, 23–24, 27, 29, 40–41, 49, 269 (n. 36), 276 (n. 13); early lack of work of, 13, 14, 15, 18, 22; expansion of work of, 35–37, 38–39, 40, 42, 48, 49, 105; loss of members, mid-1950s, 51–53, *52*, *53*, 277–78 (n. 40); Mississippi arrests and, 97, 285 (n. 56); "Mississippi Situation," 42, 44, 55; Mississippi State Conference of Branches, 29, 43, 256–57; national office and, 13, 18, 21, 22–23, 35, 40, 42, 48, 49–50, 51, 70, 71–72, 103–4, 160, 271 (n. 61); national office and Aaron Henry, 5, 53, 76, 82, 92, 104–5, 117–18, 132, 133, 161, 288 (n. 101); white "war" against, 13–14, 22, 32–39, 44–49, 50, 54, 274 (n. 122)

See also Citizenship schools; Council of Federated Organizations; Henry, Aaron; NAACP Coahoma County Branch; NAACP Coahoma County Youth Council; NAACP Southeast Regional Office; Pigee, Vera Mae; Southern Christian Leadership Conference; Student Nonviolent Coordinating Committee

NAACP Coahoma County Branch, 40, 187, 222, 314 (n. 45); civil rights activism and, 92, 111, 113–14, 128, 249; continuation into present day, 248–49, 250, 261; "Dick Gregory Day," 108, 288 (n. 100); Emancipation Proclamation Program, 36, 47, 276 (n. 18); founding of, 3, 13, 17, 24, 27–29; Freedom Ballot Campaign, 130; Freedom Summer and, 135, 155, 157, 158; Freedom Vote and, 128–32; growth of, 1950s, 36–37; injunction against, 119,

290 (n. 5); Martin Luther King visit and, 119, 290 (n. 5); membership, 51, *52*, 60, 105, 272 (nn. 87, 88), 274 (n. 133); "Mississippi Must Change" program, 55; national NAACP and, 44, 76, 82; nonviolent direct action and, 75, 84–85, 102, 118–25, *120*, *121*, 147–52, 290 (nn. 3, 6), 290–91 (n. 7); other civil rights organizations and, 132–34, 135, 157, 293 (n. 39); shopping boycotts and, *121*, 177, 181; summer of 1965 and, 162–64, 298 (n. 121); Emmett Till murder and, 9–10, 39, 42–43, 48, 49–50, 60, 275 (n. 153); violence against African Americans and, 9–10, 13, 56, 109, 124–25; Voter Education Committee, 113, 114; voter registration and, 28–29, 47, 54, 60, 65–67, 68–69, *69*, 82, 104, 164, 175, 298 (n. 123); War on Poverty and, 212–13, 214, 220–21, 235, 236; white sympathizers and, 47, 48; white "war" against, 34–35, 36, 55–56, 57–58, 99, 102; young white volunteers and, 135, 162, *163*. See also Clarksdale civil rights; Council of Federated Organizations; Haven Methodist Church; Henry, Aaron; National Association for the Advancement of Colored People; NAACP Coahoma County Youth Council; Pigee, Vera Mae; School desegregation

NAACP Coahoma County Youth Council, 58, 162, 279 (nn. 68, 69); civil rights activism and, 63–64, 84–86, 91–95, 118, 284–85 (n. 47), 285 (n. 48); Freedom Summer and, 154–55, 157; interracial concert and, 80, *81*; school desegregation and, 37, 176, 180; shopping boycotts and, 91–95, 180; Student Committee in Support of Freedom and Justice, 180; young white volunteers and, 135–36. See also Pigee, Vera Mae

NAACP Southeast Regional Office, 19, 274 (n. 122), 280 (n. 80); declining member-

162–64, 165, 298 (n. 123), 299 (n. 126); young white volunteers for, 1970s, 260, 315 (n. 51)

—in Clarksdale, 33, 77, 80, 82, 96, 104, 108, 109, 128–29, 145–46, 159, 162–64, 260, 287 (n. 89), 315 (n. 51); African American middle class and, 3, 24, 78; African American World War II veterans and, 16–17, 40; whites and, 163

   See also Citizenship schools; Freedom Vote; Mississippi Progressive Voters' League; Voting Rights Act

Voting Rights Act, 162, 163–64, 165, 175, 177, 235, 236, 260, 298 (n. 123), 315 (n. 52)

Wade, Wilma, 259, 314 (n. 39)

Walker, K. William, 25, 27, 271 (n. 72)

Walmsely, Arthur W., 127, 290 (n. 3)

Walton, Anthony, 250–51

Ward, A. Dudley, 127, 290 (n. 3)

Ward, Jerry, 244

War on Poverty, 161, 165, 261–62, 278 (n. 50), 307 (n. 40); Civil Rights Act of 1964 and, 210, 231; civil rights movement and, 233; Clarksdale white assistance to programs of, 215–16, 223, 224, 278 (n. 50); Clarksdale white reaction to programs of, 214–15, 216–17, 220, 221, 222–24, 308 (n. 62); end of heyday of, 238–39, 241, 310 (n. 117), 311 (n. 128); housing and, 229–30; middle class benefit from, 233–34, 236, 243; Mississippi Delta, influence in, 240, 243; overview of, 211–13; sharecroppers/farmworkers and, 218, 227–28, 232, 311 (n. 121). *See also* Coahoma County Opportunities, Inc.; Community Action Agencies; Community Action Programs; Head Start; Office of Economic Opportunity

Washington, Booker T., 11, 20, 31

Washington, Mary, 96

Washington Elementary School. *See*

Booker T. Washington Elementary School

Watts, Peggie, 37

Webster, Richard M., Jr., 246

Wells, Milton, 180

Welty, Eudora, xi

Wheatley, Joseph, 193, 228, 235, 240

White, Billy, 178, 183

White, Hugh, 31–32, 273 (n. 109)

White, Walter, 13, 21, 275 (n. 151)

White supremacy, 9, 15, 46, 77, 82, 119, 128, 131, 252; black sexuality and, 95, 97–98, 100–101; federal legislation forcing desegregation and, 15, 209; school desegregation and, 29–30, 61, 170, 192, 206–7, 231; violence and, 9, 110, 114, 117

Whitfield, Ernestine, 246–47

Whitfield, Monroe, 140

Whitten, Jamie, 142, 159

Wiggers, Charles C., 192

Wilkie, Curtis, 138, 147, 174, 309–10 (n. 94); *Clarksdale Press Register* and, xiv, 82, 109, 124, 266 (n. 3), 309 (n. 80); Fourth Street Drugstore description, 134, 293–94 (n. 46); voter registration and, 163, 164; War on Poverty and, 215, 220, 240

Wilkins, Roy, 23, 35, 39, 49, 53, 72, 75, 82, 90, 103, 133, 161, 285 (n. 56); Aaron Henry and, 104–5, 132

Williams, John Bell, 13–14, 17

Williams, Pat, 200

Williams, Sandra, 200

Wilson, Mayo D., 224–25, 226, 231, 232, 240, 308 (n. 64), 310 (n. 117)

WLBT television station, 132, 261, 293 (n. 37)

Wofford, Harris, 79, 132

Woman Power Unlimited, 103

Women's Society of Christian Service, 10

Woods, Clyde, 252, 260

Works Progress Administration, xiii

World War II, 15; NAACP during, 14–15, 17–19, 269 (n. 35)